MW00352627

Helen Keller

Recent Titles in
Women Making History

Helen Keller

A LIFE IN AMERICAN HISTORY

Meredith Eliassen

Women Making History
Rosanne Welch and Peg A. Lamphier, Series Editors

 ABC-CLIO®

An Imprint of ABC-CLIO, LLC
Santa Barbara, California • Denver, Colorado

Copyright © 2021 by ABC-CLIO, LLC

Library of Congress Cataloging-in-Publication Data

Names: Eliassen, Meredith, author.
Title: Helen Keller : a life in American history / Meredith Eliassen.
Description: Santa Barbara, California : ABC-CLIO, [2021] | Series: Women
    making history | Includes bibliographical references and index.
Identifiers: LCCN 2021023102 (print) | LCCN 2021023103 (ebook) | ISBN
    9781440874635 (hardcover ; alk. paper) | ISBN 9781440874642 (ebook)
Subjects: LCSH: Keller, Helen, 1880-1968. | Deafblind people—United
    States—Biography. | People with disabilities—United States—Biography.
    | Women social reformers—United States—Biography.
Classification: LCC HV1624.K4 E66 2021 (print) | LCC HV1624.K4 (ebook) |
    DDC 362.4/1092 [B]—dc23
LC record available at https://lccn.loc.gov/2021023102
LC ebook record available at https://lccn.loc.gov/2021023103

ISBN: 978-1-4408-7463-5 (print)
        978-1-4408-7464-2 (ebook)

25 24 23 22 21   1 2 3 4 5

This book is also available as an eBook.

ABC-CLIO
An Imprint of ABC-CLIO, LLC

ABC-CLIO, LLC
147 Castilian Drive
Santa Barbara, California 93117
www.abc-clio.com

This book is printed on acid-free paper ∞

Manufactured in the United States of America

Contents

Series Foreword

We created this series because women today stand on the shoulders of those who came before them. They need to know the true power their fore-mothers had in shaping the world today and the obstacles those women overcame to achieve all that they have achieved and continue to achieve.

It is true that Gerda Lerner offered the first regular college course in women's history in 1963 and that, since then, women's history has become an academic discipline taught in nearly every American college and university. It is also true that women's history books number in the millions and cover a wealth of topics, time periods, and issues. Nonetheless, open any standard high school or college history textbook and you will find very few mentions of women's achievements or importance, and the few that do exist will be of the "exceptional woman" model, ghettoized to sidebars and footnotes.

With women missing from textbooks, students and citizens are allowed to believe that no woman ever meaningfully contributed to American his-tory and that nothing women have ever done has had more than private, familial importance. In such books we do not learn that it was womens' petitioning efforts that brought the Thirteenth Amendment abolishing slavery to Abraham Lincoln's attention or that Social Security and child labor laws were the brainchild of Frances Perkins, the progressive female secretary of labor who was also the first woman appointed to a presidential cabinet.

Without this knowledge both female and male students are encouraged to think only men—primarily rich, white men—have ever done anything meaningful. This vision impedes our democracy in a nation that has finally become more aware of our beautiful diversity.

The National Bureau of Economic Research said women comprise the majority of college graduates in undergraduate institutions, law schools, and medical schools (56 percent in 2017). Still, women's high college attendance and graduation rates do not translate to equal pay or equal economic, political, or cultural power. There can be little argument that American women have made significant inroads *toward* equality in the last few decades, in spite of the ongoing dearth of women in normative approaches to American history teaching and writing. Hence, this series.

We want readers to know that we took the task of choosing the women to present seriously, adding new names to the list while looking to highlight new information about women we think we know. Many of these women have been written about in the past, but their lives were filtered through male or societal expectations. Here we hope the inclusion of the women's own words in the collection of primary documents we curated will finally allow them to speak for themselves about the issues that most mattered. The timeline will visually place them in history against events that hampered their efforts and alongside the events they created. Sidebars will give more detail on such events as the Triangle Shirtwaist Factory Fire. Finally, the chapter on Why She Matters will cement the reason such a woman deserves a new volume dedicated to her life.

Have we yet achieved parity? We'll let one of our subjects—the Honorable Ruth Bader Ginsburg—remind us that "when I'm sometimes asked when will there be enough [women on the supreme court]? And I say when there are nine, people are shocked. But there'd been nine men [for over 200 years], and nobody's ever raised a question about that."

Introduction: Why Helen Keller Matters

The 1880s were characterized by tremendous transformation and unease in the United States as the nation entered the world stage as an economic and political force. When Helen Adams Keller (1880–1968) was born in the small southern town of Tuscumbia, Alabama, no one anticipated she would become a world-known writer and activist for the Deaf and Blind, women, people of color, and the working people. Concepts of gendered dependence, interdependence, and independence played out through Keller's life in a way that makes her both unique and universal. After the Alabama-born Deaf-Mute-Blind girl learned how to communicate, she entered a world of ideas where her physical limitations did not impede her success. Keller matters because she culturally delineated new female semantics and rhetoric related to disability, self-identity, and self-help.

Democracy in America is a political institution challenged from those on the outside who deplore it and from those on the inside who ignore it. Today we must deeply examine marginalized populations of the past within a framework of white supremacy to understand how it harms everyone. Helen Keller was a white woman who was profoundly marginalized by her double-disability of being Deaf-Blind. She acted through direct democracy with liberal and conservative actors reflecting the aspirations and concerns of common people.

Despite living with a teacher-guardian-promoter Anne Sullivan Macy, who occasionally misled, misinformed, and mistreated her, Keller developed an equilibrium within the pendulum of a political culture that swung between capitalism and individualism. For Keller, politics was not a polite invitation to participate. Politics called unrelentingly upon Keller's self-expression—it was a *calling* and *call to action* ultimately defining her as a significant female historical figure within American society.

Keller demonstrated a plucky, generous, and determined character. When a possibly preventable childhood illness made her Blind-Deaf-Mute, circumstances unceremoniously propelled her onto a public stage. Keller groped for a means to communicate and relate to seeing and hearing people. Solutions and challenges to Helen Keller's family dilemma of dealing with their disabled daughter were shaped by the legal doctrine of coverture.

Coverture is the legal status of a married woman who is considered to be under the protection and authority of her husband. The family employed Anne Sullivan, a single woman considered to be feme sole to teach young Keller, while her mother Kate Keller, a married woman, was considered feme covert. Sullivan acted independently as a single woman as Keller's guardian; once she took Keller to Massachusetts, Sullivan held more power in Keller's life than her biological mother.

Society believed husbands/fathers under coverture acted in the best interest of wives, children, and dependents, and the court systems upheld these notions. Americans assumed Sullivan acted altruistically as Keller's guardian by devoting her life to her student. Sullivan, who was visually impaired, in curating information about her student accentuated this characteristic to protect position and control. Sullivan effectively developed Keller into a brand from the shadows. Sullivan's aggressive teaching style became a point of contention as other educators accused her of abusing this position.

Rights and benefits of parents were legally derived from their duties under common law practice. Society assumed children belonged to their parents since wives were historically treated as property of husbands. Some people challenged Sullivan, who behaved as if Keller was a possession, questioning whether she truly acted in Keller's long-term best interests.

When Alexander Graham Bell, a proponent of articulation, or teaching the Deaf to speak, steered Keller to the Perkins Institute, he placed her on a path of assimilation with the speaking world. The pros and cons of institutional training of the Deaf-Blind became part of Keller's broader debate between charity- and state-supported social reform for the disabled. However, for Sullivan, the debate became personal when white male educators challenged her credibility as a teacher and "miracle worker."

When Keller was about ten years old, Sullivan served as her guardian, one who looks after and is legally responsible for someone who is unable to manage their own affairs. Determined to communicate with others, Keller demanded of her guardian, training to learn to speak . . . articulate words. Within the Victorian society, Helen Keller appeared to be an exotic figure striving to communicate; her touching a man's face who was not a relative was an accommodation for her disabilities. Keller's uttered speech was a lonely sound. While she was learning to speak, Keller could only communicate orally when someone familiar with her speech patterns could translate what she said to others.

Keller belonged to a tiny minority of Deaf-Blind individuals. Once Keller could speak, she viewed herself as "restored" to her human heritage. Keller believed human creativity and speech were interrelated. She credited speech with transforming her from merely existing to living. Keller felt indebted to her teacher-guardian Anne Sullivan for her restoration. In her quest to speak, Keller promoted a controversial pedagogy of speech training or articulation in schools serving the Deaf and Deaf-Blind.

Deaf-Blind children were more likely to attend schools for the Deaf than schools for the Blind because the disability of deafness was considered to be more difficult to overcome. Prior to Keller, Perkins Institute for the Blind in Boston, Massachusetts, was the only school to establish trust funds for Deaf-Blind students grown with bequests, donations, or subscriptions (Best, 1919). Institutions during the second half of the nineteenth century promoted education and assimilation for the disabled and increasingly became places where the disabled were institutionalized and removed from families. The American School for the Deaf in Hartford, Connecticut, was the first school to accept a Deaf-Blind student, Julia Brace. Perkins Institute was the first to attempt to become a "dual school" when it accepted a Deaf-Blind student named Laura Bridgman.

Keller aspired to be an active citizen when poverty shaped lives of women, people of color, and children and when literature on poverty spoke only to white males. Her primary cause was related to the Deaf-Blind, or what she referred to as the "double shadow of blindness and deafness" (Lash, 1980). Keller's career as a fundraiser started when she was a child. Perkins Institute director Michael Anagnos encouraged ten-year-old Keller to employ a letter writing campaign to garner resources for another Deaf-Blind child Thomas Stringer to receive special education.

The Keller family's extreme financial hardships meant they could not pay for their daughter's special education. This led Sullivan to become Keller's promoter in addition to teacher and guardian. Alexander Graham Bell and other supporters established a subscription to fund Keller's special education. Not all Keller's supporters were as esteemed within the capitalist system as Bell. Before his death, Arthur Keller, upon hearing that a vaudeville promoter had approached Sullivan with a lucrative offer, threatened to put his eldest daughter into show business or on exhibit to help the family climb out of debt.

Keller and her teacher-guardian were determined to live outside of an institutional setting. Sullivan, born into poverty, had spent her formative years in an almshouse and objected to institutions based on her experiences. Keller and her teacher-guardian railed against the disabled being placed in care facilities away from family where they could be forgotten, yet they also resisted returning to limited opportunities for learning and personal expression with Keller's family in the South. The financial path for both women became burdensome once they became bound to each other by financial trusts established for Keller's financial well-being. These arrangements tied Keller to Sullivan as long as she lived. The trusts motivated Sullivan and other caregivers to separate Keller from family, any potential marriage partner, friends, and institutions in order to retain control over money.

Helen Keller was first a subject and then a contributor to a children's magazine called *St. Nicholas* edited by Mary Mapes Dodge. Keller's words were first published when she was ten years old. Sullivan, desperate to establish herself as an important educator, without earning teaching credentials, encouraged Keller to send a story called "The Frost King" to Michael Anagnos. Sullivan did not understand how embellishing a published work and calling it original was wrong. Keller later reflected, "I think if this sorrow had come to me when I was older, it would have broken my spirit beyond repairing."

The plagiarism accusation was not substantiated, but it became a defining moment Keller never forgot. The intense public scrutiny related to "The Frost King" prompted Keller to retreat from public life. Sullivan convinced Helen to write her story for the American children's magazine *Youth's Companion*. Multiple editors with the *Youth's Companion*, which offered readers natural history and moral tales, introduced Keller to transcendentalist ideas. Dodge eventually recommended teenage Keller should write her own story as an autobiography, describing her experiences as a Deaf-Blind individual.

Keller and Sullivan's interdependent-codependent relationship made them financially dependent upon white male capitalists. To be an adult "dependent" like Keller was a status abhorrent to American individualism and democracy. For example, a homeless man is dependent; he is not obliged to pay property taxes; if he is clever, he can make his way by bartering services for food and temporary shelter. However, the transient who does not pay taxes is disenfranchised and *dependent* upon the generosity of others.

The populism Sullivan supported, the political sensibility centered on promotion and protection of the common man's interest over the society's elite, enabled her to make Keller a lifelong dependent. Populism, while it appeared to be egalitarian, rejected science that builds upon knowledge with testable explanations about the universe and contained biases of white supremacy, which labeled Keller as abnormal, as someone who needed a caretaker, as a dependent. Populism rationalized the need for common woman Sullivan in Keller's life as a savior and labeled her a "miracle worker."

Keller wanted an education to be the best person she could be, but Sullivan proved to be a taskmaster to her ambitious student. At Radcliffe College, Keller put all of her energy into earning a college degree with honors, but her honors did not match Sullivan's ambitions. Despite this, Keller demonstrated how no physical obstacle could hinder intellectual achievements of the human mind once it has been opened. Capitalists found Keller's story of persistence over adversity to support capitalist notions of individuality. Horatio Alger, Jr. was a prolific American author who wrote rags-to-riches stories where protagonists raised themselves from poverty to sensational success through thrift, hard work, and moral fortitude. When Keller decided to go to college, she became a new kind of role model for white upwardly mobile women.

Keller's ability to write, turning abstract ideas into natural idiomatic English, garnered her a lucrative contract with *Ladies' Home Journal* to write a series of articles about her life. Keller's consistent denial of suffering in these articles reflected a Victorian literary aesthetic first presented in a book by Sarah Chauncy Woolsey called *What Katy Did* (1872). Woolsey's story contained a wheelchair-bound protagonist Katy Carr who learns to be "the heart of the house." Keller never wanted society to feel sorry for her, but she also sent a message that the disabled did need accommodation when she asserted, "Nobody likes a grumpy cripple" (Lash, 1980).

An education at Radcliffe College in an era when science gave Keller tools to develop abstract ideas and logic to figure out problems and apply transcendental approaches characterized by individualism, self-reliance, integrity, harmony, and equality to life. Despite being a world-known writer, *Bartlett's Familiar Quotations* included a single example of Keller's writing demonstrating these principles from *The Story of My Life* (1903): "The mystery of language was revealed to me. I knew then that 'w-a-t-e-r' meant the wonderful cool something that was flowing over my hand. That living word awakened my soul, gave it light, joy, set it free." *Bartlett's* never used any of Keller's pithy political observations.

Though Keller learned from many teachers, Anne Sullivan shaped Keller's image and brand more than anyone else. Sullivan started a romantic relationship with John Albert Macy as he helped Keller transform the series of articles into an autobiography *The Story of My Life* (1903). Keller and Sullivan offered a Victorian Deaf-Blind educational model where a "motherly" woman, remaining in the background, pours all of her energy into a single "childlike" student.

Pennsylvania philanthropist William Wade, who initially inspired Keller by this model, started a grassroots initiative to identify and assist the Deaf-Blind in the United States and Canada. William Wade eventually challenged their Victorian construct of womanhood when a teacher "mother figure" usurps the student's natural parents, sometimes projecting ambitions that are not sustainable throughout the student's life. Wade compiled the first censuses of the Deaf-Blind in North America published in 1900, 1904, and 1908. Following the examples of Frederic Douglas and W.E.B. du Bois, he was first to present multicultural faces of Deaf-Blind culture (Wade, 1908). However, as Helen Keller's sole information vector, Sullivan omitted vital information about her own past and the broader world with her own biases, so Keller never questioned Sullivan's authority.

A census of the Blind, Deaf, and Deaf-Blind in 1910 revealed there were only 584 Deaf-Blind individuals in the United States. Historically, experts on the Blind blamed deaf-blindness on epidemics like scarlet fever and spinal meningitis, accidents, or heredity. Educators of the Blind resisted support for "dual-school" educational programs for the Deaf-Blind. As early as 1871, the American Association of Instructors for the Blind argued, "Deaf-mutes and the Blind differ . . . they cannot be intimately associated without unpleasant results." Dual schools, where there are departments for the Blind and Deaf, were considered to be "unfortunate" as "injustice is done to the Blind" (Best, 1919).

Coverture enabled capitalism to drive American politics into the late twentieth century when married women could establish credit in their own names or without their husbands' signatures. Literature discussing social reforms during the Gilded Age focused on men and fostered a myth of the "American dream" of a nation attracting individuals (whether citizens or not) with aspirations of building a better life. The Keller-Sullivan-Macy household in Wrentham, Massachusetts, challenged traditional gender power dynamics. When Anne Sullivan married John Macy, the subscribers to Keller's trust assumed he as her husband would support his wife. The legal doctrine of coverture declared a husband and wife became but one person in marriage—with the person being the husband. John Macy felt entitled to benefit from Keller's popularity, but he was unwilling or unable to put in the work that Sullivan Macy put in to sustain the "Helen Keller" brand.

The legal change shifted the power dynamics in the household. John Macy could not support his wife as a writer, and Keller could not support a household by writing alone. She tried to become an influencer or bell-wether of change in the new century through essays. Keller's life and activism placed her in three periods of female reform movements related to family stability, including child labor reform (1870–1930), child welfare (1890–1930), and women's suffrage (1900–1920). Keller acted within a spectrum of middle-class white American female conversations related to roles of charity and philanthropy on public health, as many activist women did before American women had the vote.

Keller's contradictory persona defied individuals, institutions, and reformers who felt they could determine her best interests were better than she could. She politicized disability by identifying preventable economic barriers inherent in capitalism. Keller was appointed to Massachusetts Commission for the Blind in mid-1906. She researched blindness and disability, focusing on how social welfare reforms helped the Blind, the causes of blindness, and employment opportunities for the Blind. Keller did not remain on the Commission for long, but she soon discovered that while women did the bulk of the work their voices were silenced.

More than anything, Helen Keller shaped her own story. She held unconventional views about how women should or should not rely upon male "protectors," the use of charitable or government funds for educating the disabled, and the use of the money she earned through her writing. Being Deaf-Blind and reliant upon abstract ideas to construct perceptions of the world, Keller employed semantics, or logical aspects of meaning, derived from experience. Believing disability was a by-product of urban poverty and unregulated industry, Keller became a Georgian socialist in 1909. She believed public ownership of economic production, distribution, and exchange diminished preventable illnesses and disability.

Some critics called Keller a freak; a person with an unusual physical abnormality who behaved in a wild or irrational way. These people also claimed Keller merely impersonated a hearing-sighted person. Her critics could not have been more wrong. Keller studied situations with trained logic before contributing a controversial article called "The Truth Again" to *Ladies' Home Journal*. Keller offered pragmatic logic citing legislation to make the case for protective universal treatment of infants possibly exposed to infection if mothers had sexually transmitted diseases that would prevent blindness.

Mark Twain, who observed the striking individualism characterized in the politics of the Gilded Age, introduced a notion that Helen Keller was a figure like Joan of Arc. Participating in democracy, she sought to defend unalienable rights of every American to "Life, Liberty, and the pursuit of Happiness." As a socialist, Keller offered a minority political ideology. As a pacifist, Keller stood on the wrong side of *bullying* politics, fostering white supremacy simmering beneath the polished veneer of a government promoting political readiness as part of the Preparedness Movement prior to American entry into World War I. Keller remained in a self-expressive limbo. She was active to a lesser degree than socialist friends and associates who were imprisoned for publicly stating opposition to the war. Keller frustratingly could not participate in this community she identified with because of the extent of her disabilities; she could only write and learn about activities secondhand.

Throughout her public life, Keller was accused of relying upon her teacher-guardian-promoter or handlers in order to discern and describe sensations authentically. However, Helen Keller's persona shaped her authentic cultural voice. Within the world of ideas, Keller was never disabled in her thinking. She was a commentator on the importance of language acquisition and use. Her battle to gain a voice conveyed how she valued speech and conversation (as in behavior and action) and the very nature of human communication. Keller consolidated themes from leading American thinkers at the turn of the twentieth century, carrying them to the start of the Civil Rights Movement. She utilized logic and abstract ideas to speak not only to her interests but also to those interests related to wanting freedom of expression, social justice, and educational equity for marginalized people. Her rhetoric tied notions of oppression, suppression, disenfranchisement, and the marginalized to the burden bearers of the world . . . the workers.

Characteristics of Helen Keller's rhetoric remained consistent throughout her public life and exhibited her religion, mysticism, and remaining sensory perception. Keller is the most famous Deaf-Blind writer in the English language, but she was not alone. A Deaf-Blind community for two centuries has been offering multiple prisms through the written word for understanding the spectrum of Deaf-Blind experiences. Keller did not choose to write about herself. Writing, by its nature, is a solitary pursuit, and Helen Keller beyond everything else strived to connect with people. However, once her story became known, publishers and editors recognized it to be singular and dramatic.

Keller's life also coincided with a media revolution bridging nineteenth-century print-dominated media with the radio, motion pictures, and television-driven media of the twentieth century. In many ways, her life thrived more within the nineteenth-century print culture where her mosaic of abstract thinking was developed. Within twentieth-century social constructs created in the media, a Deaf-Blind woman could be manipulated and revised to suit contemporary sensibilities whether they were true to her persona or not. No other Deaf-Blind individual has yet matched Helen Keller's longevity on the public stage speaking to marginalized people with a sustained message.

Helen Keller matters because she illustrates how mass media systematically silenced women with political voices. Media situated Keller within a narrative where she was labeled as Deaf, *dumb*, and Blind well into the 1950s. Keller was a media darling until she challenged mainstream thinking on topics of socialism, disability, and the roles of women and people of color. Over a century ago, Keller's message decried capitalism as unsustainable. Financial security was elusive for Helen Keller and Anne Sullivan Macy; like many disabled, both women struggled to maintain an independent household. The disabled typically did not control property, making them physically and emotionally dependent. There was no question Helen Keller was a lifelong dependent, and this shaped her choices and relationships. After being unable to call for help when Sullivan Macy fell seriously ill during a lecture tour, adult Keller lived with the constant fear that if she died first, her guardian-promoter would become destitute.

As long as Keller played the expected role of an innocent female in public life, the news media treated her like an inspiring human-interest story. Once she expounded on socialist and pacifist views, then the media, argued her views were not her own. Keller's radicalism ultimately silenced her when she contradicted herself on capitalist philanthropists, opening the door for the press to brand her as hypocrite. Even today, Keller is recognized more as a "cripple who made good through hard work and perseverance" (Lash, 1980) than as an anti-capitalist and social justice activist who developed informed arguments related to disability over a lifetime.

Keller employed Anne Sullivan's husband John Albert Macy as her private secretary. Despite being a media man, he could not control how Keller and his wife were portrayed in the news media. Macy collected fifty clippings about Keller that were published in American newspapers over a two-year period. He found editors more motivated to print a "story" to sell newspapers than to publish facts. He discovered that over thirty news pieces were mostly incorrect, containing themes fabricated in newsrooms; ten were entirely fictional, and five were untrue and damaging to Keller. Macy stated, "And under all this is not a touch of malice, for that person [Keller], the entire press, and public are friendly." He concluded, "Imagine the lies that are told about a person to whom the editors (or, rather, the owners) are indifferent or unfriendly" (Macy, 1913a)!

Anne Sullivan Macy could not offer Keller religious instruction, so friends helped her embark upon a spiritual path embracing Emanuel Swedenborg's writings. Alexander Graham Bell's assistant John Hitz, Jr. introduced Keller to Swedenborg's work after Reverend Phillips Brooks died, who was engaged by Sullivan Macy for Keller's religious training. Emanuel Swedenborg was an eighteenth-century Swedish scientist, philosopher, and theologian who wrote *Heaven and Hell* (1758) with ideas about afterlife. As a teenager, these ideas allowed Keller to explore the notion of death after a life well lived, bringing her to a life with sight and hearing.

Helen Keller matters because her rhetoric connected the sense of touch to working-class issues. Keller faced mortality as a toddler in the relatively rural South. If she had not survived, death would not have been due to heredity or accident; it would have been due to a possibly preventable illness. If she had not survived, her birth and death may not have been recorded as it is today under the law; birth registrations were not required in many states until after World War I. Keller was peripherally active in female-dominated Progressive movement to register and document child births and deaths to bring about federal and state support for preventive medicine for children.

By involving audiences, Helen Keller engaged them: this made her successful as a lobbyist. She delivered a rhetoric starting with the difficulties of Deaf-Blind people and then transitioning to the difficulties of workers and average people. As Keller matured and met people outside of her immediate circle, her rhetoric became a chiaroscuro of right and wrong, light and dark, reflecting the conflict between absolutes. She moved from simple narrow to broad concepts to create understandable contrasts, "Let us here and now resolve that every Deaf child shall have a chance to speak, and that every man shall have a fair opportunity to make the best of himself" (Einhorn, 1998).

The Deaf-Blind are marginalized because their double disability isolates them from human contact. Helen Keller invited listeners to participate in her reasoning and to refute her arguments. She challenged listeners to criticize themselves or deny experiences common to all human beings. Keller used a universal logic to connect her hand functions to the work of anyone's hands to demonstrate how *hand* represents the struggle within marginalized groups in society. Keller utilized themes from her distant cousin Reverend Edward Everett Hale, related to helping others by *lending a hand*. Keller's rhetoric contained action steps presented in powerful absolutes, such as "Up, up, something must be done" (Einhorn, 1998).

Helen Keller could not physically take part in protest actions without drawing attention away from her causes; she was careful to donate her own earned funds when she was able to. Socialist rhetoric shaped what Keller deemed worthy of energy especially during the Great Depression; her semantics of light and dark, vision and blindness, and hearing and deafness offered paradoxical contradictions in logic. For example, Keller argued capitalists were con artists despite receiving financial support from them. Anne Sullivan Macy's inability to manage funds meant the two women were compelled to approach wealthy capitalists for support.

Keller's political life coincided with the emergence of the silent film industry in California when women in the state voted in local and state elections. Silent films fostered political literacy with short dialog titles sometimes including political messages. A silent film called *A Man without a Country* (1917) appropriated a story by Keller's cousin Edward Everett Hale with the same title to attack pacifists and conscientious objectors during American Preparedness operations while entering World War. Both Keller and Hale were pacifists, so the use of *A Man without a Country* (1863) to support a war that Keller believed was an assault on the workers of the world would have been an affront.

Hollywood created a propaganda machine during World War I when an early docudrama of Helen Keller's life was made. Historian Francis Trevalyan Miller approached Keller in January 1918 with an idea to do a film about her life, arguing moving images with dialog labels offered a new universal language. Desperate to earn more income, Sullivan Macy convinced Keller to accept $10,000 to take part in producing a Hollywood silent film called *Deliverance* (1919). The project offers the first visual record of Keller in the context of popular culture. Producers exploited the pair to create a silent film not in line with their life values.

Keller and Sullivan Macy as women had little control over how much the film perpetuated a white supremacy myth of Keller as a *super*-disabled white woman, depicting her attending Radcliffe College and outpacing classmates in spite of her disability. Viewers saw a cultural dichotomy between American-born Helen who embraces affluence while a fictional immigrant character Nadja sinks further into poverty. At one point, Keller dreams of love after reading a braille book becoming Circe, the goddess of magic that conjures up a handsome sailor in a beautiful Isadora Duncan-styled scene performed along the California coast. *Deliverance* shows Keller riding a horse, typing, gathering flowers, and flying in an airplane as

---

REVISING HELEN KELLER'S BRAND IN SILENT MOVIES

Francis Trevalyan Miller asked Keller and her guardian-promoter Sullivan Macy to involve supporters including Mary Thaw and wealthy friends to finance the Helen Keller Film Corporation established in May 1918. Keller hoped the project would not be confined to events in her life, but also be relevant to people around the world. She wanted it to "bring many vital truths that shall hasten the deliverance of the human race."

Despite the perceived universality of the medium, Keller struggled to conform to silent film production expectations. When *Deliverance* was released, Helen knew her message went against the dominant public voice. "I felt the tide of opportunity rising and longed for a voice that would be equal to the urge that was sweeping me out into the world" (Keller, 1929). She did not anticipate how the producers would override her wishes to present history accurately.

Produced in three acts, *Deliverance* told Keller and Sullivan's story in a hodgepodge of different scenarios reflecting the shifting events, gimmicks, and fantasies used to turn Keller into something she was not . . . a glamor girl. Framed in an allegorical scenario where young Helen develops a rivalry with an immigrant girl named Nadja, the first act became a simplified version of *The Story of My Life* using stereotypes of the South and immigrants.

Keller was depicted as "without knowledge, without thought." Sullivan enters the film's narrative as the "eternal feminine" teacher from the North, who uses love and patience to civilize Keller when her Southern mother Kate Keller proves ineffectual in breaking her daughter out of her isolation. Once Sullivan helps Keller to read, they travel north where Keller learns to articulate to escape her "prison of silence." As soon as she learns to speak, the dialog label reports, "I am not dumb—now."

her family looks on at the advent of the airline industry. However, it fails to chronicle World War I hospitals where Blind veterans received rehabilitation. In her late thirties during the filming, Keller still appears in her Radcliffe commencement cap and gown, showing she has overcome her disabilities, "I can speak . . . my voice will be heard through the generations" (Helen Keller Film Corporation, 1919).

The third act of *Deliverance* depicts Keller in cameo appearances with Anne Sullivan Macy, Kate Keller, and her uniformed brother Phillips Brooks Keller. The film's narrative suggests Keller's wholeness is due solely to Sullivan Macy. Kate Keller as a Southern woman gets further marginalized as she stands on the sidelines. The film would not have been produced without Mary Thaw, the wealthy widow who supported Keller and Sullivan Macy through financial tribulations and brought in capitalists to broker creation of the Helen Keller Film Company.

In a typical Hollywood ending, adapting Mark Twain's point about Keller being a modern American role model like Joan of Arc, Keller mounts upon a horse and sounds a bugle surrounded by the flags of many nations. The dialog text reads, "I must join hands with my fellow men! I send out my Spirit, like a bugle call to lead Humanity joyously to the heights" (Helen Keller Film Corporation, 1919). The last dialog title states, "Only those are Blind, who do not see the truth. Only those who are Deaf do not hear the oracle of their better selves" (Helen Keller Film Corporation, 1919).

Deliverance delivered a gendered political view in relation to the South with depictions of Sullivan Macy as an active feme sole and Kate Keller as passive feme covert. Ironically, producers released *Deliverance* on the same day women garnered the right to vote with the Nineteenth Amendment, toward the end of World War I. It was not a box-office success. Film distributer George Klein eventually removed the Nadja storyline and released the docudrama to be shown in schools. Keller reflected, "We are the kind of people who come out an enterprise poorer than when we enter it" (Keller, 1929). In the end, white males only gave Keller and Sullivan Macy token voices in how their story was told. Mary Thaw was forced to mediate with the film producer on *Deliverance* to include *some* truth in the story.

Being visible on the public stage, Keller and her guardian-promoter Sullivan Macy lost credibility as disability role models. While Keller's dominant white positionality frustrates the disabled today, she was a white Deaf-Blind woman from a marginalized disability group. When Dr. Harry Best compiled the definitive treatise *The Blind* (1919) before the American Federation for the Blind was established in 1921, he did not include Keller or her teacher. Within the white-dominated Blind activist community, this suggests Keller remained marginalized as a white Deaf-Blind woman despite the fact she operated a grassroots informational clearinghouse with minimal infrastructure out of her home beginning in about 1906.

Helen Keller matters because she reached working-class communities with affinities to socialism where they were. Vaudeville, American variety shows, reached their heyday as part of an emerging populist consumerism only to decline with the emergence of the silent film industry. The actors and dancers and acrobats happily went through their acts and allowed Keller to touch them to sense their lives. Keller experienced a revelation of how performers played out roles in the productions revealing their real lives and how everything else was make-believe. Perhaps this revelation inspired her desire to travel and explore different cultures.

Helen Keller and Anne Sullivan Macy entered vaudeville from winter 1920, before the death of Kate Keller, until spring 1924. Vaudeville offered Keller better pay than literary or lecturing work did, but it was then a grubby industry on the decline. Helen persuaded Sullivan Macy, who was offered more lucrative stage work when Keller's father was still living. Times were rapidly changing. A major shift in Keller's life occurred when her mother died. Sullivan Macy became Keller's sole and dominant "motherly" guardian, which meant she answered to nobody regarding her adult ward.

The Deaf-Blind woman who was sheltered for most of her life achieved new freedom on the stage. Later when speaking on radio, Helen felt similar emotions to when she was filming *Deliverance*, like she was talking to ghosts. Thomas Edison once compared Keller's voice to the unpleasant sound of steam exploding. Speaking on the radio demanded incredible concentration from Keller, because she became disoriented by the slightest vibration or distraction. When appearing for radio, Keller felt no life vibrations, no shuffling of feet, no echoes of applause, and no odors of tobacco or makeup, only a blank void in which her voice floated.

Vaudeville audiences were especially open to Keller, and she gained a more active place in this community by communicating directly with working-class audiences. While contracts required they get paid in advance, managers took advantage of the pair, and some did not pay them anything at all, costing Keller and Sullivan Macy thousands of dollars. Being part of an entertainment industry, any woman also risked her reputation as a "lady." Mary Thaw was shocked by the working-class vaudeville performers surrounding Keller's act when she saw it with friends and family.

By 1924, the American Foundation for the Blind seemed to counter Harry Best's assumptions regarding the significance of Keller and Sullivan Macy's contributions to issues of the Blind (Best, 1919). However, Keller's political views undermined her message to some AFB constituencies. Keller maintained, "Superficial charities smooth the way for the prosperous" (Lash, 1980).

There are several newsreels featuring Keller talking to presidents still in existence. She appeared with a contemporary First Lady Grace Coolidge,

Helen Keller reads Grace Coolidge's lips during a visit to the White House on January 12, 1926, as the First Lady headed the list of patrons for an AFB fundraising campaign. While Keller attended Radcliffe College, Grace Goodhue, after marrying Calvin Coolidge, joined Clarke Schools for Hearing and Speech in Northampton, Massachusetts, to teach lip reading to Deaf children. She developed a lifelong commitment to the educations of Deaf children, utilizing lip reading rather than sign language. (Library of Congress)

the first presidential wife to earn a four-year college degree. Before marrying Calvin Coolidge, Grace studied elocution and lip-reading at Clarke School for Hearing and Speech and taught lip-reading to Deaf children. Grace Coolidge did not speak publicly about her political views including women's rights, but she was active in the Red Cross. Ironically, neither Keller nor Coolidge spoke before the newsreel cameras.

Through her work for American Federation for the Blind (AFB), Keller's lobbying increasingly influenced important civil rights legislation and initiatives related to the disabled and African Americans. Helen Keller was among those marginalized when she did this work, and she continually feared the financial fortunes of those closest to her because of her unpopular views. This changed in 1929, when Mary Thaw, a friend of Keller and Sullivan Macy since the mid-1890s, died and left a bequest enabling them to pay debts and finally gain financial security.

FILM MAKING CONSULTANTS RECAST HISTORY

In the decade following World War II, women's roles in film culture were redefined to be submissive and feminine or aggressive and sexual. Helen Keller, an aging icon of innocence, received new treatment in a documentary. In 1952, when Keller was seventy-two years old, filmmaker Nancy Hamilton partnered with actress Katharine Cornell and hired Nella Braddy Henney as a consultant when they produced a fifty-five-minute documentary. *The Unconquered* (1955) put the spotlight on Keller, showing her with greater independence—moving about in her home and recounting her accomplishments with her secretary, Polly Thomson.

Around the same time, producers of *The Girl in the Red Velvet Swing* (1955) hired Mary Thaw's daughter-in-law, Evelyn Nesbit Thaw, to be a film consultant for a fee of $10,000. Evelyn Nesbit's impoverished mother hired her teen-aged daughter out to be a photographic model and showgirl. Nesbit's beauty drew attention from New York City architect Stanford White and Mary Thaw's son Henry Kendall Thaw, who vied for her. Nesbit could not marry an already-married White, so she married Henry Thaw who became a sociopath, luring poor youths into situations where he could physically abuse them. Henry Thaw murdered White in front of multiple witnesses, and Nesbit became a key witness for her husband in the famous Thaw-White murder trial.

The real Mary Thaw was prejudiced against Nesbit because being an actress was a disreputable career for a woman; Nesbit was a showgirl who claimed the son of another man was a Thaw. Mary Thaw rejected Nesbit and used all of her resources against her daughter-in-law. When Nesbit was hired as a film consultant, she used the opportunity to create a new narrative of her nemesis. In one scene, Mary Thaw is depicted visiting Nesbit in her bedroom and takes responsibility for her son's mental illness, saying she spoiled him with "too much love."

Mary Thaw as a feme sole widow likely offered the most significant financial support to Keller during critical moments. When Sullivan Macy died, feme sole companion-secretary Polly Thomson (despite a lack of education) retained a position of trust in Keller's household over a cleverer feme covert Nella Braddy Henney, who held Keller's power of attorney. Throughout her life, Helen Keller remained a dynamic persona in control of her destiny even while being physically dependent upon caretakers. Anne Sullivan who held strength as feme sole before she married John Macy would have regained that status if she had chosen to divorce him. Catherine "Kate" Adams Keller as feme covert lost control of her eldest daughter, Helen Keller, to Sullivan, but she eventually established an adult relationship with her daughter as a feme sole widow.

Helen Keller's biographical documentary *The Unconquered* (1954) opens with an homage to Keller's love of nature by showing a bird in the trees at their home Arcan Ridge in Connecticut; later, a pet bird appears in the house. With careful crafting, with consultation from Henney, Keller appears more independent doing chores, organizing her wardrobe, and maintaining an office. Keller disrupts crystals in a lamp, and the viewer is informed crystals were the last thing Keller remembered seeing before going blind.

The Unconquered utilized archival film and included the only moving images of Anne Sullivan Macy speaking as she described how Keller learned to speak her first word, "it." Despite learning to speak, most of the included MovieTone newsreels describe Keller as "blind, deaf, and dumb." Much of *The Unconquered* appeared to be staged. Ultimately, Keller remained silent while her posh new friend Cornell narrated. It received an Academy Award and featured Keller experiencing a special dance choreographed by Martha Graham where she could touch the male and female dancers with similar access that she would have to touch statues in a museum.

Helen Keller wrote one more account about her teacher-guardian-promoter in *Teacher Anne Sullivan Macy: A Tribute by the Foster-child of Her Mind* (1955). The tribute opens with a quote from George Bernard Shaw, "This is the true joy in life, the being used for a purpose recognized by yourself as a mighty one." The quote seemed more appropriate to Keller than Sullivan Macy, but few understood how tightly Keller's and Sullivan Macy's lives were interwoven. Helen characterized herself as a humble instrument of God, but she attributed her accomplishments to her teacher. The sentimental, sad account demonstrated the growth of a woman who felt she still could not communicate freely. Aware of her teach-guardian-promoter's failings, Helen Keller remained loyal to a flawed woman who undermined her to desperately maintain a position in society.

Produced when Helen Keller was seventy-seven years old, William Gibson's three-act play, *The Miracle Worker*, based upon Keller's autobiography *The Story of My Life* (1903) and adapted from his 1957 *Playhouse 90* teleplay, was produced within contemporary cultural contexts of the early Civil Rights Movement. Nella Braddy Henney also worked as a paid consultant on the project, while Gibson's wife Margaret Brennan Gibson, a prominent psychologist, shaped its psychological aesthetic.

The Miracle Worker presented Keller's prelinguistic volatility within a chiaroscuro aesthetic of light and dark that reflected her rhetoric of light and dark. Keller's *wild* childhood and educational breakthrough was simplified and presented on the theatrical stage, television, and film. Gibson reveals Sullivan's beginnings to the audience but not to Keller. The volatility of their early relationship and its abusive undercurrents do not require explanation because the audience does not know that the pair will be financially bound or even how this is a story propelled by economic catalysts within a transforming America. *The Miracle Worker* created a single dominant story obscuring the bulk of Keller's life and work.

In the story, twenty-one-year-old Sullivan demands total obedience with physical force with Keller to the point of separating her from family to make Keller totally dependent upon her. Despite family resistance, Sullivan immediately instills discipline to teach Helen to communicate by fingerspelling (spelling words into her hand), beginning with "d-o-l-l" for the doll that Sullivan gave Keller as a present. With Keller's educational breakthrough in fingerspelling, the intervention, instruction, or breaking of Keller's former self came as a brutal rite of passage.

As with the earlier silent film *Deliverance*, Gibson's story unfolds in the New South, where women have reimagined new narratives about a shattered way of life. Keller's father, Arthur Henley Keller, in reality became a part of the marginalization of the growing white poor, which he resists through his politics. *The Miracle Worker* depicts the Keller family as middle class and does not examine the economics shaping their true drama. Sullivan is a strong-minded Northern woman of Irish descent, navigating through the postbellum South. Sullivan confronts radically different notions of race, class, and gender.

Helen Adams Keller's real life appears like a mosaic of abstract ideas as she moves through paradigm shifts defining social justice before the Civil Rights Movement. Her unique life matters as it was constructed within a narrative of the legal structure of coverture. The dominant takeaway from this volume and what this life in American history adds to women's history is its examination of how the lives of Helen Keller, Kate Keller, and Anne Sullivan Macy reflected the broader female power dynamics derived from coverture. Under civil law coverture, the roles of feme sole (unmarried women or widows) and feme covert (married women) create a social construct of women within roles of passive and active agency.

Coverture has been the overarching instrument to codify white male supremacy where men gained control of women's labor (including child baring), property, and contract-making abilities whether they embodied inclinations toward love or avarice. If a story's denouement occurs when the conflict or mystery in the plot has been solved and all events lead to an emotional conclusion, then Keller's story appears not very interesting after the death of her inscrutable teacher. However, Helen Keller continued her work past the point when many retire, dramatically expanding the scope of her life's work after Anne Sullivan Macy's death.

Coverture shaded relationships among women. Later in life, a new generation of promoters including Nella Braddy Henney entered Keller and Sullivan Macy's lives, hoping to use the "Helen Keller" brand to profit. Yet another woman named Mary Elizabeth Switzer would consolidate federal resources as the director of the Office of Vocational Rehabilitation to out of Keller and Sullivan Macy's shared vision services for the Deaf-Blind. Helen Keller continued to grow as an individual to change perceptions of disability.

Helen Keller's life was unique within a spectrum of women codified by coverture. Despite a wealth of information and documentation, Keller, an unmarried woman with a famous name, remains as inscrutable as she was in her "no world" before Sullivan Macy's arrival. Helen Keller may have lived as feme sole in a dependent role, but she strategically leveraged her dependent status connected to her disabilities to achieve a lasting position of recognition and strength as a vibrant, modern independent-thinking woman. Helen Keller, and her many thought formations, remain relevant today.

1

Intersections: Alone We Can Do So Little

Helen hoped poet Oliver Wendell Holmes would be at Perkins Institute for the Blind that day. She knew she could not accomplish much by herself, and her new Deaf-Blind friend Thomas "Tommy" Stringer needed the support of the community. Helen's teacher Annie Sullivan was there, always her guide and always her interpreter. The director of Perkins Institute, Michael Anagnos, would help too. The tall Greek director knew how to draw attention to Perkins Institute's newest Deaf-Blind charity case. Boston philanthropists would come to hear Helen Keller speak, and she would ask them to fund the boy's education.

The audience was curious to see the Deaf-Blind wonder from Alabama. A photograph of Keller wearing a simple homespun dress made by her mother, Catherine "Kate" Keller, with her face in profile and a short, straight haircut, provided a glimpse of a compelling child, and not just because she could not see or hear. To the gathering, familiar with another Deaf-Blind woman named Laura Bridgman, Helen was unique among girls her age. She was far more interested in poetry than shiny ribbons, but more than that, she seemed to transcend her disabilities.

As the moment approached, Helen stood behind the imposing six-foot-eight-inch-tall Reverend Phillips Brooks. Not knowing how to answer Helen's questions about God, Annie had once approached the Episcopal clergyman to give her student religious instruction, and he'd become a

1

friend. Seemingly oblivious to the crowd gathered to see the young phenomenon who could move so far into the world, and so quickly, without having seen her own reflection in a mirror, Helen Keller was near, yet she was out of reach.

Strangers intimidated the girl who gave the impression of being precocious with her easy smile and outstretched hands. Helen sensed stillness instead of an audience behind Reverend Brooks, and this made her nervous. She might as well be addressing the people for money over a stonewall with Brooks standing between her and the vibrations from the audience that would offer a sense of the space.

Tommy Stringer, trapped in a hospital bed for a few years, had traveled a similar journey as Helen. He shared some characteristics with Helen's angry self before she could communicate. For five years, Helen had lived in a world she considered to be a "no world" as a "phantom." She did not want Tommy to struggle for special education opportunities. To be Deaf-Blind-Mute, the girl believed, was to be an imprisoned ghost . . . one of the loneliest people . . . *a specter*. She had experienced the frustration of being unseen and unheard as well as the sense of the surreal nonphysical reality of being invisible. Like a few other individuals who lived before her and who lost hearing and sight at a young age, Helen understood the condition of being completely forgotten by the dominant society . . . *of living in apparent oblivion.*

Helen's earliest notions of the world were tactile; she learned about her closest environs through touch, smell, and taste. She could not structure these sensations within her consciousness. Without sight and hearing, Helen could not grasp ideas of empathetic nature, mind, death, and God. As an adult, she told people, "I was like an unconscious clod of earth. There was nothing in me except for the instinct to eat, drink, and sleep" (Keller, 1955).

When Helen poked animals, as she did in her frustration, she was unable to see them wince or hear their cries of pain. The girl could not communicate her own pain to those around her. Some thought Deaf-Blind people were little more than animals, and therefore, they formed an inaccurate idea about the Deaf-Blind being less than human. Not knowing how to help Helen, some in the family thought the girl might be "feeble minded."

Standing behind Reverend Brooks, Helen felt love mixed with guilt when she remembered the distance separating her from her mother, Kate Keller, in Alabama. In a serendipitous object lesson in the association of ideas, Helen at the age of five discovered how to utilize a key to unlock her future. With the pantry key, Helen locked her mother in a closet adjacent to the kitchen, where the family stored food. For three hours, the household desperately searched for Kate while Helen gleefully sat on the front porch steps, feeling a daring sense of control.

The great anger and frustration at discovering she was *different* motivated Helen's defiant act of entrapping her mother. It revealed a paradox of her character to her family: Helen loved her mother but also resented her for not rescuing her from her isolation and bringing into the family circle. When Helen was caught out, Kate and Arthur decided to find Helen a responsible companion. Kate's entrapment pointed toward Helen's desire to escape her silent, dark closeted space enclosing her life.

While Kate's "little bronco" could be mischievous, Helen also possessed a sweet and loving disposition. Kate's period of being stuck in a dark pantry made her understand the extent of Helen's desperation. This primitive action was Helen's first effective communication in absolutes describing her Deaf-Blind experience; Kate was compelled to feel Helen's meaning and do something. Kate prodded her husband, Captain Arthur H. Keller, to seek help for Helen. Kate understood Helen's urgent, desperate cries for help even if her daughter did not.

Helen and Tommy joined a spectrum, continuum, and history of Deaf-Blind people reflecting a variety of circumstances around the world. In the hall of Perkins Institute, Helen clutched the back of a sturdy chair as Reverend Brooks spoke to the crowd. Helen recognized a cause greater than herself, as she tried to help another Deaf-Blind person in need. When Helen and Tommy lost their sight and hearing, they were not alone in entering a frontier of struggle.

Helen and Tommy had both started individual journeys to exceed society's expectations and their own. Within the spectrum of Deaf-Blind children, the point when they lost sight and hearing could determine how they were educated or rehabilitated. Unknown to Helen, there was another Deaf-Blind girl named Katherine "Katie" McGirr born in New York, who was born three weeks before her. McGirr lost her sight and hearing during a snowstorm when she was eight years old. She learned to communicate and eventually supported herself and her mother and worked long enough to qualify for a small pension from the State of New York (Rocheleau and Mack, 1930).

When Helen Keller was young, Americans were on the move via trains, steamships, and electric trolleys. The Agricultural Revolution and Industrial Revolution led to advances in manufacturing and transportation, creating an industrial working class. Conversely, this was also a time of growing poverty in America when employees of manufacturing companies could not afford to purchase what they made with their own labor. Poverty resulted from job loss or injury and led families to be unable to have access to sufficient food and shelter. Families in urban centers lived in tiny one-room tenement apartments with no privacy along the streets with little or no sewage. Families in rural communities would not have a qualified — doctor nearby, so they would rely upon quack doctors, patent medicine cure-alls, or talismans. Poverty, more than contagion, created conditions where families could not care for children during world epidemics because there was little hygiene or no place for them to go that had clean air or space to maintain social distance.

Disability could significantly impact a person throughout life. The disabled would require help to accommodate the special needs to participate in everyday life. In urban frontier America, epidemics had left disability in their wake. Smallpox, cholera, measles, typhus, yellow fever, malaria, meningitis, and other viral infections traveled through communities causing deafness, blindness, and disfigurement. If families were poor, their ability to combat epidemics was handicapped by lack of information about possible cures and resources to care for and rehabilitate family members. Gender also impacted which child would get the most help. Since boys were thought to be potential wage earners, more resources were used to keep them well fed and educated; if they got sick, they were given more time to recover and could do light work outside as part of their rehabilitation. Girls in large families were more likely to be neglected in illness, and if they recovered, they were given indoor domestic tasks of caregiving for younger children.

Children's literature contained cautionary tales about preventing disability or moral lessons about coping with disability. As the Industrial Revolution started, the disabled could live independently by receiving supplemental income, food, and clothing from local church parishes if they proved they were "worthy" poor. Many Blind individuals, including war veterans, readjusted to new living conditions with rehabilitation training or therapy.

A chapbook called *Happy Poverty, or, the Story of Poor Ellen* (1817), published to support the Baltimore General Dispensary, is representative of the disability literature's emphasis on plucky heroines. Ellen, the protagonist in the story, becomes Blind at the age of six and grows to exemplify a modest female Christian life. Ellen receives a small stipend from her local church parish. She supplements earnings from spinning by caring for another disabled woman. This story initiated an American literary tradition of depicting the disabled women discovering happiness in adversity in order to teach all women how to live with adversity.

Alice Cogswell's first teacher, Lydia H. Sigourney, was born shortly after the United States ratified the Constitution during the Early Republican Era (Kete and Petrino, 2018). She lived through the War of 1812 and the Civil War. Sigourney was friends with Emma Willard, who was a pioneering proponent of female education and who established the Troy Female Academy in Troy, New York. Sigourney believed women develop "ideal self" through aesthetic education to achieve harmony and to foster social justice in life. Sigourney believed educational equity was key to American

INSPIRING SPECIAL EDUCATION IN THE UNITED STATES

Alice Cogswell (1805–1830) contracted the "spotted fever," also known as cerebrospinal meningitis, a serious brain infection causing inflammation of the spinal cord. It caused her to lose hearing when she was two years old. Alice's father Mason Cogswell (1761–1830), a doctor living in Hartford, Connecticut, did not know how to educate her.

Thomas Hopkins Gallaudet (1787–1851) moved next door when Alice was nine years old. He noticed she played alone and did not interact with other children. After the War of 1812, the British finger alphabet was still used and evolved into the American "old alphabet."

Alice's father and Gallaudet discussed starting a school for the Deaf in the United States. Gallaudet traveled to Europe to learn methods for teaching Deaf children, but in England, he experienced resistance to sharing information so soon after the War of 1812. Gallaudet went to France and recruited a teacher for the Deaf Laurent Clerc, who brought the Sicard system for teaching sign language to the Deaf to America.

Alice went to a small school for white and Black girls in the home of Mrs. Wadsworth in Hartford, where Lydia H. Sigourney (1791–1865) taught in a schoolroom. Sigourney was one of the most popular American female writers of her day. She found Alice to be engaging and taught her to read, write, and sew. Alice mimicked the other students and demonstrated an interest in music vibrations.

Alice Cogswell inspired Sigourney to develop individualized instruction methods utilizing different modes of communicating and experiencing the world. Alice died shortly after her father died from the effects of tuberculosis. She remains an important figure in American Deaf history demonstrating the Deaf are intelligent and capable.

prosperity, meaning she wanted to educate all Americans including African Americans, the disabled (including the Deaf and Blind), and Native Americans.

Sigourney briefly connected with two Deaf-Blind girls from different generations (Julia Brace and Laura Bridgman) at her small girls' school. Julia, the daughter of a poor cobbler living in Hartford County, Connecticut, was born in 1807. Like other girls, Julia helped her family as soon as she was able to by caring for her younger siblings and by helping around her father's business. She contracted typhus fever, an infectious disease transmitted by fleas, lice, and mites and sustained high fever when she was five years old, which caused her to lose her sight and hearing.

Julia's family could not cope with taking care of her, and she was treated as inferior within her family. Despite being the daughter of a shoemaker, Julia's father did not provide her with shoes or socks during the cold winter months. One night, Julia knelt on the floor and felt her siblings' feet were protected while hers remained bare. She could not communicate her distress when she discovered she may be less valued or loved than her siblings.

Poverty became a visible threat to communities in the United States after a financial panic in 1819 when low-wage jobs became more seasonable and precarious. Julia developed skills that demonstrated she was worthy of receiving community aid. She played with remnant pieces of leather and thread her father rejected for making shoes and created little bonnets and lacelike Vandyke collars for her cat. A local benevolent society considered the sixteen-year-old Julia worthy of assistance, and she was admitted to Sigourney's small day school in Hartford, Connecticut, where Alice Cogswell was a student.

Julia, unaware of her posture, often sat with her head drooping. Julia could not express her thoughts in language, and she seemed unaware of her double disability. Sigourney taught Julia refined sewing and knitting skills. Having taught and observed Alice, Sigourney recognized Julia as affectionate, animated, and expressive, which the teacher and poet interpreted as *happiness*. Sigourney thought Alice and Julia seemed to have developed rich inner lives, and she created character studies of them.

Sigourney recognized that those who were Deaf-Blind from a very early age didn't get any opportunity to develop any "treasury of knowledge" from experience or from listening to familial conversations to connect basic abstract ideas. While Helen Keller lost her sight and hearing at eighteen months, Katie McGirr, who was about the same age, lost her sight and hearing when she was eight years old. Katie had time to grasp by listening to conversations and by connecting basic ideas before becoming Deaf-Blind; the extra six years for developing communications skills gave Katie a developmental advantage over Julia and Helen.

Julia's parents relinquished guardianship of their Deaf-Blind-Mute daughter to the community's benevolence. At Sigourney's school, local gentlemen visited to observe and test Julia's remaining senses with a game: they gave her their watches for her to feel and then switched them among themselves to confuse her. Thinking it was her sense of touch that she used, each asked Julia to return the watches to the proper owner. However, it was Julia's strong sense of smell that led her to always return each watch to the right owner. As a consequence of the repeated tricks, Julia became very cautious, and she rarely succumbed to temptations to which other more affluent students did.

Julia's humility impressed potential donors to the school. Anyone offering Julia a gift was always asked if it was truly meant for her so that nobody would be offended. Sigourney taught Julia basic signs to communicate instructions, approval, or disapproval. She mimicked other girls who read books to occupy their time by patiently sitting for hours holding a book before her eyes as if she was reading. Sigourney wrote an account of Julia's early life called "The Deaf, Dumb and Blind Girl" for *Juvenile Miscellany* (May 1828) to inspire awareness and support for charitable institutions serving the Deaf and Blind.

Julia learned to produce textiles by sewing with a needle weaving with a shuttle or by tatting with a crochet hook. Julia's constructed counterpanes, bedcovers quilted with small pieces of calico fabric, were sold at the school to earn money for her clothing and board. However, Julia grew frustrated when she could not learn to communicate like other students. Not understanding why she was different, Julia spread a newspaper before her cat and put her finger to his mouth. When Julia reasoned that the cat was not reading aloud like a student, she perceived him to be obstinate and shook the cat in displeasure.

After Alice Cogswell inspired Thomas Gallaudet, Laurent Clerc, and her father, Mason Cogswell, to establish the American School for the Deaf in 1817, it became the first residential school for the Deaf in the United States to receive federal aid. Julia Brace was admitted as the American School's only Deaf-Blind student when she was twenty-one years old. For a Deaf-Blind student, the American School was a large, disorienting facility. Julia explored and memorized step-counts for her room and all of the stairs, so she would not miss steps or sit in the wrong chair at the dinner table.

Julia was fastidious and tidy: her small wardrobe was organized so she could dress herself independently. If something was out of place, Julia immediately discovered it and returned it in the right spot. She mended her clothing to extend usefulness and save on the cost of replacing garments. American School students learned Laurent Clerc's modified manual signs from Old French Sign Language devised by monks, which he adapted into American Sign Language (ASL).

Julia learned how to communicate with word-building by manipulating wooden letters and pins on a cushion to form words. She never learned sign language used in the Deaf community; being the only Blind-Deaf student in the American School, Julia's blindness made her inscrutable to the Deaf students who teased her because she was different.

When Julia learned to communicate by spelling out words, she became the first Deaf-Blind American celebrity. Educational reformers used her story in didactic literature to teach children how to behave in adversity. Julia's experiences demonstrated how children and adults who became disabled as a result of illness or accident could learn to adapt to new circumstances. Julia attracted the attention of many visitors who observed her practicing domestic skills, including sewing and knitting. They waited for long periods to watch her thread a needle with her tongue and then contributed money to the school.

The American physician Dr. Samuel Gridley Howe, who established the Perkins Institute for the Blind in Boston, Massachusetts, traveled to Hartford during the early 1830s to meet Julia. A handsome adventurer and war hero in a distant conflict in Greece, Dr. Howe hoped to develop teaching methods for Deaf-Blind children much younger than Julia. Perhaps thinking he would develop the first "dual school" to accommodate Deaf-Blind students, he observed Julia closely to determine if she could be taught to speak.

Howe faced challenges in funding an expanding vision for Perkins Institute; he hoped the meeting would publicize how an education from his school could produce a more animated Deaf-Blind individual than the American School (Showalter, 2016). In his quest for a Deaf-Blind child to educate as an "experiment," Howe discovered seven-year-old Laura Bridgman at her family's New Hampshire farmhouse in 1831. He wrote to Sigourney ten years later, saying Julia and Laura should meet, suggesting Laura might inspire Julia to learn the manual alphabet.

When Julia and Laura met in late 1841, each touched the other's face. Twelve-year-old Laura braided a chain for thirty-five-year-old Julia, who accepted the token. Julia tucked it in her pocket and walked away. Julia enrolled in Perkins Institute for a year on April 6, 1842. Being older than other students, Julia was less malleable and was unable to grasp abstract thinking needed to connect words and objects. Julia returned to the American School as a boarder and employee. Julia eventually retired to her sister's residence in Bloomfield, Connecticut, before the Civil War and lived there until her death in 1884, when she was buried in an unmarked grave.

Five Deaf-Blind students attended Perkins Institute during Dr. Howe's lifetime, starting with the daughter of a New Hampshire Baptist farmer named Laura Bridgman who was born in 1829. The Bridgman family was hit hard by a scarlet fever epidemic a few years later, which killed two of Laura's sisters. Bridgman and Helen Keller both had blue eyes and light brown hair, and both were about two years old when they lost sight and hearing. Laura also lost her sense of smell and taste and knew no means to express self, hunger, thirst, pain, or joy other than with a few basic signs.

Laura Bridgman retained little recollection of self or family. Her father, Daniel Bridgman, remained detached from his Deaf-Blind-Mute daughter, but her mother, Harmony Bridgman, continued to show Laura affection. Laura mimicked behaviors of those around her, mostly following Harmony around the house and learning to sew and knit. Laura's delicate hands and fingers wove in and out through intricate needlework projects. The girl's communication was very limited, but her friend Asa Tenney introduced her to a few phrases of Native American sign language. Over time, Laura's demonstrations of frustration escalated as she took out anger on her dolls and people around her.

Eight-year-old Laura arrived at Perkins Institute on October 4, 1837. Dr. Howe initially perceived Laura Bridgman to be "a beast." He convinced Daniel and Harmony Bridgman to make him Laura's guardian so he could control her spiritual and educational path forward. Gender roles and disability converged during this complex time of educational reform; Julia and Laura became models for female disability. At a time before Darwin published his treatise for the nonscientific community, *On the Origin of Species by Means of Natural Selection, or, the Preservation of Favoured Races in the Struggle for Life* (1859), Laura began to demonstrate what Howe understood to be a feminine human soul. Once she was educated, Laura appeared to become a passive "good" disabled girl celebrated in Victorian literature and culture.

In the development of each child who became Deaf-Blind before acquiring some sense of language and speaking, there came an increasing understanding of being *different* from other humans but not understanding the cause. Like Julia Brace, Laura sat and held a book before her eyes and moved her lips as she sensed other students did while reading.

Dr. Samuel Gridley Howe based his teaching of the Deaf-Blind on the ideas of French philosopher Denis Diderot, who believed touch offered alternative symbolic language (Dickens, 1842). Howe planned to teach Laura using two tactile methods: embossed printed or raised-type cards and fingerspelling using a manual alphabet. He had a few tools for instructing a Deaf-Blind student. He needed to either create a grassroots language of signs for every individual object or idea based upon Laura's natural language or teach her an existing language in common use. A knowledge of letters used to create combination, like what Julia Brace learned, would allow Laura to express ideas to others with word combinations.

Dr. Howe decided to use the latter: the first method would be quick but ineffective, but if he achieved the second more challenging method, it might be "very effectual." He worked along with Laura for the first few weeks, and then he delegated her instruction to Miss Lydia Hall Drew who was housemother at Perkins Institute. Howe and Drew utilized Emma Willard's premise where teaching commenced with familiar objects and then broadened to build confidence in students.

Howe and Drew started with daily exercises utilizing imitation and memory; this process was mechanical, similar to "teaching a very knowing dog a variety of tricks." Laura imitated her teachers' actions. Howe used familiar items brought from Laura's home. He devised raised-type labels featuring names for a knife, fork, spoon, key, and chair. He encouraged Laura to touch and feel each object, and then he passed her fingers over the label. Once Laura experienced feeling the label and object together, then he pasted the label on the object *connecting them* and encouraged her to feel them again.

Laura's teacher pasted labels on objects. The girl understood the labels were not alike, but after her first forty-five-minute lesson, she puzzled as to why. After many repetitions of the lesson, Laura figured out how the raised-letter labels connected to specific objects. She matched the label for "chair" with the chair. Once she did this, matching labels to items became a game, and Laura was delighted when she discovered word labels meant something.

While the Deaf can see to acquire sign language, the Deaf-Blind must learn to finger spell by touch and feel. Dr. Howe and Drew taught Laura how a word was made up of letters. Then they mapped the alphabet by tracing letters upon the palm of her hand to create primitive fingerspelling. Lydia Drew remembered, "I shall never forget the first meal taken after she appreciated the use of the finger alphabet. Every article that she touched must have a name, and I was obliged to call someone to help me wait upon the other children, while she kept me busy in spelling the new words."

Dr. Howe commissioned a case of metal types consisting of four sets of alphabets so one set remained in alphabetical order. Laura could move the other three sets freely to learn the alphabet and build words. Within three days, Laura mastered the order of alphabetical letters. Once she learned words, she never tired of learning to spell. Word-building was a clumsy way to communicate, but once Laura realized she could connect abstract ideas, she grabbed hold of this means to receive and share ideas.

Dr. Samuel Gridley Howe's work with Laura Bridgman reflected educational advances in literacy training at the start of the Industrial Revolution in the United States when inexpensive mass media technology emerged. Laura's parents relinquished their daughter's guardianship to Dr. Howe for her education, room, and board. Dr. Howe couched Laura's story in the framework of how her imprisoned soul through religious conversion embraced human contact. Stimulation became a catalyst for Laura's transformation. Her interest in learning intensified, and her face lit up with human expression as she learned to communicate. The first report of Laura's breakthrough appeared three months after her lessons started: she learned one hundred nouns and a handful of verbs.

English novelist Charles Dickens donated a large sum of money to print an edition of his *Old Curiosity Shop* (1841) in braille. A year later, Dickens wove Howe's narrative about Laura Bridgman in his travelogue *American Notes for Circulation* (1842). The author described Perkins Institute as an important location in Boston with an extensive description of the school and Howe's work with Laura to show that with an education the Deaf-Blind girl was no longer *a dog or parrot*. According to Howe, Laura was "an immortal spirit, eagerly seizing upon a new link of union with other spirits" (Dickens, 1842)! The Howe Memorial Fund was established with proceeds from his memoir in 1879. A braille library housed textbooks, *Milton's Paradise Lost and Regained*, Shakespeare's *Hamlet* and *Julius Caesar*, and other plays, as well as selections from Pope, Baxter, Swedenborg, and Byron.

Harmony Bridgman visited six months after her daughter, Laura, arrived at Perkins Institute. Harmony stood with tears, watching her daughter remain oblivious to her presence. Laura brushed up against the visitor and touched her to discover who she was. Then Laura turned away from her mother, thinking she was a stranger. Harmony handed Laura a strand of beads that she wore at home, and Laura recognized the beads, putting them around her neck. But there was no connection after six months.

Harmony tried to caress her daughter, but the girl preferred not to be touched. Harmony next gave Laura another familiar object from home. This prompted Laura to examine the visitor more closely. When the girl figured out the visitor was actually her mother, she clung to her. When it was time for Harmony to go home, she walked Laura to the door. The mother and daughter embraced there. Laura took Harmony's hand and then grasped Miss Drew's hand. Laura dropped Harmony's, weeping, and then she returned to Perkins Institute holding Miss Drew's hand because she had grown fond of her teacher.

Laura learned to write with a pencil using a pasteboard a year later on July 24, 1939. Laura occupied herself with sewing and knitting, but as her vocabulary expanded, she amused herself within an inner landscape like Alice Cogswell and Julia Brace did. When left alone, she seemed quite content soliloquizing slowly in the *finger language*. Howe reported, "In this lonely self-communion she seems to reason, reflect, and argue . . ." (Dickens, 1842).

The Deaf-Blind were isolated and longed for human connection. When Laura became aware someone was nearby, she would become restless until she could sit close next to the person, hold their hand, and converse with them by sign language. However, once Laura entered Howe's world, she became ensnared in an environment of scientific and social investigation, and she was unable to leave.

While Laura's intellect remained inscrutable, she became Howe's leverage to challenge Darwinists because she demonstrated the human capacity for learning language, which was thought to separate humans from animals. Laura was Howe's specimen, a quaint living relic who never aspired to normalcy. At Perkins Institute, Laura Bridgman was exhibited like Julia Brace earlier at the American School to attract donations. Dr. Howe treated Laura like a daughter; she lived with him and his sisters Lizzie Howe and Juliette Howe until he married poet Julia Ward in 1843. Howe was eighteen years older than his heiress wife and about a foot taller.

The couple traveled during an eighteen-month honeymoon, leaving Laura at Perkins Institute and causing her much anxiety. Under the laws of coverture, Dr. Howe took control of his wife's large estate and invested it badly.

Lydia Sigourney met Laura to observe and compare Laura Bridgman with Julia Brace. Of the two, Julia retained her sense of smell, which allowed her to identify people and situate herself within spatial contexts. Laura learned arithmetic, geography, and history. She chronicled her daily experiences and non-rhyming poems in a journal. Laura's fame as the Deaf-Blind woman who could word-build eclipsed Julia only because she had learned the skill earlier in life.

Laura Bridgman was intelligent; she intuitively used silence to leverage power and achieved a kind of *broken* physical power from mastery of movement and stillness. She only smiled when something pleased her. Laura communicated anger, frustration, and loneliness to those closest to her. Her lack of smell and taste made it easy for her to starve herself literally; this led Perkins Institute staff and students to walk on eggshells around her. Laura learned to distinguish different degrees of intellect in her own specimens—the Blind students—and she regarded newcomers with contempt if she discovered their weaknesses. Laura preferred companions she could communicate with and manipulate. For example, she took advantage of schoolmates to make them wait upon her.

When Perkins Institute opened to the public on Saturdays for "Exhibition Days," students dressed in their finest clothes and prepared to demonstrate certain exercises and talents. Laura was easily excitable, and her teachers worried she drew more attention than the Blind students. Thousands of visitors arrived to watch the novelty of Laura reading and pointing out locations on a raised-letter map. Like Julia Brace, she could thread a needle with her tongue. Tourists asked for keepsakes and followed her story in the newspapers, evangelical journals, and ladies' magazines.

Boston's influx of poor Irish immigrants because of famines started to dominate the Boston political establishment. During the 1850s, famous abolitionist Dorothea Dix hoped to establish a special trust for Laura so that she could have a paid Irish companion. Dr. Howe wanted to control Laura as her guardian-teacher-promoter in the way he could do with his wife Julia Ward Howe under coverture. Ironically, he was a bad money manager and declined Dix's offer because he did not want to deal with female-controlled fund. As a consequence, for some time Laura had no companion at all.

Perkins Institute would twice try unsuccessfully to return Laura Bridgman to her family, but they did not know what to do with her after her communications breakthrough was achieved because she was still too disabled to contribute to the family household economy. However, Scottish phrenologist George Combe relocated to Boston and befriended Howe.

AMERICA AS A SCAB NATION OF IRISH POOR

Today scab is understood to mean someone who takes the place of a worker who is on strike. However, during the late nineteenth-century, American industry consistently underbid other nations by employing quicker, lower standards of work, underselling, and manufacturing goods by using unfair methods. The breathless and exhausting work pace in American workshops was not seen in Europe. Wretched conditions causing workplace accidents and extended economic depressions brought on the ruin of thousands of families.

Between 1885 and 1895 during Helen Keller's early life, consecutive industrial depressions swelled the numbers of unemployed men with families living in poverty to a point of desperation that the nation was moved to pity. American workers seen as scab workers labored more intense, longer hours with lower wages than workers in other industrial nations. By the turn of the twentieth century, the United States was known as a scab nation.

Life spans of working-class men decreased by ten years, and working-class women and children were forced into the labor market. The unemployed overran urban lodging houses, and the number of vagrants increased dramatically. Alcoholism became a rampant cause for family desertion and domestic violence. Petty crimes like vagrancy and drunkenness became noticeable in urban areas. Gaunt, hungry unemployed laborers wandered as transients into urban industrial centers begging for work, rough food, and shelter.

Unemployment was especially high for Irish families, and low wages for men meant women and children went to work to help support families. Exploitation of child labor meant that adult employees were easily replaceable by lower-waged child workers. Soon the unemployed Irish immigrants flooded northern almshouses.

Combe's most famous work, *The Constitution of Man* (1828), influenced science more than the work of Charles Darwin. Combe studied Laura and funded a single teacher devoted to her studies and care.

After the Civil War, New Englanders increasingly perceived the Irish who emigrated to escape the Irish famines to be the lowest class of whites. The Irish were stereotyped as waves of them arrived; their hardships often continued, and where there was hardship and poverty, there were often subsequent preventable deaths. When Irish-born Thomas Sullivan received twenty-five dollars from his brother John Sullivan who worked on a "Yankee" farm in a village called Feeding Hills, Massachusetts, he used it to immigrate to America. Sullivan was alternately a charming storyteller and a hot-tempered, illiterate alcoholic. He and his wife Alice Choesy Sullivan settled in an old boardinghouse with other Irish families in an old shabby colonial-style house called "The Castle."

Their first child Joanna Sullivan was born on April 14, 1866. She was christened in a cathedral in nearby Springfield, Massachusetts, and her family called the girl Annie. The growing family lived in poverty, which meant young Annie wore shoes too small for her feet, so they did not develop properly. What little money Thomas Sullivan earned as an unskilled farm laborer often went to his drinking, leaving his family destitute. Annie contracted bacterial infection known as trachoma at the age of five, and the condition left her nearly blind.

Thomas Sullivan was unable to hold a job, and consequently, he became increasingly abusive toward his daughter. When Thomas was drunk, Alice learned to hide Annie. Their living conditions bred diseases. When Annie was eight years old, her mother Alice contracted tuberculosis and died, followed by two of her four siblings. Thomas could not cope and abandoned his remaining three children. With Annie's poor vision and her younger brother James "Jimmy" Sullivan suffering from a tubercular hip, Mary Sullivan remained the healthy sibling.

The derogatory term "tramp" was first used to describe the homeless and unemployed in the *New York Times* in February 1875. Civil War veterans learned to live outdoors (a skill they'd learned in the war) and carried guns. Tramps were routinely attacked and sometimes burned to death. Within the context of consecutive depressions, the affluent became increasingly hostile toward the poor. Little is known of Thomas Sullivan after he left his children with his brother John and his wife Bridget Sullivan, but his eldest daughter Annie never forgave him for abandoning his children.

In the nineteenth century, stories about disabled children rarely had happy endings; children with visible disabilities dependent upon family were sent to almshouses—early hospitals provided hospitality and shelter to the poor and needy. By early 1876, Annie with her bad vision and her lame brother Jimmy became too much for her uncle's family to cope with. On Washington's birthday during the centennial year in 1876, Annie and Jimmy were told they were taking a train ride to Springfield when the two actually were headed to a state almshouse located in Tewksbury, Massachusetts. A "Black Maria," a black hearse-like police prison transport vehicle pulled by horses, transported Annie and Jimmy on the final leg of the journey. They were terrified as they approached the huge, desolate institution housing one thousand inmates.

Tewksbury served many functions: it was a hospital, a lying-in hospital, a mental asylum, and a homeless shelter. Tewksbury was also a punitive workhouse providing only the coarsest food and clothing. Annie remembered being treated like a "foreign" pauper with intentional harshness (Henney, 1933). A clerk tried to separate Annie and Jimmy into gendered wards when they were admitted, but Annie refused. She created such a scene they dressed Jimmy in a girl's pinafore, or apron, and placed them both in the deadhouse where bodies were stored for burial.

To pass the time, Annie and Jimmy were given police gazettes and a popular magazine for women called *Godey's Ladies' Book*. Middle-class Victorian children cut up colorful lithographs from magazines as popular pastime, so Annie and Jimmy cut pictures from the magazines. They mounted them on the walls in their little corner area of the deadhouse, creating a primitive picture gallery. Annie remembered, "Our artistic efforts were encouraged by the doctors and attendants. They would show the exhibition to visitors with great gusto" (Wagner, 2012).

Jimmy grew increasingly sick. A doctor informed Annie, "Little girl, your brother is going on a journey soon." Annie understood what death meant. She had witnessed her mother dead not so much earlier, lying still, cold, and strangely white. Annie had also watched men enter the ward bringing coffins to remove the dead without ceremony. She lunged at the doctor in a rage. He shoved her back and threatened to send her away. Annie knew she needed to control herself.

Jimmy died as Annie slept, and he was removed. It was dark still when she awoke to feel for Jimmy's bed and found it was removed. Filled with terror at his absence, she froze, sure her little brother was already dead. The girl arose and ran to the deadhouse. She lifted the latch and discovered everything was dark inside. Annie could not see Jimmy's bed at first. She reached out her hand and touched its iron rail, and she clutched it with all of her strength and slowly pulled herself closer.

Annie felt Jimmy's cold body under the sheet; soon her screams brought people running. The orderlies tried to separate the girl from her brother's corpse. They dragged her back to her ward, but Annie kicked, scratched, and bit them until they dropped her on the floor and left her.

An aged, disabled women hobbled close. She tried to lift Annie, but the effort was too much and she groaned. Annie slowly lifted herself up and helped the woman back to her bed. The old woman comforted Annie until she allowed her tears to flow in an emotional release.

In the morning, Annie returned to the deadhouse where the orderlies allowed her say goodbye to her brother with hugs and kisses. At a time when middle-class Americans had developed elaborate, sentimental mourning rituals, the poor were not allowed to express the same emotions over their dead. One of the residents said, "Come away now; you can see him after breakfast. You must control yourself. Making such a fuss does no good."

The matron took Annie outside, where they picked some white lilacs symbolizing purity and innocence to shroud Jimmy. Men brought a small coffin, but Annie was not allowed to watch Jimmy being placed in the coffin; then the girl was allowed to view her dead brother and place the lilacs she'd picked over his cheeks.

When Annie realized they were taking Jimmy away, she ran after them, but the doctor stopped her before they reached the gate. She begged to follow. The small group walked down a long narrow path and arrived at the pauper's burying ground in a bare sandy field. The grave was already dug, and the men quickly lowered Jimmy's small coffin without ceremony. When Annie heard the sound of sand shoveled over the coffin, she could bear no more and fell to the ground with her face in the weeds, sobbing.

The men left quietly when the work was done. The doctor turned to Annie and said, "Come now, we must return to the hospital."

A grave digger approached Annie and said, "Look, little girl, here are some flowers for Jimmy's grave" (Wagner, 2012). Annie, with tears in her eyes, took the scented geraniums symbolizing melancholy and tenderly planted them in the sand.

Annie grew to believe the Tewksbury staff did not serve the poor but viciously repressed them. On returning to the hospital, the doctor told Annie a priest had been called, but he could not come because he was sick. The doctor explained this was the reason there was no proper burial service. Annie Sullivan was desperately alone. She never returned to the deadhouse after that day and never embraced a religion.

After a time, the Tewkesbury staff transferred the resentful girl twice to Sisters of Charity Hospital in Lowell, Massachusetts, for eye surgery to improve her vision. Annie returned to Tewksbury and was placed in the hospital ward where women gave birth, so she came in contact with regular inmates.

The ward was depressing. Patients were not separated by age or seriousness of illness; its frosted windows prevented patients from seeing the gardens, and the windows were locked in case patients tried to escape. During the sticky summer months, with no ventilation the stench was like a sewage dump. Rats and other vermin ran free in overcrowded wards, and some attendants mistreated the inmates. Amid ongoing noise and wailing, Annie ironically found herself comforted by a community of Irish women. She roamed the almshouse, making herself useful by visiting fellow inmates. Not knowing how to read or write, she borrowed books from the library and asked inmates to read them aloud to her. Glimpsing the world through books and magazines, Annie learned people beyond Tewksbury's walls lived differently.

Missionaries with biases about the poor visited Tewksbury and made impressions on the visually impaired orphan. Female residents made fun of those who offered prayers to the poor and then left them to fend for themselves. Missionaries questioned inmates about their lives, and they responded with misleading answers. Most did not want to be judged based on the circumstances that had drawn them to such an awful place. Once the missionaries left, the residents appropriated their hymns with raunchy lyrics relevant to their life experiences.

Some female inmates observed male inmates of Tewksbury with disdain. They described them derisively as the "procession of the *Horribles*." This phrase was derived from Boston's Fourth of July tradition where young people dressed up in grotesque costumes like those of tramps, petty thieves, pickpockets, professional beggars, drunkards, Blind men, lame men, and deformed and hunchback men. Massachusetts's tradition of holding parades featured people wearing comic and grotesque costumes commemorating the Battle of Bunker Hill. It had started in 1875 when the term "tramps" was coined with an event called "The Antique and Horrible Parade."

Annie's memories of men showing cunningness, glaring with pleasant expressions, and others so ashamed that they lowered their eyes made lasting impressions. She witnessed the staff readily shame men who were decent working people. It did not matter if the men were only temporarily unemployed or transients on the road, all were treated like tramps. Some women disparaged their own sex partners. These observations informed the girl's relationships throughout her life as she felt ashamed of her own visual disability and tried to keep her time at Tewksbury a secret.

When "officials," men with impressive beards like Frank B. Sanborn came, residents were informed to be on their best behavior. Sanborn had established the American Social Science Associations and the National Conference of Charities and Corrections (Wagner, 2012). He knew Ralph Waldo Emerson, Henry David Thoreau, and Boston's famous Alcott family. Tewkesbury's staff prepared for these inspections with great care to cover up the notorious conditions: toilets were cleaned and windows were opened, and the smell of ammonia burned the residents' lungs for days. Anyone misbehaving during these visits received no dinner and lost any privileges.

Annie Sullivan remembered how residents were told to behave like human beings, not wild animals, "We knew if we did not behave, we would get it." Female reformers visited wearing dresses with trains they lifted with their right hands to avoid picking up the inmate's germs. Once the wedding for the daughter of a railroad tycoon was held on the Tewksbury grounds. Annie later lamented, "Oh, the money spent could have furnished us poor with so many things that we really needed" (Wagner, 2012).

While an inmate at Tewksbury, Annie learned to fend for herself amid disabled, diseased, criminal, and insane castaways. When residents told Annie about an upcoming visit by Sanborn, she was advised he could change her life. Annie Sullivan became determined. With hands outstretched in a very un-Victorian posture, the girl propelled herself before visiting dignitaries including six-foot-four-inch-tall Sanborn and cried out: "Mr. Sanborn, Mr. Sanborn, I want to go to school" (Wagner, 2012)!

Frank B. Sanborn responded by procuring a spot for Annie as a charity case at Perkins Institute for the Blind in Boston, Massachusetts. He knew

Dr. Samuel Gridley Howe's son-in-law, Michael Anagnos, who was now the institute's director. Perkins Institute had built relationships with noted writers ever since its founder, Dr. Samuel Gridley Howe, had married the daughter of a wealthy Wall Street banker. Julia Ward Howe had made connections throughout the region, but her husband did not believe women should have intellectual lives outside the home.

When Dr. and Mrs. Howe traveled to Europe with their daughter Julia Romana Howe, they took a side trip to Greece, where a bearded young philosophy student named Michael Anognostopolous acted as Howe's translator and secretary. Julia Romana was very shy and uncomfortable in crowds, so when she formed a romantic attachment with Michael, her father did not question the attachment or the man. Michael shortened his name to Anagnos when he came to America, as an investigation would have revealed Howe's future son-in-law was already married and divorced and had a son named Polychronos Anognostopolous.

Annie Sullivan was fourteen years old when she arrived at Perkins Institute in October 1880. She spoke with a slight Irish accent and could neither read nor write. The girl from Tewksbury almshouse did not even know her own birthday when she was enrolled, but Annie was a quick learner. She retained some eyesight so she could make herself useful around the school of Blind students.

Perkins Institute employed only female instructors to teach Black and white students. Comparable to Boston's public schools, Perkins Institute taught braille, geography, arithmetic, algebra, geometry, history, grammar, rhetoric, composition, English literature, civics, natural history, physics, anatomy and physiology, philosophy, and Latin. Perkins taught with *The Moon System of Embossed Reading* for Blind that had insensitive senses of touch to distinguish finer letters and braille for letters and music notation.

Male students learned vocational skills to make brooms and to weave caning for furniture. Female students learned the domestic skills of knitting, crocheting, and sewing with needle and machine; beadwork; and spinning finely worsted yarns. Perkins Institute also opened a store located on Avon Street in Boston where student-manufactured mattresses, featherbeds, welcome mats, and brooms were sold during open hours on Thursdays. The shop was also a repair enterprise for upholstering furniture, re-seating cane-bottomed chair, and renovating older mattresses and featherbeds with proceeds going directly to the Blind manufacturers.

A forty-year-old shipmaster's widow named Mrs. Sophia C. Hopkins became Perkins Institute's housemother shortly before Annie arrived, and she treated the girl like a daughter. Sophia's only daughter, Florence Hopkins, had died when she was sixteen years old. There was no place for the new girl to go during school breaks when other students returned to their families. Annie desperately feared being returned to Tewkesbury. Mrs. Hopkins owned a house in Brewster, Massachusetts, built by her father along the Cape Cod shoreline. The housemother offered the truculent teenager a coastal refuge when needed.

Annie met Michael Anagnos during an "Exhibition Day" when wealthy donors were invited to see the students exhibit their talents. Mrs. Hopkins asked Annie to collect plants from the various cottages. When the teenager went to the housemother's cottage where she resided with Laura Bridgman, she explored and discovered Mrs. Hopkins' stash of cosmetics. Annie could not resist the temptation. At a time when proper Victorian girls wore no makeup, she liberally applied face powder and rouge without asking permission.

Returning to the exhibit hall, Annie came face-to-face with a tall, slender Anagnos, sporting eastern-styled whiskers, leading a tour. The director promptly told Annie Sullivan to wash the makeup off. The pair soon developed an odd relationship, alternating between sparring partners and playful father-daughter team. The teen had no respect for position and aggravated Anagnos's mother-in-law, Julia Ward Howe, who was the grand dame of Perkins Institute. Annie perceived Mrs. Howe to be a wealthy Boston Brahmin, though in fact she had little money. Samuel Gridley Howe's bad investments had left his widow with a meager budget, compelling her to protect his good name in order to keep funds flowing into Perkins Institute.

Annie remained at Perkins for seven years. The director gave Annie the nickname "Miss Spitfire." She never shook off her Tewksbury experience. Miss Spitfire retained a subconscious feeling of shame and pessimism alternating with self-assertion and self-justification, dark rage, and depression. Most of Annie's classmates scorned the Irish-Catholic girl who struggled with bronchial infections, and they laughed at her shabby clothing. Annie always believed that even if she did not have a penny she should face each day with her chin up. Tewksbury became Annie's secret, but it gave her a *shattered power* of the poor determined to move up in the world.

Annie's favorite teacher in her first year was Miss Mary C. Moore. The aging teacher overlooked Annie's hair-trigger temper, but she recognized the teen as an underdeveloped child, which made her also astonishingly mature. Moore taught Annie grammar and spelling, which gave the girl faith in herself. Under this loving tutelage, Annie realized if she was going to make anything of herself, she would need to navigate the conventional order of Victorian society.

Annie developed detachment: she was rarely shocked, pained, grieved, or troubled by the things she saw. Annie and Jimmy were cast out of the family that did not know how to deal with their disabilities without a backward glance. While Jimmy died, Annie disappeared as a charity case. The

Tewkesbury staff knew where she went. Nobody expected the visually impaired girl to make anything of herself with no resources, but they were also aware of the trauma she survived from neglect and abandonment by an abusive alcoholic father. As the story goes, Annie's uncle John Sullivan and his wife Bridget Sullivan visited Tewksbury once and asked about Annie and Jimmy. They were told that Jimmy had died and Annie had gone away, but nobody told them where.

Mrs. Sophia Hopkins befriended Annie and offered her accommodations during school breaks. Sophia's brother, Frank Crocker, was a grocer who knew all of the local gossip. He shared it with Annie, making her feel part of a community. Hopkins's home in Brewster was filled with china and silver and a personal library of books including a volume *Birdie and his Friends* (1873) by Margaret T. Canby, which included a story called "The Frost Fairies."

Annie resided with Laura Bridgman in Sophia Hopkin's cottage. Annie remembered Laura, now in her fifties, sitting quietly by the window like Whistler's Mother in the painting by James McNeill Whistler. Laura's sightless eyes were turned toward the window, like a flower drawn to the light. Laura taught Annie the manual alphabet. Annie's fingers soon rang, rippled, danced, buzzed, and hummed with words. She learned to create perceptive, audible, and other qualities to bring her Deaf-Blind roommate into abstract sensory contact with touchable environments, even better than Dr. Howe could have. Annie never allowed the silence to be silent.

Since Annie retained some vision and Anagnos's wife was extremely shy, he mentored Miss Spitfire, who in turn helped promote Perkins Institute. Anagnos trusted Annie and deployed her to talk to Boston newspaper editors about getting free advertising. Annie excelled through six years of study at Perkins Institute and graduated valedictorian of her class. Of Perkins Institute's valedictorian, Anagnos observed: "The furnace of hardships through which she passed was not without beneficial results . . . An iron will was hammered out on the anvil of misfortune" (Wagner, 2012).

The notion of possibly returning to Tewkesbury after graduating terrified Annie. Mary Moore wanted Annie to go to a normal school to learn how to be a teacher, and Anagnos promised to find resources for her to do so. Annie Sullivan gave herself a middle name "Mansfield" at Perkins Institute to make herself appear more affluent. In her commencement speech, Annie "Mansfield" Sullivan stated, "Every man who improves himself, is adding to the progress of society, and everyone who stands still, holds it back."

Annie Sullivan travelled with Sophia Hopkins to Brewster over the summer. No one knew how Annie would support herself with impaired vision and a delayed education. At the same time, Laura Bridgman became one of the most famous women in the world because she excited sympathy and interest in her disability. As Lydia H. Sigourney had bridged the lives of Deaf-Blind women Julia Brace and Laura before, Annie Sullivan would soon bridge Laura and Helen Keller. While Sigourney was an elegant writer, essayist, and educator, Annie Sullivan was a scrappy pauper with ambition. Both women had strong views of tactile teaching from personal observations of life, but only one would become a household name.

2

Interventions

Everyone in America knows the "story" of Helen Keller, though her real biography remains obscure. She was born in Tuscumbia, Alabama, on June 27, 1880. The town was located between the tribal lands of the Cherokee to the east, the Chickasaw to the west, and the Muscogee (Creek) to the southeast. Tuscumbia was named after the Cherokee chief Tashka Ambi. Its broad main street was lined with shops with large houses peeking behind large magnolia trees. Beyond the pastoral town, Captain Arthur Henley Keller and his wife Catherine "Kate" Everett Adams Keller dealt with the dilemma within their household; their Deaf-Blind daughter Helen grew increasingly wild, and the couple did not know how to intervene. They did not want to institutionalize their eldest child, but they were increasingly concerned for their youngest daughter's safety as Helen's temperament became increasingly volatile when she began to understand she was different from everyone in the household.

The Keller family lived in a homestead at the end of a dirt lane called "Ivy Green," built in 1820 by Helen's grandfather David Keller. The house was now dressed in English ivy climbing the fences, and the property exuded a warm scented appeal from its trees and flowers. The nearby Tennessee River ran red with the soil of the region. It was one of Alabama's oldest river ports and lay close to a canal constructed at Muscle Shoals.

Helen's father Arthur served in the Confederate Army at the siege of Vicksburg, Virginia. He had two grown sons from his first marriage to

Front view of the Keller family home, Ivy Green, in Tuscumbia, Alabama, where Helen Keller spent the first eight years of her life. Photographer W. N. Manning took the photograph of the simple 1820s era white clapboard house designed and built by Keller's grandfather, David Keller, on February 2, 1934, during the second year of the Historic American Buildings Survey initiated by the National Park Service as a "make-work" program during the Great Depression. Located opposite from Andrew Jackson's house in Tuscumbia, Alabama, Helen Keller was born in a plantation office built and converted into a home by her father, Arthur Henley Keller, for his second wife, Catherine "Kate" Keller. (Library of Congress)

Sarah E. Rosser, also from Memphis, who had died when she was in her late thirties in 1877. Captain Keller's second wife, Kate, got along with her younger stepson, William Simpson Keller, who was a teenager when she joined the family, but her older stepson, James McDonald Keller, deeply resented his father and Kate for marrying only a year after his own mother's death. James retained a healthy skepticism for his father and challenged his stepmother who held a more liberal view of the world than many in the family.

After the Civil War, Captain Keller built a small house consisting of a large square room and a smaller one, where he and Kate resided. The Little House was covered with vines, climbing roses, and honeysuckles, nearly hiding its porch, like an arbor of yellow roses and Southern smilax attracting hummingbirds and bees. The Kellers and their Black employees raised and manufactured much of what they needed on their farm, including fruits and vegetables along with chickens, turkeys, pigs, and sheep. Blacks made up more than half the population of Tuscumbia, yet they remained largely invisible.

In Kate's garden, young Helen first explored nature. She followed scents from spot to spot to orient herself with familiar landmarks; she also recognized plants by their shape and by the texture of their leaves and blossoms. Helen groped her way along the boxwood hedges using hands above, feet below, tracing paths at the ground level, guided by her sense of smell. Later in life, she impressed friends when she determined the difference between purple and white lilacs by scent.

The Keller family owned a summer cabin called Fern Quarry that was surrounded by ferns and thick woods, located on a mountain ridge about fourteen miles from their home. It was located near the entrance of an abandoned pit where limestone was extracted. The family spent summers and celebrated the Fourth of July at their cabin where Arthur and his friends hunted, told stories, and played card games.

No longer affluent, the Kellers needed to watch their resources. An economic depression beginning after the Panic of 1873 and continuing through the decade before Arthur and Kate married made life difficult for many Southern families, white and Black. This depression and others impacted the South more dramatically than North due to Reconstruction, a process of restoring civil government of the former Confederate states and establishing political civil rights of African Americans. The social and economic dislocations of both the war and Reconstruction made the region vulnerable to economic fluxes.

While in the North the numbers of homeless reached points when they could not be reabsorbed into jobs, in the South the remnant plantation system economy was partially deconstructed after slavery and the war ended in 1865. Freed slaves gained new opportunities for education, obtaining land grants, and running for political offices, though the vast majority of freed persons lived in dire poverty. New "gray economy" enterprises emerged where Blacks could be employed in occupations they once performed as slaves and invest earnings in small businesses to garner some economic independence, but for many, life after slavery was not very different from life before.

As the overall Southern economy went into a free fall, white business owners like Arthur Keller were caught without sufficient cash resources for them to maintain properties and businesses. As Blacks became consumers patronizing or bartering with Black-owned businesses, the economic losses for white employers were deeply felt and resented. Many white Southerners including Arthur continued to believe Blacks were less human than whites and resented any gains made by nonwhites.

Economic uncertainty stressed the marriage as Arthur struggled to support his growing family as a cotton plantation owner and the editor of a small weekly local newspaper, the *North Alabamian*. As a proslavery Southern Democrat, Arthur turned his newspaper into a publication with a Democrat's voice. After the Union victory in the Civil War, Republicans took control of Congress and enacted Reconstruction to establish and enforce civil and voting rights for African Americans. In the early 1870s, Southern state legislatures rolled back many of the Republican reforms with Jim Crow laws to enforce racial segregation and to suppress the ability of Blacks to vote. A lawyer before the Civil War, Arthur could be a man of limited ideas, and he did not adapt his actions to the changing economic and political landscape.

Helen's mother was an Arkansas-born, Memphis belle with periwinkle blue eyes and suffragist sympathies. Kate thought she had escaped Memphis's dangers from a particularly intense epidemic of yellow fever. Efforts at quarantine came too late, so roughly half of the town's residents fled the city as the fever raged, infecting over seventeen thousand residents and killing more than five thousand people, including her father, General Charles William Adams, on September 9, 1878. Kate soon married Captain Arthur Henley Keller.

Kate came from a respectable family before becoming the second wife of a widower twenty years her senior. She moved from living in a major Southern river port center to a frontier where she did not know how to darn a sock, let alone maintain a household. Cloth and clothing production were important for female social networking, so Kate learned how to cut and sew clothes for her family. She learned by taking mending home to Memphis so that her mother's Black servants could teach her how to do these tasks. She learned to treasure her pretty workbasket that stood on three legs above the floor, containing her sewing supplies. While Kate generally lived within the same Southern notions of race that her husband did, by the time Helen was born, Kate and Arthur sometimes went days without speaking to each other.

Kate was overjoyed with her baby girl, who she named Helen Adams Keller. Helen started speaking at six months, and one of her first words was "wa-wa" for *water*. By the time Helen was a year old, she was walking and talking. "What wonderful eyes you had," Kate later told Helen. "You were always picking up needles and buttons that no one else could find" (Lash, 1980).

When Helen was eighteen months old, she contracted an illness, possibly scarlet fever, although no one diagnosed it. Global scarlet fever epidemics occurred throughout the nineteenth century. There was no known local outbreak of scarlet fever around Tuscumbia; Helen's illness happened toward the end of a decade-long cycle of pandemics. The family doctor ascribed Helen's illness to a brain fever with stomach congestion. She ran a high fever for many days, and the family was not sure she would survive. Then the fever vanished, so the family felt relief.

VICTORIAN NAME CHOICES AND MEANINGS

Helen Keller's story is a story of identity. During the American Victorian Era, coverture legally covered a woman's identity. When a woman married, her husband's name covered her own, and she became Mrs. (husband's name). She needed to wisely choose a husband with a good name or that name could bring down her future fortunes and those of her children. Helen Keller and Annie Sullivan garnered nicknames Billy (Keller) and Bill (Sullivan), a masculine name derived from the name William (English compound of two words "wil," meaning "will or desire," and "helm," meaning "helmet or protection").

Kate Keller chose the name Helen (Greek meaning "light") and her maiden name Adams (British meaning "son of Adam") for her first daughter, showing her family lineage connecting to New England roots and the second president of the United States, John Adams (1735–1826), who was a political philosopher and Founding Father. The surname Keller (Swiss-Germanic meaning "cellar") referred to winemakers who stored their product in a cellar. Ironically, the first Keller in America, Swiss-born Casper Keller (1736–1819), was a pioneering teacher of the Deaf in Zurich, Switzerland. The family called her "Little Bronco," referring to her wild streak.

Annie Sullivan's surname was Sullivan (Irish meaning "dark-eyed") and birth name was Joanne (feminine version of Hebrew name John meaning "God is gracious"). The family called her Anne or Annie (derived from the Hebrew name Hannah meaning "grace"). When Annie Sullivan attended Perkins Institute, she gave herself a middle name "Mansfield." Mansfield (a Celtic place name referring to a field by the hill called "Man" meaning "a mother") was made popular with Jane Austin's *Mansfield Park* (1814). Michael Anagnos called her "Miss Spitfire" because of her hair-trigger temper.

Kate noticed that when the sun streamed brightly onto the infant's face she did not turn away. Kate tried waving her hands in front of Helen's face, but she did not react. Kate next held a lamp in front of Helen's eyes, and still there was no sign the baby could see the light. Kate realized her baby girl was blind. Soon after, Kate noticed that Helen, who loved food, did not react to the dinner bell. Kate shook a homemade rattle close to Helen's ear, but she did not respond or move. Kate became frantic. She shook the rattle harder near Helens ears, but there was no response. Helen was so young that she had no consciousness of being Blind, Deaf, and Mute.

Arthur Keller chronicled Helen's condition for his newspaper readers, first hopefully and then with resignation. Kate worked through her pain of dealing with a Deaf-Blind-Mute daughter with Helen clinging to her skirts. There was no place to retreat, so she buried herself like a workaholic in domestic production for the homestead. As with other middle-class Southern women in a society turned upside down, Kate did not complain about family problems. Kate became a knowledgeable poultry farmer and supervised the family's Black workers in farming crops and livestock. She also manufactured jams and jellies, which became well known in the community. With hired farm laborers, Kate learned to manufacture her own butter and lard, as well as cure bacon and ham from the farm's pigs that could be bartered or sold. Now largely unknown in American cuisine, lard is the semisoft white fat manufactured from the fatty parts of the pig. Leaf lard obtained from the "flare" fat surrounding the kidneys and inside the loins has little pork flavor, and it was ideal for use in baked goods, especially flaky, moist piecrusts.

In Victorian America in the South, middle-class women were much more isolated than in the North because they were more likely to live in rural areas. Kate was an Episcopalian who found comfort in attending church. The sensibilities of common law dictated that marriage offered women their primary social network and protection. Female subordination within the family along with children and Black servants, husbands argued, reflected their subordination under common law asserting, "Influence by reason when you can, by authority when you must."

Arthur was generous host even in the worst circumstances. Kate did not complain publicly if she disagreed with Arthur, but she suffered silently, and her nature changed. Her mouth showed every etched line related to the family's hardships. Kate stopped talking about herself. The Southern belle from Memphis became so reserved she rarely revealed her deepest thoughts even to her family, but it deepened her sympathy for the pain of others. Kate confided in a friend, "Fate ambushed the joy in my heart when I was twenty-four and left it dead."

Kate focused on her family as Helen initially remained unaware of how she was confined in her Deaf-Blind-Mute "no-world." Humans use language, a system of spoken and written words, visual symbols, and gestures to express thoughts and ideas. Helen could not hear people speak or see their mouths move; therefore, she could not learn language as a seeing or hearing person would. Helen's world appeared to be dark and silent, but she utilized touch, taste, and smell, and she *adapted.*

Helen and Kate communicated using simple grassroots manual signs. Helen devised her own signals to communicate needs with family and household staff. Helen stroked her cheek to communicate "Mother." Helen's earliest memories of her father, Arthur, dated to when she was about five years old. She remembered navigating through drifts of newspapers to find him alone holding a sheet of paper close to his face. Helen wondered what he was doing and imitated his movements and gestures to figure out the mystery. Arthur wore reading glasses, so Helen's sign for "Father" was created by making the shape of spectacles with her fingers before her eyes.

Helen generally clung to Kate's skirts following her mother from task to task; otherwise, she groped to move from place to place. The Deaf-Blind-Mute girl learned to assist women in the households with sewing, knitting, and basic cleaning tasks like Julia Brace and all girls, as soon as they were old enough to handle needles without pricking themselves. As she grew, Helen sensed that other children younger than herself in the household learned to communicate differently.

Helen sometimes stood between two people talking and touched their lips, but she could not understand what they were doing. The Deaf-Blind girl frantically moved her lips and gesticulated without any result. She eventually reasoned others could somehow do something with their mouths to receive what they needed, and she could not. This realization made Helen so angry she threw tantrums until she exhausted herself. Helen did not know what the emotion of *play* was, as something so common within the whole of humankind. She was not socialized enough to grasp the abstract notion of play as a means to experience fun, relaxation, entertainment, and learning in a way to develop living skills. Helen grew increasingly restless, difficult, and uncontrollable.

Helen experienced her immediate environment with her remaining senses through touch, smell, and taste (Keller 1903). One of Helen's favorite tasks was gathering eggs of guinea fowl in the long grass. She explored the family's property freely, tactilely examining every object she could reach. She visited sheds where the family stored corn harvests and the stable where Arthur's horses and cherished hunting dogs lived, and their female setter tolerated the wayward girl.

Helen wanted freedom of movement, but without sight or hearing, she did not have much physical liberty without groping for signposts. Inside and outside, the Deaf-Blind girl preferred to sit on the grass or floor because being grounded offered comfort. When the cows were milked, the farmhands allowed Helen to touch them. Sometimes a cow did not appreciate Helen's curious grasp of her udder and let her know it with a sharp switch of her tail. Helen got bruised and scuffed during her meanderings, but she could not complain. Whether it was her inability to communicate or her stubborn determination to remain independent, her family got the notion Helen simply did not feel.

The Black servants on the homestead taught Helen how to fold and put away laundry. She excelled at this task, utilizing her sense of smell to distinguish the owner of each article of clothing by its residual smell. The little girl also helped to knead dough balls, make ice cream, and grind coffee. Helen enjoyed tangling with other children over remnant cake batter.

Helen passed time in the kitchen with the family cook, Belle, and her daughter, Martha Washington, who was about three years older than Helen. Martha, familiar with the Deaf-Blind girl's moods and tricks, translated Helen's crude communications with others in the household. In her growing frustration, Helen alternated between temper tantrums and giggling when happy.

Helen learned tactile lessons from everything she touched. She helped feed the hens and turkeys that congregated near the kitchen steps. One day, a bold turkey grabbed a tomato from Helen's hands and ran off with it. Inspired by the gobbler's tenacity, Helen and Martha Washington snatched a newly frosted cake and took it to the woodpile and ate the whole thing. Helen learned the hard way not to gorge on sweets from her unhappy stomach.

Arthur Keller, although increasingly short of cash, still indulged Helen. He gently directed her through the gardens and never failed to bring her the juiciest and most fragrant, first-harvested grapes and berries of the season. His fortunes improved in 1885 when President Grover Cleveland appointed him U.S. Marshal for the Northern District of Alabama with a steady income and increased political stature in the community.

Strong and active, Helen understood some of what was going on about her. When she was five years old, Kate had another daughter named Mildred Keller. Helen regarded her baby sister as an intruder, even as she became familiar with the curves and dimples on Mildred's hands. Helen's jealousy of the baby led her to overturn Mildred's cradle, and the baby would have been seriously hurt if Kate had not caught her before she fell to the floor.

One day, Helen spilled water on her apron and unthinkingly spread it out while sitting in front of the open fire in the sitting room hearth. The apron was not drying fast enough, so Helen held it over the flames, and the fire suddenly leapt to life. In a moment, her clothes caught fire and Helen cried out. Her nurse came quickly and put out the flames with a blanket. Helen was not badly burned, but her parents feared that she would get herself into other situations that she would not get out. They also scared as she got stronger, she would cause more damage and disruption in the household.

Helen's few signs became inadequate. She later remembered, "My failures to make myself understood made me throw tantrums." This realization of *difference* made Helen angry, and she increasingly threw fits when she kicked and screamed until she exhausted herself. Helen felt as if invisible hands held her back. She struggled, "Resistance was so strong in me. The tempest made me lash out sometimes daily, sometimes hourly."

The girl was determined to have her own way regardless of the consequences. She knew her storming was wrong, and she felt regret, but it did not deter her from throwing tantrums to manipulate situations. After fits of frustration in the house, Helen would go outside and hide her hot face in the cool leaves and grass. Helen's bucking behavior garnered the nickname "Little Bronco," especially when she kicked her nurse.

To Kate's distress, some relatives soon labeled the troubled Helen as wild, a destructive animal, and possibly mentally defective. An Alabama law enacted before the Civil War specifically banned carnivals from abandoning Deaf individuals in towns for the locals to support. The Deaf and Blind were among the "unwanted" to be pitied, shunned, abandoned, and ignored as monstrosities. However, Arthur's sister Eveline "Eva" Keller recognized Helen had potential, *if someone could reach her mind.*

Helen played with Black children living at Ivy Green. She noticed they moved their lips and uttered sounds. So too did Mildred, who was much younger than herself and other family members. Helen moved her lips too, but to no effect. She knew that she was *different,* and the difference made her very angry like other Deaf-Blind children who had lost sight and hearing early in life. Helen felt like an *outsider* in her own home; she could feel her own cries, but others only heard the girl's quacks. Sometimes, Helen held her playmates' mouths very hard, not understanding she was hurting them. Once Helen was playing with Martha Washington, who had been instructed to entertain her, and Helen cut off some of her corkscrew curls.

Despite Helen's growing wildness, Kate resisted institutionalizing her "Little Bronco," even as she grew harder to manage. At almost six, Helen was strong for her age, and Kate worried about how Helen would cope when she became a teenager and would be interested in boys. Kate worried that Helen's challenges might one day make her vulnerable to sexual assault.

Kate Keller toured the Alabama Institute for the Deaf and Blind located in Talladega, Alabama, which was located over a hundred miles from Ivy Green. When she visited the private "dual school" school that had sixteen white students enrolled in it, she found it offered industrial training in manufacturing brooms and weaving cane chair or baskets, offering no path to economic self-sufficiency. While Deaf-Blind boys learned shoe repairing, the girls learned less than what Helen learned at home. If Helen attended this school, Kate reasoned, she would be unable to marry or live with any independence. Her daughter would be compelled to enter an asylum as an adult where she could be thrown in with the poor, the insane, and the intellectually challenged.

Kate read English author Charles Dickens' *American Notes for General Circulation* (1842). The travelogue chronicled the education of an older Deaf-Blind-Mute woman named Laura Bridgman, who lived at the Perkins Institute for the Blind in Boston, Massachusetts. The desperate young mother saw similarities between Laura and her "Little Bronco." Dickens found Laura's voice to be *an uncouth noise* that was rather painful to hear. However, it was over forty years since the account had been published, and Kate reasoned Laura's teacher Dr. Samuel Gridley Howe must be long dead, and perhaps Howe's methods may have died with him.

Kate learned from the account how Boston fostered public institutions and charities supporting the needy with either State support or assistance. A superintendent and trustees directed Perkins Institute for the Blind, and students from adjacent states including Maine, Vermont, and New Hampshire paid for board and instruction. Each student opened an account so that families, benefactors, or their home state could contribute to their special education. Kate thought her husband Arthur might like this model because they could afford some schooling for Helen if it helped to socialize her for.

Dickens' travelogue and the progressive education scene in Boston offered Kate hope. Students at Perkins Institute learned similar skills as those in the Alabama Institute so they could earn tuition with the skills learned, and anything that was earned over tuition and board the students could keep. Arthur would appreciate Helen having the ability to work for tuition and board; Perkins Institute was not an almshouse. Dickens described Perkins Institute as a place of "working bees in the hive," an industrious community within the New England sensibility working to improve lives.

Students attending Perkins Institute, according to Dickens' account, did not wear uniforms; they demonstrated "their own proper character, with its individuality unimpaired; not lost in a dull, ugly, monotonous repetition of the same unmeaning garb" (Dickens, 1842). Perkins Institute had a spacious music hall with an organ and a map room for learning geography. Dickens observed the faces of the Blind did not conceal their inner thoughts. "A man with eyes may blush to contemplate the mask he wears." Dickens synthesized Howe's methods for teaching Laura in terms Kate could understand and then explain to Arthur.

Helen's parents discussed their options and did research, and they came up with the idea of hiring a paid companion and teacher for their daughter to see if she could be educated at all. This would help Kate to focus on her domestic duties without Helen tugging at her all the time, and perhaps Helen's sister Mildred would also benefit.

Arthur and Kate took six-year-old Helen on a two-day train ride to visit an oculist named Dr. J. Julian Chisholm residing in Baltimore, Maryland, in 1886. The train ride was exciting, and Helen made friends easily during the journey. A woman gave her a small box of shells and Arthur made holes in each shell so Helen could string them. The activity kept her happy and content for a while. When the conductor made his rounds, she clung to his coattails while he collected and punched the tickets. The conductor allowed Helen to play with the hole-punch used to mark the tickets, and she sat curled in a corner of the car making little holes in the cardboard bits.

When Arthur and Kate Keller approached Chisholm for a consultation, he could offer no assistance because there was no known operation or cure to restore Helen's sight and hearing after years without use. Chisholm suggested the family visit Alexander Graham Bell, who lived only thirty-five miles away in Washington, D.C.

*   *   *

Before the Civil War, sign language (or manual education) was the predominant educational tool for teaching the Deaf. Alexander Graham Bell changed all that. Bell married a Deaf woman Mabel Gardiner Hubbard, and his mother, Eliza Grace Symonds Bell, was Deaf. Bell and his father, Alexander Melville Bell, invested time and resources into speech and elocution science. Some people later speculated George Bernard Shaw's iconic play *Pygmalion* (1912) was loosely based upon Bell's parents. Alexander Graham Bell's research on hearing and speech led him to experiment with hearing devices, culminating in Bell being awarded the first U.S. patent for the telephone in 1876.

Bell taught speech at Boston University from 1873 to 1877, but he never actually taught a Deaf person to speak. He felt sign language imprisoned the Deaf, making them outsiders. His bias toward oral communication for the Deaf contradicted the parallel movement within the Deaf community to teach and use sign language (Bell, 1883). Bell was a proponent and taught *visible speech*, or lip-reading, which was a challenge for the Deaf-Blind like Helen.

Bell promoted integrating the Deaf into mainstream society, and he opposed Deaf marrying Deaf and segregating themselves in small communities (Bell, 1916). Bell asserted Deaf children remained mute, not because they couldn't hear, but from a lack of instruction. Bell railed about how no one taught the Deaf to speak. He wasn't wrong. At the time, the American School for the Deaf located in Hartford, Connecticut taught only sign language and not methods for speech articulation.

Bell argued written words related directly to abstract ideas that are expressed do not require the intervention of manual language. He felt Deaf children should be taught written English to communicate with commonly used regional vernacular language. Bell argued the manual alphabet was a backward approach harkening from a more primitive time when humans gestured and used pantomime. He believed acquisition of sign language hindered the acquisition of the English language with idiomatic expressions. "It makes Deaf-Mutes associate together in adult life, and avoid the society of hearing people . . ." (Bell, 1883).

In his *Memoir upon the Formation of a Deaf Variety of the Human Race* (1883), he describes familial experiences with the Blind. Here, he expressed concerns about a tendency for the Deaf to select Deaf marriage partners, which he asserted was an undesirable "calamity to the world" (Padden and Humphries, 2005). He proposed remedies and reforms, including eliminating special schools for the Deaf, prohibiting the use of sign language among Deaf children, and discouraging Deaf teachers from teaching Deaf children, against which Deaf activists today rail in the ongoing controversy of fostering Deaf culture or integrating the Deaf into mainstream society where they are marginalized.

Dr. Chisholm likely sent a letter of introduction to Bell about young Helen Keller who grew up in Alabama. The tall inventor's daughters, Elsie and Marian, were a little older than the Deaf-Blind-Mute girl. Once Arthur, Kate, and Helen arrived at Bells' residence, Captain Keller dropped off an introductory note, or calling card commonly used in Victorian society, asking if he could bring his Deaf-Blind-Mute daughter Helen for a consultation. Bell quickly dispatched an affirmative reply.

When Arthur and Kate brought Helen into his house, Bell knelt to allow Helen to explore his facial features with her hands. The girl was inscrutable as she discovered his bushy beard, prominent nose, and thick mustache. Helen's small fingers paused upon his lips as he articulated her name. Then she touched his stiff collar, silk tie, waistcoat, and watch chain. The inventor's home and fashions revealed far more affluence than her small-town home. Bell tried to read Helen's expressions and later described her face as "chillingly empty."

Bell led the three visitors into his parlor, a Victorian sitting room designed for receiving guests, and invited Kate and Arthur to sit (Gray, 2006). Bell gently pulled Helen close to him, and she climbed into his lap, where she continued her exploration. She discovered the inventor's pocket watch, and Bell obligingly set to chime on command so Helen could hear its vibration. To his delight, Helen responded to it with a hint of a smile.

Bell found Helen untutored, unmanageable, and unhappily isolated, but in possession of the senses of smell, taste and touch. Bell was beguiled when he saw an inner light beneath Helen's expressionless face, which made him conclude the girl could be educated.

After the Kellers left, Bell consulted with a Washington expert on educating the Deaf, named Edward Miner Gallaudet, the son of Thomas Hopkins Gallaudet who cofounded the American School for the Deaf and Dumb in Hartford, Connecticut. The pair was somewhat adversarial since Gallaudet was the leading proponent of manualism—the use of sign language for teaching the Deaf. He professionally pushed back on Bell's notions of importance of articulation for assimilation into the dominant hearing community as superintendent of the Columbia Institution for the Deaf (now Gallaudet University) in Washington, D.C.

As Bell studied deaf populations, he developed the opinion that sign language offered harmful results in deaf populations: "Can it be wondered at, therefore, that such a child soon tires of home?" There was no doubt in Bell's mind Helen would thrive in an environment where a Deaf child could learn to communicate. He observed that schools for Deaf and Deaf-Blind break up families, "little by little the ties of blood and relationship are weakened" (Bell, 1883), and the institution becomes their home, as was the case with Julia Brace at the American School for the Deaf in Hartford, Connecticut.

Bell steered Helen's parents toward Perkins Institute instead of the American School because he favored speech. Bell wrote about the thorax in his scientific papers as if it was a metaphoric vault in which Helen found herself entrapped. He wrote, "We find ourselves in a dark room or vault with a door in the roof. The floor of this vault . . . is a soft membrane or muscle . . . dome-shaped like the top of an umbrella . . . the most extraordinary thing about this room is, that the floor is in constant motion, heaving upwards and downwards in regular pulsations . . . the walls also are in motion, the hole room is alternately increasing and diminishing in size" (Bell, 1916).

Kate and Arthur feared their daughter might never live an independent life. Helen, as a person with little sense of the world around her, desired independence. She dreamt in form of sensations devoid of sound, thought, or emotion other than fear. Helen later remembered, "I often had a dream that I ran into a still, dark room, and while I stood there, I could feel something heavy falling without any sound that caused the floor to shake up and down violently" (Jastrow, 1900). Every time this happened, the girl awoke with a jump. As Helen learned more about her environment and the objects in her world, the dream stopped haunting her.

The Kellers believed that Helen would need some kind of guardian-caregiver throughout her life. Her extreme challenges resulted from the timing of her loss of sight and hearing before there was a chance for her to acquire any language comprehension. Arthur and Kate were unaware about a girl named Katherine "Katie" McGirr, three weeks older than Helen, who lost her sight and hearing after getting caught in a snowstorm when she was eight years old (Rocheleau and Mack, 1930). The later difference in the point of disability after learning some speech and reading made a dramatic difference in how McGirr would be educated and rehabilitated.

After consulting with Gallaudet, Bell contacted Michael Anagnos, director of the Perkins Institute of the Blind, where his late father-in-law Dr. Samuel Gridley Howe had earlier taught Laura Bridgman to word-build and use the manual alphabet. Bell wrote Anagnos a letter on behalf of Arthur Keller to ask if the director could refer an experienced teacher for a Deaf-Blind girl in Alabama named Helen Keller. Anagnos decided Helen Keller might become another Laura Bridgman. He suggested a recent graduate, twenty-year-old Anne "Mansfield" Sullivan, could be able to travel to Alabama to become Helen's instructor and companion.

Nobody knew what Annie Sullivan would do when she returned with Mrs. Sophia Hopkins to Perkins Institute for the Blind in the fall after

Louisa May Alcott's "Blind Lark"

As Kate and Arthur Keller sought help for their daughter Helen Keller from Alexander Graham Bell, Boston author Louisa May Alcott published a story about a Blind girl called "The Blind Lark" in the November 1886 issue of *St. Nicholas*. Alcott's fictional nine-year-old Blind character Lizzie Davis living in tenement poverty was inspired by Michael Anagnos's sentimental idea for developing kindergarten at Perkins Institute for the Blind, and she turned him into a fictional character named Mr. Constantine.

Alcott created poverty as a geographic character; Lizzie Davis, her brother Billy, and widowed mother reside in a squalid one-room apartment. Mrs. Davis works in a factory job, leaving Lizzie and Jimmy behind. The Blind girl passes time singing tunes. Nearby laborers teach her new tunes out of pity, especially after Billy dies. Lizzie prays to join her brother in heaven. A passer-by gossips, "It will be a mercy if the poor thing doesn't live; blind folks are no use . . ." Her companion laments, "Yes, Mrs. Davis would get on nicely if she hadn't such a burden. Thank Heaven, my children aren't blind."

Miss Grace brings Lizzie flowers, telling her about a school for the Blind. She visits again accompanied by a Blind student who has learned to read raised type tactilely. Lizzie hopes to sing to earn a place in the school. Miss Grace introduces her to Mr. Constantine, who believes Lizzie could use her voice for fundraising.

Lizzie attends an "Exhibition Day" event displaying students' needlework and projects. Visitors purchase items and explore exotic maps and books designed to teach the Blind. Her success in performing earns her a spot at the school as a charity case. Mrs. Davis is proud of her daughter who has learned to read aloud.

graduating as valedictorian. Recently widowed after his wife, Julia Romana Howe Anagnos, died in March 1886 from typhoid fever, Anagnos, was entrenched in the Perkins Institute family. He trained his unproven protégé Annie, and he wondered how he could use her ambition to his advantage. After hearing from Alexander Graham Bell, Anagnos corresponded with Captain Arthur Keller about his daughter, Helen. Anagnos thought the wild Deaf-Blind-Mute girl might be useful to Perkins Institute. In a letter, Kate Keller described her daughter Helen as a strong, ruddy, and unrestrained child like a young bronco. She said perhaps Annie "Miss Spitfire" Sullivan could tame the girl to become the second Laura Bridgman at Perkins Institute.

Laura Bridgman, no longer a fragile greenhouse flower in 1886, lived on as a monument to Dr. Samuel Gridley Howe's pioneering teaching experiment. Laura used her talents to help younger students with sewing projects. Annie, who was a companion to Laura in Mrs. Hopkins cottage, never liked sewing because she never mastered Laura's secret way of threading a needle with her tongue.

Annie's news of being hired as companion and teacher to another Deaf-Blind girl named Helen Keller excited fifty-seven-year-old Laura, who offered advice. Laura dressed a doll purchased by Blind students at Perkins Institute for Annie to take to Helen as a gift and Laura told Annie she could use the doll for Helen's first object lesson. Annie prepared for her first waged assignment by reading Howe's reports about teaching Laura.

A young volunteer at Perkins Institute named Harriet "Hattie" Freeman denied herself a fancy bonnet to give Annie the thirty dollars she needed to make the train trip to Alabama. As Annie prepared to travel to her first job, a Polish-born experimental psychologist named Joseph Jastrow visited Laura Bridgman to learn about her dreams. Sophia Hopkins' little cottage where Laura lived was adjacent to Perkins Institute's main building. Jastrow greeted the tall, thin woman wearing large spectacles for their interview. "She was very lively, and one could almost read her feelings by her face" (Day, 2013).

Anagnos, Hopkins, and a Perkins teacher named Miss Fanny S. Fanny S. Merritt Merritt, who replaced Annie's favorite teacher Miss Mary C. Moore, accompanied Annie to the train station. Anagnos gave Annie the thirty dollars on loan from Hattie along with a small garnet ring symbolizing strength and safety in serving others. Mrs. Hopkins packed a sack lunch for the long journey.

Annie had never traveled alone on a train. She had more confidence as she boarded the train than she had when she and her little brother Jimmy Sullivan started their journey to Tewkesbury, but that wasn't saying much. Annie smiled nervously, knowing her life experience to date had prepared her to face challenges. She later reflected, "Life certainly plays queer tricks on us" (Lash, 1980).

Annie "Mansfield" Sullivan traveled to Tuscumbia, Alabama, carrying the doll in her little carpet bag that held everything she needed to start a new life. The two-day train ride from the bustling Boston, Massachusetts, to the sleepy little train platform in Tuscumbia, Alabama, was the farthest distance Annie had traveled in her life. It was as far from her past as she could conceivably go. Michael Anagnos did not give the Kellers the specifics of Annie's experience or credentials, but the young woman was motivated and extremely creative.

Unsure of when Miss Annie Sullivan would arrive, Kate Keller and her stepson James Keller drove to the station to meet every train for two days. With basic signs, Kate conveyed she was leaving to get the woman at the train station in the wagon, and she instructed Helen to wait on the porch until her return. Despite his resentment toward his stepmother, James remained an important presence in his half-sister's life. Often, only he could moderate Helen's wild behavior.

Annie arrived from Boston on March 3, 1887, to serve as Helen's teacher with a monthly salary of twenty-five dollars and room and board (Keller, 1903). For the young woman who arrived at Perkins Institute as a charity case, this seemed like a fortune. Kate became disturbed when she saw Annie's badly inflamed right eye, still recovering from a recent surgery. However, nobody was more anxious for the twenty-one-year-old Northerner to succeed than Helen's mother.

Annie approached the girl with tumbled hair, wearing a soiled pinafore apron over her dress, standing in the doorway. The first impression of the woman who had worn shoes sized too small for her growing feet while living in poverty was how Helen's black shoes were tied with white shoestrings. The two misfits would perhaps make a perfect fit. Helen was attractive without the mannerism of some Blind children. Helen was a healthy weight, and Annie felt her strength with a greeting rush.

Helen touched Annie's face and dress and sniffed her luggage bag to gage her identity. She had been expecting a gift or sweets and greedily searched Annie's bag. Feeling a keyhole, the girl made a sign of turning a key, pointing to the bag. Kate tried to wrestle the suitcase from her daughter. Annie distracted the girl with quick hand movements, luring her with a watch to get her to follow into the house and upstairs to help to unpack. Helen snatched Annie's bonnet to mimic her mother's motions when she arrived home.

Once Anne unpacked, she immediately began to teach Helen an object lesson to finger-spell by spelling out the word "D-O-L-L" into Helen's hand. Annie placed the doll dressed by Laura Bridgman into Helen's hands. Annie next clearly nodded her head in an exaggerated way into Helen's hand to establish an association between the letters spelled and the doll.

Helen did not comprehend Annie's unfamiliar actions. She felt Annie's hand and mimicked the motions of fingerspelling and then pointed to the doll. Annie took back the doll intending to give it back to Helen when the girl spelled "d-o-l-l" correctly. Helen misunderstood, believing the unfamiliar visitor took the doll away for good, and she threw a tantrum.

Annie ran to the kitchen to get a piece of cake for a different bribe. Annie held the cake under Helen's nose so she could get a whiff of it and finger-spelled "C-A-K-E" into her hand. Helen imitated the letters rapidly, and Annie rewarded her with the cake. Helen scarfed it down, believing that Annie would take the treat from her as she had the doll. Thus, the first object lesson failed because Helen could not connect fingerspelling with the object and reward.

Annie Sullivan observed Kate Keller critically; she needed to gage herself by someone who was not Blind. Only seven years older, Kate was not as old as her mother-figure Sophia Hopkins, but the young mother carried a weight managing her daughters and stepchildren. Annie wondered how such a sensitive, high-strung woman like Kate Keller could endure grinding labor and not complain. Kate appeared reticent and aloof, but her poise was a character trait Annie awkwardly aspired to emulate.

Conversely, Annie reported how Kate was "careless about everything, yet good-hearted and sincere" (Lash, 1980). Annie perhaps exaggerated the descriptions to make herself seem more sophisticated by reporting how Kate's house looked, "as though a hurricane had passed over it, around it, and through it." The inexperienced teacher soon discovered how a "discussion with Mrs. Keller was a test of one's metal." The young mother loved politics; an intellectual and ardent suffragist, Kate always responded quickly to questions with vivid phrases.

In Annie's opinion, Captain Arthur Keller was a genial storyteller, but not an intellectual. She described Arthur as hospitable, arrogant, and "most exasperating," because his logic was "playing leap-frog blindfold" (Lash, 1980). Annie wrote to Mrs. Hopkins about how listening to the talk of people with Confederate sensibilities, "you would think that they won every battle in the Civil War" (Lash, 1980).

The young teacher reported observations of the Alabama household and her student to Michael Anagnos and Mrs. Hopkins. Her letters revealed how she resisted demands for a more experienced teacher. Annie hoped to avoid direct confrontations that would result in her being fired and returned to an institutional setting like Tewksbury if she failed in her first job. For one who had spent her life in institutions of one sort or another from the age of eight years, Annie was amazed the family appeared to raise nearly everything needed to sustain their household on the homestead.

Annie threw herself into teaching Helen. The girl seemed like Laura Bridgman, so Annie hoped to bring her under control without breaking her spirit. Annie continued to study Dr. Howe's reports about teaching Laura, but she found underlying shortcomings in his approach. After living with Laura's peculiar otherworldly dialect, Annie observed the characters of the people in the Keller household.

Annie also observed how Helen's fifteen-month-old cousin learned by imitating and assimilating information from her environment (Wagner, 2012). One of Annie's problems with her new charge was a result of the Kate and Arthur not disciplining their daughter. Annie wrote to Mrs. Hopkins, telling her Helen "is very quick-tempered and willful." It was easier for them to indulge Helen than to interact with her or to say no. Annie was only a little older than Helen when she had entered institutional settings like Tewksbury and later Perkins Institute: she believed people with disabilities must be self-disciplined to survive.

Victorian families came together for meals, where they shared experiences of the day and taught children manners. At breakfast, Annie observed Helen wandering from person to person, groping for bits from each plate, and it upset her. Annie wondered if her student was going to be allowed to act like a dog begging scraps, or worse, *a tramp* entitled to help herself to anything she wants.

The new teacher forcefully attempted to get Helen to eat food from her own plate with a spoon. She escalated the situation by demanding authority at the table, confronting the family dynamics. Annie ordered everyone to leave the dining room except for Helen. She then locked the door, placing the key out of her student's reach. It was a bold move since Helen once used a key to lock her mother in the family's pantry to get attention.

Once the family was gone, Helen dropped to the floor, where she started to kick and scream. Annie coolly sat down to eat her cold breakfast. Helen approached the stranger who had defied her routine and pulled her chair out from under her. The resistant girl subsequently and unrelentingly pinched Anne the way she pinched a grandmother she did not like. Helen hurled spoons at Annie and pushed and shoved her for over several hours. Annie gave what she got in this messy battle of wills, returning again and again to compel Helen to pick up the spoon again and eat the cold, stale food in front of her.

Not succeeding, next Annie repeated the action of folding a napkin for Helen to learn. Annie repeated simple processes over and over, trying to teach Helen by rote because she had already demonstrated she could imitate or mimic actions. When the battle ended and Helen did what Annie demanded of her, the exhausted teacher allowed Helen to join her family outside. Whether or not Annie understood how discipline and structure was part of Howe's educational methods, she experienced how Laura's manipulative personality got in the way of socialization. Annie unknowingly conducted what twentieth-century social workers would call an intervention when she removed Helen's family and forced the child to eat from her own plate. However, within minutes of everyone returning to the house, Helen bossed her beleaguered family into submission. Anne's small bit of progress was immediately undermined.

Annie needed to remove Helen from her family to immerse her in total learning. She argued Arthur and Kate needed to relinquish their daughter in order for her to learn. Over the next several days, Annie's *tough love* in epic battles made everyone in the household cringe.

At one point, Annie insisted Helen sit down in a chair when she preferred to stand or sit on the floor, and the Blind girl's fist flew, hitting Annie and knocking out two of her teeth. Annie wrote to Sophia Hopkins about how Helen's untaught, unsatisfied hands "destroy whatever they touch because they do not know what else to do with things" (Lash, 1980). The young teacher had never come across a child of Helen's age with such strength and endurance; Annie wrote to Sophia, "Fortunately for both of us, I am a little stronger, and quite as obstinate when I set out . . ."

Helen was bright, but she was not engaged with learning because there were no signposts or boundaries. After a week of small steps forward and backward, Annie convinced Kate to isolate Helen with her alone in the unused Little House. Annie argued she could work intensely to teach Helen fingerspelling without the family to distract or undermine her efforts.

While Arthur bristled at the young Northern stranger in his household, his sister Eveline "Aunt Eva" Keller came to Annie's defense, saying, "Miss Annie is going to be Helen's salvation; she must learn obedience and feel her dependence upon Annie" (Lash, 1980). Kate and Aunt Eva finally convinced Arthur to do what Annie asked.

Captain Keller took Helen on a long carriage ride to the Little House, using a circuitous route so the girl's senses could not inform her how really close she was to home. Annie allowed Helen to keep her favorite doll, and a young Black servant stayed with them to maintain the fireplace, and their cook, Belle, brought food.

Annie just needed a small breakthrough to prove to Michael Anagnos she had potential to be a good teacher using methods from Perkins Institute in order to secure future employment if this job panned out. She just needed to get her single student to grasp the connection of feeling the manual alphabet finger-spelled into words in her hand and basic object lessons. Annie attempted handing Helen an item and using her fingers to spell letters into Helen's hand. However, Helen, like Laura, did not readily connect the wiggling finger movements to objects.

After a week, Kate and Arthur wanted their daughter back. Annie was afraid the old disruptive patterns would resume. Helen resented the woman separating her from her parents, who tried to control her, and she refused to give in. Not one to give up easily, Annie remained with Helen day and night in the Little House for two more weeks, constantly spelling into her hand the words and ideas of things going on around them.

Helen's father challenged the young teacher's ability to control Helen when he considered sending her back to Boston. Annie demanded total obedience from Helen, which meant her total dependence on her teacher for food and rest. Helen could not make the connection between letters and words spelled into her hand with meaning. In desperation, Annie tried to make the exercise into a game made up of letters: when Helen asked the name of something, she patted Annie's hand and pointed to the object.

Helen slowly warmed to Annie and began to demonstrate an excellent memory and remembered more than twenty words, but the girl could not delineate their meanings. Annie reported an initial breakthrough to Sophia Hopkins on March 20, 1887, "A miracle has happened . . . the wild creature of two weeks ago has been transformed into a gentle child" (Lash, 1980). On the cusp of a greater breakthrough, Arthur brought Helen's favorite family dog to Little House for a visit. The girl hugged her pet with joy and sat down on the floor next to her. Helen took the dog's paw in hand and tried to teach the animal how to finger-spell "D-O-L-L" with her other hand.

Anne Sullivan Macy fingerspells from a book into Helen Keller's hand and Catherine "Kate" Keller watches, c. 1914. Some mothers of Deaf-Blind individuals suffered when surrendering children to institutions or teachers who could provide special education opportunities. Helen Keller's most profound life lessons would come from navigating her dominant relationships with her mother and her teacher-guardian. (Library of Congress)

After returning to the family's house, Helen, like Laura Bridgman, made a major breakthrough on April 5, 1887. She asked Annie how to finger-spell "W-A-T-E-R." In her desperation, Annie decided there might be another way. After some thought, Annie led Helen to a water pump and made her hold the cup under the spout as she pumped the water. She guided Helen to hold a mug under the spout as she pumped, all the while fingerspelling "W-A-T-E-R" into Helen's free hand.

Annie handed Helen a cup and spelled the word, "C-U-P." Then Annie poured some liquid into a cup and formed the letters "W-A-T-E-R." Helen stood for a moment transfixed; she looked puzzled by the sensation of the water spilling over her hand as if it startled her. Helen confused the two words, spelling *cup* for *water* and *water* for *cup*. Then Helen became frustrated as Annie kept repeating the words over and over. With her body at full attention, the girl focused on the motions of Annie's fingers as the cool stream of water flowed over Helen's hands.

Helen suddenly dropped the mug. She felt a stir . . . a memory . . . a connection . . . as if she was awakening. Helen's face lit up with revelation; she finally made the abstract connection between a finger-spelled word and the object sensation, the cold *something* flowing through her fingers. Helen connected with the outside world when she discovered the *key* to the world of ideas.

Sensations, thoughts pressed forward and receded quickly; thoughts, sensations awakened in her brain and spread throughout her. Helen began to spell the word "w-a-t-e-r" repeatedly. She remembered a distant connection of language meaning between a sound she had made before losing her sight and hearing, "wa-wa" and "water." "W-A-T-E-R" spelled out as that wonderful cool *something* flowing over her hand.

Now Helen understood that objects have names and her teacher was spelling these names into her hand. This unlocked a whole new world of learning for Helen. She began to reason about the parts of nature she could touch. Helen could communicate better than Laura Bridgman because Annie Sullivan soon introduced her to the ability of constructing graceful and even poetic sentences. Helen dropped to her knees and touched the ground, asking Annie for its name. She reached for the pump and asked for its name, and then the trellis. Annie finger-spelled each word out for the girl. Helen at last touched Annie, and her teacher finger-spelled "T-E-A-C-H-E-R" into her hand. Within a few hours, Helen had added about thirty words to her vocabulary. The transformation of Helen Keller, from a wild, undisciplined "little bronco" into a motivated learner, had begun.

3

Helen's Pen Pals

Nobody had expected much from Annie "Mansfield" Sullivan when she journeyed to Tuscumbia, Alabama. Much less prepared than other special education teachers, she seemed unlikely to draw the Deaf-Blind-Mute girl Helen Keller out from her five years in an isolated "no world." Annie had a meager education and precarious eyesight, but she was motivated to prove herself to the world. However, the world was much larger than the one she had learned about in the geography classroom at Perkins Institute, where a giant three-dimensional globe revealed geography to blind fingers. Maps produced in relief along the walls depicted states from Maine to California with pins to mark capital cities, raised lines to mark mountain ranges, and grooves for rivers so that students could follow them to their opening points to a lake, larger river, or the ocean. Annie, visually impaired like the Blind students, learned to interpret and draw maps at Perkins Institute as she became a young lieutenant for the director, Michael Anagnos, who treated her like a daughter.

In Alabama, after Helen's fingerspelling breakthrough, Annie engaged her student in conversations using the manual alphabet during their waking hours. Annie wove a spell so Helen eventually finger spelled thoughts even as she dreamed. Frustrated with life at Ivy Green with Captain Arthur Henley Keller and his wife Catherine "Kate" Everett Adams Keller trying to control how she taught their daughter who was her only Deaf-Blind-Mute student, Annie employed her considerable letter writing skills to lift herself and Helen out of the world at Ivy Green.

Annie taught Helen letter writing as a way to connect to children beyond her isolated home. Annie's lifeline was letter writing with Perkins Institute staff, including director Michael Anagnos and housemother Mrs. Sophia C. Hopkins. Both received information from their young lieutenant in Alabama. In return, both offered Annie sound advice on developing Helen to conform to society in the North, even if Miss Spitfire did not heed it.

Annie, comparing herself to Kate Keller, started to resent her impractical education as a charity case at Perkins Institute. She felt it did not equip her for this physically and mentally challenging job. Annie keenly observed her new environment and believed it was absurd to teach Helen language like a school marm who sticks to arbitrary rules in a classroom environment. Annie felt children did not learn speech by memorizing lists of words and grammar patterns; she saw learning was best done with total immersion in life.

Annie abandoned Howe's lock-step pedagogy and started to speak into Helen's hand in the same way as Kate talked into Mildred Campbell Keller's ear. Mrs. Hopkins gave her a little red dictionary, and it proved to be her most useful tool. Annie never spoke baby talk into Helen's hand; she always used complete sentences with gestures to keep her student interested and stimulated her to engage with language. As with Laura Bridgman, Annie became the storyteller with her fingers communicating quivering soap bubbles, insect noises, and the murmur of trees; fireside vibrations, the rustling of silk, a door creaking, and the pulsing of blood in the veins could be conveyed with touch.

Helen Keller's sight entered through her fingers and not her eyes; she *listened* to vibrations with her hands and not her ears. She heard the gobble of turkeys and the squeal of pigs by feeling their sounds when she touched their bodies. Similar to other Deaf-Blind people, Helen possessed no sense of direction or distance. In her familiar home environments, she oriented herself with landmark furniture objects. For example, if a carpet was moved, Helen got disoriented and needed to relearn the room arrangement. Throughout her life, the girl found sitting on the floor or ground gave her orientation and a sense of balance.

Annie taught Helen everything she knew about objects and subjects as quickly as her student asked. As Helen's knowledge and vocabulary grew, she returned to subjects again and again, eager for more information to build her internal knowledge base. Sometimes a new word revived memories or experiences engraved upon her psyche. Helen later remembered, "Everything that could hum, or buzz, or sing, or bloom, had a part in my education" (Keller, 1955).

Most importantly after being stuck in a "no world" for five years, Annie taught Helen how to play and laugh once she learned obedience. One morning, Annie, who had experienced a dark childhood, entered the parlor where Helen, her younger sister Mildred, Kate, and Arthur were talking. The young teacher laughed merrily, "throwing out breezes of glee" to her student and throughout the space. The woman, who frequently disappeared so others would not see her habitual depressions, raised Helen's hand to her face as she finger-spelled "L-A-U-G-H." Annie tickled Helen while her family was around. Annie spelled the word again repeatedly as she guided Helen through the processes of romping, swinging, tumbling, jumping, hopping, and skipping.

Annie afterward spent her days outside, guiding Helen along winding dirt roads and traversing familiar woodlands and meadows toward Keller's Landing, an abandoned wharf along the Tennessee River. Helen smelled the natural odors. Annie smarted when Helen only tolerated her mother's kisses. As their meanderings started, she aspired to build trust with her student. Annie spelled "I love Helen" into her hand.

Helen asked, "What is love?"

Annie drew the girl close, touching Helen's heart, and spelled, "It is here." Helen became aware of her own heartbeats, but she was puzzled because she did not understand emotions she could not touch.

Helen smelled violets in her teacher's hand and asked in half-words, half-signs, "Is love the sweetness of flowers?"

Annie responded, "No."

Helen struggled to understand the notion of abstract ideas, and she paused. The girl pointed in the direction of the warm sun. "Is this not love?" she asked (Keller, 1903, 1929, 1955).

The sun seemed to hide behind clouds with intermittent showers, so Helen worked on a learning exercise inside. She strung graduated beads of different sizes into symmetrical groups and made some mistakes, and Annie pointed out the mistakes so Helen could correct the order. She concentrated to figure out what the right sequence should be. Annie touched her forehead and finger-spelled, emphasizing the word, "T-H-I-N-K."

Helen had a revelation regarding the process going on between her hands and her mind connecting an abstract notion about size perception. She remained still, apart from fingering the beads spread in her lap, while her mind fixed upon the *abstract* notion of love. When she felt the warmth of the sun again, Helen asked Annie, "Is this not love?"

Her teacher replied, "Love is in the clouds and in the sky and in the sun. It is all around you." Still, Helen did not understand. Annie gave Helen her first nature lesson when she demonstrated the sun and rain helped plants and animals to flourish. She explained, "You cannot touch the clouds, but you can feel the rain and know that the flowers and the thirsty earth drink it up after a hot day." Annie touched Helen's arm, "You cannot touch love either, but you feel what it pours into everything."

Kate Keller's affinity for birds inspired Annie to keep a few pigeons in her room. The teacher sometimes released them from their birdcage and chased them around the room, so Helen felt the air motion from their wings to understand the movement of flight. The birds grew to trust the Deaf-Blind girl, and they would light on her head and shoulders to allow her to feed them. Through this process, Helen learned to understand their pecks, sounds, and fluttering. Birds became Helen's natural teachers even if she could not see or hear them.

The student and her teacher seemed to grow up together; as Helen's knowledge of her environment grew, Annie's grew too. The young teacher had never seen a rabbit until she arrived in Tuscumbia, Alabama. Much to Kate and Arthur's delight, Annie grew fascinated with watching the lopsided motion of their rabbits chewing their food. She tried to control their chewing motion so it was straight up and down, but the rabbits never obliged the stubborn teacher.

Annie continued connecting Helen's lessons to nature, so Helen became acquainted with birds and flowers as peers. This sensibility was similar to Native American sensibilities that they lived within the natural order rather than subduing it. The girl was such a voracious learner, Annie struggled to stay ahead of her student after sharing Mother Goose rhymes.

Annie wrote to Mrs. Hopkins, "My mind is undisciplined, full of skips and jumps . . . I need a teacher quite as much as Helen." Her student's parents Arthur and Kate soon worried Helen was too immersed in the pursuit of knowledge. Their little girl now preferred fingerspelling to eating her favorite treats. Arthur summoned the same family doctor who had not been able to diagnose Helen's ailment, causing her to become Deaf-Blind-Mute, and he pronounced how Helen was thinking *too much*. The girl had fallen in love with a world of ideas and language.

Annie Sullivan, as a Northerner, may have been scornful of the segregated post-Reconstruction South, but on their rambles, she discovered some Southerners were often more equitable to Blacks, and in some ways expressed more tolerance of *difference*, than Northerners. Pervasive poverty among whites troubled her, but as the pair wandered into poor Black neighborhoods, they found the residents generous with hospitality. Helen and Annie received fruit and berries and sometimes fried chicken before continuing on their way.

The impetuous teacher made nature lessons a game as they explored the geography about the homestead. Helen and Annie excavated dams and erected sand sculptures along the riverbank to study its geography. The pair explored shells and tadpoles and rocks and fossils in this natural laboratory as they learned about the world together.

Helen enjoyed smelling the layered fragrances in a nearby woodlands. Once on a ramble, the pair stopped by a wild cherry tree not far from Ivy

Helen Keller and Anne Sullivan, c. 1891–1894, a time period when the pair frequently relocated to find a good education for Keller. At this time, Keller made excuses for her teacher's occasional cruelty. Many familiar with the pair wondered about Sullivan's tension, contrasting the teacher's personal ambition with her ambition for her single student. (Library of Congress)

HELEN KELLER'S VICTORIAN ENTERTAINMENTS

Middle-class Victorian Americans enjoyed leisure time and some disposable income, allowing them to consume popular culture entertainment including games, hobbies, and camping. For the sighted in Victorian America, with hobbies like scrapbooking and creating decoupage objects, there seemed to be a human need to explore and collect "paper" objects and then organize and repurpose them in ways that created new understanding. Even impoverished orphans Anne Sullivan and her younger brother James "Jimmy" Sullivan created a gallery with discarded magazines at Tewksbury almshouse and demonstrated creativity.

When Helen Keller lost her sight and hearing, she entered a metaphorical twilight where she could not experience many of the pastimes others took for granted. Helen's earliest sensation was linked to shiny, glistening cut crystals hanging from a table lamp. Keller delighted in watching an open wood fire. She insisted on staying up beyond her bedtime to watch the flames and sparks, giggling as they danced up the chimney. Once she became Deaf-Blind, Keller entertained herself exploring her parents' garden or helping around the house, but she was not conscious of entertainment as having fun.

On their Alabama homestead, Captain Arthur Keller never failed to bring home guests for dinner; he was a noted recounter of humorous stories. At the end of long days of domestic chores, Kate Keller joined family and guests in trick-taking game of cards called euchre. Euchre was a common game of the lower classes and was one of the most popular American card games along with poker. Sullivan introduced Keller to play as means for learning, but she could not join in card games until she gained access to a special deck customized with embossed braille to identify each card. Keller entertained herself by reading when she could enjoy poetry and literature independently.

Green. The morning started out clear, but the weather changed quickly. Helen, with some help from her teacher, scrambled up a tree to a seat in the branches (Keller, 1929). Annie thought it would be nice to have lunch in that spot and went home to fetch some food from the Black cook named Belle.

The sun's warmth disappeared, and Helen smelled unusual odors arising from the earth. She sensed the energy from an oncoming thunderstorm nearing, and overtaken with fear and alone, Helen felt disoriented and cut off from solid earth. She froze in terror as leaves stirred after the stillness. The tree seemed to shiver and vibrate, and the wind sent forth a blast, so the girl clung to the branch with all of her strength. The tree swayed and strained as twigs snapped and showered down about Helen. She wanted to jump to the ground but could not move. Larger branches lashed her all about. Annie finally returned and promptly helped her climb down to earth.

It was a long time before Helen considered climbing another tree. However, the following spring, the subtle fragrance of a mimosa tree seduced the girl until she instinctively stretched, like a cat after a long sleep, and reached out her hands to feel her way to the end of the garden to touch its familiar quivering blossoms. Helen made her way through the shower of mimosa blossoms. Up, up, up she pulled herself up despite the bark scraping her hands, higher into the tree. There the girl sat with quiet fulfillment until someone came looking to get her.

The young teacher gained her student's trust and became increasingly possessive, while the teacher's mentor, Michael Anagnos, working twelve hundred miles away in Boston, hoped Perkins Institute for the Blind would be credited with transforming a wild Southern Deaf-Blind-Mute girl into a gentle, socialized little girl with a soul like Laura Bridgman. Helen was totally reliant upon her teacher's descriptions and interpretations of cultural ideas. Annie Sullivan recognized that while discipline was Helen's path out of isolation it might not reach her spirit. Annie needed advice, so her letters to Boston detailed and exaggerated the truth a bit to tell her mentors what they hoped to hear—how their valedictorian followed Dr. Samuel Gridley Howe's course and educational theories used at Perkins Institute to successfully teach Helen.

Annie Sullivan was not Dr. Samuel Gridley Howe, and she was not always patient with her student. For example, when Annie wanted to break her student of a nail-biting habit she slapped Helen on the side of her head in frustration and then tied the girl's hands behind her until she stopped biting her nails. The cruel tactic curtailed a nervous habit that Helen likely started when Annie separated her from her family. However, to stop all hand communications for a Deaf-Blind-Mute individual was cruel and would not be tolerated at Perkins Institute from any teacher then or today.

As Annie poured words and ideas into Helen's hands, her vocabulary grew to a hundred additional words in a month. The student perhaps sensed her teacher's excitement when she received replies to letters, or perhaps Annie prompted Helen to correspond with Blind girls at Perkins Institute. Helen was eager to learn to use a special stylus to create raised letters on a braille slate with a poking action. After accompanying Annie to the post office to mail some letters, Helen produced a short, scattered letter to her cousin Anna right before her seventh birthday. She asked Annie to place it in an envelope and mail it. The writing in each of Helen's letters improved quickly, so she soon wrote to "the blind girls" attending Perkins Institute.

As Helen's vocabulary grew, Annie likely directed her to write to adults, including Michael Anagnos and Alexander Graham Bell, to demonstrate her progress as a teacher and to show off her student. Consequently, the school director and inventor shared letters with friends, prompting further correspondence with philanthropists who might help Helen and Annie. One of Helen's first pen pals was a Blind poet and inventor living in Kentucky named James Morrison Heady, who had attended Perkins Institute as a boy.

Heady invented the "talking glove" designed with letters on each part of the fingers to allow anybody to communicate with a Deaf-Blind individual.

Helen's descriptions of family were simple and happy. By September 1887, her vocabulary increased to six hundred words. Arthur Keller was astonished and wrote to Anagnos telling of Helen's "phenomenal" progress in basic mathematics beyond learning to read and write. In November 1887, Helen wrote directly to Anagnos, informing him how her father had commissioned a photograph of her, and Annie would send it. She told Anagnos about her desire to correspond with Blind girls at Perkins Institute and signed her letter, "Good-by Helen Keller."

Aside from a protruding left eye, Helen was very photogenic. Anagnos and Bell shared every picture of Helen Keller with the media, so her story was transmitted to the world via newspapers. Anagnos called Helen's progress a "miracle," and he hoped to establish a connection between Annie's success and Perkins Institute by leaking Annie's news to the press with exaggerations.

Around the same time, Helen also wrote to Alexander Graham Bell, telling him she remembered visiting him and feeling the vibrations from his pocket watch, after visiting an oculist Dr. J. Julian Chisholm in Washington, D.C., to get her eyes examined. Helen promised to send Bell a photograph. Bell became one Helen's first pen pals to exploit her progress to advance his crusade for educating the deaf oralism to be part of the speaking world.

Bell learned the one-handed manual alphabet and braille to better communicate with Helen. He correlated Helen's fast-learning pace with Annie's tactile educational methods. Helen began to learn idiomatic English with fingerspelling, resulting in her learning semantics, or language meaning, within cultural contexts that were more advanced than other Deaf-Blind-Mute individuals like Julia Brace or Laura Bridgman. As a child, Bell made Helen feel as though if she had more time, she too could become a great inventor.

Bell leaked all of Helen's letters and a photograph to *Science Monthly* in 1888 to interest the scientific community with her story. Journalists soon appeared at Ivy Green to report the latest details of Helen's progress. Annie could not control the publicity. Fearful of someone with more credentials replacing her as Helen's teacher if the stories were too impressive, Annie railed, "The truth is not enough to suit the newspapers, so they enlarge upon it and invent ridiculous embellishments."

Already restless with Arthur and Kate's continuing involvement in their child's education, Annie grew increasingly possessive of Helen. She corresponded with Michael Anagnos and Mrs. Hopkins to keep their support. However, Anagnos, who was having trouble raising money for Perkins Institute's new kindergarten initiative, saw an opportunity to cultivate a grassroots celebrity who had been taught by a recent alumna by utilizing Dr. Howe's teaching methods.

Anagnos wrote to Arthur and Kate inviting Helen, her mother, and Annie to visit Perkins Institute as his guests so Helen could be among a community of Blind girls. The family accepted, unaware they might be relinquishing their eldest daughter to Helen's teacher.

In May 1888, Helen, Kate, and Annie traveled north to Boston, Massachusetts. When they visited the new kindergarten at Perkins Institute, they entered the cast room where Helen passed her hands over sculptures to read their expressions, and her fingers explored Dante's prominent nose. The "Touch" schoolmistress taught Helen how to identify three-dimensional objects using her fingers. Helen learned the basics of modeling clay, making bead baskets, and knitting socks with four needles.

Helen, who was developing her gift of connecting abstract ideas, discovered an old spinning wheel in the art room prepared for weaving flax; she excitedly fingered into Annie's hand. "Flax! It is blue!" Annie had informed Helen of how only the flax flower is blue.

Helen responded with a quote from Henry Wadsworth Longfellow's narrative poem "The Wreck of the Hesperus" (1842) to make her point: "Blue were her eyes as the fairy flax, her cheeks like the dawn of day."

"Yes," Annie responded. "The poet referred to the flowers" (Hall, 1889; Keller, 1903).

The vibration of the tambourine in the music room delighted Helen. When a Blind girl sat down to play the piano, Helen's countenance changed as her face lit up at the chance to be sociable. The girl played a popular skirt dance that was often performed in vaudeville theaters, in which female dancers manipulated long, layered skirts with their arms to create a motion of flowing fabric.

Helen could scarcely stay still *to listen*; her hands and feet kept constant time with the music vibrations. She sensed the beat and pulsation of music by sitting at the piano and resting her hands on it to feel the varied degrees of the instrument's throbbing, vibration, and rhythm while Annie spelled out the singer's words into Helen's hand.

Helen participated and understood the significance of her first Christmas at Perkins Institute. When Helen arrived at Perkins Institute, she learned to connect Christmas sensations with the holiday's religious meaning when she experienced it within a tight-knit Blind community. The scent of the great Christmas tree planted in the center of the children's lodge wafted everywhere and excited Helen's sense of smell. Students spent a week decorating it, and Helen helped to hand-trim the tree and climb a ladder to affix ornaments, apples, and tinsel to its branches. Other students attached the little slender candles that once lit made the tree glisten (Keller, 1906).

Blind students did not entirely appreciate gift reminders of their blindness, but local charities told them to be grateful in their affliction. Gifts were placed in the tree so that the sweet-smelling branches seemed to nearly break under the weight of the parcels and decorations. The kindergarten students preferred stories capturing their imagination instead of bleak religious tracts. Older students received books with raised print like Kate Douglas Wiggins' *The Story of Patsy* (1889) depicting a disabled waif in a San Francisco slum or Lewis Carroll's *Alice in Wonderland* (1865).

On Christmas Eve, Helen was restless at bedtime, anticipating last-minute surprises. During the Christmas tree festival, Helen discovered one student would not receive any gifts. She went to her own stash of possessions and brought out a treasured mug to give to the child (Hall, 1889). In the morning, the students went into the parlor to pass their hands over the tree. The Blind children joyfully played, so strangers walking among them assumed they were just playing because in their wild gyrations they never ran into a tree, knocked over a chair, or stumbled into a fire in the hearth (Keller, 1906).

In early 1888, Helen, Kate, and Annie returned to Tuscumbia, Alabama, after their first explorations in Boston. Annie, motivated to return to the

HELEN'S CHILDHOOD DREAMS AT PERKINS KINDERGARTEN

Polish-born psychologist Josef Jastrow was interested in experimental and anomalistic psychology, and he studied the dreams of the Deaf-Blind (Jastrow, 1900). Helen Keller was unaware how she spelled with her fingers in her sleep or how she laughed out loud in her dreams about playing. Sometimes she dreamt friends spelled short, vague messages into her hands. Helen felt her dreams reflected conversations and events going on around her as if her mind acted like a mirror in which faces and landscapes as well as abstract thoughts thronged.

In one of Keller's dream landscapes, she wandered in a natural mansion constructed of leaves and flowers; the landscape was wavy and graceful. She could see openings between the leaves that permitted pure air to pass. Keller learned in her dream how the flowers would never perish, and this discovery thrilled her until she awoke.

One of Keller's last sights before losing her vision was dangling crystals from a lamp in her parents' home and she relived that sensation visiting Niagara Falls. She did not remember seeing or hearing in dreams, except for one time when sunlight appeared to flash suddenly in her eyes so she became so dazzled she could not think. When she looked up, someone hastily spelled in her hand, "Why are you looking back on your babyhood?"

Helen Keller felt there were places in dreamland where she could and could not enter. Otherwise, she was free to wander through nature or be with friends. She often dreamed of her mother Kate Keller or sister Mildred Keller because they lived at a distance. Anne Sullivan rarely appeared in Keller's dreams, but she feared if Sullivan was torn away by circumstance, she would dream about her. Once Keller learned how to read, she dreamt nightmares of war.

familiar North, taught Helen the patterns of raised dots needed to read braille texts in a few months to add to her skills. Michael Anagnos, now a widower, continued to treat Annie Sullivan like a daughter. He took responsibility for Annie's education at Perkins Institute and gave her significant financial assistance. Anagnos and housemother Sophia Hopkins corresponded regularly with Annie, hoping to gain control of the situation in Alabama, but Annie did not want to be told how to teach Helen.

Helen's delayed learning and her curiosity led her to ask questions younger children would ask. The girl wrote another letter to Anagnos thanking him for sending a desk to her in Alabama, saying she used it to write a letter to her mother who was visiting family in Memphis. Helen's correspondence increasingly demonstrated her socialization. She showed herself to be a charitable young person worthy of investment, even as she wrote of placing money in a church collection basket after a service.

Unaware that the public was interested in her life, Helen innocently responded to letters from Anagnos with a beguiling openness and honesty. As soon as the Perkins Institute director received correspondence from her, Helen's letters were published in Boston newspapers. Mrs. Hopkins also started corresponding directly with Helen to gage the girl's level of socialization to learn if the girl would fit in at Perkins Institute.

Michael Anagnos and Alexander Graham Bell, in conspiring to bring attention to connections between Helen Keller and their respective initiatives, discovered Boston activist Reverend Edward Everett Hale and Kate Keller were distant cousins. When Anagnos received Helen's letters, he soon forwarded them to Hale to publish in his family newspaper *the Boston Daily Advertiser*. After reading Anagnos's account of Helen, Hale wrote to Helen's father, Arthur Keller, claiming kinship.

On January 15, 1888, Helen wrote to her mother's cousin, demonstrating in the letter that she understood the roles of people around her (Keller, 1903). Helen told Hale she would like to visit Perkins Institute in June. Unknown to Annie, her train ride to Tuscumbia eight months earlier was paid by Hale's secret girlfriend, Harriet "Hattie" Freeman. The single college-educated naturalist who volunteered at Perkins Institute and Reverend Hale's parish, discretely took an interest in Annie and her student. Once Hale started corresponding with Helen, he signed his letters to her in braille with pinpricks similar to how he coded private messages to his girlfriend in correspondence.

Annie, increasingly frustrated with the heat and slowness of life in Alabama, started to maneuver and cajole supporters into welcoming her and her student back to a more familiar climate in the North. In March 1888, Anagnos traveled to Alabama to assess the progress of Annie's protégé firsthand. While Anagnos hoped to manipulate Annie, the young teacher masterfully manipulated her mentor to keep her position with Helen.

EDWARD EVERETT HALE'S MASTERPIECE OF PATRIOTISM

Reverend Edward Everett Hale is best remembered for his Civil War tale, *The Man without a Country* (1863), subtly questioning light and dark aspects of American patriotism during times of war. The story's protagonist Philip Nolan, a Southerner, in a moment of youthful braggadocio during a military hearing for treason arrogantly damns the United States. Nolan shouts, "I wish I may never hear of the United States again!"

The court grants Nolan's boastful wish, sentencing him to a life of exile upon the high seas where he must live in a Robinson Crusoe-like isolation from his homeland. Stripped of all national identity and news from home, Nolan enters an experience of sustained limbo familiar metaphorically to a Deaf-Blind individual. Separated from society in meaningful ways, the one female from home he meets during a shipboard dance shuns him.

After enactment of the Slave Trade Treaty (1807), Nolan's ship rescues human cargo and frees them. Nolan acts as translator and experiences a nervous breakdown after Black men communicate they would not prefer freedom in distant lands, but would rather earn freedom to return to their families and homelands.

Perhaps Nolan was modeled after Eustace Dauger (1640–1703) depicted in Alexander Dumas' *The Man in the Iron Mask* (1850), where Dauger became a phantom and the subject of false new stories. Nolan retreats into an inner landscape where his homeland's symbols are allowed. Nolan's true character emerges in his actual heroic self, but his homeland never pardons him. During his fifty-five years in exile, Nolan faces death during the Civil War. Having long since repented his youthful follies, Nolan's companions realize he was a man who submitted to a fate he demanded.

Annie strategically communicated Anagnos's likes and dislikes to Helen so she knew how to create the desired impression. For instance, Helen learned he frequently traveled to Greece to visit family, so she knew to write she desired to learn about different countries.

When in May 1888, Helen, Annie, and Kate boarded a train to Boston, Kate and Arthur did not realize their daughter would not return home again other than for visits. On the way, they stopped first in Washington, D.C., to meet President Grover Cleveland. Helen tried to kiss the president; being unused to precocious children, Cleveland pushed the Deaf-Blind-Mute child away. They also visited Alexander Graham Bell's family. Helen's "Southern belle" charms led women in the Bell household to be a little standoffish. His daughters Elsie and Marian Bell, who were about the same age as Helen, were jealous of how their father paid so much attention to the Deaf-Blind girl. The sisters caused mischief by taking Helen to their secret hiding place on the roof of a stable, but the athletic girl came to no harm from the adventure.

Helen was admitted as an unofficial student at Perkins Institute. She had free run of the extensive braille library, gymnasium, and collection of stuffed birds and animals. She learned a whole new set of contextualized smells and textures. Helen learned to navigate larger spaces as she required more familiar places for her little fingers to make contact with walls and furniture signposts. Anagnos did not allow Arthur Keller to pay any tuition, and he ceased to pay any salary to Annie. Helen took classes in basketry and clay modeling and studied French.

Kate, Helen, and Annie met Edward Everett Hale in late May 1888. He was careless in his dress and refused to waste time on shaving and barbering. Kate's cousin was a prodigious worker trying to reform social, political, and economic issues. He was the grandnephew of American Revolutionary War soldier and spy Nathan Hale, whose last words as an illegal combatant at a Manhattan hangman's noose were "I regret that I have but one life to lose for my country."

Reverend Hale was the son of the *Boston Daily Advertiser* owner and married to Emily Perkins, who was the niece of the famous abolitionist author Harriet Beecher Stowe. With such familial connections to the highly publicized scandal related to popular pastor Lyman Beecher and Elizabeth Tilton, Hale went to lengths to keep his extramarital relationship with Hattie Freeman a secret. Now a pioneering environmentalist and naturalist who filled his columns of the *Transcript* with reports on New England streams, woods, and wildlife, Hale had been a geologist in his youth. Mount Hale in New Hampshire was named after him for a forestation campaign. Hale introduced Helen to New England trees and wildflowers as well as stonewalls and green pastures as he connected their significance regionally to the people.

Although Hale recognized Annie Sullivan's extraordinary efforts on Helen's behalf, he also saw the girl was totally dependent upon her teacher. Annie's desire to stay out of the grasp of poverty prompted recklessness. Hale once observed, "There are famous men who started out life poor, but they persevered, conquered many obstacles, and succeeded in all their undertakings, and were happy. But there are other men, who have brains and they struggle and struggle, and cannot accomplish what they set out to do, or if they do, they wear themselves out in the process so that they cannot enjoy their success."

Hale and his wife, Emily Baldwin Perkins Hale, hosted a party for Helen, to which they invited five neighborhood girls (Day, 2013). Helen explored a bas-relief of Jesus and John the Baptist in the home, asking questions in rapid succession. Hale wrote to Hattie about his observations of Helen's sensory skills and intelligence and reported how Kate was lovely, "glowing with happiness." Hale and Hattie secured accommodations for Helen and Annie within their social circles during summer breaks at Perkins Institute, because Arthur Keller did not allow Helen's teacher any vacations.

Hale wrote a poem inspiring Helen in her efforts for other Deaf-Blind children: "I am only one, but I am still one. I cannot do everything, but still I can do something; And because I cannot do everything, I will not refuse to do the something that I can do" (Lash, 1980).

Helen lived up to the persona established in her correspondence, immediately becoming the institutional darling, while Annie was treated like a returning hero almost two years after graduating as valedictorian. Anagnos concocted commencement exercises when there were no graduates. Helen appeared to eclipse the resident Perkins Institute star Laura Bridgman at her jubilee celebration when she finger spelled a poem to a standing-room crowd. She did not become a "second Laura"; by exhibiting the manual alphabet, she became a new sensation.

Helen met the Blind students who had received her correspondence. Hale later reported to Freeman, "Our dear little Helen was the light and the life of the whole thing." She made sounds of "coo-oo-oo" with laughter and was affectionate, moving as if dancing across a stage. Hale added how Annie Sullivan called Helen "baby."

Before Laura Bridgman's jubilee celebration, Annie took Helen to visit her, like Lydia Sigourney had introduced Laura to the elder Deaf-Blind-Mute woman Julia Brace. Having lived with her in Mrs. Hopkins's cottage, Annie knew Laura, and Annie told Helen about their similarities. Both had been of the same age when they lost their hearing, both had blue eyes and light brown hair, and both had started their education at the same age.

Annie and Helen found Laura sitting motionless like a statue near a window, crocheting lace. Laura recognized Annie's touch. Helen reached for Laura's dainty, cool hands and they felt like flowers growing in shady places. If tidy Laura was like a greenhouse flower, then Helen was a wildflower. The two Deaf-Blind females kissed according to the custom. Helen reached for the lace Laura was crocheting, and the older woman snatched it out of her reach, stating, "I'm afraid your hands are dirty."

Intrigued by the Deaf-Blind woman since her teacher had first described her, Helen wanted to feel the older woman's face, but Laura shrank away. The elder female chided Annie, "You have not taught her how to be gentle." Then she turned to Helen. "You must not be forward with calling upon a lady."

Unsure of herself, Helen characteristically sat on the floor to gain a sense of equilibrium. This only seemed to agitate Laura, who jerked her young visitor up and spelled, "You must not sit on the floor when you are wearing a clean dress. You will mess it up." Next, Laura instructed Helen, "You must remember many things once you understand them" (Keller, 1903).

HELEN'S FIRST DEAF-BLIND FRIEND

Michael Anagnos hoped to expand operations and sought another new Deaf-Blind prodigy to draw attention to the work at Perkins Institute for the Blind. He decided to use the occasion of Laura Bridgman's jubilee celebration of residing at the school for fifty years to introduce two new Deaf-Blind girls to Boston society: nearly eight-year-old Helen Keller and nine-year-old Edith M. Thomas (Rocheleau and Mack, 1930).

Thomas was born in Chelsea, Massachusetts, on October 8, 1878. She was a precocious girl, determined and practical, who lost her sight as a result of scarlet fever and diphtheria when she was four years old. Thomas then lost her hearing when she was six. Edith talked after becoming deaf but eventually slowed to single-word utterances and then stopped speaking completely for a long time; her last word was "kitty."

Thomas attended the new Perkins Kindergarten when she was eight years old. She started learning the manual alphabet, but apathy to instruction kept her from progressing. Thomas was self-reliant and independent; she was more of a *doer* than *communicator*. She resented the constant prodding associated with language training but entered Perkins Institute after graduating from the Kindergarten when she was twelve years old.

Thomas enjoyed history and the natural sciences, and she was athletic. She excelled in woodwork as well as knitting and sewing. Edith could draft a clothing pattern, cut it, and stitch it by hand or assemble it on a machine. After relying upon the manual alphabet for seven years, Edith was determined to learn to speak aloud or articulate. She eventually spoke with those who knew her well, but she never made herself vulnerable by speaking in public like Helen Keller.

In her eagerness to kiss Laura goodbye, Helen accidentally trod upon Bridgman's feet, further annoying her. Helen sensed in Laura's cool stillness a frustration that made her feel like a bad little girl described in Sunday school books. A year later, Laura Bridgman was dead.

Annie Sullivan taught Helen Keller to write idiomatic English characterized by special linguistic meaning that was not immediately clear from the usual meaning of the words used. This knowledge differentiated Helen from Laura Bridgman, who could write words but could not communicate poetically. While teachers or guardians wrote for Alice Cogswell, Julia Brace, and Laura Bridgman, Helen began communicating for herself through letters. To public perception, Helen's disabilities imprisoned her because she could not verify impressions entirely through her own experience. However, Helen's remaining senses of smell, touch, and taste along with her ability to express herself artfully drew famous thinkers to her.

Helen enchanted scientists, poets, philosophers, clergymen, and celebrities interested in corresponding with a Deaf-Blind child. Michael

Anagnos, like Helen's father Captain Arthur Keller, was an attorney and journalist before becoming the director of Perkins Institute. Anagnos published sentimental descriptions of Helen's "miracle" in their annual reports in 1888: " . . . As if impelled by a resistless instinctive force she snatched the key of the treasury of the English language from the finger of her teacher, unlocked the door with vehemence, and began to feast on its contents with inexpressible delight . . ."

In early July 1888, Helen, Annie, and Kate stayed with Mrs. Hopkins in Brewster, Massachusetts. This offered Helen her first visit to the seashore. Someone was always available to read to her from children's books in Hopkins's library that her late daughter read. Reverend Hale was the family minister to Oliver Wendell Holmes, Sr., and he introduced his cousin to the poet. Holmes belonged to Julia Ward Howe's social circles, and he praised her husband for his work with Laura. In Holmes's *The Autocrat of the Breakfast-Table* (1858), he wrote, "He asked not whence the fountain roll / no traveler's foot has found, / but mapped the desert of the soul / untouched by sight or sound" (Lash, 1980).

Boston's literary elite already knew Laura Bridgman's story, but beyond superficial similarities, Helen exhibited a completely different temperament from Laura, just as her teacher Annie Sullivan came from a very different background from Dr. Samuel Gridley Howe. Holmes praised his friend, "To Laura Bridgman" in about 1850:

> *Be thine the task, O! Generous Howe, to guide the imprisoned guest, through Nature's ample fields to draw the curtain of her wealth aside, and show the pleasure that the true science yields; to tread the path by learning seldom trod, that leads "from nature up the nature's God.* (Lash, 1980)

Holmes always tinkered with words, or *something*. He owned a microscope he used to examine things, and when he tired of it, he adapted the contrivance with some small improvements and developed a stereoscope. If Holmes took out a patent, he would have become a very wealthy man, but this was not his style. Though he joked about the large sums he lost, Holmes wanted people to enjoy his experiments, so he gave the technology away free.

Likewise, Helen's fingertips kept her busy as her conduit to the world. Her little fingers retained tactile mental landscapes of facial and hand contours of those who increasingly pulled the girl into new worlds of ideas. Helen studied insects at Perkins Institute and learned about butterflies. She wrote to the poet, "I am studying insects in Zoology, and have learned many things about butterflies." Her letters charmed Holmes with their guilelessness as she reached out to him. "I am sorry you have no children to play with sometimes." Holmes always responded to Helen, and he sent her some shells from Greece to foster her interest in nature.

To truly read involves selecting mental images, filtering thoughts, and marking important events and locations in life journeys while navigating illusion and allusion. Helen easily received impressions from stories spelled into her hand, so when her teacher read Charles Perrault's tale called *Little Red Riding-Hood* (1697) Helen subsequently dreamt about a wolf rushing toward her. The animal sank his teeth into her flesh. Helen tried to scream, but no sound escaped her lips. The dream stopped haunting her as she began experiencing events outside of herself.

The first book Helen read independently in braille was *Little Lord Fauntleroy* by Frances Hodgson Burnett (1849–1924), originally published in serial form in *St. Nicholas Magazine* (Keller, 1903). As Helen's reading improved, the lack of braille books available in Alabama became frustrating. Helen had a strong memory for nuance and abstract concepts, and Annie introduced her to idiomatic expressions known naturally to native speakers in America with her finger-spelled phrases so she could take in symbolic knowledge to understand physical realities.

Helen had already learned the manual alphabet (sign language) and the braille alphabet (an alphabet of raised dots), so she could read and write. Helen and Annie stayed with Mrs. Hopkins during the winter break when everyone left to be with families, and Michael Anagnos traveled home to Greece to visit family.

In February 1889, Helen wrote to Reverend Hale about how Annie taught her about the importance of kindness, especially toward Mildred. Helen wrote, "My teacher says, if children learn to be patient and gentle while they are little, that when they grow to be young ladies and gentlemen, they will not forget to be kind and loving and brave. I hope I shall be courageous always" (Keller, 1903).

During the summer of 1889, Helen and Annie experienced their first separation when Annie underwent another eye surgery. The pair reunited in September at the same time when Dr. Samuel Gridley Howe's daughter, Florence Howe Hall, wrote an article about Helen appearing in the children's magazine *St. Nicholas*. Hall, a Pulitzer Prize recipient, hoped to brand Helen as a product of her father's teaching methods. Hall offered a little dig at Annie when she suggested that Helen as the Blind-Deaf-Mute girl from Alabama came to Perkins Institute in late 1887 to get real training.

Hall explained that despite being "dumb," or speechless, Helen showed aptitude for learning and "imitated the motions of people whom she did not see, indeed, but *felt*." The term "dumb" during the Victorian era was synonymous with "mute." However, today when someone is described as dumb, it is a derogatory term meaning the person is exhibiting a lack of thought or intelligence. Hall attempted to tell Helen's story to "mute" her; however, with Annie's guidance, Helen soon communicated directly through writing letters and getting her words published.

Hall suggested that since Helen learned to talk with her fingers, her natural, or sign, language was gradually laid aside. She shrewdly challenged Annie's accounts of Helen's progress in the court of public opinion, suggesting it was incredible a six-and-three-quarter-year-old Helen had learned 450 words in four months. "On the first day of March 1887, the poor child was almost like a dumb animal: she knew no language—not a single word, nor a single letter. In July, of the same year, she had not only learned to talk fluently with her fingers, but had learned also to read raised type, to write a neat square hand, and to write letters to her friends" (Hall, 1889).

Helen's letter-writing campaign from her home Ivy Green won her friends and admirers far and wide when they were published in newspapers and magazines. A Pennsylvania land developer named William Wade—an English mastiff to Helen in Tuscumbia while she was at Perkins Institute in November 1889, and she named it Lioness. Wade was drawn to Helen after reading one of her letters published in *St. Nicholas*, in which she wrote about her dog.

Helen and Wade became pen pals, and he soon extended his friendship to the Deaf-Blind throughout the United States and Canada (Keller, 1913). Wade contacted Deaf-Blind children scattered throughout the United States to encourage them to embrace learning. Wade was practical in his efforts by supplying books, typewriters, sewing machines, printing presses, and other materials or seeking employment opportunities to make them feel self-sufficient.

Helen wrote directly to John Greenleaf Whittier in November 1889 about his poems called "In School Days" and "My Playmate" (Keller, 1903). She impressed him by discussing elements of his poems. Helen wrote to her mother about being invited to Whittier's home in the spring; she asked for permission to visit him. Helen reported that the poet had advised Kate to feed the mastiff from her hand so that she would learn to be gentler than if she were allowed to eat with her father's hunting dogs. Helen asked her mother to convince her father Arthur Keller to write to her.

Introduced to a new world filled with epistolary relationships based upon the exchanging of letters, Helen optimistically believed she and her teacher Annie had made friends. The challenge with letter writing (like with email and texting today) is the writer does not how people truly respond to words communicated. Helen's wily and insecure teacher sent mixed messages to supporters and sometimes pitted powerful men against each other. Annie Sullivan's secrets consumed her, so she did not pay attention to how her words might precede her and her student Helen Keller in the world. As a result, surprises and undercurrents dogged the pair when they next traveled north to Boston, Massachusetts.

4

Articulating Helen

Men could conceal their failures in Victorian America by developing secret identities. Rarely did Americans question the societal threat of maintaining dirty secrets until news of the tragic Greely Expedition to the North Pole surfaced in 1881. Frederick F. Kislingbury, a member of the expedition, met a tragic end after the federal government bungled a delivery of supplies. Exhumations eventually confirmed rumors that desperate survivors had resorted to cannibalism. The attendant scandal thrilled and shocked Gilded Age Americans, who reveled in the exposure of the expedition's secrets. However, women, especially single women like Annie Sullivan, needed to be extremely careful of secrets connected to identity because men could use those secrets to manipulate and control them. Annie remained ignorant of Reverend Edward Everett Hale and Michael Anagnos's secrets, but they knew about her sordid but blameless childhood at Tewksbury. The thrilling Greely Expedition revealed a dichotomy in American culture shaping Helen Keller's life; Americans were intrigued by the "sordid" because they could judge and shun others, yet this element also drew them to the innocent "goodness" exemplified by Helen.

This placed the ambitious teacher Annie at a disadvantage in navigating a man's world because she was blameless but not innocent as well as worldly but not jaded. Annie's biggest disadvantage was her ignorance of the consequences of challenging men who dominated the world she hoped to conquer. Annie was a force of nature; she did not restrain her ambition or words, which her student Helen Keller recognized as a "love of perfection (Keller, 1955)." While revelations of savage behavior in the Arctic horrified Americans, they sought diversion by placing childlike innocence on a pedestal. The country noticed Helen Keller because she was an anomaly as she listened through her fingers and was unable to utter feminine sounds. If nature could not reach the girl through her ears and eyes, it would engage her remaining senses of smell, taste, and touch.

When alone in the outdoors, Helen spoke to birds with her own unique squawk, assuming they would not judge. She had already mastered the art of gesticulation, using vigorous gestures to emphasize words she could not articulate. However, Helen Keller was not the only disabled child nature spoke to; there was a famous Blind pianist Thomas "Blind Tom" Higgins, who was born a slave in Georgia to Charity and Mingo (O'Connell, 2009). Higgins was within the autistic spectrum and possessed a gift for taking sounds around him and transposing them in music. Higgins's hearing and memory made him sensitive to the vibrating acoustic environment from nature.

When he was eight years old, Higgins's owner "loaned" him to a promoter Perry Oliver. Oliver exploited the Blind prodigy to become a very wealthy man. It was easy for Oliver to manipulate the information that Higgins received to keep him ignorant of how his blindness and the color of his skin led audiences to perceive him in ways that made his concerts particularly profitable for his guardian.

Helen was as dependent upon her guardian-teacher-promoter Annie Sullivan as Higgins was on his guardian-promoter Perry Oliver. While like Higgins, Helen could receive vibrations through her sense of touch, she always felt her greatest disability was her inability to hear the world around her. Helen and many Deaf-Blind-Mute individuals agreed on deafness being the harshest part of their double disability because it socially isolated them. Helen's most profound desire was to learn to articulate her thoughts to speak to the world.

With no money coming from her father, Helen and Annie spent breaks from Perkins Institute with its housemother Mrs. Sophia C. Hopkins or affluent friends. Nine-year-old Helen met Joseph Edgar "Uncle Ed" Chamberlin and his wife Ida Elizabeth Atwood Chamberlin, who were Perkins Institute supporters. She and Annie spent weekends and holidays at the Chamberlin's Red Farm home in a suburb of Boston called Wrentham, Massachusetts. Red Farm on the shores of King Phillip's Pond became a gathering place for literary, political, and artistic figures, where notables such as Edward Everett Hale and Bradford Torrey congregated.

Chamberlin's family could not afford to send him to college, so he helped an older brother Everett Chamberlin establish a newspaper in Chicago. He obtained a poor man's liberal arts education by borrowing books from the Chicago Public Library. Uncle Ed Chamberlin and Ida had six children, one an adopted son. Chamberlin was a pioneering environmentalist and naturalist. He filled his columns "The Listener" in the daily newspaper *Boston Evening Transcript* with reports on New England streams, woods, and wildlife.

Chamberlin became an editor and writer for the children's magazine *Youth's Companion* also headquartered in Boston, and he introduced Helen and Annie to his assistant editor Bradford Torrey at the Boston Commons. As employees of the *Youth's Companion*, Chamberlin and Torrey were writers of natural history and moral tales for young people. The ornithologist gave Helen a tour of the urban public park. Torrey devoted much of his time to the study of birds, their habits, peculiarities, and domestic traits. He knew Henry David Thoreau as a spiritual economist and an artist and hoped to share Thoreau's naturally affinity for the common and ordinary to his young Deaf-Blind friend.

Torrey was a singular kind of man. Even his appearance was odd, with his receding closely cropped hairline, arched brows over fragile spectacles, and a beard that sprang in all directions. Torrey was a romantic in pursuit of a song. He followed his own methods for understanding birds and humans with an ornithologically educated sensibility. While Annie introduced Helen to the vibrations of common pigeons, Torrey listened to birds in nature and learned to understand their characteristics. Torrey's experience allowed him to focus on Helen's abilities to smell and touch in understanding his feathered friends.

The ornithologist escaped into Helen's innocent world to explain how transient bird visitors to the Boston Commons tarry a few days a season (Torrey, 1900). Torrey followed the vibrations of bird conversations as they traveled from tree to tree and in and out of shrubs. The transients feared they were wrong stopping in the public park in the first place, but they put up with the discomforts of the situation until after sunset.

As Torrey spoke, Helen traveled from tree to tree, feeling a variety of barks and leaves in the way she touched a person's hand to identify and remember them. Torrey observed his young colleague with a scientific satisfaction as he communicated to Annie, who translated everything into Helen's hands.

Torrey described how a yellow-bellied woodpecker showed up in the Commons one October morning; it was the only yellow-bellied woodpecker he had ever seen. The woodpecker stayed in the company of chickadees and other birds before taking up quarters in maple tree near the Ether monument. Also known as "The Good Samaritan," it was near the northwest corner of Boston's Public Garden. The woodpecker remained four days alternating between the maple tree and a nearby tulip tree. Torrey decided the woodpecker was a genuine connoisseur of trees, asserting the Boston Commons' maple was no ordinary wood.

The ornithologist could not resist offering Helen a tidbit of humming-bird gossip to pass on to her mother. Kate Keller had Scottish Campbell kin, so Torrey stated, "The Duke of Argyll once argued no bird can ever fly backwards" (Torrey, 1900).

Helen responded, "No?"

Annie swiftly whispered his words, spelling the manual alphabet into Helen's hands as she enjoyed learning alongside her student. Torrey con-tinued, "Well, I hate to dispute the noble Scot." Annie's translations built in intensity. "But I am compelled to report after observing these hum-mingbirds at their work, they have never heard his theory!" Helen giggled. Torrey continued, "At any rate, they very plainly did fly tail foremost; and did that not only in dropping from a blossom, which might be just an opti-cal illusion." Torrey paused, to see if Helen was still paying attention, before continuing, "But they also backed out of the flower tube in an upward direction" (Torrey, 1893, 1900, 1906).

Helen's subconscious thoughts showed as she unconsciously imitated the hummingbird's motion with her hands, as she was prone to do when deeply focused. Torrey, excited by her joy, continued at a more excited pace, "I once saw a hummingbird exploring the disk of a sunflower in the company of a splendid monarch butterfly!"

Helen reached out and touched his face to feel the laughter beneath the surface about to erupt. "Yes, the hummingbird must have known the sun-flower was very popular because it was appearing in so many gardens along his path." Torrey caught his breath, and Annie laughed, before he offered a conclusion, "For only a few moments before, the same bird chased an Eng-lish Sparrow out of the garden and across Arlington Street and up to a rooftop . . . to the delight to at least one patriotic Yankee."

Helen's whole body was alive to the conditions about her. She laughed and gesticulated, encouraging her new friend to continue. Torrey did not need much convincing; he continued, "There is nothing unusual about see-ing hawks flying over the city and they have a famous taste for sparrows making their home in the Commons." He described how a hawk perched for a while on a fence post along Arlington Street near a passing carriage. Then the hawk swooped down, peering into a bed of rhododendrons before choosing a tree where he perched while men passed beneath, watching and waiting.

A small company of sparrows flew along. One sparrow, intent upon showing off before her comrades, swooped down upon the hawk and gave him a jab before rejoining his companions. Torrey described how the spar-row appeared to laugh in scorn. "There! Did you see me give that big guy a peck? I am not afraid of any old big bird!" Torrey looked at Helen and then at Annie, hoping they got his message about a "little gal" with the big mes-sage. He paused, satisfied at the story's revelation, in the style of Thoreau, of illustrating the ascendency of spirit over matter. Not able to leave the point, Torrey asked Helen, "Do you know what Thoreau's peculiarity is?"

Helen responded, "What?"

Torrey and others had observed Helen pressed to play a public role at a young age. The bird man stated, "Thoreau insists upon being himself." Torrey continued, "Society is kind of a self-constituted militia, a protective association, an army where everyone must keep in step."

Helen nodded, and Torrey looked at Annie, seeking her approval. "Thoreau liked solitude, and in other words, he liked to think." Helen paused and began to stroke another nearby tree. Each trunk offered a particular story to tell the Deaf-Blind girl. She listened with her fingers and smelled with her nose while Torrey paused to greet the tree too. He saw something similar between Helen and the ecologist, "Thoreau much preferred the society of trees" (Torrey, 1906).

Helen nodded. She grasped the abstract ideas of transcendentalism, living simply in natural surroundings and not feeling the need to finger-spell with Torrey. He continued, "Thoreau found fellowship with the trees too." Helen smiled as his word got spelled into her hand. "They were his kin, which is not to say that he enjoyed looking at them as objects of beauty." Torrey observed as Helen articulated in her own manner in her own space. Contented, he continued, "Thoreau lived in a world of his own, a world of ideas." She appreciated his insights as Torrey observed, "He was strangely indifferent to much of what other men found absorbing" (Torrey, 1906).

Helen Keller would be all right if she could be independent of others for communications; relying upon Annie to continually speak for her undermined the girl's self-identity. She uttered a sound of affirmation. Torrey decided to press her, "Thoreau could get on without a daily newspaper . . ." At this, Arthur Keller's daughter stopped and grabbed his arm, *No!* The bird man finished his sentence, "But not without a daily walk."

Helen laughed out, but Torrey caught her arm to make his point. "Thoreau was more anxious to live well, according to an inward standard of his own." Torrey recognized how people wanted to *handle* Helen, even his dear friends Ed and Ida Chamberlin, but he hoped to put the girl's mind to rest. Many in Boston had observed Annie's desire to dominate her student. They had seen her attempts to look affluent: the ambitious young teacher once spent an entire month's salary on a velvet fur-lined cape! Torrey offered Helen thought model, "Thoreau set a low value on money. It *might* be of service to him, he once confessed to me, but in general he accepted poverty" (Torrey, 1906).

The girl was perceptive; she sensed there was more to Annie's life than she let on. Despite her flair and drama, Annie carried great sorrow. For instance, despite all of Annie's efforts to present a strong front, Helen caught her teacher reading a book very close to her eyes and asked her about it. Annie could see best in the morning when the light was strong, but Helen discovered her vision was so poor she could only see about an inch beyond her nose.

Annie took Helen into the tenement neighborhoods to sensitize her; this was the only hint of her harrowing past shared with her student. When visiting the poor, Helen sensed the narrow, dirty streets. In those grimy alleyways, half-clad, underfed children gathered; young Helen reached out to them. They sometimes shrank away as if avoiding another blow. Poverty was a surreal abstraction haunting Helen; she perceived some adults living in poverty as "all gnarled and bent out of shape" (Lash, 1980).

Torrey did not miss Helen's perplexed expression. Everyone surrounding her was concerned with money; they possessed no sensibility of tangible-free resources. Torrey told Helen Thoreau's mantra, "Simplicity, simplicity, simplicity! Simplicity of life and devotion to the ideal . . . simplicity is the root of spiritual economy and free will." The bird man seemed to read into the girl's thoughts, and he quietly added, "Fame is a plant that blossoms on graves . . . botanists would say 'a late flowering perennial, to be found in old cemeteries'" (Torrey, 1906).

Helen asked, "Do you think I could live like Thoreau?"

Torrey understood her question was not about intellect, but rather her need for privacy and solitude. He wondered if the girl craved solitude or just space to be herself. Helen had dealt with celebrities like Laura Bridgman. She was no greenhouse flower like Laura, living a sheltered live in an institution. Torrey thought for a moment and said, "But life was never as simple as Thoreau attempted to make it, and he, like others, was conscious of a mind divided" (Torrey, 1906).

Helen asked, brashly finger-spelled through Annie, what he meant. In their conversation, Torrey, Helen, and Annie absentmindedly circled the same tree again and again as it if were part of their debate. Torrey saw Helen's fingers continually returning to the aged curvilinear bark as if to see if the tree was drawing some conclusions.

Perhaps Helen's tree friend once met Thoreau's fingers too during its long lifetime. The little man wearing spectacles reached for a metaphor for Helen to chew on. "Thoreau's attainments as a naturalist have been in turns, like a pendulum exaggerated and belittled, one extreme following like another." The girl looked up in her characteristic way, as if the sky was written in braille, and laughed in appreciation. Torrey continued, "Thoreau's work, humorous or serious, transcendental or matter-of-fact, was all from his own tree" (Torrey, 1906).

Helen fondly stroked the tree bark. Torrey smiled. "Thoreau knew his local flora and fauna by his own method: he was sympathetic." Helen understood what the ornithologist was trying to convey. He observed, "Nobody was more successful at getting inside a bird than Thoreau."

Helen told him, "I am never alone; everything is through my teacher." Torrey immediately understood. Everyone in Boston quietly wondered how to reach Helen without always having to go through her mercurial teacher.

Torrey replied simply, "Helen, you are your own person with your own path. By inclination and habit, Thoreau liked to see and do things for himself . . . that was a mark of his individualism and the chief mark of his genius." He paused, "You need to pursue your path because Annie will not always be there."

Life without her teacher was unimaginable to the girl. Torrey sensed Helen's agitation and changed the topic to give her time to digest what he had said. Helen focused her attention back to the tree trunk. Torrey continued, "Did you know that Thoreau knew Ralph Waldo Emerson and they lived in the same house for a while?" Torrey knowingly whistled and then concluded, "Thoreau preferred the company of nature to Emerson." Helen gently swatted her friend and laughed (Torrey, 1906).

HELEN'S LESSONS FROM FICTIONAL CHARACTERS

On March 1, 1890, Helen wrote to Oliver Wendell Holmes, Sr. asking him about a book called *The Story of Little Jakey* (1875) by a Blind writer Mrs. Helen Aldrich de Kroyft. The fictional Blind orphan named Jakey captured Helen Keller's attention. She wrote Reverend Phillips Brooks, "Why does the dear Father in Heaven think it is best for us to have great sorrow and pain sometimes?" (Keller, 1903).

Literacy, the ability to read, provided Keller with her sense of self-worth as she pieced together abstract ideas and reached for broader significance and information by touch and smell. Comparing and contrasting how Cedric, the protagonist in Francis Hodgson Burnett's *Little Lord Fauntleroy* (1886), and Jakey developed, Keller discerned Jakey's life was harder than Cedric's because Jakey was poor *and Blind*.

Keller already connected an author's experience to what they produced. Keller wrote to Reverend Brooks, "I am so happy and so was Little Lord Fauntleroy, but dear little Jakey's life was so full of sadness." Keller related to Jakey's vulnerability due to his disability, and she asked Brooks, "Do you think that poor Jakey loved his Father in Heaven more because his other father was unkind to him" (Keller, 1903)?

Keller wanted to understand why a virtuous Blind character felt hardship, "God did not put light in Jakey's eyes, and he was blind, and his father was not gentle and loving." Keller then asked, "When people do very wrong and hurt animals and treat children unkindly, God is grieved, but what will he do to help them to be pitiful and loving?"

Brooks responded, "It is the power of love which is in our own hearts. Love is the soul of everything . . . the more we love, the more near we are to God and His love."

Fictional characters including Little Lord Fauntleroy and Jakey became Helen's "dear little friends." She wrote to the readers of *St. Nicholas* magazine, asking, "I wonder if anyone as read a sad sweet story called Little Jakey?" Helen asserted, "Jakey is the dearest little fellow you can imagine." The two characters introduced Helen to the deeper aspects of poverty. Helen wrote, "I used to think before I could read that everyone was always happy, and at first, I was grieved to know about pain and great sorrows, but now I understand that if it were not for these things people would never learn to be brave and patient and loving" (Keller, 1894).

Annie never developed deep religious practices. As Helen read more and more books with religious themes, her teacher felt uncomfortable answering Helen's questions about death and the afterlife. Helen asked her teacher, "Why can't people see God?" Annie responded, "This human body we live in is a veil that prevents us from seeing him" (Lash, 1980). She demonstrated this concept by making Helen stand on one side of a screen made of Japanese paper while she stood on the other side. They were quite hidden from each other and could not touch each other, yet by little signs, Helen could tell that her teacher was still there.

Annie did not feel comfortable talking to Helen about God. She contacted a prominent Boston Episcopal leader named Reverend Phillips Brooks without consulting Michael Anagnos. Brooks addressed Helen's most pressing questions using simple language to tell Helen that God loved her and that she was one of His children. When Helen understood, she said, "O yes, I know him, I just forgot his name."

Brooks wrote to Helen, "I do not see how we can help thinking about God when he is so good to us all the time" (Keller, 1903).

Helen's club of older literary pen pals grew when she learned to type and gave up her writing board altogether. She wrote to Holmes that she had read one of his poems to a gathering of students at Perkins Institute for the Blind on Washington's birthday and had shared his shells from the Greek island of Palos. She wrote, "I have learned many things about butterflies . . . they do not make honey for us like the bees, but many of them are beautiful as the flowers they lite upon, and they always delight the hearts of little children" (Keller, 1903).

Holmes's servant followed Helen's progress in the news with keen interest; she had a blind sister living in an asylum and told the poet one of Helen's visits to the residents was inspirational. Holmes loved Helen's letter for its childish natural openness and printed it in his column "Over the Teacups" in the May 1890 issue of the *Atlantic Monthly*. To Helen, he wrote, "I am delighted with the style of your letters. There is no affectation about them, and as they come straight from your heart, so they go straight to mine" (Keller, 1903). Annie was pleased.

Holmes later observed, "The life of an individual is like a child's dissected map, if I could life a hundred years maybe I could put the pieces together to make a properly connected whole." When they returned home, Helen asked Annie to read her *The School-boy* (1878), because it was not available in raised type. Helen remembered with Holmes, "I saw through his eyes and heard through his ears" (Keller, 1903).

Celebrating her second Christmas Eve at Perkins Institute, Helen sent homemade gifts home to Alabama to show her family what new crafts she had learned. Helen made a watchcase for Kate, knit mittens for Mildred, but she purchased a handkerchief for her father because she had run out of time. Arthur Keller sent his daughter money that he could not really spare so she could purchase gifts for her new friends to hang on the tree at Perkins Institute as was the tradition. Helen and Annie remained with housemother Mrs. Hopkins when Michael Anagnos traveled home to Greece to visit family. Annie alienated colleagues at Perkins Institute when she curried favor with Anagnos. The director increasingly embellished and exaggerated Helen's progress to publicize Perkins Institute's programs.

In Norway, Ragnhild Kåta (1873–1947) lost her sight, hearing, smell, and taste when she was three-and-a-half years old as a result of scarlet fever. Norwegian writer Hallvard Bergh met Ragnhild in 1887 and wrote about her plight to Elias Hofgaard at the Hamar Institute for the Deaf in Norway. Hofgaard accepted Ragnhild as a charity student when she was fourteen years old. School was a difficult transition for her because Ragnhild was suspicious of strangers and did not want to be touched. Ragnhild bit, screamed, and clawed Hofgaard early on, but he established a trusting relationship with her.

Hofgaard used a "speaking method" on bright deaf students with good results, but many experts were shocked when he used the method with Ragnhild. Hofgaard reasoned a Deaf-Blind child might better apply learning to speak than using the finger alphabet. Hofgaard taught Ragnhild to pronounce the letters first and then to combine two letters into a syllable and finally multisyllabic words before trying to attach meaning to what until then had been presented as a complicated object lesson game.

Words were associated with objects over several days. Once she began to associate words with ideas, then she learned to understand others by placing her hand on their lips as they spoke. Then Ragnhild learned to write and to read braille. In 1889, Ragnhild met with Mary Swift Lamson, who had once taught Laura Bridgman at the Perkins Institute. Lamson reported that Ragnhild could already speak simple sentences.

Ragnhild Kåta's story inspired Helen to learn to speak; she did not want every living creature to wonder why she opened her mouth and nothing came out. At Helen's continued insistence, Annie contacted Miss Sarah

Fuller, who was principal of the Horace Mann School for the Deaf in Boston, the oldest public day school for the deaf in the United States. Annie-impetuously figured if Miss Fuller was successful in teaching Helen to articulate words, then *she*, Annie, could take credit for something Dr. Samuel Gridley Howe could not do with Laura Bridgman.

Horace Mann School catered to students aged four to sixteen (Brown, 1880), as a free public day school situated near the center of Boston for local deaf-mute students. While Helen and Annie lived at Perkins Institute, most students admitted to the Horace Mann School lived with families to practice what they learned. Students learned symbols of visual speech in order to lip-read and take classes in reading, diction, geography, arithmetic, and other grammars school subjects. Helen did not have to pay the $150 out-of-state tuition.

Once admitted the school, Sarah Fuller started Helen on one of eleven speaking lessons on March 26, 1890, and continued into July. The deaf learn how the vocal cords feel when air is forced upon them to create sound by placing a hand upon the throat to understand the physical sensations of making particular sounds orally. Students learned spoken language using hand mirrors so they could see how the tongue, teeth, and lips looked and felt when producing a given sound because these elements helped them to lip-read.

Fuller showed Annie how to feel vibrations of the articular (the movable organs including tongue or glottis used in the production of speech sounds) with the other hand on the lips to imitate the shape of a mouth. Helen could not determine the right breathing pressure needed to utter sounds. As she learned the elements of speech only Fuller and Annie could understand her, but they did not develop Helen's vocal organs properly. When Alexander Graham Bell described the thorax, which plays a major role in breathing, he did not include the muscular partition separating the diaphragm from the abdomen that inflates the lungs to power the voice. Fuller and Annie tried to build up Helen's speech without understanding how working the vocal organs in voice production was necessary to enunciate word sounds properly.

After her first lesson in articulation, Helen wrote to Reverend Brooks, "Last evening I went out in the yard and spoke to the moon. I said, 'O! moon come to me!' Do you think the lovely moon was glad that I could speak to her?" She continued, "My parents are delighted to hear me speak. I was so happy to give them a happy surprise." Proud of her accomplishment, Helen stated, "I-am-not-dumb-now."

As Helen worked diligently at learning to speak, Annie who wanted to own Helen's progress, grew more evasive in her reports to Anagnos and Mrs. Hopkins. Helen's father Arthur Keller, a popular local storyteller, shared his cleverest anecdotes with Helen so she could tell them to her friends. After she learned to speak, Helen still finger spelled to herself, but she wanted to stop using the manual alphabet for communication. Helen prematurely asked Annie to tie her fingers in paper until the habit was broken during her waking hours, but those close to her still used it because it was more convenient and faster. She later explained, "Constant practice makes the fingers very flexible and fast, about as fast as typing on a typewriter" (Keller, 1929).

* * *

Annie wanted Helen to empathize with the poor. She told Helen, "The world treats the poor harshly, but they do not strike back." Annie offered Helen a hint of how she had experienced poverty without giving details. "The poor are usually kind. It is only the respectable and rich who think up ways of being cruel" (Lash, 1980). In *Little Lord Fauntleroy* (1886), the poor but noble protagonist Cedric offered Helen a good example of dealing with hardships with grace as he bore the weight, even though it exhausted him, and "was willing to accommodate himself even to circumstances which rather overpowered him (Burnett, 1886)." A situation arose in the story when the earl conducted an experiment with his grandson and heir Cedric. The old man pressed his full weight upon the shoulders of seven-year-old Cedric, and the elder leaned upon him like a crutch to see if the boy possessed the courage to carry the burden.

Cedric seemed to enter Helen's inner world with imaginary conversations; her love of reading led her to write to popular child actress Elsie Leslie Lyde. Articulating words required socializing with seeing-hearing children. *Little Lord Fauntleroy* by Frances Hodgson Burnett was the first braille book Helen read on her own. Annie told Helen that Elsie Leslie was portraying her favorite character Cedric in the touring stage version.

After the business that Elsie's father owned failed, the desperate family hired Elsie out to Joseph Jefferson's theatre troupe, and she played Little Meenie in *Rip Van Winkle* when she was four and a half years old. Being an actress was a disreputable career for a girl from a good family, even if Jefferson was wildly popular (Lyde, 1977). Elsie's Methodist parents did not want their daughter to use the family name on stage, so she dropped her surname.

The young actress convinced author Mark Twain that she could perform both the roles in the stage version of his book *Prince and the Pauper* (1882). Twain liked Elsie, and she became friends with his youngest daughter Jean Clemens, but the little celebrity could be manipulative. At first Twain stated, "Impossible! Impossible! You are not twins, Elsie!" Elsie's familiarity was insufferable. He added, "Besides, where under the sun could I find another child like you?"

Elsie responded, "But I want to play both parts."

"Dear girl, you will make my story longer than *Hamlet!*"

Elsie was a smooth talker, "That's okay, sir. I can learn it." However, the girl did not want to stop playing with Jean to go to the theater and negotiated, "I don't want to go."

Twain responded, "Why, Elsie, some little girls would give anything to be an actress, and think how many people are depending on you to be there."

"I don't care," Elsie said. "I'm going to stay here with Jean."

"My goodness, you are a stubborn little rat," the author replied.

Elsie started crying; few children were part of her social circle. Twain relented and offered to drive her to the theater. She went with him obediently, not wanting him to think she was a *stubborn little rat* (Lyde, 1977).

Elsie, like Helen Keller, cultivated pen pals everywhere and maintained a lively correspondence with them throughout her life, including Eleanor Roosevelt who was one year younger. She remembered, "I like to write letters, but I like to get the answers still better."

When Elsie performed Cedric in the production of *Little Lord Fauntleroy* to audiences in Boston, she won the city's heart. Bostonians loved her so much they did not want the production to move on to New York. Boston civic leaders wrote to the New York Society for the Prevention of Cruelty to Animals and Children, saying they feared the girl was being overworked and under educated. Elsie was less educated than Helen in reading and writing. While nobody ever raised this issue for Thomas Higgins, the letter suggested Elsie's working conditions would have far-reaching and negative impacts on all child entertainers. Legislation was enacted requiring children under seven years old to get special work permits to perform on stage to limit exploitation of child performers by greedy parents, guardians, and promoters.

When Annie told Helen how the Bostonians were concerned about Elsie getting a proper education, she concluded, "I am learning to speak with my mouth. I can say 'Elsie.'" Helen wrote to Elsie, "I want very much to touch you because I cannot go to the theater and see you play for I am very blind, and I could not hear your voice because I am deaf." The girl concluded, "I thought Cedric was a lovely little boy. I should dearly love to see you dressed like a beautiful prince."

Elsie's mother was afraid seeing a Deaf-Blind child might upset her daughter, but her fears vanished after Reverend Brooks took them to the Perkins Institute to meet Helen and Annie. Elsie enjoyed Perkins Institute, though she thought it was sad the Blind could not see the beautiful gardens, grass, and trees on the grounds. Brooks took Elsie, her mother, Annie, and Helen for a carriage ride. Less than a week later, Helen visited Elsie backstage after a Saturday matinee. Elsie told her mother, "I think she is one of the bravest people in the world, don't you?"

Elsie made an impression on Helen, who wrote to her newest pen pal, "You cannot imagine how happy it made me to touch your lovely hair and sit beside you in the chair." The pair soon shared a patron, John P. Spaulding, known as the "Sugar King." Helen and Elsie became Spaulding's "two darlings" and renamed him "King John" (Lyde, 1977; Lash, 1980).

Spaulding, like many, could not understand Helen's articulation. "If I can't understand you, I can always love you." He was more interested in Helen than Elsie and offered Helen and Annie shares of Sugar Stock. He also sent Helen about $300 per month. When Arthur Keller who was falling into debt discovered this, he asked Spaulding for $15,000, which he deposited in his bank with the interest going to Helen's education.

Mark Twain, and his friend Charles Dudley Warner, coauthored a book called *The Gilded Age: A Tale of Today* (1873) satirizing greed and political corruption in America after the Civil War (Twain, 2001–2015). The Sugar Trust, known as the American Sugar Refining Company, was a nationwide monopoly that controlled 98 percent of the American Sugar Market. Sugar manufacturing was hard work, fueling slavery in subtropical climates. However, Spaulding and his brother Mahlon Spaulding established the Revere Sugar Refining Company in East Boston as one of the few sugar companies not controlled by the American Sugar Refining Company.

Spaulding, a bachelor, resided in an elegant hotel while he built a palatial estate on ten acres of land on Pope's Hill in Dorchester, where Helen and Elsie visited with Annie serving as their chaperone. Helen remembered, "Mr. Spaulding took us down to his country place in Dorchester for dinner, and after that, all during Elsie's engagements, we saw Mr. Spaulding almost every day, and when we did not see him, great boxes of roses and sweets came to us" (Keller, 1903).

At eleven years old, Helen's vocabulary increased to include smatterings of Greek, Latin, and French. Perkins Institute for the Blind started admitting a few Deaf-Blind students to their kindergarten. Helen developed relationships with children with similar challenges, including Elizabeth Robin, who was born in Texas in 1884. Elizabeth had lost her hearing and sight at about eighteen months like Helen due to catarrhal fever. Elizabeth exhibited strong individuality when she was admitted to the Perkins Kindergarten in December 1890. When she graduated to the Perkins Institute, she studied English, arithmetic, zoology, botany, geography, and other topics. She learned knitting and sewing and woodcarving. Elizabeth was a tidy person, but she did not have Helen's curiosity. Elizabeth lamented, "New things are not easy for me."

Helen and Elizabeth visited historic and cultural places. Elizabeth's family did not know the manual alphabet, so she learned articulation. Elizabeth, like Helen, became more demonstrative with education. Elizabeth only resorted to the manual alphabet with her friend Edith Thomas, who

---

PEN PALS CONNECTING HELEN KELLER TO EARLIER GENERATIONS

Oliver Wendell Holmes, Sr. introduced Helen Keller to John Greenleaf Whittier after she learned to speak. Keller wrote to Whittier on his eighty-third birthday, "Dear Kind Poet . . . If I were with you today, I would give you eighty-three kisses . . . one for every year you lived" (Keller, 1903). Whittier, a Quaker poet, was happy to receive her kind words. "I had two or three hundred others, and thine was one of the most welcome of all." Then he observed, "I do not wonder thee thinks eighty-three years a long time, but to me it seems but a very little while since I was a boy no older than thee, playing on the old farm at Haverhill."

The Quaker poet knew Dr. Samuel Gridley Howe, who asserted the primacy of speech for deaf education because he felt only speech was humanizing. Howe did not respect ideas from the Deaf about Deaf education, because he felt deafness made this community ill-equipped to decide. Howe felt the most that could be done for the deaf in this view was to mask the inferiority by teaching the deaf to appear to be able-bodied. This oralist mindset hampered the Deaf-Blind who sought self-determination; oralists dealt with this double-disability by trying to make it invisible or to make the Deaf-Blind speak.

Whittier connected Helen with two earlier Deaf-Blind women: Julia Brace and Laura Bridgman. Julia attended the girl's school operated by Lydia Huntley Sigourney who was an antebellum poet known as the "Sweet Singer of Hartford." Whittier had composed Sigourney's epitaph: "She sang alone, ere womanhood had known / The gift of song which fills the air to-day: / Tender and sweet, a music all her own / May fitly linger where she knelt to pray."

---

also could not be understood when she articulated or recited in public demonstrations at Perkins Institute.

Helen learned about a Deaf-Blind boy named Thomas "Tommy" Stringer's while she was learning to articulate. He was born in Washington, Pennsylvania, and had contracted spinal meningitis as an infant and had become Deaf-Blind. When his mother died, his poor father could not care for him. Tommy was admitted to a hospital almshouse because he needed constant care; his existence consisted basically of lying in a hospital cot with no communications with anybody.

A sad event for Helen became an opportunity for Tommy. A policeman in Sheffield, Alabama, shot Helen's dog, Lioness, who was running unleashed in a public square in late 1890. The girl was devastated, and the event angered townsfolk. Lioness had not disturbed anyone. Not wanting the officer to get into trouble, Helen stated, "I am sure they never could have done it if they had only known what a dear good dog Lioness was" (Keller, 1903)!

Lioness's death became the catalyst for Helen to help Tommy. Friends far and wide raised $300 to purchase a new dog for Helen (Keller, 1903). She was grateful to learn there were so many friends willing to help, but Lioness could not be replaced. Helen accepted the money on Tommy's behalf to add to a fund Michael Anagnos had established for the Deaf-Blind boy so that he could attend the Perkins' Kindergarten for the Blind in Jamaica Plain, Massachusetts.

Everyone at the Perkins Institute was excited to have Helen on hand to help raise money for Tommy's education. She tried to recruit Oliver Wendell Holmes, Sr. to speak for her. "If you come, will you speak to everyone to ask the kind Bostonians to help brighten Tommy's whole life?" She continued, "I want you to see baby Tom, the little blind and deaf and dumb child who has just come to our pretty garden" (Keller, 1903). However, Holmes declined Helen's invitation; he could not bear to ask people for money.

The girl personalized letters dictated by Annie and addressed to children for newspapers and newspaper editors. She painstakingly wrote about eight letters per day describing Tommy's plight, with Annie standing over her to make sure the spelling was correct. She next wrote to Reverend Phillips Brooks, now the newly elected bishop of Massachusetts. Brooks was a good choice. He warmed to Helen's invitation that stated, "Our dear little human flower, Tommy, is here in the child's garden. He is a poor, little helpless bud now, but we know that he will grow strong and beautiful in the dear God's warm sunshine." Helen had unintentionally started a movement to create awareness about the needs of disabled children.

Tommy Stringer arrived at Perkins Institute before he turned five years old on April 10, 1891 (Rocheleau and Mack, 1930). The boy did not walk but crept. He appeared unaware of his surroundings, except when food was placed into his mouth and someone moved him about when necessary so he would not get bedsores. His caregiver at the almshouse had been a night nurse, so Tommy's sense of time was reversed with day as night and night as day. Helen understood that Tommy's real plight with poverty was more precarious than Jakey's fictional challenges.

Many people saw the blond boy as a "little beast." He displayed temper and stubbornness, tearing and destroying everything in his reach like Helen did. When the Ladies' Visiting Committee of Perkins organized a fundraising reception at the Kindergarten for Tommy's education, Anagnos was delighted Helen could attract the attention of Boston's wealthiest families. Perkins Kindergarten utilized Friedrich Froebel's manual training methods for early education.

Upon hearing news of the reverend's elevation, Helen spelled out, "I don't know what a bishop does, but I am sure it must be good and helpful." While Brooks normally commanded the attention of crowds, on the day of

Tommy's fundraiser, everyone was really there for Helen. Brooks appealed to the group on Helen's behalf, "Helen is asking her friends to help her in this work, and surely the appeal of one child on behalf of another cannot go unanswered" (Keller, 1903).

Anagnos likely marveled at Annie Sullivan's ability to control Helen. None in the room was quite certain where Helen stopped and Annie started. However, many in the room were already convinced the young heroine was simply a pawn in her teacher's ambitious schemes to outshine Perkins Institute founder, Dr. Samuel Gridley Howe. Stringer's fellow Deaf-Blind classmates included Edith Thomas, Elizabeth Robin, and Helen, and Perkins Institute staff photographed the four together each facing different directions.

While Annie created celebrity Helen, the student created her teacher with her breakthrough and fast language acquisition. Anagnos's father-in-law, Dr. Howe, first taught Laura Bridgman how to communicate with word building, but Annie expanded his work with tactile teaching in nature outside of institutional settings where Helen learned to communicate with idiomatic expressions. While Annie was an independent survivor, she was dependent upon Helen's celebrity status to prove that her educational ideas were not a freak accident.

Annie increasingly became dependent upon Michael Anagnos for travel, clothing, and other expenses. Anagnos kept Annie's secret about her time at Tewksbury to himself because he could control her with it. "Miss Spitfire" worked hard and earned her education, graduating from Perkins with honors. Anagnos quietly observed his protégé, who was a wily natural leader carrying the Perkins Institute banner through a convulsing world. However, Annie increasingly pitted Helen's benefactors against each other.

Annie Sullivan needed her young protégé Helen Keller to prove she was better than those who had once snubbed the poor little Irish girl who had arrived alone at Perkins Institute without a nightgown or toothbrush. Annie stayed close to Helen, and she stayed in the background lest someone speak of her secret, but in the back of her mind, she calculated how Tommy Stringer could fit into her job security. The pair had already navigated changing finances with Helen's family and found new friends and supporters cultivated by the charismatic young teacher. Several years passed after Frank B. Sanborn plucked Annie from Tewksbury almshouse. Despite a lack of teaching credentials, Annie Sullivan now basked in the glow of her alma mater.

Sanborn and Howe's widow, Julia Ward Howe, with her daughters, Florence Howe Hall and Maud Howe Elliott, wondered how secure the relationship between Annie Sullivan, her student Helen Keller and Perkins Institute was, and how they might have to "spin" the periodic rebellions of the unpredictable Miss Spitfire (Wagner, 2012).

Many in the room considered Helen Keller to be a wonder child, but she was oblivious to the hushed murmurs in the room. People congregated to see Helen standing behind Reverend Brooks, grateful he was the fastest talker in Boston. Yet Maud Howe Elliot described Helen's voice as "the loneliest sound I have ever heard, like waves breaking on the coast of some lonely desert shore."

Thomas Stringer's event raised a substantial amount but not enough to assure his full tuition and board to go through the two-year program at the Kindergarten. Helen continued the effort with a letter writing campaign to newspaper editors. Annie undoubtedly organized and dictated some of the letters utilizing Anagnos's training in publicizing Perkins Institute when she was a student.

Sanborn and the Howe family increasingly received clues "Miss Spitfire" was not only an "ingrate" for not acknowledging what she and her student received from the prestigious Perkins Institute but also a "false friend" to the Blind (Wagner, 2012). They were astounded how a woman raised in a poorhouse with so little formal education could replicate Dr. Howe's work in teaching Laura Bridgman. They wondered if Michael Anagnos had placed too much trust in her loyalty.

When Tommy arrived at Perkins Kindergarten, he appeared to be another apathetic learner like Edith Thomas. Helen and Annie became the boy's first interim teachers until a permanent teacher was secured. Tommy was not socialized, so he started with lessons in discipline, regular habits, and obedience needed to learn the manual alphabet. Annie and Helen utilized the same tactile touch method used with Helen. Every time Tommy received bread to eat, the letters "b-r-e-a-d" in the manual alphabet were formed with Tommy's fingers and repeated in his hand by his teacher's fingers. Annie demonstrated customary love and determination with her new student.

Helen wrote to her pen pal William Wade, "Little Tommy, our sweet human plantlet, is here in this pretty child's garden, and teacher and I will give him his first lessons." In her letters written home to family in Alabama, Helen never conveyed how instrumental she was in helping Tommy's fundraising initiative come to fruition. Helen's mother, Kate Keller, received extensive correspondence in Alabama reporting news of her daughter and her teacher's adventures. Probably the only person who understood the nature of Helen and her teacher's relationship, it must still have stung when her daughter wrote, "Love is our very life, and my teacher seems a part of myself."

Michael Anagnos encouraged Helen and Annie to visit nearby schools to demonstrate Helen's progress for outreach and public relations. Helen was very effective in this role as she exchanged goodbye kisses from each girl and surprised everyone by remembering each name perfectly. In

Helen Keller was already a published writer when she posed for this publicity photograph; she was positioned in profile so her protruding left eye was not visible, between 1891 and 1894. Annie Sullivan sent the director of Perkins Institute for the Blind, Michael Anagnos, a story attributed to twelve-year-old Keller, leading to accusations of plagiarism, but their supporters stood by them. (Library of Congress)

visiting other schools, they were advertising Perkins Institute in the region and creating awareness about the education of the Deaf-Blind. On May 15, 1891, Helen's public speaking engagement after Tommy Stringer's event occurred when she, Annie, and a Perkins Institute teacher Miss Fanny S. Marrett visited students at the female boarding school called the Abbot Academy in Andover, Massachusetts.

An Abbot Academy student named Adeline G. Perry chronicled their visit in an article, "A Visit from Helen Keller," published in the June 1892 issue of *St. Nicholas* (Perry, 1892). Perry downplayed Annie's teaching abilities with Helen, suggesting the Deaf-Blind girl could learn more quickly at Abbot Academy. Perry was judgmental in describing Helen's monotonous, unmodulated voice, "It is a pitiful and rather trying experience to see a person in such a sad condition here. Of course, her articulation is very imperfect; but when she speaks slowly, one can understand what she says quite well."

Helen met about thirty Abbot Academy students, articulating something pleasant to each. She touched every student's face, hair, and dress to fix their features in her mind. One student brought up the Minutemen in civilian militia companies during the American Revolutionary War. Helen quoted from Ralph Waldo Emerson's "Concord Hymn," sung at the Completion of the Battle Monument on Independence Day in 1837: "Yes! And 'fired the shot heard round the world.'"

To Helen, it was dreadful when men killed each other, and she revealed her pacifist tendencies when she said, "I think it is not good to be afraid of death and to be ready to fight for one's country." She concluded, "My father wouldn't be afraid to die; he fought in the Rebellion" (Perry, 1892).

With educational institutions competing fiercely for money, Abbot Academy faculty invited their families to meet the young celebrity. Their literary magazine the *Abbot Courant* reported, "She seemed utterly unconscious that girls were crowded around her on all sides—behind the sofa where she sat in state, on the floor in front of her, and in a big circle all around her—and seemed to enjoy the talk as much as we did" (Morris, 2016). Throughout the reception, the students noted that Helen was devotedly attached to Annie. Every few minutes, she would caress her teacher with a loving smile.

Helen peppered conversations with literary metaphors and similes. A student gave her a familiar East Coast flower called a Jack-in-the-pulpit and asked, "Does he preach?"

Quick to catch the pun, Helen responded with a reference to Reverend Phillips Brooks who was very tall, "Oh, yes. He preaches to all the other flowers, but he is not so large as Dr. Brooks" (Perry, 1892).

A student asked Helen what games she played. Helen responded, "Yes, I love to play, but I like best to study, and I love poetry." She told the girl that her favorite poet was Oliver Wendell Holmes and asked her about her favorite poet.

Miss Marrett spoke about teaching methods for the Blind, alluding to the writing of Charles Dickens. Annie finger-spelled a question to Helen, "How does Dickens write?" Nobody responded for several minutes; then Helen's face lit up, and she responded with another pun, "All of er Twist!"

After the visit, a student lamented, "Think of her being so grateful for what she has, and see what a pig I am" (Morris, 2016)! Another student ate dinner that night with her eyes closed "so as to be in sympathy" with their recent guest.

Helen's basic ability to articulate carried her to a new plateau of communicating, but it was not enough for her teacher to claim an achievement more significant than Dr. Howe's. Annie Sullivan was growing bolder and more ambitious as she attempted to forge a future for herself and her student. She started to sidestep men in positions of authority including Arthur Keller and Michael Anagnos. Anagnos, on the other hand, hoped to rein his protégé in regarding Helen's instruction. He asked Arthur Keller to have Helen and Annie at Perkins Institute for the next academic year. Arthur said no because Kate Keller was expecting another baby, and he did have resources to support Helen's tuition. Anagnos responded with generous assistance.

Unfortunately, Helen's second dog, a mastiff given to her by William Wade and named Lion, bit Annie (Lash, 1980). Everyone feared the dog carried rabies. Helen and her teacher once again separated so Annie could travel to New York City's Pasteur Institute for treatments and Helen stayed with friends up north. Kate Keller bore a son on Independence Day, and Helen asked her parents to name him after Reverend Brooks.

High on their success in getting Helen to publicly speak on multiple occasions, Helen and Annie traveled Tuscumbia, Alabama, in early fall 1891. Helen entertained her family with a fairy story about the changing season that she called "Autumn Leaves." Kate and Arthur enjoyed hearing the story about "The Frost King" who lived far to the north in a land of perpetual snow. Excited by how Helen's family received the story, Annie Sullivan sent the story to Michael Anagnos as a birthday surprise. Annie, who avoided reporting details of how she diverged from the director's wishes in guiding her student, sent the story as part of her first report in over a year and a half. Anagnos was delighted and published an extensive report of Helen's progress, innocently exaggerating bits here and there. Helen's story would take on a life of its own and would haunt it's authors, changing the course of their lives.

5

Money Talks

In Boston, prominent men placed Helen Keller on a pedestal, but the Deaf-Blind girl just wanted to be a girl. Men appeared to direct efforts on behalf of Helen and her teacher Annie Sullivan in the public sphere, while their wives and philanthropic women stepped up in the private sphere of women to organize assistance through epistolary campaigns. Helen was totally dependent upon her guardian and failed to pick up clues of how her guardian acted "strangely" until she was fifteen years old (Keller, 1955). Helen sensed Annie did not behave like other women in her life, but she could not or chose not to articulate the meaning of "strangely." Perhaps Annie did not recognize how her impetuous ambition undermined her student's equilibrium, but for the Deaf-Blind teenager, trust was key to all of her relationships.

Perkins Institute for the Blind aggressively competed with other educational institutions for funding. Director Michael Anagnos delighted in the notion of using Helen's original children's story to promote the school. He promised to publish "The Frost King" in their magazine called *The Mentor*. The young teacher became annoyed when she felt his publicity machine reported exaggerations without consideration of their impact of making a child's life public knowledge.

Annie liked Helen standing high up on a pedestal, at least until it became too tall for the teacher to climb. The *Goodson Gazette*, a weekly newspaper of the Virginia Institution for the Deaf, Dumb and Blind, soon picked up the story. A reader recognized striking similarities between

Helen's story and "The Frost Fairies" in Miss Margaret T. Canby's picture book called *Birdie and His Fairy Friends: A Book for Little Children* (1874). The environment was ripe for other Deaf and Blind institutions to bring Perkins Institution down a peg with accusations of plagiarism. The *Gazette* accused Helen's influencers of publishing the piece without vetting it.

Annie sidestepped reporting her curriculum for Helen, and nobody accused the teenager of fraud. Helen would do anything for her teacher who did not understand the notion that taking someone else's ideas and passing them off as one's own was wrong. The accusation of plagiarism humiliated Anagnos because Perkins Institute had branded itself among philanthropists as a moral reform institution for the disabled.

Anagnos interrogated Helen and Annie and then started a curt correspondence with Helen's father Captain Arthur Henley Keller since Helen had "written" the story in Alabama. Annie became defensive. She said her mentor Mrs. Sophia C. Hopkins had read the story to Helen during a visit in 1888. Anagnos, Frank B. Sanborn, Julia Ward Howe, and her daughters realized Annie Sullivan had presented herself as the sole gatekeeper and protector of Helen Keller, but in doing so, she placed the school into quagmire.

Meanwhile, Helen told everyone the story was original. Annie broke news of the accusation to her student on January 30, 1892. The girl wrote in her diary, "Someone wrote Mr. Anagnos that the story which I sent him as a birthday gift, and which I wrote myself, was not my story at all, but that a lady had written it a long time ago . . ." She could not bear being considered a liar. "My heart is full of tears" (Keller, 1903).

Michael Anagnos initiated an internal investigation at Perkins Institute. Staff interrogated Helen for two hours. She remembered, "The blood pressed about my thumping heart and I could scarcely speak except in monosyllables." When supplied with a copy of Helen's story, Canby responded that she felt flattered Helen would remember the plot so clearly after having it read to her once. She rejected the accusation of plagiarism, asserting, "Under the circumstances, I do not see how anyone can be so unkind as to call it a plagiarism." The author was shocked someone Helen's age would remember her story and embellish it to "really improve the original" (Keller, 1903).

Arthur Keller responded to Anagnos's letter, stating nobody in the family knew the origins of "The Frost King." He wrote that Helen's relatives and friends in Alabama could not communicate with her well enough to convey Canby's story in such detail. His letter removed blame from Helen and the family and implicitly planted it with Annie Sullivan.

Anagnos's investigation resulted in a split decision as to whether Helen was innocent, so he voted "not proven." Helen's teacher was caught in a lie. The girl thought, "I had disgraced myself. I had brought suspicion upon those I loved best" (Keller, 1903).

Alexander Graham Bell supported Helen. He wrote to his wife Mabel Gardiner Hubbard Bell, "We all do what Helen did; our most original compositions are composed exclusively of expressions derived from others" (Gray, 2006). Bell wanted Helen in the public eye and dispatched an employee based in Boston, Mrs. Annie C. "Aunt Polly" Pratt, to investigate. Bell hoped Helen had written the story when Annie was at the Pasteur Institute in New York City being treated for rabies after a dog bite. Pratt interviewed Helen and Annie in early February 1892, but discovered nothing conclusive.

Bell invited Helen to his regular Wednesday night get-togethers with scientists, which included math professor Simon Newcomb, an aviation pioneer Samuel Pierpoint Langley, Thomas Gallaudet, and Bell's father-in-law Gardiner Hubbard who had established the National Geographic Society.

Helen Keller (aged fourteen, in a rare photograph showing her protruding eye) and Alexander Graham Bell in early July 1894, while attending the American Association to promote the Teaching of Speech to the Deaf Conference, in Chautauqua, New York. After Anne Sullivan's credibility as a teacher was challenged, Bell invited Anne Sullivan to present a paper at the conference, and she experienced such panic in presenting that Bell read the paper for her. Bell opened many doors for Keller, and she dedicated her book *The Story of My Life* to him, saying he "taught the deaf to speak and enabled the listening ear to hear speech . . ." (Library of Congress)

Michael Anagnos, Helen, Annie, and Miss Fanny Marrett visited a young Boston painter named Albert H. Munsell in his studio on February 22, 1892, after Munsell asked to paint Helen's portrait. While Munsell painted Helen, Anagnos prompted Marrett, who was a friend of Annie's, to subtly ask Helen about "The Frost King." Helen revealed how Annie had initiated the story (Lash, 1980). When the accusation of plagiarism arose, Annie instructed Helen to answer questions saying Perkins Institute's housemother Mrs. Sophia C. Hopkins had read the story to her when she was visiting her home in Brewster, Massachusetts. The teacher directed her student to say, if asked, she had written "The Frost King" from *her own imagination*.

Lost in the questions was the iconic portrait Munsell created of pre-teen Helen Keller as she sits reading a braille book positioned on her lap. Helen's hair is loose over her shoulders and her face is slightly upturned with light pouring to the side without the protruding eye. She wears a white blouse with puffed sleeves under an emerald green jumper. Helen's expression is thoughtful.

Once the truth slipped out in the session, Helen became agitated. She admitted Annie had read the story to her in 1888 when they had first visited Mrs. Hopkins' seaside home. Annie was desperate and out of her depths. Annie blamed Anagnos for publishing too much information about Helen and raising expectations, yet she sent out the story in hopes of staying in the director's good graces after neglecting to inform him of her progress for eighteen months (Lash, 1980).

Three weeks after the fated sitting, Munsell suggested to Annie how Helen's hands were good and strong for sculpting. Helen had learned to model clay at the Perkins Kindergarten, but the desperate teacher hoped Helen might show herself to be a prodigy in a new area. She read biographies about famous sculptors to Helen, but to no avail. The girl tried sculpting in clay, but the work tired her hands. Annie pushed her student to keep trying, but she could not produce anything promising.

Annie began behaving more like an exploitative promoter than a teacher. Her ambition for Helen got the better of her temper, and she slapped Helen with cold wet clay in frustration. Realizing she was wrong, Annie exclaimed, "Please forgive me, Helen! I don't see you as Deaf-Blind." Remorseful for striking Helen, she added, "I love you too much for that, but I should remember you are human, and I should not be so ambitious and let you relax sometimes" (Lash, 1980).

Helen started a pattern of rationalizing her teacher's mercurial behavior. Her confidence was so badly shaken, Helen stopped reading and communicating. Annie pushed her to write a short article, "My Story," for the family magazine called *Youth's Companion*, where friends Joseph Edgar Chamberlin and Bradford Torrey offered support. Annie prodded Helen, and the result was a piece "written wholly without help of any sort by a deaf and blind girl, twelve years old . . ."

As Helen regained her confidence, her favorite painter Albert H. Munsell visited and described his recent trip to Venice. Helen's gregariousness returned when she wrote to her mother, "His beautiful word-pictures made us feel as if we were sitting in the shade of San Marco, dreaming, or sailing upon the moonlit canal." She wrote to Kate about her hopes of visiting Venice with Munsell one day, "You see, none of my friends describe things to me so vividly and so beautifully as he does" (Keller, 1903).

"THE FROST KING" REVELATION

Annie Sullivan and Helen Keller adapted "The Frost King" from a story by Margaret T. Canby. The story tells of a benevolent builder who painted the trees in the fall. The Frost King has two neighbors: a churlish King Winter and Santa Claus who is good natured. Mr. Sun undermines King Frost's work, so he sends frost fairies to help Santa Claus, but they follow their own follies and get distracted. Mr. Sun's actions unexpectedly create beautiful fall colors, and when the Frost King sees the children's delight, he forgives the fairies, and everyone joins forces with Mr. Sun.

Both versions of the story appropriate myths of Santa Claus. The Keller-Sullivan narrative contains an energetic dynamic with stylistically straightforward writing. They explicitly describe the Frost King as the developer of benevolent plans to relieve poor and unhappy children, like an otherworldly version of Alexander Graham Bell: "Wherever he goes, he does many wonderful works" (Keller, 1903).

Nobody knows how much Keller influenced the story; "The Frost King" demonstrates the vitality of Sullivan's abilities as a storyteller inherited from her Irish-born father Thomas Sullivan and her energetic translations through fingerspelling. This version creates tension between King Frost (ice) and King Sun (fire) who simply do not agree as to the "best way of benefitting the world." Both stories concluded with questions, but Keller's is more sensory than the original. This story reveals, for the first time, the lengths Anne Sullivan would go to in order to protect her position by promoting Helen Keller as a miracle girl and herself as master teacher.

Helen and Annie attended Edward Everett Hale's seventieth birthday celebration to show Boston society their spirits were not broken. After Helen's successful appeal for Thomas Stringer, Michael Anagnos recruited her to help draw attention to Perkins Kindergarten. Helen and Annie conceived of an idea to raise money with a tea party. Helen, utilizing a strategy Anagnos taught Annie when she was a student, wrote to Boston newspaper editors, who published her letters publicizing the tea party. The Ladies' Visiting Committee selected the reception date to be on kindergarten pioneer Friedrich Froebel's birthday and the location to be held at the home of Helen's benefactor John Spaulding. Helen invited supporters including Reverend Phillips Brooks, Oliver Wendell Holmes, Sr., Edward Everett Hale, John Spaulding, Alexander Graham Bell, John Hitz, Frank B. Sanborn, and a Unitarian minister named Reverend Minot J. Savage.

Helen asked Holmes to speak for her, but he was ill, so her cousin Hale spoke instead. Hale simply stated, "Ladies and gentlemen, I am here as Helen's retained counsel." He continued, "She came to see me last week, dear child, and said, as she could not speak, she wanted me to speak for her. I asked her what I should say?"

Helen stepped up to speak for herself, "I want to say something to you myself. I cannot speak very well yet, but my heart is full of thoughts and I must express some of them. Kindness is like rain in April; it makes everything grow. Your kindness will make the little plantlets here grow and blossom. Think how happy we will be when Tommy's mind bursts beautiful and bright from behind the clouds that hide it now" (Keller, 1903).

Despite the recent controversy, Helen Keller was an effective fundraiser. Annie stood in the background and her protégé performed like a professional. Helen's short performance at the tea brought in over $2,000 in donations to the kindergarten. Michael Anagnos hoped to keep Helen connected to Perkins Institute *without her teacher.* He was like a second father to Helen and Annie, but now he bitterly resented Annie. When Perkins Institute closed for summer in June 1892, Helen and Annie traveled to Tuscumbia, Alabama, where they stayed until December. Helen and Annie would never return to Perkins except as visitors for ceremonial purposes

Helen and Annie arrived at Arthur Keller's summer cabin called Fern Quarry built on a mountain ridge about fourteen miles from Tuscumbia, Alabama, near an old, abandoned limestone quarry. Helen awoke mornings to the vibrations of gunfire and the smell of strong coffee. Men played cards in the evenings and bragged about their hunts and women barbecued meals. Although pastoral, the trip was not easy. Cash was scarce. Kate Keller's one-year-old son Phillips Brooks Keller and her stepson James Keller suffered from typhus fever, and no hired help was not available because there was no money to pay salaries. Arthur Keller was deep in debt with all of his property mortgaged. In desperation, Arthur asked his eldest daughter to give him money she had earned from her article for *Youth's Companion.*

When Helen happily handed over her first earnings to her father, Kate uncharacteristically held her hands to her face in combined shock, horror, and pride. Helen's teacher matched what her student gave, contributing another thirty-five dollars so the family could subsist for two months. Kate turned toward her younger children with tears in her eyes . . . perhaps less certain for their futures than her Deaf-Blind daughter.

When Arthur took off for two weeks to deal with a local election, Kate and Annie were left to carry water a quarter of a mile and a mile along the railroad track for Phillips's milk. Even when Arthur was around, he and his beleaguered wife argued over money, leading others to choose time in the woods over tensions in the cabin. Before the 1892 presidential election, the family prompted Helen to write to First Lady Frances Cleveland wishing well her baby girl named Ruth, born a few months after Phillips. Helen's political correspondence probably reflected her father's interest in retaining his appointment as a federal marshal by incumbent president who was a Democrat.

*   *   *

Money matters kept Helen and Annie on the move. Helen met her pen pal William Wade at his home in Oakmont, Pennsylvania. The teenager enjoyed his English mastiffs and made friends with his donkeys. Helen recognized Wade by the smell of his pipe tobacco that matched the scent that permeated his letters. She threw her arms about his neck and hugged him. Wade had straight brown hair, a wild curly mustache, and beard and wore spectacles. He was a man of simple tastes who avoided ostentatious occasions as well as the pedantry of the highly educated. Wade introduced Helen and Annie to his neighbor, Reverend John D. Irons, a Presbyterian minister who introduced Helen to Latin and mythology. While studying with Irons, Helen wrote a poem called "Autumn."

William Wade contacted Alexander Graham Bell as his grassroots movement commenced to seek out and financially assist Deaf-Blind children in accessing educational opportunities. Wade and his wife found practical ways to entertain Deaf-Blind acquaintances. He commissioned Blind craftspeople to manufacture special game sets so the Deaf-Blind could play chess, checkers, and card games. Wade gave one Deaf-Blind girl a sewing machine, to another he gave books to copy, to another he sent dolls to dress, so that they could earn a little money and gain a sense of independence.

Bell took Helen and Annie to Niagara Falls (Gray, 2006). Helen sensed it as a light force, imagining she was hearing the roar of a mighty cataract. She sensed her proximity to the water and felt its roar by placing her hand near it as if it was a soft pillow. The natural landmark made an impression on Helen's subconscious, lasting throughout her life.

Helen dreamed she saw her teacher dressed all in white standing at the edge of Niagara Falls. In her dream, Helen did not recognize Annie at first and thought she might be an angelic apparition. Then Annie was swept out of sight, and Helen ran toward her, thinking she had plunged into the whirlpool. Her teacher arose on the crest of a giant wave, and Helen seized her, holding fast. When Helen recognized Annie, she intensified her efforts in vain. In the dream, Helen could not draw Annie to shore; she could only prevent her from sinking. Helen tried to thrust herself between her teacher and her destruction. Annie, not appearing to recognize Helen, threw herself upon the shore and vanished. Helen was unable to let go of the fact that the apparition had ignored her; that seemed worse than all of her quarrels with teacher combined.

THE DEAF-BLIND AT THE 1893 CHICAGO WORLD'S FAIR

Alexander Bell hosted Helen Keller and Anne Sullivan at the World's Columbian Exposition in Chicago after going to Niagara Falls. World's fairs and expositions showcased progress and the idea that life inevitably improved as a result of technological advancement and healthy living even though it occurred during a great economic depression in the United States. Keller drew attention as she toured the White City, and many Chicagoans hoped the fair might spur economic rejuvenation.

Negro Day was held in late August, and Frederick Douglass and Ida B. Wells distributed pamphlets describing the accomplishments of African Americans. The Chicago Woman's Club became a major sponsor of events and recruited women representing 126 organizations from 27 countries. Over 350,000 women attended a week of simultaneous seminars held during the World's Congress of Representative Women.

The president of the Chicago World's Fair offered the Deaf-Blind special accommodation. Unsuspecting crowds observed Keller and Bell roaming amid the exhibits. She touched and smelled exhibits and tasted the newly developed snack of caramel popcorn and peanuts called Cracker Jacks.

Sullivan left Keller in the care of Miss Carolyn H. Talcott, a young teacher at the Rochester Institute who was attending a meeting of deaf teachers in Chicago. The two explored the exhibits together. Psychoanalyst Joseph Jostrow headed the Psychological Section that Keller attended, where he collected "psychophysical and reaction time data" from thousands of attendees.

A British-born Deaf-Blind man named Clarence J. Selby resided in Chicago. He met Keller, and they both could articulate but they could not hear each other, so they conversed in manual language. Selby said, "I think I enjoy my life as well as many people that can both hear and see" (Selby, 1898).

An economic depression caused by tightening credit set in after the financial Panic of 1893. Helen's widening circle of male benefactors were conscious of her father's feelings when they worked on her behalf. They may not have approved of Captain Arthur Keller's politics, but they understood one absolute truth among men: if the economic security and ability to obtain credit for a man's family was lost, he would become a different kind of animal in the face of insolvency. A man could change and become a mercenary and be extreme in his approach to family relationships. Arthur paid Annie no salary, so the teacher and her student became reliant upon the goodwill of institutions and spent vacations with their wealthy friends.

William Wade wanted to establish a fund for Helen's education. Wade approached Alexander Graham Bell, who approached Edward Everett Hale and Joseph Chamberlin, before Bell approached Arthur. Helen's father did not want to accept the help from Northerners. He eventually relented and responded, "While I am reluctant, after consideration and knowing the disinterested and unselfish motives that prompted it, I am giving my consent to any plan you have in view for the welfare and happiness of Helen and Miss Annie's future" (Lash, 1980).

In April 1894, Bell sent Reverend Hale a check for $1,000, asking him to be a trustee for a college fund for Helen. On Helen's fourteenth birthday, Bell sent her a cockatoo that she named Jonquil because it was covered in white and gold feathers. Jonquil liked to perch on the teenager's foot, rocking back and forth as she read. Jonquil seemed curious about the teen's extended silences so different from others in the household, and he sometimes placed his sharp, hooked bill in her mouth. This unexpected and uninvited action sent ripples of terror down Helen's spine especially when the bird darted off, with a fiendish *squeech*, and alighted on the back of a dog or on somebody's head. Although Helen, like her mother Kate, loved birds, Jonquin threatened her equilibrium, and her father could not allow his Deaf-Blind teenager to lose her equilibrium if it could be prevented. Arthur tried to find Jonquil another home, but news of his antics preceded him, and he eventually found a home for the curious bird in a local bar (Keller, 1929; Lash, 1980).

Alexander Graham Bell's assistant, John Hitz, Jr., befriended Helen and became a foster-father figure, or godfather, assuming the spiritual guardianship over Helen and Annie. On the occasions of her fourteenth birthday, Hitz presented Helen a special gold watch. The timepiece was not originally manufactured for a Blind person; Hitz had obtained it from a German ambassador who thought it was impolite to obviously consult a pocket watch during meetings. The ambassador had taken the watch to a jeweler, who modified it with little rounded markers on the edge so that he could discretely feel the time in his pocket with his fingers.

Helen and Annie, upon Bell's invitation, traveled to attend a meeting of the American Association to Promote the Teaching of Speech to the Deaf held in Chautauqua, New York. They met John D. Wright and Thomas Humason, who started a progressive school for the deaf. The school taught lip-reading as well as arithmetic, physical geography, French, and German .They made arrangements for Helen to attend with Annie the first sessions at the Wright-Humason School for the Deaf in New York City in October 1894.

Wright personally gave Helen lessons in articulation, showing her how to use her fingers placed at a speaker's neck to feel the vibrations of sounds. Completely dependent upon Annie, strangers immediately noticed Helen constantly reaching for her teacher for reassurance, like a small child. Helen was also different from the other students because she required technology, specifically three typewriters, to communicate. She started a voluminous correspondence when other girls of her age were learning about courting boys.

Annie set Helen apart and controlled how she received current news and information. The school's cofounder quickly observed how Helen's teacher demonstrated uncanny insight into the motivations underlying human action. He also noticed how Annie frequently took advantage of this power to manipulate circumstances to her advantage. Annie did not want the pair to become reliant upon any single source of income. She continually maneuvered between Alexander Graham Bell and John Spaulding, working the two men against each other while in New York City, to obtain financial help.

Helen accompanied friends to New York theater and opera performances and learned the main action points from her companions' finger play. She received information about people in social settings when she felt sensations while shaking hands. Helen discovered hands could be very eloquent in speaking about a person: a hearty handshake gave Helen genuine pleasure; some hands revealed impertinence; and the hands of joyless people were like holding on to a northeast storm . . . cold. Like the Deaf-Blind-Mute girl Julia Brace, generations before, who was tested to match watches to their owners to garner donations, Annie encouraged her student Helen to use her sensory skills for wealthy men to cultivate supporters.

Helen and Annie met literary critic Laurence Hutton and his wife Eleanor Hutton who were active in New York City's literary society (Lash, 1980). Hutton introduced Helen to Mary Mapes Dodge, who had earlier published some of Helen's letters to child readers in *St. Nicholas* magazine. Dodge was the first to suggest that Helen and Annie should write an autobiographical book about their experiences, so Annie started keeping a journal of her experiences. Kate Douglas Wiggins had written *The Story of Patsy* (1883) about poverty in San Francisco that featured a crippled angelic waif attending the first kindergarten located in a San Francisco slum.

New York society interacted with Helen differently than Boston society. Helen perceived a strangeness in her teacher, who frequently suffered from melancholy and depression after leaving Perkins Institute for the Blind, where she found her first stable home as a charity case. With the acquisition of speech, Helen developed self-identity. This led to battles of will between student and her guardian. Helen began to recognize her teacher was not always logical and frowned upon rhetoric requiring critical thinking skills. Helen later remembered, "I tried not to argue with her—and I seldom succeeded . . . her comments flew out spontaneously, highly colored, and pithy, leaving me dazzled, delighted, and dumbfounded all at the same time" (Keller, 1955).

Through Hutton's contacts, Helen became somewhat of a Deaf-Blind "seraphim" in New York society; she possessed a robust vocabulary to create sophisticated rhetoric with a fiery passion to do God's good work. At a gathering in their home, the Huttons introduced Helen and Annie to Mark Twain and financial magnate Henry H. Roger.

Twain offered searing critiques of the conflicting emotions of the Gilded Age, a post-Civil War boom characterized by inequality inherent in industrialization. Gilded Age fostered monopolies, conspicuous consumption, and greed and materialistic excess of rapid economic growth and conversely extreme poverty and inequity when unions fought for an eight-hour workday.

Helen, who devoured books in braille, entered Hutton's library. Smelling the critic's vast library, the teen exclaimed, "Oh, the books, the books, so many books. How lovely!" Mark Twain recalled, "The girl began to deliver happy ejaculations in her broken speech" (Twain, 2001–2015). William Dean Howells, an author of realist novels. In literature, realism or naturalism faithfully represents reality objectively without the sentimentality of Victorian children's book writers like Kate Douglas Wiggins. Howells was also editor of the *Atlantic Monthly* and a Swedenborgian. He sat next to Helen on a sofa during Hutton's luncheon. Howells let Helen put her fingers to his lips so that she could lip-read his stories. Howells' wife, Elinor Mead Howells, was an architect who had designed Howells House near the Harvard Yard located at 37 Concord Avenue in Cambridge Massachusetts.

Mark Twain recognized Helen to be perceptive through her sense of smell. "Without touching anything, and without hearing anything, Helen seemed to recognize her surroundings clearly." After a few hours, someone at the gathering asked if Helen could feel the textures of the skin of the guests' hands to identify them. Annie promptly responded, "Oh, she'll have no difficulty with that" (Twain, 2001–2015). Soon a game began like one used on Julia Brace, who was tested with identifying gentlemen's watches.

Everyone filed past Helen offering their hand in a greeting before going into the dining room for lunch. Twain greeted Helen with a pat on the head and moved on. Suddenly, Annie called the author back because Helen had not recognized his handshake. Twain gently patted Helen's head again, and the girl responded, "Oh, it's Mr. Clemens." The writer wryly wondered how Helen could feel "the wrinkles of my hand through her hair" (Twain, 2001–2015). Later, amused, Helen told him that she had recognized him by smell.

Twain first interpreted Helen's responses to be a contrived mind-reading performance. When Twain told Helen a story, she responded with appropriate laughter in the right places, an easy unpracticed laughter her teacher could not control. When Annie asked Helen what Mark Twain was known for, the girl responded audibly, "For his humor." Twain chimed in simultaneously as Helen continued, " . . . and for his wisdom." As their relationship deepened, people found it characteristic in Helen and Twain's conversations that the Deaf-Blind girl often finished the author's sentences.

Twain was particularly tender with Helen as he saw her as a modern Joan of Arc. She soon wrote to her mother Kate Keller, "I think Mark Twain is a very appropriate *nom de plume* for Mr. Clemens because it has a funny quaint sound, and goes well with his amusing writings, and its nautical significance suggests the deep and beautiful things that he has written."

Helen built up memories and inner landscapes derived from book descriptions spelled out into her hands. Twain thought Helen's inner images were sometimes more beautiful than what he experienced with all of his senses combined. To Helen, the warm sun brought out odors that made her think of red. Coolness emerged from odors creating a sense of green or a sparkling color brought to mind soap bubbles quivering under her hand as she washed dishes. Twain quipped with chagrin after Helen described the face of one of his friends, "I thank God, she cannot see" (Twain, 2001–2015)!

Helen attended the Wright-Humason School for two years and studied physical geography with great interest. Helen learned how the winds develop and "how the vapors ascend from the ends of the earth, how rivers are cut out among the rocks, and mountains overturned by the roots, and in what ways man may overcome many forces mightier than himself" (Keller, 2000).

Laurence Hutton introduced Helen to another naturalist John Burroughs, who asserted, "The Kingdom of Heaven is not a place, but a state of mind." Burroughs perceived the realism in Helen, describing her as "drenched in the sunshine and sweetness of the out-of-doors world . . . freed from the complex trappings of modern society" (Burroughs, 1905). Burroughs was different from Bradford Torrey who taught Helen about the vibrations of birdcalls; Burroughs was a leader in the nature conservation movement with a literary gift for describing perceptions of the natural world.

Burroughs argued philosophically how the living acted with spontaneity and self-direction through intelligence. He, like Helen, had been once accused of plagiarism. At a time when the world was exploring sound technology as a means to record disappearing languages of Indigenous people and "rustics," Burroughs asserted while the rock and the tree grow, beside it, the birds, rodents, and insects occupy the same location. He stated these entities are made of the same essential stuff, but the same intelligence in the living is not recognized in the inanimate.

Helen described Burroughs to Eleanor Hutton, "He has the same gentle ways as John Greenleaf Whittier and makes one feel that he lives very near our Father all the time" (Keller, 1903).

Burroughs used an analogy of a phonograph record technology to make his point. At the time, science was not capable of analyzing the intelligence of a rock just as a listener could not discover the deep meaning of a Beethoven sonata recorded in the *latent* grooves of a phonograph record. The new audio medium according to the naturalist was like the rock—inanimate, yet it still contained intelligence. Conversely, the Deaf-Blind appeared to be inscrutable to the seeing and hearing world. Science was eager to understand Helen as a vital force. Helen seemed to reflect *soul*, *spirit*, and *intelligence* that Science attributed to humanity. Simply by existing in this changing world, Helen presented a natural paradox.

Annie Sullivan did not enjoy New York; she felt its intellectual and literary circles judged her. New York City was expensive, so Annie audaciously pleaded for funds. Their benefactor John Spaulding grew very sick, and there was no provision for the pair in his will. Annie was invested in Helen's success because of the continuing talk among special education supporters about her credentials to teach an increasingly spectacular disabled student who was now accepted among American literary greats. The "Frost King" incident made public Annie's most private fears about who she was and what her prospects without Helen Keller might be.

William Wade, who watched over Helen and Annie as much as they allowed him to, introduced the pair to Mrs. Mary Copely Thaw, who was a grand society dame residing in Pittsburgh, Pennsylvania. Mary Thaw's late husband William Thaw, Sr. had earned his fortune in logistics, banking, and railroads that emerged out of a freight business in Pennsylvania. When her husband died in 1889, Mary Thaw managed his $12 million estate for their children and her stepchildren. Wade knew William Thaw, Sr. had donated money to establish Pittsburgh's Western Pennsylvania School for Blind Children established in 1890. Mary Thaw was thought to exemplify moral integrity, but she could be a formidable presence known to protect her family and friends through sheer determination.

Mary Thaw was a wealthy widow active on the public social scene in Pittsburg, but there were secrets related to the mental health of several family members she fiercely kept private. Mrs. Thaw, like so many other Americans, did not want nasty questions anywhere near her family about the worst of human behavior that arose during the earlier Greely Expedition. She enjoyed the company and connection with the innocent Deaf-Blind teenager and asked Helen to report when she arrived safely back at New York City after visiting Wade. Helen wrote to Thaw on October 16, 1895, to describe how porters made their train ride home pleasant. She wrote, "Someone is ever ready to scatter little acts of kindness along our pathways, making it smooth and pleasant" (Keller, 1903).

Helen's German teacher Miss Olive L. Reamy at the Wright-Humason School learned the manual alphabet. After Helen acquired a small German vocabulary, Reamy immersed Helen in German. She made more progress in German than in any of her other studies in New York. Within a few months, Helen had acquired a good enough understanding of German so she could read Friedrich Schiller's *Wilhelm Tell* (1804). Schiller, a German philosopher and poet with ideas similar to Henry David Thoreau, offered Helen a practical roadmap to her *ideal self*.

Julia Brace's teacher Lydia Sigourney would have been knowledgeable about Schiller's writing. In an age before Victorian "self-help," Schiller argued how developing a personal life as an entity of beauty could be transformed for a broader good. Contemplating lives of beauty in words enabled the reader to reshape personal beliefs and to transform thoughts into action. Schiller suggested that with self-transformation during lifelong self-education, individuals could achieve freedom and subsequently social justice and transform "blind compulsion" into the work of "free choice."

Annie Sullivan separated her charge from her family as she became increasingly aware of her own educational shortfalls. Annie became more defensive and critical of the Wright-Humason School's faculty, and reported to Bell's assistant John Hitz of how teachers at the school demonstrated apparent "stupidities." Bell, with his own agenda, was delighted by Annie's reports and invited her to deliver a paper at a convention for teachers of the deaf. Meanwhile, when Edward Everett Hale, recruited to organize an education fund for Helen, visited Bell, he witnessed the inventor's tremendous wealth firsthand.

Helen and Annie's financial security upended when their benefactor John Spaulding died intestate in February 1896. At this time, Helen figured out that if she hoped to stay with Annie, she needed to find a way to support her teacher for the rest of her life. Prior to his death, Spaulding had given Helen's father Captain Arthur Keller $15,000 (which in 2021 would be $467,111) for her education without a will to define how to deal with the transaction. Arthur deposited the money in his own account with the interest going to Helen's education, but he was caught short when Spaulding's heirs demanded its return. They settled on a repayment for $10,000, but with everything mortgaged, Keller was unable to raise the cash.

Annie held firm to the notion that her security lay with Helen's respectable reputation. When the pair crossed paths with vaudeville promoter Benjamin Franklin Keith, on a train from New York to Boston, Keith offered to present Helen and Annie on the stage for $500 per week, which in 2021 would be $15,570. This was very good money, but Annie turned down the offer because respectable Victorian women did not perform in vaudeville. When news of the offer and denial reached Helen's father, who was struggling to hold his family together financially, he was indignant.

Captain Arthur Keller, angry that Annie had passed on Keith's lucrative offer, wrote to Mrs. Hopkins, who managed Helen's education fund established by Wade, Bell, and Hale. Arthur demanded the money be turned over to him as Helen's true guardian. He argued that he would otherwise be compelled to hire Helen out to raise the funds to repay his debt by performing in public.

Despite Hopkins's implication in the "Frost King" incident, she stood firm as the manager of Helen's educational fund, refusing Arthur's suggestion of his daughter performing on stage. For a girl from a respectable family to perform publicly on stage would be shameful. Hopkins told Annie it was dreadful Helen's father could contemplate removing Helen from school to publicly exhibit her disabilities for profit. Kate Keller was mortified.

Helen's father Captain Arthur Keller supported Democrat William Jennings Bryan in his bid for the presidency in 1896. At stake was the gold

---

EXPLOITING CHILDREN AS FREAK PERFORMERS

Helen Keller was a natural performer before her father Arthur Keller considered putting her on public exhibit like Thomas Higgins. The Deaf-Blind girl attended theater performances with someone describing action on stage into her hands, so it seemed she was amid the action, but Keller never crossed paths with the Blind-Autistic spectrum piano prodigy.

Harpers' Magazine editor Laurence Hutton viewed Keller as a perfectly clear, fresh soul without guile, writing Keller was a "revelation and an inspiration to us. She made us think and shudder, and think again." Hutton harshly described other prodigies of American stage. He grouped together Keller's friend Elsie Leslie Lyde, a dwarf Charles Stratton known by his stage name as "General Tom Thumb," and pianist Thomas Higgins who was born into slavery.

Higgins, likely the last legal slave in America, was the first African American to perform in the White House in 1860 (O'Connell, 2009). Unable to care for himself, Higgins's well-being throughout life depended upon the goodwill of his guardian and concert promoter Perry Oliver. Higgins remained unaware of being a slave because he started performing as a child.

Now considered an autistic savant, Higgins's special cognitive abilities allowed him to accurately echo sounds around him in compositions. Oliver marketed Higgins beginning at the age of eight as a "Barnum-style freak" performer. The superstar made his guardian wealthy but was frequently compared to a bear, baboon, or mastiff.

Helen Keller compelled Hutton to look at the disabled with less bigotry, but the critic still observed how phenomenal stars in novelty acts occupied "the neutral ground between the amateurs and the monstrosities." Hutton used racist language, arguing Higgins could never pass as a great stage performer because he was an underdeveloped human being like "learned pigs and the trained monkeys" (Hutton, 1891).

standard for American currency employed since 1879, and Bryan supported the free silver forces within the Democratic Party. While the United States today has a flat currency produced by a central bank that controls how much money is printed, during the nineteenth century, currency was backed by a metal commodity. Gold possessed a higher value than silver and therefore was a more potent standard, but silver was more highly available and therefore more ideal for widespread trade. The populist Democrat Bryan recognized the need to distance the party from the unpopular policies of the Cleveland administration. The free silver forces quickly established dominance at the Democratic convention for working-class voters, and Bryan repudiated Cleveland, calling the gold standard "not only un-American but anti-American."

Helen, away from home in the North, surrounded by affluent supporters and under Annie's guardianship, wrote to her mother. After the death of John Spaulding, Annie's deep-seated fears about returning to poverty took hold. Her sixteen-year-old student wrote to her mother, Kate Keller, to suggest to her father be more moderate in his politics and not offend Helen and Annie's financial supporters. Within a few months, Captain Arthur Keller unexpectedly died.

Helen attempted to return to Tuscumbia, Alabama, for her father's funeral. Her mother, Kate Keller, advised her not to come. There was too much to sort out with the family's troubled finances and caring for two children. Always private in her grieving, Kate wanted the family out of the public spotlight, which would inevitably follow if Helen returned to Alabama.

John Spaulding's passing was "the greatest sorrow" the teenager had experienced. However, Helen was devastated by the loss of her father; she did not know the depth of her feelings for him until he was gone. Frantic, sobbing, and unable to find a train to get her to her mother in time for the funeral, Helen wrote to Alexander Graham Bell, "How shall I bear it!" Conversely, Annie never desired to reconnect with her father, Thomas Sullivan, so she could not comprehend the depth of Helen's grief. Annie assumed Helen felt the same way, or worse, she was in denial her student was capable of such feelings. Annie lamented, "I never dreamed she could feel such sorrow . . . she bears her affliction so patiently, I thought her emotional nature was dulled" (Lash, 1980).

There was a desperation in Annie Sullivan, who resented Daughters of the American Revolution in New England as much as the newly established Daughters of the Confederacy, who sought to retell the Civil War as a noble "Lost Cause." Annie did not know how she, as the daughter of a poor Irish immigrant, fit into America's changing power dynamic. She still found herself with few choices for employment beyond being Helen Keller's teacher-guardian. Annie did not have the disposition to look backward, yet she could not see into the future.

During this shadowy time, a dark-haired woman travelled to Feeding Hills, Massachusetts, where Joanne Sullivan was born, with a mature male companion with a flowing beard harking from Washington, D.C. Under the guise of seeking records for a pension, the woman approached Annie's uncle John Sullivan's elderly wife. Bridget Sullivan sharply regarded the visitors, questioning the woman, and did not ask them who they were. After the couple left without the answers they had sought, Bridget remarked to friends, "If Annie Sullivan is alive, that was Annie Sullivan."

With financial supporter John Spaulding and Helen's father Captain Arthur Henley Keller dead, Helen and Annie's New York friends were concerned the pair would soon be destitute. A letter from Laurence Hutton arrived in London for Mark Twain in November 1896, informing him Helen needed help (Twain, 2001–2015). Twain, on a world tour, had remained in seclusion after his eldest daughter, Olivia Susan "Suzy" Clemens, returned home early, developed spinal meningitis, and died. Twain and his wife, Olivia Langdon Clemens, were mourning Suzy as the letter arrived from Hutton, who proposed raising $50,000 for a pension fund for Helen.

Hutton and Twain exchanged correspondence regarding the merits of a permanent fund versus a subscription fund for their Deaf-Blind friend and her guardian. Twain believed a permanent fund would be too hard to establish considering the ongoing economic depression and suggested growing a temporary fund for Helen's college expenses until a permanent fund could be established. Twain advised Hutton that if people declined making the large donations needed for the permanent fund they could suggest twenty-five-dollar annual subscriptions to build up a permanent fund.

Twain had earlier introduced Helen and Annie to his own patron, Standard Oil magnate Henry H. Rogers and his wife Abigail "Abbie" Gifford Rogers, who had helped him to get out of his financial woes. Rogers had made his fortune in the oil refining industry by consolidating the industry. Known as "Hell Hound Rogers," he masterminded the Standard Oil Trust as one of the last great "robber barons." As a realist, Rogers believed that life feels no need to compromise. Unlike Andrew Carnegie who retired from the steel industry using the same unscrupulous tactics before becoming a philanthropist, Rogers remained a modest man, and therefore, his generosity was not known until after his death.

Twain wrote to Abbie about a scheme Eleanor Hutton had devised to develop a permanent fund to support Helen and her teacher. Twain suggested, "The thing is for you to plead with Mr. Rogers for this hampered wonder of your sex . . ." (2001–2015). Twain hoped that Rogers would interest the other Standard Oil chiefs, including John D. Rockefeller, to support Helen's cause.

Twain, Hutton, and Rogers hoped that by making money available to Helen and Annie, they would learn how to manage it. Annie, who only understood subsisting, never understood the concept of saving money, and she did not appreciate being managed. On Christmas Eve, Hutton sent Twain a message about Rogers receiving letters from Abbie Rogers and Eleanor Hutton, and how their scheme to involve the women had achieved its objective. Rogers would support Helen's education, and he would leave Helen an annuity in his will.

Helen decided she wanted to go to college. At the Wright-Humason School in New York City, Helen continued to correspond with Mary Thaw as she worked on improving her oral communication, math skills, French, and German. Helen described how it took her a long time to prepare her lessons with her disabilities, and she worried how her teacher strained her eyes. Helen wrote to Thaw, "Sometimes it really seems as if the task which we have set ourselves were more than we can accomplish; but other times I enjoy my work more than I can say" (Keller, 1903).

After leaving the Wright-Humason School, Helen and Annie returned to Boston. Helen would have been welcomed to any woman's college, but the teenager was determined to go to Harvard College, which did not admit women. Not to be discouraged, Helen decided to go to the Cambridge School for Girls operated by Arthur Gilman to prepare for entrance exams. Gilman and his second wife Stella Scott Gilman, also from Alabama, established the Private Collegiate Instruction for Women, known as the Harvard Annex, which became Radcliffe College. William Wade soon contacted Arthur Gilman, asking how he could help his friend Helen to make her dream a reality.

Once admitted to the Cambridge School, Arthur Gilman designed a course that was expected to take five years to complete, but Annie, tired of financial turbulence, hoped to condense it to two years (Lash, 1980). Annie's rush to accelerate Helen's studies created tensions with Gilman, who disagreed on how to manage Helen. Annie sat by her student's side in classes to interpret even though Helen had already intellectually surpassed her teacher. With her own vision challenges, Annie struggled to read everything Helen needed to learn except the material available in braille. Annie researched words and ideas in dictionaries and encyclopedias to prepare so she could immerse Helen in topics like with those they studied in Alabama.

Annie believed maintaining good health was key to Helen's pathway to freedom. She felt "greater physical self-confidence gained from swimming and riding a tandem bicycle supported good health. Annie aggressively pushed Helen physically and mentally as she studied her most challenging subject, geometry. Helen remembered, ' . . . sometimes a composition I wrote did not please her, or I could not solve a problem in geometry, or some other stupidity angered her—it seemed as if a thundercloud passed over me" (Keller, 1929).

Helen took preliminary entrance exams for Radcliffe College in June 1897. Gilman administered her tests in a separate room so Helen could use her typewriter and not disturb the other examinees. Helen's high marks in English impressed Gilman. Over the summer, Helen and Annie stayed in Wrentham with Joseph and Ida Chamberlin.

Prior to her birthday, Helen explored acquiring a tandem bicycle of her own. She wrote to Twain's friend Charles Dudley Warner asking him about bicycles. The teenager wondered if he recommended a "sociable" or a Columbia tandem as one of her friends suggested. The "sociable" was considered safer, but in her opinion, it was heavy and awkward and "has a way of taking up a better part of the road" (Keller, 1903). The tandem bicycle was developed in the 1880s and got its name from its "fore and aft" seating arrangement. Bicycling became popular in the late 1800s when they became chain-driven, more affordable, and safe for women to ride wearing corsets and long skirts. The League of American Wheelmen lobbied for safer roads for biking, but Victorian women of different sizes needed to figure out how to ride bikes designed for men and then pay to have alterations made to bikes. Helen told Warner she and Annie both rode with divided skirts, but Annie who steered in front preferred a man's wheel, while Helen wanted to peddle from a "lady's" seat behind.

In the fall, with encouragement from his wife, Gilman offered Helen's sister Mildred Keller a scholarship, hoping to entice Helen to stay longer to bring attention to the school. When Helen and Annie returned to the Cambridge School, Gilman took credit for Helen's success.

Sophia Hopkins visited Helen and Annie. She reported to Gilman how she had found Helen in "a state of collapse." Hopkins was concerned about how Annie was cutting Helen off from companionship with students her own age. Hopkins blamed Gilman for Helen's ambitious schedule, but he responded by telling her that Annie controlled Helen's schedule. Hopkins held a "stormy" meeting with her "foster daughter," unhappily concluding Annie's personal ambitions led her to press Helen harder than necessary.

The level of effort Helen needed to keep up with other students was daunting. Annie attended every class with Helen to translate lectures and books not printed in braille. Gilman accused Annie of overtaxing Helen with geometry. Once Helen experienced a very intense menstrual cycle; her guardian ordered her to rest over the weekend, taking Helen out only for brisk walks in the snow. Gilman believed Annie worked Helen with a level of impatience and cruelty that would get the school's faculty dismissed. He wrote to Kate Keller, Alexander Graham Bell, Eleanor Hutton, and Sarah Fuller at the Horace Mann School for the Deaf informing them of the situation.

Alexander Graham Bell paused to warn Annie to slow down. Eleanor Hutton wrote to Annie, offering advice that she should not rush Helen in her studies. She wrote, "Mr. Hutton says the people who succeed in life, make haste, slowly . . . Don't be too ambitious for her" (Lash, 1980).

Gilman worried Annie was alienating Helen and Mildred from him. He hoped to separate Annie from the Keller sisters and become Helen's legal guardian to keep her at the Cambridge School. He wrote to William Wade suggesting Annie's perceived change in behavior had developed out of her growing feelings of inadequacy at the school because she did not have credentials for professional teaching.

The epistolary evidence escalated when Wade responded, describing how his wife could not bear how Annie had treated Helen on a recent visit. Wade reported to Gilman how Annie forced Helen to retype long papers even for small typos, "We were all distressed" (Lash, 1980). Sophia Hopkins wrote to Helen's mother, "Miss Sullivan's ambition for the child has warped her judgment" (Lash, 1980).

Kate Keller subsequently wrote to Annie, " You know how largely I have left her to you, and I hope you love and have enough confidence in me to believe that only the firm conviction that it is injuring Helen to be pressed in this way could make me oppose myself to your ambition."

Alabama-born Stella Gilman, growing concerned about her husband's health with the growing stress of the situation, wrote to Kate Keller, "Perhaps you have noticed wherever Annie has been she has fallen out with those who have tried to do good for Helen" (Lash, 1980).

Mrs. Hopkins wrote to Gilman, "For dear Helen's sake we should now do what is necessary to protect her . . . Annie needs to understand that Helen is not her property." In turn, the director of the Cambridge School wrote to Kate Keller, describing how Annie pressured Helen to accelerate studies and how it was badly impacting her health.

Gilman reminded Kate how before his death Arthur Keller had hoped to remove Helen from her teacher's control. Gilman offered to pay the widow's travel expenses to come to Boston. "Miss Sullivan has boasted frequently to me and others that she has complete control over Helen, that she can take her from this school at any moment, transfer her to Europe or elsewhere, and, in fact, do what she pleases without your interference." Gilman concluded that he believed "the mother has a right to her child."

Kate responded promptly, giving Arthur Gilman approval to cut Helen's schedule and authorized him to act as Helen's guardian. Gilman made the mistake of showing Kate's telegram dated December 8, 1897, to Annie. It simply ordered, "You are authorized to act as Helen's guardian."

Helen had just finished her Greek lesson when Annie approached her. Annie's hands uncharacteristically shook, so Helen asked, "What is it, Teacher?"

Annie had difficulty in fingerspelling. "Helen, I think we are going to be separated."

Helen responded, "What! Separated? What do you mean?" Helen later recounted, "When Miss Sullivan left, it hit me hard . . . I did not enjoy my studies." The teenager was humiliated by not being consulted. "Miss Sullivan's judgment was flung aside as if of no value!" It was after this event that Helen began to capitalize on her title for Annie, "Teacher," as if to affirm her guardian's importance in her life. Annie approved, and the title stuck (Keller, 1929; Lash, 1980).

Annie escalated matters by threatening to remove Helen and Mildred from the Cambridge School. Arthur Gilman visited Helen who was distraught, but the teen refused to talk to him. Gilman and Annie held a hasty exchange. He wanted Helen and Mildred to stay with him and his wife Stella. Helen simply refused.

When Gilman told Helen how other teachers had reported Annie's cruelty and how her own father wanted Helen and her teacher to be separated, Helen was stunned. The teen retorted, "My father knew how I love my teacher and he would never separate us!"

Annie interceded, "Don't, dear child." She immediately left the school, leaving Helen and Mildred in a state of agitated confusion. Annie sent Kate a telegram. "We need you."

That night, Annie walked toward Charles River intent upon drowning herself. She felt an angelic presence restrain her and the words "not yet." She walked on and eventually spent the night with Sarah Fuller, the principal of the Horace Mann School.

The next morning, Helen joined the other students. Quick to defend Annie, she stated, "Mr. Gilman lied when he said I was working too hard on weekends." The situation was too reminiscent of when Michael Anagnos, the director of Perkins Institute for the Blind, had confronted Annie with charges of plagiarism based upon the opinions of other teachers.

Sophia Hopkins and Eleanor Hutton backed down from their own observations and protested Gilman's extreme move to separate Helen and her teacher. Kate Keller tried to backtrack by writing to Annie how she believed they shared Helen as their child. Kate asked Annie if she was trying to bring herself and Helen to utter ruin after working so patiently to develop Helen as a well-rounded person (Lash, 1980).

Eleanor Hutton alerted Arthur Gilman about how Helen's trust fund was intended only for Helen and Annie. "In the event of any separation of the beneficiaries, the trustees will need to return the funds raised to the various donors." Mary Thaw was also a major patron for this trust, and she would not support changes in the arrangement.

Kate Keller arrived in Cambridge, Massachusetts, to discover her daughters in hysterics but otherwise in good health. The widow was as dependent upon Annie as her eldest daughter. Kate reversed her decision. "Mr. Gilman had made cruel use of the authority I had given him to distress my children . . . I certainly never dreamed of Miss Sullivan being forced away from Helen. I always felt that Helen was partly your child" (Lash, 1980).

Helen Keller was isolated as long as she was under Annie's protection; she could not socialize freely with students, and she did not receive information of current events unless her teacher mediated. In early December, Helen wrote to Mary Thaw about her desire to be like other girls her age. Helen may have been seeking help without knowing it, as she had done when she locked her mother in a pantry as a child. Helen instinctively understood there was something "strange" about Annie and their situation beyond her own disabilities. Helen wrote, "I cannot help wishing sometimes that I could have some of the fun that other girls have . . . but I must not waste my time wishing idle wishes . . ." She concluded, "It is only once in a great while that I feel disconnected and allow myself to wish for the things I cannot hope for in this life" (Keller, 1903).

Ultimately, money talked in Helen's life. Michael Anagnos and Florence Howe Hall offered olive branches to Helen, which the teenager did not accept after they both challenged Annie. Arthur Gilman, after experiencing the phenomenon of Annie's tactics in controlling her ward, traveled to New York to lobby Helen's fund managers so as to not allow the fund to bind Helen to Annie, telling them it would be disastrous for the Deaf-Blind girl. Word of his interfering with her financial security reached Annie, who became furious. "All the powers on Earth cannot separate Helen and me" (Keller, 1903; Lash, 1980). As money spoke, it mandated how Helen and her teacher Annie Sullivan would be financially bound for life.

6

The Boundless Universe

Helen Keller and Annie Sullivan were again set adrift in late 1897 after clashing with the director of the Cambridge School for Young Ladies. They weathered another storm, but their actions reinforced speculation about Annie controlling Helen to preserve her own interests. Directors at Perkins Institute for the Blind, the Wright-Humason School, and the Cambridge School wanted Helen to continue connections with their respective institutions. They retreated from Helen's temperamental teacher, Annie Sullivan. A positive outcome of the recent dramas was that Annie stopped treating Helen like a child. The teenager wanted a college education to develop her ideal self; the path remained rocky with a guardian inclined to give and take offense. Helen appeared to embody confidence and self-esteem, but her teacher did not disguise negativity, which her student described as a "porcupine of principles" (Keller, 1955).

Kate Keller and her children Mildred Keller and Phillips Brooks Keller embraced Annie Sullivan into their family after Captain Arthur Keller died. Kate and Mildred exited Helen's spotlight in Boston, Massachusetts, to resume private lives in Alabama, while Helen and Annie traveled to the Boston suburb of Wrentham, Massachusetts, to regroup with Joseph E. "Uncle Ed" Chamberlin at Red Farm. Despite his change of heart about binding Helen and Annie financially with a trust, Uncle Ed quietly observed the successful public experiment using subscriptions to create an educational endowment for Helen.

Chamberlin dedicated his "The Listener" column to Helen's education on April 7, 1897. He surmised college might open Helen's mind to deeper soul perception and help her develop her individuality and self-expression. The teenager might not be a genius, but she possessed intriguing soul perception. Chamberlin wrote, "One feels, when engaged in conversation with her, as if one were in closer communication with the soul itself" (Lash, 1980).

Chamberlin did not expect prodigious intellectual output from a college-educated Helen, but he hoped she would not be restricted to intellectual boundaries from a conventional institutional Deaf-Blind education. Uncle Ed's wife Ida Chamberlin suggested Annie establish a school for the Deaf-Blind training to secure some financial independence. However, no-nonsense William Wade became concerned that Annie, who had never formerly learned teaching methods, had deliberately trained Helen to be dependent.

Wade believed Annie, without basic credentials, would never garner government financial support to establish an educational enterprise like the one Ida proposed. The young woman reared in poverty could not manage money. Wade felt Annie's labor-intensive one-teacher-to-one-student model required teachers to devote lives and careers to a single student (Wade, 1908). Helen's guardian managed to alienate all the educators who supported Helen.

Harvard University only admitted male students, but the teenager had set her sights on Arthur Gilman's other educational endeavor, the Harvard Annex, which was reorganized as Radcliffe College in 1894. Helen prepared for Radcliffe entrance exams with tutoring twice a week from math instructor Merton S. Keith. Keith taught Helen to break down algebra problems into abstract ideas. Keith expanded what Helen had learned from Reverend John D. Irons who had coached her in geometry, Greek, and Latin. Helen and her guardian relocated to a boardinghouse in Boston to be near him so Helen could study five days a week.

Deaf-Blind students did not have algebra workbooks with braille or raised-type texts corresponding to the mathematical symbols. Helen needed to construct geometrical figures on a cushion with curved wires and memorize the lettering of the figures and other aspects of a geometric proof. Keith coached her to practice clear reasoning and seek conclusions calmly instead of jumping to fast conclusions.

Orison Marden met Helen and Annie in their home on Newbury Street in 1899 (Marden, 1905). On Helen's lap was a small red cushion affixed with an array of wires representing geometrical figures in her current algebra problem. Helen transcribed physics, algebra, and geometry problems with a braille writer, a machine like a typewriter with six keys. She pressed combinations of keys at the same time, like a pianist plays a chord, to

HELEN KELLER AND A NEW THOUGHT GURU

Dr. Orison Swett Marden (1848–1924) was an American writer who offered common-sense principles for obtaining a well-rounded, successful life. Many of his ideas were based on nineteenth-century New Thought philosophy inspired by Phineas Quimby (1802–1866). New Thought holds that God is everywhere and that true human selfhood is divine. Mary Baker Eddy, founder of Christian Science, was a patient of Quimby's before she disavowed his influence in developing her theology.

Marden was orphaned at the age of eight years and hired out into a series of foster homes. As a teenager, he discovered a book in an attic by Scottish reformer Samuel Smiles (1812–1904) called *Self-Help* (1859). Smiles argued how poverty was a consequence of laissez-faire government that promoted bad economic practices. Reading Smiles' book, Marden was motivated to improve himself through education. He worked as a hotel employee to earn science, medical, and law degrees.

Oliver Wendell Holmes, Sr. and Ralph Waldo Emerson influenced Marden's thinking about the ideal self when he asserted, "We make the world we live in and shape our own environment." Marden, who embodied Algeristic qualities of hard work, leveraged his hotel experience to build a hotel and a resort empire. He established the magazine called *Success* in 1897. Marden's popular writing was distinctively American in tone, emphasizing how success comes as a result of cultivating individual development, "The golden opportunity you are seeking is in yourself."

Keller, because she appeared to be governed by animal impulses before she could communicate with words, seemed to reflect Marden's rhetoric of animal magnetism. Fixated upon Keller's transformation from a phantom Deaf-Blind individual to a woman with intellectual potential, Marden questioned how Keller's inquisitive mind demonstrated what it means to be human.

create characters. Marden asked Helen about the strange contraption, and she replied, "I am trying to prove that the sum of the areas of two similar polygons, constructed on the two legs of a right triangle, is equal to the area of a similar polygon constructed on the hypotenuse" (Marden, 1905).

Marden asked Helen about ambitions after finishing school. She replied, "I think I should like to write . . . for children." Helen, still less than confident from the controversy after the "King Frost" story, continued, "I tell stories to my young friends, but they are not original yet . . . many are translations from Greek mythology and fables."

She told Marden that while Charles Kingsley's satire of Darwin's *The Origin of Species* (1859) called *The Water-Babies: A Fairy Tale for a Land Baby* (1863) and Lewis Carroll's nonsense fantasy novel called *Alice's Adventures in Wonderland* (1865) were popular, she said, "But none of them can surpass the Greek tales."

Helen impressed Marden with her power of expression using gesticulation as she illustrated her passion for Greek culture. He asked her if she wanted to visit Greece. Inspired by a gift of Greek shells from Oliver Wendell Holmes, Sr. and her onetime friendship with Michael Anagnos, the director of Perkins Institute, Helen responded, "Oh yes! It is one of my air castles, that I have long dreamt of since I was a little child" (Marden, 1905).

"Do you think the dream will come true?"

Helen had a rich dream life recorded by Josef Jastrow, who had studied the Deaf-Blind including Laura Bridgman. In one of Helen's vibrant dreams, she climbed to the stars and she sprang up into the air by the force of a strong impulse (Jastrow, 1900). The teen could not see or hear, but her mind guided and interpreted events. Higher and higher she rose until close to the stars she sensed their intense light and heat that prevented her from approaching closer. Helen clung to invisible wings, fascinated by the constant play of light and dark from rolling spheres in her dream images. She suddenly lost her balance, not knowing how or why. Then down, down, down, she rushed through empty space, violently striking a tree before sinking to the ground. Helen remembered the shock woke her up, and she thought all of her bones were broken to atoms, but then she went on with her day.

Helen slowly replied to Marden, "I hope so, but I dare not be too certain, the world is full of disappointments and vicissitudes, and I have to be a little conservative" (Marden, 1905).

The older man was surprised by the nineteen-year-old's use of the word "vicissitudes," meaning unpleasant changes of fortune. In many ways, the young woman possessed depths beyond her years. Not tied to superficial entertainments connected to mirrors, Helen's actual self appeared to be self-contained. The teen directed her own path even if a guide was necessary to move through the physical world. Helen felt she was self-directed after she handed her father her first earnings in his time of need.

Marden observed Helen's love of everything Greek. He blithely suggested she must possess the soul of an old Greek.

Helen laughed. "Oh, no, not the soul of an old Greek, but the soul of a young Greek" (Marden, 1905).

Annie chuckled as she translated, "She caught you there."

Marden asked Helen if she liked to wear pretty things. Helen stretched the truth when she responded, "I used to be very fond of dress, but now I don't care about it so much; it is such a bother." Helen, who preferred comfort to confining corsets, laughed. "It would be fine if we're made with feathers and wings like the birds, then we would not have to worry about what to wear, and we could fly where we pleased."

Helen experienced beauty deeply by smell, touch, and taste. She enjoyed visiting museums, and the superintendent of the Museum of Fine Arts,

Boston, General Francis William Loring gave her special permission to approach and touch three-dimensional art deeper than a half-inch bas-relief (Keller, 1903). Loring often accompanied Helen and a friend in the beginning. Helen nearly cried when she touched the statues depicting violent acts because they felt so real to her.

"I suppose," Marden suggested, "you would fly to Greece first?"

Helen became wistful remembering her family and responded, "No, I should go home first, to see my loved ones" (Marden, 1905).

The words Helen read entered her consciousness. When she read a violent account of war in a history book about Queen Victoria's reign called *Sixty Years a Queen* (1897) by Sir Herbert Maxwell, imagery of the Bibighar Massacre, when British soldiers were killed along with women and children during the Siege of Cawnpore in June 1857. The accounts gave her nightmares for several days when she dreamt that she was in a small prison. At first, she saw a skeleton hanging upon a wall; then she felt a strange, awful sound, like heavy iron being cast down and heartrending cries. Twenty men were executed. Helen rushed from room to room, trying to lock doors in futile efforts to save the remaining men. She watched cities burning with men being dragged into the fires, and she could not speak. Amid the conflagration, Helen grasped men, trying to pull them from the fire, but they slipped beyond her reach. Helen awoke in sickening horror. Realizing it was a new morning, the fresh air chased her phantoms away (Jastrow, 1900).

Helen told Marden about her interest in the Peace Congress her cousin Edward Everett Hale had attended. During the Universal Peace Congress held in Chicago in 1893, Hale called for an annual court of arbitration to coincide with the Columbian World's Fair. Revealing her early pacifism, Helen told her interviewer, "I hope the nations will carry out the project of disarmament. I wonder which nation will be brave enough to lay down its arms first!"

Marden asked, "Don't you hope it will be America?"

"Yes, I hope so, but I don't think we will." Helen thought for a moment, "We are only entering this world stage, and I am afraid we like it." She paused again, "I think it will be one of the old, experienced nations that has had enough of war" (Marden, 1905).

Marden asked Helen what was essential for successful living, as she prepared for college. Helen mused for a moment. She responded, "Patience, perseverance, and fidelity" (Marden, 1905).

Then he asked, "What is the most desirable thing in life?"

Helen understood how many people had helped her. Annie smiled when the teenager responded promptly, "Friends" (Marden, 1905).

Marden asked, "But what about material possessions? What would you prioritize? Wealth or education?" Helen had sensed the dissipation of affluence with its toll on her family and responded that education was more important because it would prepare her for a life of service. Helen stated, "I have so long been nothing in the world that I have made up my mind that I must be something before I die."

*　*　*

Helen Keller passed her exams in elementary as well as advanced German, French, Latin, English, and Greek and Roman history (Keller, 1903). She remembered learning four things before attending Radcliffe College: "to think clearly without hurry or confusion, to love everybody sincerely, and to act in everything with highest motives, and to trust in dear God unhesitatingly." Helen was twenty years old when she entered Radcliffe College in September of 1900 as a freshman.

Helen Keller reads a braille book (possibly during her time at Radcliffe College) from a library seen behind her. Keller could often be found sitting on the floor reading braille books that opened up her lifelong exploration of the world of ideas. While at Radcliffe College, Keller became close friends with Lenore Smith, who learned to finger spell so she could accompany Keller on adventures when Anne Sullivan was not available. (Library of Congress)

Annie Sullivan was not inclined to learn languages. Annie could no longer lead Helen in her studies, because the studies were too advanced; Keith continued as Helen's tutor throughout her first year. Annie's life was in conflict between outward circumstances and a changing ideal world found in the books she read. From her childhood while borrowing books at Tewksbury almshouse, Annie believed everything worth knowing could be found in books.

Annie shared her love of literature with Helen, who read her braille *Bible* so much her fingers rubbed down the dots. Literature in general shaped the younger woman's utopia; she felt a home negotiating the world of abstract ideas. Braille gave Helen independence, so she could read without interpretations from others. Helen stated, "In literature I am not disfranchised."

Radcliffe College did not accommodate Helen's special needs, but she had learned logic. Helen's exposure to great thinkers gave her perspective, so she knew the difference between controlling arguments and collegial arguments. This gave her an authority that Annie could not control. Helen remembered what Alexander Graham Bell had said when he disagreed with someone, "Perhaps you are right. Let us see how far our ideas on the subject agree. I may be the one who needs enlightenment."

Radcliff staff, perhaps aware of how Annie slurred Arthur Gilman, did not want Helen as a student. Many thought Annie might help Helen to cheat, so all of her tests were conducted with Annie out of the room (Lash, 1980). Annie dominated Helen, but the guardian-promoter was changeable. Annie once told Helen, "I change whatever theory I form about life every now and then—and that keeps the boredom at bay." Helen sensed unanswered questions from her guardian. Helen reasoned, "Throwing aside one's conclusions on impulse is like pulling up seeds to see if they are sprouting—harmful" (Keller, 1955). Explaining her thoughts in relation to her guardian, Helen later wrote, "Our illusions are broken, our ideals change, friendships vanish, and everything we are familiar with vanishes" (Keller, 1955).

Suffering from frequent headaches, Helen refused to consult doctors for fear her guardian would be accused of overworking her again (Lash, 1980). Helen periodically refused to eat, feeling tired and weak, and she became anemic, lacking enough healthy red blood cells to carry adequate oxygen to the body's tissues.

Helen's nightmares featuring her guardian were reported to psychologist Joseph Jastrow, but they were not published. In one nightmare, Annie seizes Helen's hand forcefully dragging her toward an abyss. In another, the pair stand at the foot of a stairway rising to the stars, and Annie orders Helen to climb. When Helen refuses, Annie strikes a match, holding it close to Helen's face, compelling her to swallow it. Helen wrestles out of

Annie's grasp and rushes blindly in the opposite direction with Annie in hot pursuit.

Helen desired friends as a college student, but her mother Kate Keller and Annie both sheltered her. Kate harbored fears Helen would get sexually assaulted without Annie as a chaperone. Annie's experiences at Tewkesbury made her alternatively resentful and cautious about men and flirtatious and rebellious of men in roles of authority. Annie later told a biographer, "My distrust of men . . . go back to those walls."

Helen occupied her time in study to compensate for lack of accommodations. Radcliffe students took part in the new bicycle riding craze that had started in the 1890s when the "safety bicycle" allowed riders to achieve higher speeds. Bicycles gave young female students personal mobility, and they could ride wearing bloomers. Students loved to bike ride because it was physical activity outdoors that offered women visibility and a sense of power, so they encouraged Helen to ride a tandem bicycle. Helen preferred horseback riding because she benefitted from a familiar natural rhythm and balance of the horse since she had learned to ride as a child. Being Deaf-Blind, Helen could not ride a regular bike, so she and Annie experimented riding a bicycle called a "sociable," which allowed two people to ride connected bicycles side by side. She and Annie tried it while wearing divided skirts, but Helen felt awkward, and it took a while for her to get used to taking so much space in the roadways.

Annie allowed Helen to socialize with students her own age if they learned the manual alphabet (Lash, 1980). This allowed them to look after Helen and freed up time for Annie to do other tasks. Helen enjoyed being social. "Many times during the long winter evenings we sat around an open fire with a circle of eager, imaginative students, drinking cider, and popping corn as we joyously tore into philosophy and literature . . ." (Lash, 1980).

As Helen prepared for her freshmen final exams, individuals and organizations asked for her to lend a hand. A commission approached Helen to start a lay campaign that resulted in the formation of the National Committee for the Prevention of Blindness. Helen joined a group established by the Women's Education and Industrial Union in Boston to promote the welfare of the adult Blind.

Helen brought emotional depth to public appearances, and when asked to say a few words at the dedication of the New York Eye and Ear Infirmary, New York journalists reported she wore a dark skirt and white shirtwaist. Her few words were slowly and laboriously uttered before Joseph Jefferson read her written message. The actor read, "In spite of the harsh words that are spoken against this great city, I find here a wide human sympathy." Helen described how New York received the hungry from every country and faith, offering them opportunities for education and assistance. She hoped to promote employment opportunities for the Deaf-Blind over buildings with handsome facades. "A human being who does not work is not a member of society and can have no standing in it . . ."

William Wade visited Helen and Annie as he worked on a grassroots census of Deaf-Blind people in the United States and Canada (Keller, 1903). He was the first American to identify the Deaf-Blind as a distinct disabled community with special needs. The Deaf-Blind were geographically scattered. Government agencies found it hard to address their needs. Wade collaborated with Alexander Graham Bell and his Volta Bureau to turn his quest into the first nongovernmental census of the Deaf-Blind in 1901.

Wade discovered practical approaches for Deaf-Blind reforms (Wade, 1901). He offered a moderate voice, and this sometimes placed him in an adversarial position to Annie. Wade argued the Deaf-Blind were better off learning the manual alphabet. Those teaching the manual alphabet were only required to teach with "intelligence, patience, and devotion." Wade wanted to help Helen in her studies; he wrote to her, "I want a list of all the books you will need during the college course, and I will have them copied in braille for you." In helping Helen, Wade helped disabled workers. "This will enable me to help about twenty Blind persons to earn a little something, and it will delight my heart to feel that I am making your college work easier" (Keller, 1903).

Helen agreed, but she could not predict what books her teachers would assign. She wrote to Wade, "No barrier of the senses shuts me out from the discourse of my book-friends."

Linguist George Lyman Kittredge became one of Helen's favorite Radcliffe professors, who approached the past through language and collected New England folktales and songs (Keller, 1929). Kittredge once quipped, "There are three persons who know what the word 'Victorian' means, and the other two are dead." He introduced Helen to the idea of how idiomatic language development is closely tied to cultural history. She took his Shakespeare class and read six plays and virtually memorized the texts to discover what Shakespeare said and "what he meant when he said it."

Helen's composition teacher Charles Townsend "Copey" Copeland stated Helen possessed an "excellent *ear* for the flow of sentences" (Lash, 1980). He and other essay readers for English 22 agreed Helen was the best freshman writer at Radcliffe, *or Harvard*. Tired of her doing what many freshmen did by retelling myths, Copey encouraged Helen to write about her own truly unique experiences. Taking the freshman and her guardian aside, Copeland told Helen, "We want more of you and less of what you have read."

Helen just wanted to be like all of the other students and to forget her own limitations. She responded to her professor, "I see the folly of attempting to hitch one's wagon to a start with a harness that does not belong to it . . ." She promised, "Henceforth I am resolved to be myself, to live my own life, and write my own thoughts when I have any . . ." (Lash, 1980).

Within the first few weeks of Helen's second year at Radcliffe, *Ladies' Home Journal's* editor William V. Alexander summoned her from Latin class to talk. In an unprecedented move, Alexander invited the sophomore to write a series of stories about her life. Annie as her guardian convinced Helen to sign a contract with publisher Curtis Bok for a proposed $5,000 for five essays.

Helen was thoughtful in her studies; she developed an awareness of the past . . . her past. In November 1901, she wrote to her cousin Edward Everett Hale, who had planned on memorializing Dr. Samuel Gridley Howe at an event celebrating the centennial of his birth. Helen reflected upon what her life might have been if Howe had not "taken upon himself the responsibility of Laura Bridgman's education . . . should I be a sophomore at Radcliffe College today—who can say" (Keller, 1903)? Helen wrote to Hale, "I think only those who have escaped that death in life existence from which Laura Bridgman was rescued, can realize how isolated, how shrouded in darkness, how cramped by its own importance is a soul without thought or faith or hope."

Radcliffe College required all of Helen and Annie's efforts to keep up with assignments, but the pair savored their new relationships. Students elected Helen to be the vice president of the class, but she declined because she had to devote all of her spare time to assignments. Annie encouraged classmates to help Helen to complete readings and assignments. A married classmate Lenore Kinney Smith learned the manual alphabet. Classmates gave Helen a Boston terrier to keep her company, and she named him Phiz.

Lenore's husband was a Harvard geology student Philip S. Smith, and her ability in fingerspelling opened new dialogs for Helen. The couple resided in a boardinghouse for married students, and they soon became a vital part of Helen and Annie's small circle of friends. The Smiths introduced Helen and Annie to a twenty-five-year-old fellow boarder named John Albert Macy, a Harvard English instructor and associate editor for *Youth's Companion*, where Joseph E. Chamberlin and Bradford Torrey worked.

For Helen, Phil's friend John became a combination of friend, brother, and advisor. In late 1901, Macy helped Helen with writing assignments and her essays for *Ladies' Home Journal*. He learned the manual alphabet so Annie would not restrict their conversations. The English lecturer recognized Helen's unexpected gifts as a communicator. He observed how she utilized expressive gestures with her hands as few white Victorian women did.

Helen derived pleasure from touching great three-dimensional works of art. Josef Jastrow gave Helen a medallion of Homer, the author of the *Odyssey*, for her study. Helen perceived the ancient Greek poet as being a fellow Blind person who groped his way from camp to camp, singing of life, war, and human achievements. John remembered, "Helen's hands have been her instruments of communication for so long they have mutated, as it were, to become as quick-shifting as the eye, and therefore express some the things that we say in a glance" (Macy, 1902).

John Macy was bohemian in nature. Helen's mannerisms and physical communications intrigued John like many others. Once Annie let him into their confidence, and he was the first man to have this access, John saw the informal Helen . . . the little bronco who was less corseted than other young Victorian ladies. Helen was physically strong; she sat on the floor when she could. In an age when women were taught to be malleable and submissive, Helen's manners held no affectation; they were practical to make life easier for her and those around her. The young Deaf-Blind woman was dependent upon others for most things, but she was economical in her dependence so as to be less of a burden.

Helen expressed more through her hands than by speaking to people. John found himself mesmerized by the young Deaf-Blind woman as she kept up with the rhythms of quick ragtime tunes. John observed, "The reason for her gesturing habits is that she was never chilled into self-conscious reserve by seeing that the rest of us have dumb and silent fingers" (Macy, 1902). He was impressed by her physical strength and bravery; John told friends how she hiked through the woods and never complained if she got scratched and bruised. However, Helen did not complain about adversity by choice.

John and Annie communicated differently with Helen while using fingerspelling. Annie was quick and dramatic, while John put his words together carefully as if he was writing a novel. His hands were seldom still even when he was not spelling for Helen. Her finger-reading of the manual alphabet was as fast and efficient as Annie's but in a different way from John. Helen did not feel each letter as a reader sees each separate letter in a word or as a television viewer sees each detail, but she gained a mental picture through inductive contextualizing. Helen could tell by John's gestures whether he was arguing or joking, or simply carrying on an ordinary conversation with friends.

Annie encouraged Helen's learning through the constant stimulation of touch. She wrote a poem describing Helen's child hands as she first learned to use them to communicate to the broader world:

Hands, understanding hands,
Hands that caress like delicate green leaves,
Hands, eager hands,
Hands that gather knowledge from great books—Braille books—
Hands that fill empty space with livable things,
Hands so quiet, folded on a book—

Hands forgetful of words they have read all night,
Hands asleep on the open page,
Strong hands that sew and reap thought,
Hands tremulous and ecstatic listening to music
Hands keeping the rhythm of song and dance.

(Harrity and Martin, 1962)

Annie groomed Helen to be emotionally measured in public appearances. As Helen received her formal education at Radcliffe College, John and Annie shaped Helen's image in magazines like *Youth's Companion*. The pair informed Helen's autobiographical articles in *Ladies' Home Journal*. Helen's family was not happy with how they were portrayed. Her mother Kate Keller was particularly distressed by Helen's candor in describing her violent behavior during her "phantom" years before the language breakthrough, probably because they reflected upon her own hardships mourning her father's death in a yellow fever epidemic and Helen's disabilities caused by another epidemic.

Annie had fostered Helen's communications skills beyond teaching her to explore environments to responding to outside communication with correctly spelled words and proper (and even lyrical) grammar. Now John helped develop Helen's essays into an autobiography, *The Story of My Life* (1903), where she chronicled how she came to sense and understand the world despite being Deaf-Blind.

Words are powerful. Helen became a celebrity in popular media during her lifetime; media shaped her communications. During the industrial revolution, the telegraph and more powerful printing presses led to rapid expansion of newspapers and magazines in the United States. Helen came to fame at the cusp of print and audio-moving image media. This transition was marked by a literary and arts movement of realism when language and literacy was extremely important.

By the early twentieth century, before radio was invented, media syndicates became profitable for media moguls like Joseph Pulitzer and William Randolph Hearst, who competed for readers. Profits came from selling sensational headlines, yellow journalism, and muckraking stories that newsboys could peddle in busy business districts. While Copeland helped Helen to develop her ideal self by telling her story through the written word, John was a media man who came from a modest Nantucket whaling family. He appreciated the material trappings of affluence, but he developed his craft of writing in relative isolation.

John was willing and able to take chances and deal with unconventional situations to further his own interests. John, like Joseph Chamberlin, did not spread the notion of Helen being a "brilliant genius" (Lash, 1980). John saw himself as her intellectual superior and thought Helen was not scholarly in her interests although he conceded "her mind is stout and energetic, of solid endurance."

John knew women with more obvious capacity for scholarship. Without considering Helen's disabilities, he wrote, "I, for one, cannot see that she has the intellect of a genius, or much creative power, or great originality" (Macy, 1902). John chose to ignore how Helen's guardian-promoter might also be handicapped. Annie was not an academic, and she resented academics. John concluded about Helen, "But her heart is noble; the world has yet to see a finer spirit, a loftier and more steadfast will to do the best."

Despite employing a professional editor as her private secretary, writing still did not come easy to Helen. Her double disability meant she and John had to translate from braille to typewritten manuscripts on her manual Hammond typewriter to fingerspelling. Helen typed and retyped texts until she got it right. The creative process was agonizing. "Sometimes I feel ideas beating against my brain like caged birds; but they will not sing themselves into words . . ." (Keller, 1929).

John, as an ardent socialist, held strong biases like Annie, but John was liberal, and Annie was conservative. John shared his ideas with Helen, because Annie could be rigidly conservative; she believed women should rely upon men to move up in the world. Helen's thinking was malleable, and she could bring her thinking to his views by using logic. For instance, John's take on Henry David Thoreau was far different from that of nature writer Bradford Torrey, who knew the transcendentalist essayist as a friend. John told Helen, "Thoreau's vision shot beyond the horizon. Thoreau was an anarchist of great literary power in a nation of slavish conformity" (Macy, 1913b). He asserted, "Thoreau's ideas today could not be printed in the very magazine that published his complete works."

Annie projected much of her insecurities upon her charge. On a fundamental level, Annie Sullivan had pushed Helen's mother, Kate Keller, to the periphery long before returning to Perkins Institute. Frustrated with Helen's lack of zeal in aspiring to *summa cum laude* (with highest distinction) honors at Radcliffe College, Annie pushed her because she was so conscious to her own lack of formal education. Annie covered this when she told Helen, "Yes dear, I am your mother in heart and mind, but I do not own you. I want you to form your views independently . . ." (Lash, 1980).

Annie's inconsistencies and contradictions led Helen to believe her guardian possessed secrets to be unveiled. John could only position himself to reach Annie's heart by undermining Helen intellect. Helen's aspirations to be a writer or poet like Laura Bridgman made her open to John's lofty suggestions when Annie preferred to focus on mundane matters.

John was tall and handsome when he came into Helen and Annie's lives, but where another woman of the same age would be romantically attracted to him, Helen treated him like a brother. John was a skeptic like Helen's stepbrother, James Keller. Both were not afraid to challenge authority and did not withhold opinions. John could be sarcastic and caustic, but Helen appreciated his candor. He mixed socially with literary figures and American socialists. John introduced her to the writings of H. G. Wells, Leo Tolstoy, and Karl Marx.

John underestimated Helen's reliance upon faith to deal with hardship. Annie did not like the Swedenborgian influence upon Helen; she told Helen, "I do not believe in immortality." John concurred; trying to undermine Helen's faith, he asserted, "Swedenborg is stupendously absurd" (Macy, 1913a).

Radcliffe College inducted Helen into a broader world of ideas about religion and philosophy. Harvard professor Josiah Royce explored philosophy as a means to understand human life, the nature of human society, religious experience, ethical action, suffering, and the problem of evil. Royce felt without loyalty an individual cannot find unity and peace because in solitary moments related to loving and dying, individuals have to think and act for themselves. He connected societal interpretation of all experience to the individual interpretation of *self* within the experience of *nature*. Royce proposed utilizing the economic power of insurance to mediate hostilities among nations and reduce the attraction of war.

Whereas Helen believed that the idea is the truth and the rest is delusion, Royce taught truth has practical meaning within inner life. He argued how an individual's limitations, especially boundaries for the senses, lead the individual beyond *self* to see a bigger truth. "What an individual sees, hears, and touches is not the only reality of what is, but imperfect manifestations of the Idea, the Principle, the Spiritual . . ." (Royce, 1904). Meaning is derived and verified through shared experience and communications. Royce pointed out, "Our fellows furnish us the constantly needed supplement to our own fragmentary meanings."

The reality Royce described lay in human experience of nature, which was relevant to Helen. As *nature* offers resistance to human muscular senses and sets our boundaries, humans reason it to be external. Royce argued experiences coming from senses are verified by shared experience from other humans, and create meaning only when they are in harmony with the individual's socially colored ideas. Royce asserted, ". . . precisely in so far as you know the world as one world and intend your place in that world to be unique, God's will *is* consciously expressed" (Royce, 1904).

When John looked romantically to Annie, who was eleven years older than him, she was open to romance and open to a partner who could help her with Helen. After struggling with male authority over control of Helen's education and religious training, Annie was eager to have a man on her side. She wrote to John in New York, "My heart is impatient—impatient because of the repression and self-effacement of a lifetime." She needed

someone stable who could ground her. "My life seems a century long looking back upon it; I have not stilled its passionate unrest." However, John
was a restless, independent person. Annie wondered what his motives were
for wooing her when Helen was closer in age. "I have thought a long time of
you . . . trying to discover the reason for your love of me" (Lash, 1980).

Adult Helen remained totally dependent upon her guardian-promoter.
Annie held a monopoly on Helen because of this dependency, but would an
attractive man accept Helen in a familial equation? Despite past disappointments from men, Annie began to contemplate a life with love. She
wrote to John, "How wonderful it is! And how impossible to understand!
Love is the very essence of life itself" (Lash, 1980).

Reason had nothing to do with Annie's need for love. John saw Annie
Sullivan as the poetic fire beneath Helen; she was a feisty Irish woman.
Annie wrote to John, "For one moment I gave myself up to the supreme
happiness—the certainty of a love so strong that fate had no dominion over
it and in that moment all the shadows of life become beautiful realities."
She continued, "Then I groped and stumbled my way back to earth again—
the dreary flat earth where real things are seldom beautiful" (Lash, 1980).

John drank like Annie's father, Thomas Sullivan. She assumed John was
too refined to be abusive. However, John Macy was ambitious and soon
courted Annie and Helen as a pair. Annie was not sure that their love
would last. She wrote, "You say that we have no right to test present happiness by harping on possible sorrow. It is because your love is so dear to me
beyond all dreams that I rebel against the obstacles that the years have
built up between us." Annie "Mansfield" Sullivan needed a man to help her
navigate the new century. She asked her lover, "You will not leave of loving
me will you—not for a long time yet . . ." She tried to convince John that he,
and not Helen, was her first love: "I kiss you my own John and I love you, I
love you, I love you" (Lash, 1980).

Perhaps shaped by Annie's biases, Helen now attacked perceived elitism
at Perkins Institute in not teaching practical stills to students so they could
assimilate into regular jobs. John continued to transform Helen's articles
for *Ladies' Home Journal* into a book. Intent upon being Helen and Annie's
champion, John attempted to entrap an ailing director of Perkins Institute
for the Blind, Michael Anagnos, with a series of pointed questions. He
hoped Anagnos would back down from his allegations of Annie being
behind the controversy of "The Frost King." John asserted Anagnos needed
to act with "an obligation to truth" when he remained silent on the incident even though he expected Helen and Annie to speak well of Perkins
Institute (Lash, 1980).

Helen received mixed messages from Annie and John, who wanted to
control her, and Radcliffe and Harvard professors, who wanted her to think
for herself. Helen wavered in her opinions: she believed if a woman did not

independently garner academic distinction, she could still help other women to achieve difficult tasks to advance causes for all women. Helen's ambivalence led her to conclude, "It is not so much genius that availeth as energy, industry, and willingness to make personal sacrifices" (Lash, 1980).

Michael Anagnos and John met, but Anagnos denied there was any documentation other than his personal notes. He felt Perkins Institute took every precaution to protect Helen's rights and reputation, but he remained silent about Annie's role. While Helen's own words worked against her, Anagnos said the investigation was "instinctually friendly to her." Frank B. Sanborn, the man who removed Annie from Tewksbury almshouse and placed her in Perkins Institute, corroborated Anagnos's conclusion that the accusation was "not proven" (Keller, 1903).

With John's editing, the last 120 pages of *The Story of My Life* became a justification of Annie as a teacher. It included a defense of the "Frost King" incident. John, desperate to paint his fiancée in a positive light, took the offensive by asking, "Finally, whom, if anyone, do you hold guilty of intension to deceive, Miss Sullivan, Helen Keller, or both?" Anagnos refused to respond; he felt his feelings on the matter were personal, "I must decline to pursue this subject further" (Wagner, 2012). Anagnos chose to respond to Macy with consideration for the long-term welfare of all of the Deaf-Blind students at Perkins Institute and not just the one with the most vocal teacher: deception on Keller's part was "not proven."

John was paradoxical: he needed to feel settled, yet he needed his independence. Annie needed to control; she could be bossy, but she refused to be controlled. In February 1903, as the book was coming to completion, Annie wrote to him, "I think of you oftener than I breathe" (Lash, 1980). She needed him with her to control and asked, "Haven't you had enough of New York? Idling about clubs and going to the opera isn't so much fun is it?" Annie teased John that she had an enduring commitment to Helen with a little tug, "Aren't you longing for to come back to your twelve to fifteen hours of work every day? And me?"

Helen's mother, Kate Keller, objected to one passage in the book when Helen described her "consciousness" before Annie arrived in Tuscumbia, Alabama. Helen wrote, "Before my teacher came to me, I did not know that I am. I lived in a world that was a no-world . . . I did not know that I knew aught, or that I lived or acted or desired. I had neither will nor intellect. I was carried along to objects and acts by a certain blind natural impetus . . ." (Lash, 1980). Kate hoped that they would omit this because it seemed to confirm what some family members thought—that Helen was incapable of being educated without Annie. Kate was not alone in resisting this description suggesting that Helen lacked cognitive depth normal to human beings. It took some convincing from Annie that "dormancy" was not the same as being "feeble minded."

John negotiated a lucrative deal for *The Story of My Life* (1903), published by Doubleday, Page & Company. It contains three sections: her story with a note from John in the preface—"Much of her education she cannot explain herself, and since a knowledge of that is necessary to an understanding of what she has written, it was thought best to supplement her autobiography with the reports and letters of her teacher, Miss Anne Mansfield Sullivan" (Wagner, 2012). John edited Annie's letters and reports and acknowledged Eleanor Hutton, John Hitz, and Sophia C. Hopkins for their anecdotes about Helen. The volume contains Keller's letters, spanning fifteen years revealing her intellectual growth along with commentary from Annie and John, who together mediated Helen's story to shape her image as well as their own.

The Story of My Life sold ten thousand copies in its first year on the market. It transformed societal attitudes toward individuals living with disabilities. Helen dedicated the book: "To ALEXANDER GRAHAM BELL Who has taught the deaf to speak and enabled the listening ear to hear speech from the Atlantic to the Rockies, I dedicate this Story of My Life" (Keller, 1903)." Mark Twain wrote to Helen, "I am charmed by your book—enchanted" (Twain, 2001–2015).

The Story of My Life made Helen a Deaf-Blind sage in a time when self-help books by Orison Swett Marden and others had become popular. Although middle-class American women fought for the vote, social justice, equality, and public safety reforms, few disabled individuals had access to the philanthropic support Keller received. The book brought Annie recognition. A reviewer for the *New York Sun* wrote, ". . . the wonderful feat of dragging Helen Keller out of her hopeless darkness was only accomplished by sacrificing for it another woman's whole life, and if ever the attempt is made in a similar case, it must be at the same cost" (Lash, 1980).

Dr. Samuel Gridley Howe's daughters Maud Howe Elliot and Florence Howe Hall, who had earlier profiled Helen for *St. Nicholas* magazine, coauthored the biography *Laura Bridgman: Dr. Howe's Famous Pupil and What He Taught Her* (1903) to counter Helen's book. Elliot and Hall chronicled their father's achievements and took undisguised swipes at Annie Sullivan, asserting she did nothing innovative and failed to live up to their father's standards.

Frank B. Sanborn thought the book placed Laura in a more feminine, favorable light and suggested Annie was an attention-grabbing exhibitionist. Elliot and Hall compared Laura who came from good New England stock to the aggressive Irish pauper Annie and the saucy, high-spirited hoydenish daughter of a rebel Confederate, Helen. Reverend Hale wryly observed, "Poor staid Laura Bridgman who had been brought up in all of the conventionalities of the most rigid New England propriety, used to say that Helen was crazy. It was the craziness of sweet, natural love" (Day, 2013).

LITTLE BRONCO AND THE COWBOY

Helen Keller's first biography was a radical work of literature that changed lives. Edward Everett Hale wrote to Helen saying her series of essays that became *The Story of My Life* were "very simply written, and that generally means very well written." Hale stated Helen's book and Rudyard Kipling's *Kim* were the two most important contributions to literature for 1902.

Near Elko, Nevada, a cowboy named J. J. Page ordered a copy of *The Story of My Life* directly from the publisher Doubleday, Page & Company, and perhaps there was a family connection. Page wrote to Keller describing a large cattle drive that included a two-year-old steer that was blind. Page told Keller, "He seemed to do as well as the rest." The cowboy observed how the steer always ran to the side of the herd or behind, often getting lost. Page asked Helen to write a biography of Anne Sullivan Macy because it would be interesting.

Page recognized Helen's guardian-promoter to be a great teacher for surrendering her prospects of having a home and family to serve her single student. Page concluded, "And she has kept you climing climing . . . I think Miss Sullivan theory is all rite in a Colt let them lurn by Experence. I think when she went to Alabama and took charge of that little Bronco it proved it" (Twain, 2001–2015).

Page recognized what more eloquent educators did not: Sullivan-Macy had deep insights into how children learn, and she applied them to Keller. When Mark Twain read the letter, he recognized it was written from the heart. Differing from the letters of Elsie Leslie Lyde to Oliver Wendell Holmes, Sr. that showed a lack of depth, Page's writing may have contained spelling and grammar errors, but Mark Twain called it "literature, high literature."

In late 1903, Helen predicted in an essay, "My Future as I See It," she would lobby on behalf of the Deaf and the Blind to the best of her ability. She carried serious doubts about her ability to remain independent. The idea of starting a normal school for special education teachers for Deaf-Blind students faded into the distance without the support of William Wade, Perkins Institute, and Wright-Humason School. The powerful Howe family fanned the fires Annie created with institutions, where credentialed directors vied for the same financial resources. Despite this, after graduating Reverend Hale wrote to his cousin Helen, "Now the boundless universe is yours." He added, "Now you can direct yourself" (Lash, 1980).

Helen Keller's college degree offered no path to autonomous living. Prior to commencement exercises, with a clear concept of self, Helen optimistically told classmates on June 28, 1904, "College has breathed new light into my mind and given me new views of things, a perception of new truths and of new aspects of old once . . . the end of my school days fills me with bright anticipations . . . light kindled by the thought that there is something for me to do beyond the threshold" (Lash, 1980).

Helen received a general liberal arts education, but many classmates only attended college to prepare for advantageous marriages. Influenced by Annie and John, Helen grew to think her college education amounted to nothing. "They did not teach me about things as they are today, or about the vital problems of the people." She rebelled against the curriculum celebrating "the achievements of war, rather than those of the heroes of peace." Helen argued textbooks offered "a dozen chapters on war where there were a few paragraphs about the inventors, and it is this overemphasis on the cruelties of life that

A Radcliffe College graduation portrait of Helen Keller wearing her cap and gown, reading braille, in June 1904. Keller was the first Deaf-Blind person to earn a bachelor of arts degree, graduating cum laude. A newspaper reporter remembered the audience broke into "thunderous applause" as Keller and Anne Sullivan walked up to accept the degree. Keller, who was already experienced with audiences by that time, asserted, "I felt no thunder of wild applause." (Library of Congress)

breeds the wrong ideal." She concluded, "Education taught me that it was a finer thing to be a Napoleon than to create a new potato" (Lash, 1980).

Annie and John held jaded views of the world, so out of reach of classmates, Helen came to believe higher education was in deadlock. Away from intellectual supporters including Copeland and Royce, Helen changed her views. "College isn't the place to go for any ideas" (Lash, 1980). Nobody knows exactly how Annie and John shaped Helen's thinking when she argued her college experience was not relevant to her life. "Schools seem to love the dead past and live in it."

*   *   *

Helen resisted writing about herself. For the first time in her life, she was affluent through income from *The Story of My Life* as well as a financial trust. Editors insisted readers wanted Helen's insights as a Deaf-Blind woman. The book was published as verismo, an Italian literary movement celebrating realism, and became popular. This arts movement sought to portray the passions and hardships of common folk framed within the real language of ordinary working people. Realism created newspaper-selling headlines because its most compelling stories came out of sensationalized stories of brutal murders and the activities commonplace in places like Tewksbury almshouse.

Realism was interested in preserving and celebrating regional collo-quial language that was disappearing. To this movement, Helen's striving to have a real voice was real. While college-educated Helen embodied ide-als of purity and modern womanhood overcoming adversity, "phantom" Helen filled readers' imaginations with images of the distance Helen tran-scended. John introduced Helen to the literary language of activism. "The realist, or as they sometimes call themselves, 'naturalist,' take the simpler facts of common life and weave them into stories" (Macy, 1913a).

Helen was not a realist; she was as sentimental and biased in her views of Annie Sullivan as Julia Ward Howe was about her late husband Dr. Sam-uel Gridley Howe. She was adult in years, but her isolation and total reli-ance on Annie as her guardian-promoter led Helen to be arbitrary in responses to criticism. Helen believed William Wade wrote to her mother criticizing Annie's one-teacher-to-one Deaf-Blind student model. Wade, although empathetic to Annie, challenged themes in *The Story of My Life* as "branding." He disagreed with Annie's strategy for developing percep-tions of Helen suggesting Annie was a miracle worker when Wade felt Helen was the miracle.

Helen believed Wade's words undermined the prospect a training insti-tute offered the pair to secure a livelihood. Ironically, Wade collaborated with Alexander Graham Bell's Volta Bureau to disseminate information. Defending Annie, Helen wrote to her mother Kate, "Mr. Wade is as wrong in this as he has been in other things. He is no true educator." Helen con-cluded, "In fact, he knows nothing about education, and those who know the difficulties of teaching the deaf laugh at this ignorance" (Nielsen, 2004).

John and Annie's narrative in *The Story of My Life* effectively wrote Kate Keller out of her daughter's life. Kate was as dependent upon Annie to care for her daughter as Helen. While Annie controlled access to Helen, she was increasingly dependent upon John to deal with media relations. Helen Keller was as unaware of being exploited by her guardian-promoter as was Thomas Higgins. However, John with his education could not control media any better than Annie, and this led him to resent the media.

Helen got her start in writing from the colossal American magazine industry shaped by Madison Avenue advertising agencies in New York City. Her ideal self was delineated on pages with little regard for her actual self in the present moment. John coaxed her, saying, "Helen, we should not just be intelligent readers of books, but also intelligent readers of magazines and newspapers" (Macy, 1913b) He remained critical of newspaper editors who were not responsible for maintaining ethical advertising or rejecting fraudulent advertising.

Philosopher William James argued that the best American magazines together constituted a real popular university. However, consumers paid sales taxes on flower, shoes, clothes, paint, and other ordinary commodities needed for daily life, so advertisers paid for space in periodicals and newspapers to develop branding. John lamented how periodicals and newspapers paid writers from "a fiftieth to a twentieth" of advertising income to create advertising that was visually and literarily interesting enough to attract readers (Macy, 1913b).

Helen moved within a community of intellectuals who sought to understand her as an active, dynamic, malleable individual with an expressive, striving soul. Her autobiography, though compelling, was not consistent with the complex thinker who engaged authors, philosophers, and scientists. In defense of *The Story of My Life*, John wrote, "Literature is the written record of human life, therefore biography, the life story of real human beings must lie at the core and center of literature."

John discovered some insights into his love's early life and suggested he write her story. Annie started a journal of her thoughts and activities, hoping to write her own story. She grew increasingly afraid a stranger might write her story in unflattering terms. The frequent fluctuations in Annie's health led friends including Lenore Smith, who had cared for Helen during her treatments, to warn her someone might write her story with or without her consent based upon public records (Lash, 1980).

Annie told John and Helen, "The most conscientious biographer cannot tell the whole truth about his subject, because the subject himself has forgotten so much that was once impressive" (Lash, 1980). John regarded Annie curiously, wondering if she was encouraging his feelings or warning him off. Annie continued, "One sees things differently; from day by day, the aspect of life changes, what seemed important yesterday seems trivial today . . . the years pass, and memories become dull aches."

Helen Keller had traveled far in a short space of time. She used *a voice* and smart words, but now was dependent upon two people with different agendas intent on shaping her life. Again, she was set adrift, no longer asking if she could earn a college degree, but released in a boundless universe attached to her teacher who increasingly struggled with health challenges. The college graduate was oblivious to the undercurrents in the room, unaware her guardian-promoter might be describing memory pictures she preferred to forget. "Our early recollections of childhood are very similar to dreams . . . they are pictures. When we try to put them into words, we must make connections and fill gaps . . . time and place are lost, but the image remains." Then Annie turned directly to John, apologetically in a rare acknowledgment of her feelings, "The truth of a matter is not what I tell you about it, but what you divine in regard to it" (Lash, 1980).

7

Wrentham

Helen Keller set high expectations for herself. Her Radcliffe College education demanded she commit herself to a career of service. At the turn of the twentieth century, Helen felt a college woman should learn to cooperate, meaning learn "how *not* to have her own way." The ideal college education would reveal a student's highest capacities to direct talents into achievement. Helen wanted to be a writer, but her path seemed opaque. Perhaps she could translate books for the Blind or perhaps she and Annie could still open a school in their Wrentham home. For her guardian-promoter Annie Sullivan, financial obstacles stood in the pair's path. Annie hoped to recruit editor John Macy to help, but he had his own ambitions and desires.

Helen had committed her life to public service, but she felt a woman possessed a right to *self*. Helen discouraged women from reading popular literature, encouraging them to read texts deeply for life lessons. Helen saw herself as a college graduate, but the world still saw a Deaf-Blind-Mute woman. Despite her aspirations, Helen had few options to shape her destiny and craft her own life.

Helen pushed herself into spaces where others felt she did not belong. Her supporters offered abundant advice: Edward Everett Hale encouraged Helen to utilize talents. "If you have accomplished all that you have planned for yourself, you have not planned enough." Meanwhile, Joseph E. "Uncle Ed" Chamberlin recommended that Helen and Annie purchase a small farm on some neglected land located near his family in Wrentham, Massachusetts, with an easy commute to Boston by electric streetcar.

Helen's annual income as a "recent graduate" of $5,000 would in 2021 be worth closer to $150,000 in purchasing power (Lash, 1980). This could help Helen's family in Alabama, but the trusts were established soley for Helen and Annie. Prior to graduating, Helen and Annie purchased an old farmhouse surrounded by seven acres of land for $2,000. Some of the money came from Helen's writing royalties, and for the rest, they sold stocks John Spaulding had given them before his death. The two-story house was situated on a bluff with pathways leading to woodlands thick with birds and deer. Annie rode horses with style and loved dogs as much as Helen. Annie's dog Sieglinde read her every mood, and when the dog stood on her hind legs, she placed her front paws on Annie's shoulders and licked her face.

Annie commissioned their Deaf-Blind friend from Perkins Institute Thomas "Tom" Stringer to install ropes and wired pathways for Helen so she could roam the property autonomously. A lot of small rooms were reconfigured, walls were knocked down, and a dairy and two pantries were converted into a study for Helen. On some level, Helen envisioned recreating her mother's functional chicken farm, but the absence of Kate Keller's pragmatic approach undermined their best efforts; nobody in the house was experienced in managing a farm. When Kate visited, Helen hoped for her approval, and she wrote to a friend, "She went everywhere with us, walking, driving, and taking now and then a day's ride on the electrics. All of my friends love her" (Lash, 1980).

Helen and Annie's home in Wrentham was a small, long, narrow, old farmhouse. Helen's study was a sunny room where she had some plants and there was a big window with eastern exposure. In Helen's study, two dominant works of art adorned the room: John Hitz supplied a plaster cast of Venus di Milo and Josef Jastrow gave Helen a bas-relief medallion of the Greek poet Homer. Large braille volumes and numerous curios from friends packed the bookshelves.

Helen loved being outdoors, and she had learned how to row a boat when she was a girl. During the summers, she spent hours in her boat rowing with friends. Helen relied upon someone sitting at the stern to manage the rudder while she rowed by feel and intuition, following familiar scents of water grasses, lilies, and shrubs along the banks and by feeling resistance in the water currents. Despite preferring to ride on horseback, Helen owned a sturdy two-seated Tandem bicycle. A friend piloted from the front seat while she peddled as the stoker in the back. She loved the rapid rush of air against her face while riding gave her a rush of strength and buoyancy.

Helen played fierce games of checkers and chess with friends using a special board with cutout squares so the pieces remained secure. In her special set of checkers, black pieces were flat and white pieces were curved on top. A hole in every checker accommodated a small brass knob to distinguish it as a king as opposed to a common piece.

THOMAS STRINGER GROWS UP

Helen's Deaf-Blind protégé Thomas Stringer grew into a tall, unassuming young man. He visited Wrentham during summers and created imaginative designs that would impress Alexander Graham Bell. One summer, Tome engineered a "play-elevator" in Keller's barn devised with ropes and pulleys that he used to hoist himself to the rafters and descend at will.

Stringer was good at math but like Keller had trouble with articulation. With a special teacher to help accommodate his needs, Stringer was admitted to a public grammar school in Roxbury, Massachusetts, to be assimilated as a sixth-grader in 1900. This was when Stringer discovered that he was different from the other students and asked, "Will Tom read with his eyes when a man?"

Stringer asked questions about his past, where he lived as a baby, and who took care of him. He explored the farm at Wrentham and made improvements where he deemed necessary. He inspected the kitchen, the cellar, the barn and shed, the garden and orchard, and the pond with Keller's boat. Stringer added railings to stairs, fitted the barn window with a new weight and sash, and secured a gas pipe in the barn so that the cats residing there would be safe. He constructed shelves and windowsills.

Stringer remained for twenty years at Perkins Institute, attaining legendary status as a carpenter (Rocheleau and Mack, 1930). His skills were utilized at Perkins Kindergarten to replace worn window cords and as a locksmith. He was a steady worker in the kitchen and did chores on his Monday workdays. After he graduated in 1913, Thomas resided with a guardian Mr. Lee Edgarton who was a grocer. Over the years, Michael Anagnos secured funding for him to receive an annual income of $1,000, worth almost $26,500 in 2021. Thomas also received a workbench and a tandem bicycle that he could ride with a seeing companion.

After each play, Helen followed her opponent's maneuvers by moving her hand over the board to feel the movement of pieces from one hole to another. Helen knit and crocheted during the cold winter months and enjoyed playing solitaire with her card set marked in the upper right corner with the value of the card in braille.

Helen's bedroom was situated near evergreens, and they built a balcony so Helen could walk into nature whenever she wanted. The trees came too close to the railing so she could lean over and feel the rhythm of rustling branches in the breeze. A wisteria clung to the rail on one end of the balcony with an apple tree in the garden below on the opposite side.

Helen was standing near the wisteria one May morning when a rhythmic vibration stirred beneath her hands, repeating again and again. Similar to when she would put her fingers on a singer's throat to feel a song, the pulsations stopped, and Helen felt a wisteria blossom tick against her cheek. She assumed it was a breeze or a bird swaying on the vine. The sound started again, an odd unfamiliar beat, and the young woman wondered what her ornithologist friend Bradford Torrey would think of it.

Helen remained still. Annie heard the sound and put her hand through the window and touched Helen ever so gently, like a whisper, so that she knew not to utter a sound. Annie spelled gently into her hand, "It's a whippoorwill. He is on the corner post so close to you that you could touch him, but you must not . . . or he will fly away" (Keller, 1929).

Helen now recognized the repeating song. "Whip-poor-will! Whip-poor-will! Whip-poor-will!" She followed the intonations, "Whip-poor-will! Whip-poor-will! Whip-poor-will!" The emotional song came joyously to her touch, and she sensed the tones grow louder and louder . . . faster and faster.

Annie tapped Helen's hand again, as if whispering, and spelled, "His lady-love is answering him from the apple tree. She's been there all along, hiding. They are singing a duet now." When the trill vibration stopped, Annie spelled, "They are both in the apple tree now" (Keller, 1929).

Annie seemed to have everything tied up nicely at Wrentham. Helen had never assimilated in a regular community. She needed someone to cut meat and tough food for her, but ironically, everyone on the Wrentham farm was dependent upon Helen's circumstances. Helen remained dependent upon philanthropy even as she resisted it. She challenged the very philanthropists who organized and maintained her educational trusts and financial security. Helen argued the notion of employers, offering employees insufficient wages to meet their needs, who then give money to charities. Helen asked how these people could be considered to be philanthropists who seek to promote the welfare of people in need while they create austere conditions for their workers that undermine welfare for entire families.

Despite so much support, Helen never appeared to be rich, and nobody wanted her to experience poverty. Ironically, Helen argued that philanthropists personified essentially inhumane, careless, and thoughtless societies by fostering conditions that ruined ordinary households. With socialist John Macy, already a robust drinker, trying to guide her intellectually, Helen's thinking became more radical. She used the analogy of factory girls with compromised health due to them working in insanitary workrooms. Female workers experienced high rates of tuberculosis because there were less opportunities to do light work outside in the fresh air after an illness before returning to regular work assignments. Helen felt a society *blind* to destructive economics led families to ruin so they were required to ask for mercy and charity, and then philanthropists would offer relief with a generous hand.

The distance between Wrentham and Feeding Hills, Massachusetts, was only about ninety miles, but the emotional space between Annie

Sullivan's birthplace and her current home was a world away. Annie may have been radical in some ways, but she was essentially far more conservative than John Macy due to having lived with "want" in her formative years. Abandoned by her family and taken to an almshouse had caused a lifetime of low self-esteem in Annie, who kept her own counsel, so even Helen and those closest to her did not truly know her.

Helen, Annie, and John would discuss controversial topics. Annie spelled out opinions to Helen without reserve. She was no suffragist like Helen or her mother Kate Keller, so the more they talked, the less they thought alike. Annie was pessimistic about human progress. John introduced Helen to his radical rhetoric through literature when Annie took a more earthy approach to life. As he courted Annie, he understood he was tethering himself to a cyclone. Friends and associates observed the three wildly different personalities involved in this unusual love triangle and wondered about its stability from the start.

John recognized the romanticism in Helen. He utilized the British writer Charles Dickens, who had chronicled Laura Bridgman's life, as a Romantic. John sought to persuade Helen of his socialist points in logic couched in Romantic literature. He finger-spelled, "Romanticists select from the more universal circumstances of actual life to offer dramatic revelation as we do not meet with in ordinary times and places" (Macy, 1913a). John delineated, "Dickens found extraordinary romance in ordinary romance in ordinary London streets, which he knew with journalistic realism to the last brick and cobblestone."

John saw how Helen responded, and he finger-spelled quicker, "Dickens's imagination penetrated life, real or unreal, familiar or remote, and found it rich with plot and subplot."

Helen's mother Kate Keller discovered her guardian Annie because Dickens had written in a travelogue about Dr. Samuel Gridley Howe's teaching methods with Laura Bridgman. John communicated, "Because Dickens loved human beings and understood their everyday sorrow and happiness, and he wrought into the fabric of his plots real people, *like a realist*."

Annie chimed in to get John riled up, "I can't stand how of these people are describing Helen."

John treated Helen like a little sister. "Individual vitality is what makes a good book."

Helen appeared to gaze downward. "Everybody knows the story of my life, nobody wants to read more about my life."

John wanted her to see his point of view. "You love Shakespeare and Shakespeare is the greatest biographer of all."

John Macy's exact motives for courting Annie Sullivan remained opaque. If he continued to help Helen, he could win Annie's love. Annie listened intently. Annie's secrets would be used against her if they were known. John watched Annie as he spoke to Helen, "Great books and great men, have common qualities, they are memorable for their *difference* from other books and men."

John liked being Annie and Helen's protector, and he benefited from their status. John said, "Helen, a book that is worth reading is worth reading carefully."

Helen's essays were effective, but John condescendingly felt they did not reflect a depth of thinking resulting from extensive reading, "Most written philosophy today is in the form of essays." John continued, "It is always better to be a student of literature than a mere reader."

John was ambitious. Helen was no mere reader; she was an *authentic* college-educated woman who had read with depth ever since she welcomed Cedric from Burnett's *Little Lord Fauntleroy* into her consciousness as a child. However, in this moment, John thought suddenly of the Carlyle quote, "A well-written life is almost as rare as a well spent one." He wondered who he was in Helen and Annie's story: a hanger-on or a director. John's fingers murmured into Helen's hand, "Let us be readers of literature, and then the study of literature will take care of itself" (Macy, 1913a).

Helen was evangelical in her communicating; she was direct in her rhetoric, but resisted writing autobiographical material. John drew from one of Helen's favorite writers Ralph Waldo Emerson to encourage her to explore essay writing. "Emerson's philosophy comes to us through his essays like sermons." He contrasted Oliver Wendell Holmes, Sr, with Emerson, "Holmes, your Poet, is a true essayist who discourses on *things in general*." Helen leaned into his hands. John continued, "He snatched philosophy from the library, and brought it to the breakfast table so that the poorest boarder goes to his day's work from the company of an immortal who has met him halfway" (Macy, 1913b).

Annie, who encouraged Helen through motherly nagging, nodded, happy; she was happy to have John take on this role. He concluded, "And talked to his audience without condescension." John seemed to be headed for a crescendo when he said, "All literature consists of the written opinions and ideas, the knowledge and experience of individuals." He concluded, "Helen, literature is this chorus of human voices."

Helen faced John and uttered honestly, "My voice is too weak."

John took her hands in his and lifted them to his face. "Helen, the individuality of the creative artist is lost in the magnitude of the work." Then he added, "In an essay a person addresses us with direct communication from *me* to *you*" (Macy, 1913a). The young woman seemed ready to protest, so he continued, "Helen, the great writers themselves are the best guides for one another … the poet must study the poets and the novelist must study the novelists." John added, "You already have a following. Imagine the influence you could have for good. Novels are shot through and through with economics."

John wanted Helen and Annie to follow his lead. John was a wordsmith in the household, but he sometimes felt like a third wheel. John suddenly changed tactics and sarcastically remarked, "The one great advantage of college is that it allows you four years of comparative leisure, of freedom from the day's work of a breadwinner, and a good library, so you can read for yourself."

Helen nodded. She wanted her words to mean something. John understood Helen's hesitation and simply concluded, "The great writers are wanderers, not tourists" (Macy, 1913a).

*   *   *

The writing was on the wall. Helen and Annie took a break and visited Alexander Graham Bell and his wife, Mabel, at their home on Cape Breton Island, Nova Scotia. Helen was tasked with holding the guiding ropes for the kite that was a flying contraption for humans that Bell felt was safer than a biplane. Helen felt the powerful tug of the flying contraption that was similar to something Thomas Stringer would think up. She commented, "Mr. Bell has nothing but kites and flying machines on his tongue's end. Poor dear man, how I wish he would stop wearing himself out in this unprofitable way" (Lash, 1980).

When Helen's cousin Edward Everett Hale had visited Bell's home in Washington, D.C., a few years before, he was *astounded* at the inventor's wealth. However, the inventor was also a dreamer who spent a lot of time exploring his imagination, like Helen. Bell fundamentally believed disabled people should be able to experience the full range of human emotions. He offered his young protégé Helen advice when she was alone.

One evening, with a breeze gently coming off the Bras D'Or Lake, Bell and Helen were seated alone in the wicker chairs on the porch outside the drawing room in the streaming moonlight (Gray, 2006). Her earliest supporter surprised Helen with a serious talk. "Helen, I have never been the master of my fate." Bell remembered, "When I was a young man, I loved music and wanted to become a musician, but fate willed otherwise. Ill health brought me to America."

Helen paused, curious, as he finger-spelled into her hand, "There is a tide in the affairs of men . . . the more that I look at the world, the more it puzzles me . . . we are forever moving towards the unexpected." This idea perplexed the young woman; he read her face and pointedly finger-spelled, "Helen, when Annie marries, will you heed my advice and build your own nest?" He mused about something for a moment, then suddenly said, "There are unique tasks waiting for you, a unique woman . . . The more you accomplish, the more you will help the deaf everywhere" (Gray, 2006).

Helen shifted in her chair, uncomfortable, not knowing if she was talking about her as a woman or as an icon for the disabled. He spelled into Helen's hand, "It seems to me, Helen, a day will come when love, which is more than friendship, will knock at the door of your heart and demand to be let in" (Gray, 2006).

Helen responded, "What made you think of that?"

Bell bluntly stated, "I often think of your future. To me you are a sweet, desirable young girl, and it is natural to think about love and happiness when we are young."

Helen reflected, "I do think of love sometimes, but it is like a beautiful flower which I may not touch, but whose fragrance makes the garden a place of delight just the same" (Gray, 2006). She clarified, "I cannot imagine a man wanting to marry me, I should think it would seem like marrying a statue."

Helen's mother, Kate Keller, along with Annie, resisted her dating college boys. Bell, who grew up with a deaf mother, stated, "You are young, and it is natural that you shouldn't take what I have said seriously now: but I have long wanted to tell you how I felt about your marrying, should you ever wish to. If a *good* man should desire to make you his wife, don't let anyone persuade you to forego that happiness because of your peculiar handicap" (Gray, 2006). Her advisor continued, "You have learned to speak, and I believe you are meant to break down barriers which separate the deaf from mankind. There are many tasks awaiting you."

Helen had already sensed the growing closeness between Annie and John, but in her heart, she saw them all as dear friends. Deeply sentimental like as John Macy rightly percieved, Helen found the platonic notion of romance in the excitement of ideas. "No, I feel less inclined to embark on that great adventure. I feel that a man and a woman must be equal in weathering the *vicissitudes* of life." Helen had already embarked on the great adventure as an icon of courage.

*   *   *

Helen hoped to create awareness for the challenges facing the Blind and Deaf. She, Annie, and John traveled to St. Louis to attend the Louisiana Purchase Exposition since October 18, 1904, was proclaimed Helen Keller Day (Lash, 1980). David Rowland Francis, a Woodrow Wilson Democrat, served as the president of the St. Louis World's Fair, where visitors explored modern consumer goods and popular culture. Filipinos, who had mounted an exhibit, when told of Helen's disabilities, demonstrated reverence and deference as if she were a saint, because of her glowing smiling face in ongoing adversity.

In St. Louis, crowds jammed Congress Hall to see and hear Helen Keller, with some spectators being stopped from climbing stepladders to enter through windows. Francis offered to read her address, but she had not brought a copy with her. Francis said, "Well, I understand you perfectly, so I will repeat everything you say" (Lash, 1980).

Helen inelegantly pushed her way to the podium and spoke slowly. Twin deaf boys hoisted onto a table played violins. Helen articulated, and Francis kept his hand on her arm to signal when to start and stop. After several sentences, Helen felt from the crowd that the event was going well, and when they were done, she received a rousing ovation as many in the room sobbed with emotion.

Helen was generally a private woman, so she was not prepared for the excitement at her being an international celebrity. A crowd gathered outside wanting to come in, and security guards lost control of the mob, separating Helen and Annie from their escorts. Crowds thronged Helen and tore at her clothes. Some grabbed roses that Helen carried and snatched the hat from her head as a souvenir. Francis called the guards to disperse the crowds, and six soldiers were dispatched to escort Helen and Annie through the rest of the exposition.

Meanwhile, Edward Everett Hale had organized a peace conference back in Boston (Day, 2013). Helen's cousin promoted the idea of establishing an international court of arbitration to settle disputes between countries. Hale's wife, Emily Baldwin Perkins Hale, weakened by bearing nine children remained in the private sector, while his mistress Harriet "Hattie" Freeman was a woman of independent means with a career in studying botany and science. Promoting peace movements was something that Helen and Hale shared in different ways.

Despite her modest preferences, John Macy radicalized Helen to move away from her cousin's influence from the past century. Helen was not yet aware of how she might become an activist. American sociologist Robert Hunter's *Poverty* (1904) estimated that there were at least ten million "underfed, under clothed, and poorly housed" in America. Of these, four million were public paupers who were dependent upon public or private charity for survival. Hunter's politics were shaped by witnessing the grinding poverty during the deep economic depression that had started in 1893 when Helen's father Captain Arthur Henley Keller fell so deeply into debt. Hunter came from an affluent family and worked with female social reformers including Jane Addams. He married Caroline M. Stokes Phelps, the daughter of wealthy banker Anson Phelps Stokes in 1903, and both joined the Socialist Party of America. A year later, his book *Poverty* was published.

The goal of the Socialist Party was to promote discussion of socialist ideals in colleges and universities; it elected western realist writer Jack London as its first president writer and muckraking writer Upton Sinclair as vice president. When Helen read Hunter's work, she found it derogatory to the disabled, but she adapted some of his rhetoric prescribing society's duties related to the poor to be applied to the Blind. After Massachusetts recognized the importance of providing "home education" for Blind adults in 1904, Helen researched issues of the Blind and hoped someone would create a central clearinghouse for information on the Blind because so much money was wasted in unorganized efforts.

Helen and Annie believed charity created paupers. Like Reverend Hale, Helen felt creating ongoing educational opportunities was more important than philanthropy to train the Blind to work and be self-sufficient. Helen asserted, "Never did my heart ache more than when I thought I was not fit to be a useful member of society" (Lash, 1980). Helen refined her earlier accusations about Perkins Institute for the Blind when she challenged the practicality and retention of some programs for the Blind. She felt the Blind attended schools where they lived in nice surroundings and enjoyed good music and the company of cultivated people only to return to poverty with no plan for self-support. The Blind wanted programs that made economic sense and allowed them to contribute as citizens and not as dependents. The Blind felt no greater anguish than to feel helpless, according to Helen, when "every avenue to activity and usefulness closed to them" (Keller, 2000).

Attitudes changed with economic booms and busts. The Progressive Era spanning the 1890s–1920s offered widespread social activism informed by social science throughout the United States, but it was dominated by white male scientists, and therefore, contradictory. Helen found herself caught in crosscurrents of thoughts when offered a statistic from an unnamed source asserted that less than 8 percent of the Blind in the United States who attended schools for the Blind were trained to be self-sufficient. On February 15, 1905, Helen wrote a letter to Mrs. Elliot Foster, who was secretary of the Board of Education of the Blind in Hartford, Connecticut. She suggested to Foster not to classify the Connecticut Institute for the Blind as a charitable institution or asylum. Helen wanted it to be labeled as educational because using the word "asylum" was associated with the idea of dependency. Helen argued that while it cost more to educate the Blind, it was no more expensive than the cost of educating a student in a public or vocational school. Helen cited Massachusetts and New York states as examples where public education of the Blind was essential to public school systems.

The fragile routine of Helen's home in Wrentham was challenged as correspondence flooded in when people contacted Helen in the absence of agencies for help with blind friends and family. Chores still had to be completed: making the beds, starting and stopping the windmill for power and water, cooking meals, cleaning. There was no pomp or circumstance. Annie drove John to the train station for his commute to Boston every morning and then did grocery shopping. Helen cleared the table and washed the dishes and tidied rooms, because they had not employed any servant.

Annie increasingly saw marriage to John Macy as her backup plan in the event something happened to her. John went to Helen to get her consent before announcing their tentative plans to marry. Helen approved of having her private secretary in the household in a more formal way. Alexander Graham Bell was right to alert Helen that she needed to think about a changing family dynamic.

Wrentham fostered a small social and intellectual community with Helen at the center. John Hitz visited for six weeks every summer, and they visited Hitz whenever they went to Washington, D.C. During the spring of 1905, Hitz was showing Helen and her mother Kate Keller around the capital, and he introduced the three women to Wisconsin senator Robert M. La Follette, Sr, who was known as "Fighting Bob." La Follette was married to a major peace activist Belle Case La Follette, who was one of the most influential American women in American public affairs.

The senator greeted the ladies with some perplexity. John Hitz repeated Helen's name. Surprised to see Helen in the streets, La Follette responded, "Yes, yes, I know. When people meet you, I am sure they always shake hands twice" (Keller, 1929; Lash, 1980).

When La Follette, Sr., walked on, Hitz observed with some reverence, "That's a fighter."

Kate who had a quiet passion for politics said, "Oh?"

Hitz explained that in Washington there were two ways for a politician to cross the aisle: one is to invite him over and the other is to grab him by the collar. Hitz said, "La Follette grabs opponents by the collar."

Annie had no alternative income, and John's salary from the *Youth's Companion* was quickly spent. Kate Keller was known as "Mother Keller" within the household. With Annie's dominant role in her daughter's life, Kate struggled with depression and anxiety related to their prolonged separations. Kate found comfort lurking in a small woodland near the farmhouse where she watched birds when she visited. John, sensing her retreat, introduced Kate to the writings of a noted British wit and Anglican cleric Sydney Smith. He offered advice on how to control suffering from "low spirits," and Kate reported his sayings became a "silent accompaniment to her thoughts" (Keller, 1929).

Annie Sullivan married John Macy in their home on May 2, 1905. It was a simple ceremony; Annie, who always credited Helen's mother Kate Keller with teaching her all she knew about culinary arts, prepared her own wedding cake and refreshments (Lash, 1980). Reverend Hale officiated the wedding service with twenty guests present. He led the vows as Lenore Smith finger-spelled all of the words into Helen's hand. Hale advised Annie and John: "Life begins when you are married—and not until then." Hale ironically called Annie and John's union "the most extraordinary prefabricated triangle in history" (Day, 2013; Lash, 1980).

When Helen consented to the marriage, Annie asked John to sign a rare prenuptial agreement. With the marriage, the household lost half of its income. Eleanor Hutton, the administrator for Helen's trust, assumed under coverture John would support Annie. When news reached her about Annie marrying, the allotment was cut in half. While Annie, no longer having to sustain academic support for Helen, relaxed and read for pleasure, visitors consulted with Helen on issues of the Deaf-Blind, the Blind, and the Deaf. They bombarded Helen with attention while Annie remained in the background. John first made a name for himself as literary critic and associate editor for *Youth's Companion* while living at Wrentham.

*   *   *

With her guardian-promoter married to John Macy, Helen looked for a new path for herself. She hoped to insert herself and her ideas into public addresses and published works, and John encouraged this as a professional editor. Helen wanted to apply social science learned in college and set a goal of starting a national survey of occupations for the blind.

When William Wade started a census tracking the tiny minority group of Deaf-Blind people, he found they were too scattered for effective services (Wade, 1908). Wade attempted a tactic earlier used by Black leaders to capture photographic images of the Deaf-Blind, including some of Helen's friends, in poses showing them riding tandem bikes and working in ordinary occupations so as to introduce readers to an active culture of a hidden Deaf-Blind community.

A Wisconsin-born Deaf-Blind girl named Eva Halliday asked Wade to reach out to Keller. Wade connected the two, and this became a small step toward starting a basic clearinghouse of Deaf-Blind information. Wade also connected Helen with a Deaf-Blind girl in Wisconsin named Annie Johnson who had contracted bovine tuberculosis. This was the same ailment that the fictional character Patsy contracted after drinking bad milk in Kate Douglas Wiggins's *The Story of Patsy*.

Helen responded to Johnson in a letter, saying she hoped they could be pen pals. She described how she passed time. "I thought of you this morning when I took my walk" (Keller, 1929). Helen described how she could not walk much farther from the house than Johnson could from her chair. Annie and John had a "balcony build for me up among the treetops, so I can bask in the sound to my heart's content" (Keller, 1929, 1955). Helen told Johnson she did not have young companions, so she spent most of her time reading, writing, and thinking. She also wrote how when folks visited, she liked to play pinochle with scored tricks; "it is great fun and we go almost wild with excitement over it at times."

Helen was formally recruited when an activist for the disabled, Charles F. F. Campbell, a graduate of the Massachusetts Institute of Technology, visited Helen at Wrentham. He had grown up on the London campus of the Royal Normal College for the Blind (RNC), established in 1872 by his father Sir Francis Campbell, who attended Perkins Institute (Campbell, 1931). After completing his degree, Campbell worked on vocational training programs for the Blind. He invited Helen to join a new organization called the Women's Educational and Industrial Union in Boston to promote the welfare of blind adults. Helen was already a proponent of vocational training for adults who had been blinded later in life so that they could learn new job skills.

Campbell led the development of modern vocational rehabilitation for blind adults that demonstrated the Blind could train for jobs without sight. In 1904, he established an "experiment station" to train and place Blind workers in industry at the Massachusetts Association for the Adult Blind. Campbell launched the field's first professional journal called *Outlook for the Blind* in 1907 (Koestler, 1976). The publication was a free forum discussion of topics connected with work for the Blind. It supported the development of professions and disciplines serving the Blind and their families. Campbell led the Blind People's Higher Education and Improvement Association established in 1895 by graduates of schools for the Blind as a counterpoint to the American Association of Instructors for the Blind (AAIB), which in 1905 was reconstituted as the American Association of Workers for the Blind to help professionalize services for blind adults.

* * *

Michael Anagnos died in 1906 while staying in Greece. The death created an opportunity for Frank B. Sanborn and members of Dr. Samuel Gridley Howe's family to attack Annie (Wagner, 2012). Many felt that any college-educated teacher could have taught Helen. Sanborn cited Thomas Stringer, Elizabeth Robin, and Edith Thomas as Deaf-Blind students at Perkins Institute who had gotten exposure to public school education to foster their assimilation and independence. In a shocking move, John Macy applied for Anagnos's position, although having no qualifications or mentoring as Anagnos received.

Sanborn, ready to defend his friend Anagnos, went through his papers and found evidence Anagnos was aware Helen could not have written "The Frost King." Anagnos had simply refused to distrust his protégé Annie, and he was mortified to discovered the truth. Sanborn reported to the trustees of Perkins Institute what he had found in a lawyer's brief called "Miss Sullivan's Methods."

Annie and John's account of Helen's education in *The Story of My Life* deliberately minimized and concealed the extent of Perkins Institute's role in Helen's education. Sanborn hoped to ease the relationship between Helen and Annie with the Anagnos-Howe family. He wrote to Helen about his findings, but Helen's defensive response revealed the continuing extent of Annie's complete influence over her perceptions.

Massachusetts's Republican Governor Curtis Guild, Jr. appointed Helen to fill Anagnos's former seat on the Massachusetts Commission for the Blind to investigate the conditions of the Blind. Helen's viewpoint on the causes of blindness changed when she discovered many cases of blindness were traced to industrial conditions. However, Helen sensed her boundaries in doing committee work; she could not communicate well without understandable speech.

The commission was made up of three white men and two white women; the commission did experimental work to determine how best to spend $40,000 of public money set aside for educating the Blind. The two women conducted the bulk of the research even though they had no direct voice in deciding how the funds would be appropriated. Helen argued that while taxpayers included women, if women contradicted men who collected money or the legislature, the men would smile and state in a condescending tone, "There you are! You see! Women are utterly inconsistent" (Keller, 1929). If the woman responded with any argument, she was described by the male commissioners as "unladylike."

As she participated in committees, Helen came in contact with special education leaders. Lydia Young Hayes headed the New Jersey Commission for the Blind. Hayes had lost her eyesight when she was eight years old after a bull threw her off. After a chance meeting with Annie Sullivan, Lydia's parents sent her to Perkins Institute. Lydia studied at the Kindergarten Normal School of Boston University before opening a private nursery. Helen visited New Jersey to provide testimony before the state legislature to promote the idea of "a state Commission for the Blind." As a member of the Massachusetts Commission for the Blind, she asked Hayes to be one of the program's two official teachers.

New Jersey Governor John Franklin Fort appointed Hayes to lead New Jersey's state agency for the Blind. Hayes asserted, "Education concerning the Blind should be two-fold: the education of the individual regarding his responsibility to the community and the education of the community to promote understanding of the capabilities of the individual" (Koestler, 1976). New Jersey provided state support and supervision of braille classes in public schools. Hayes worked with others to establish innovative classes where both Blind and sighted children learned side by side.

Helen Keller later corresponded with Hayes's adopted Deaf-Blind daughter named Helen Schultz, who was admitted to a program that Hayes had

---

MARK TWAIN ENTERS THE COURTROOM OF PUBLIC OPINION

Helen Keller's mother, Kate Keller, resisted any notion of Helen being exploited on stage to bring in money into the household. Respectable women did not perform on stage if they were proper young ladies. Mary Thaw started helping Keller and her teacher Anne Sullivan financially during the 1890s. Thaw was drawn into what Mark Twain described as "the most lurid cause celebre of the modern age" (Twain, 2013), when her eldest son Harry Kendall Thaw who was showing signs of mental illness shot a prominent New York City architect Stanford White in front of hundreds of witnesses (Baatz, 2018).

Harry Thaw went against his mother's wishes when he married showgirl Evelyn Nesbit. Nesbit's mother hoped to escape poverty by hiring out her fifteen-and-a-half-year-old daughter "for all of the scoundrels of New York" (Twain, 2013). Nesbit embodied the physical personification of the feminine ideal as a Gibson Girl despite her apparent ignorance and innocence. Twain knew Stanford White casually and concluded the prominent New York architect who designed Madison Square Gardens was "ravenously and remorselessly hunting young girls to their own destruction" (Twain, 2001-2015).

Helen Keller and Evelyn Thaw could not be more different in temperament. Evelyn Thaw's mother, Florence Nesbit, undermined her daughter in support of Stanford White who gave her financial assistance. Under pressure during her husband's two murder trials, Evelyn Thaw testified saving his life. Twain followed the case in the newspapers, debating whether the lurid details of her testimony should be so widely read. Twain called White a seducer who should be "flayed alive in the middle of a public plaza." Evelyn Thaw's testimony was false. She had a son by another man and later changed her story, revealing Harry Thaw to be abusive.

---

started at the Washington Street Public School in Jersey City (Hayes, 1926). Schultz had no private teacher or companion; her schoolmates helped her. She received communication through the manual alphabet from those who knew it and through printing in her palm from those who didn't. She later became proficient in reading braille and typing.

Helen hoped to reinvent herself as a social critic to limit public performances. Helen and Annie invested hours in preparation for every public appearance, and they developed a formulaic presentation. Helen and Annie met the American comedic actor Joseph Jefferson through her friendship with Mark Twain.

Jefferson felt if a performance was mediocre, there was no consolation for the audience. Jefferson told Helen, "For this is the night that the public remembers and the impression that the performer makes, good or bad remains as in the public's mind as such." Jefferson observed, "I have seen impulsive actors who are so confident of their power that they leave everything to chance . . . this is a dangerous course." Jefferson continued, "For myself, I know that I perform best when the heart is warm, and the head is cool" (Jefferson, 1889).

Helen was a natural performer; she displayed enormous charm in front of people, but she wore a mask with her bright smile no matter what was going on in her life. On a train ride from New York to Boston, a vaudeville promoter once offered Annie and Helen $500 a week to perform on his circuit. Jefferson told her, "Acting is more a gift than an art. I have seen a child impress an audience by its natural grace and magnetism. The little creature was too young to know what art meant, but it had the gift of acting."

Jefferson sought to instruct Helen be a more effective *performing artist.* The aging actor thought a minute about how to express what he needed to say in the presence of Annie, who translated what he said into Helen's hands. He continued, "The great value of art when applied to stage is that it enables the performer to reproduce the gift, and so move his audience night after night even though he has performed the part a thousand times" (Jefferson, 1889). Jefferson pointedly looked straight at Annie and concluded, "When you lose interest, stop performing" (Jefferson, 1889).

*   *   *

Helen, Annie, and John visited Mark Twain in January 1907. Remembering Helen when he had first met her, Twain likened her to a lump of clay, an "Adam being," because she appeared to him to be "deaf, dumb, blind, inert, groping, almost insentient" (Twain, 2001–2015). Twain placed Helen on a pedestal erected with his words that she could not climb down from. Twain noted, after two decades of Annie's teaching and a college education, Helen stood alone in history as a "creature who sees without eyes, hears without ears, and speaks with dumb lips." His secretary Miss Isabel Lyon met Helen and noted she was not spoiled, but "the signs of her great affliction are always present, because she is so dependent upon others" (Twain, 2001–2015).

Twain remained amazed by Helen's transformation, and like so many, he gave Annie total credit for it. Sounding like Professor Henry Higgins in *Pygmalion*, Twain bragged, "Helen's talk 'sparkles,' and she gives as good as she gets." When Twain had first met Helen at the age of fourteen, Annie had kept all worldly news from her student, but Twain concluded, "I think she now lives in the world that the rest of us know" (Twain, 2001–2015).

International visitors arrived at Wrentham for advice. Elizabeth Anrep-Nordin who taught the Deaf-Mute-Blind in Skara, Sweden, visited. Anrep-Nordin became indignant when she was not invited for an extended stay, so when she returned to Sweden, she disseminated misinformation, stating Helen offered resources to help all the Deaf-Blind to be educated. Anrep-Nordin created unrealistically high expectations, and the little farm in Wrentham suddenly gained an international reputation as a clearinghouse for information on the Blind.

Helen was inundated with mail related to issues of the Blind and Deaf linked to much larger issues of industry, labor, and economics. She wrote a groundbreaking article for the *Ladies' Home Journal* in 1907 to create awareness of prevention of *opthalmia neonatorum* caused by a mother's exposure to venereal disease (Keller, 1920). Blindness in nearly two-thirds of the blind children entering public schools would have been preventable if they had a cleansing solution applied to their eyes at birth. Helen rallied support to initiate treatments in regular pediatric procedures in hospitals.

Helen's focus shifted from prevention of blindness to special education programs. She felt the Blind had minds that could be educated, hands that could be trained, and had ambitions, and the public could help the Blind to make the best of themselves so they could "win light through work" (Keller, 1920). Before the American birth control movement started in 1914, Helen asked why it was not illegal to bring disabled children into the world to grow up in soul-destroying poverty, but it was criminal for a physician to tell a mother how to protect herself and her family by seeking information about birth control. She also argued blind children needed places where there was plenty of room for play and where they could learn farming and gardening. She asserted, "The blind individual is neither a genius, nor a freak, nor an idiot" (Keller, 2000).

John Hitz, who introduced Helen to the writings of Emanuel Swedenborg during the 1890s, became increasingly weak (Keller, 2000). Helen and her mother, Kate Keller, visited Helen's friend Lenore Smith in Washington, D.C. in 1908, and John Hitz met their train. They had walked a short distance when Hitz collapsed with a heart attack. Lenore summoned an ambulance, and Helen and Kate followed him in a carriage, but he died on the way to the hospital. Helen was able to say goodbye to her friend, passing her hand over his face and kissing him.

John Macy regularly spent his work week in Boston where he was an editor at *Youth's Companion,* and he slept over at the Boston men's club called St. Botolph's Club located on Newbury Street (Lash, 1980). His lifestyle did not come cheap. Another financial supporter Henry H. Rogers passed away in September. Rogers and friends had set up Helen's monthly annuity so she received one hundred dollars a month, and when Annie and John married, the amount was cut into half to fifty dollars. When Helen died, the principal for this annuity would not go to Annie or John; it would go to a charity chosen by Rogers.

Seemingly oblivious to schemes unfolding beneath her nose, Helen got her hands on every book Robert Hunter wrote. Poverty was a complex subject in books, which rarely addressed people of color, women, and dependents. In his book called *Socialists at Work* (1908), Hunter described socialists as missionaries ministering to tired workmen. He argued that Abraham Lincoln's rhetoric demonstrated the character of the socialist movement. Lincoln frankly discussed important matters with thorough and painstaking thinking and clear and forceful repetition of ideas with logic. Helen argued as "Americans remained unconcerned, it was *blindness*, a disregard for the causes of poverty, to believe that is charity merciful" (Keller, 2009).

Hunter observed how luxury of the Gilded Age could only be enjoyed by the ignorant. Only the cruelest of men could sit at a feast unless blindfolded while those around him was going hungry. Helen believed capitalism fostered poverty and disability. She applied Hunter's logic in her rhetoric; Helen did not view pauperism as an economic issue; pauperism was a moral issue. Like her cousin Edward Everett Hale, Helen did not support relief assistance because it destroyed self-respect.

Wrentham required continual maintenance. Annie, Helen, and John often left work unattended to attend meetings and social functions. They tried unsuccessfully to renovate the farm: deer devoured their apple trees they planted, they purchased horses that were not trainable and insane, and their chickens always died. They took in feral pets. As urbanites, they resisted allowing more people into their little circle who could offer practical guidance.

Helen enjoyed the "hermit life" that Wrentham countryside offered despite interruptions and distractions. John Macy enjoyed the bohemian life in Boston, but he accumulated debts. He could escape his increasingly bossy and moody wife Annie, who behaved like his second mother. John negotiated writing deals for Helen and worked as her editor, so he felt entitled to a share of her income without consulting with Annie.

While Helen was diverted by growing tensions at Wrentham, a Harvard-educated Blind activist named Robert I. Irwin, who was Harvard educated, took charge of teaching the Blind (Koestler, 1976). Irwin independently navigated public transportation during his daily commute before it was accessible to the Blind. He successfully secured state financing to hire special education teachers at higher salaries to teach the Blind in public schools in Cleveland, Ohio. Irwin and a few other blind educators worked on the premise: "If you wish to train the Blind to compete with the sighted, you must provide the blind children with at least as good teachers as you provide seeing children" (Campbell, 1931).

* * *

In her dream that was Wrentham, Helen considered Edward Everett Hale to be "the living embodiment of whatever was heroic in the founders of

Mark Twain and His Institutionalized Daughter

Mark Twain's youngest daughter Jean Clemens (1880–1909) was a day older than Helen Keller. Jean Clemens was educated at home until she was sixteen years old before attending school in Elmira, New York, where she started experiencing epileptic seizures. Twain and his wife Olivia "Livy" Clemens searched for treatments for several years, even taking Jean to Sweden to receive the Kellgren treatment for seizures.

Jean dressed in white as did her father, Mark Twain. She was tall, fair-skinned, and considered to be a classic beauty. Jean enjoyed quiet family retreats in the woods where she passed the time in her favorite pursuit of wood-carving. She learned how to type in 1899, so she could transcribe her father's manuscripts. Family employees manufactured stories about Jean's outbursts, leading Twain to admit her to an institution in Katonah, New York, in 1906. Once institutionalized, Jean became entirely dependent upon caregivers.

Twain testified before Congress with Edward Everett Hale in March of 1908 on the topic of copyright legislation, hoping his writing could offer an income for his surviving daughters when he died (Twain, 2001–2015). Helen remembered Twain's deep sadness when she and Annie last visited him. Jean visited home in Stormfield, in Redding, Connecticut, in late 1909 because she had not had an attack in months. Twain remembered, "She had been shut up in sanatoriums, many miles from us. How eloquently glad and grateful she was to cross her father's threshold again!" Jean died on Christmas Eve after a seizure by drowning in her bath. Twain died only four months later.

New England." Helen's joie de vivre garnered Hale's genuine affection. Helen, her mother Kate, and Annie had entered Hale's life in May 1888 after his secret lover Hattie Freeman gave Annie the thirty-dollar train fare to Alabama. Hale wrote to his lover, describing his cousin Kate Keller as a "pleasing person, glowing with happiness, as indeed she may be, in the presence of a constant miracle." Hale dismissed Kate and her substantive role as Helen's biological mother, as Annie eclipsed her in her daughter's life before *The Story of My Life* wrote Kate out of Helen's narrative.

When Alexander Graham Bell sent Hale a check for a thousand dollars to start an education fund for Helen, it became the catalyst for an annuity binding Helen to her guardian for life (Day, 2013). His liberal Unitarian beliefs along with this of Bishop Phillips Brooks framed Helen's belief systems. Hale's paradoxes and literary themes of alter egos and double lives reflecting his age became embedded in Helen's character. Hale could be extremely tolerant and sometimes blind to the weaknesses of others, yet he was bound by societal conventions.

When *The Story of My Life* was published, Hale described Helen's extraordinary sensory and mental abilities. The book, and Hale's initial assessment of Helen, reinforced her emotional dependence upon her teacher. Annie was described as a miracle worker, but few questioned how this dependence might limit Helen's potential. Hale who had officiated at Annie and John's wedding perhaps knew it would not last. Hale maintained societal norms, as Freeman brought youth, energy, and optimism into his life.

The idea for the poem Helen dedicated to her cousin posthumously came to her while she and John were building up old stone walls in one of their fields. As Hale's health deteriorated, Helen imagined the men who had built the walls long ago. She touched the stones in the walls they had mended to hear their stories. "We are the dust of continents past and to come..."

John and Helen rambled or drove through the country roads, and they would sit under the Great Oak at the edge of Lake Wollomonapoag. Helen felt the stonewalls around Wrentham were like New England tapestries of stone, alive with memories from ancestors. She wove themes with ideas from philosophers she had studied and knew from rambles and from books she loved. The project was illustrated with photographs of Helen simply dressed during her explorations of the landscape. Helen submitted a poem containing local history, called *Song of the Stone Wall*, to Century Company in 1909, and earned $300, worth about $8,600 in 2021.

The *Song of the Stone Wall* was rich in sentiment but demonstrated that Helen was oblivious to conflicts among "ancestors" in history and the undercurrents within relationships in her current life. Helen remained in the dark as Anne's marriage to John Macy started falling apart. Hale died shortly before Helen's twenty-ninth birthday. She remained innocent in her opinion of her cousin when she wrote, "Though a herald and proclaimer of peace, he could fight stubbornly and passionately on the side of justice." John perceptively asserted, "The trouble with the generation that is now happily passing is that it did little else than strive for individual fortune" (Macy, 1916).

Helen credited conversations with psychologist Josef Jastrow, conversations sprinkled with humor, as her inspiration to write her second book, *The World I Live In* (1909). The project started as a series of essays in *Century* magazine to demonstrate how Helen used her senses of touch, taste, and smell to understand her environment. She raised the consciousness of readers regarding unrecognized and underdeveloped senses. Helen pointed out how people commonly neglect to develop all of their senses. "Touch brings the Blind many sweet certainties which our more fortunate fellows miss, because their sense of touch is uncultivated. When they look at things, they put their hands in their pockets."

8

What Is in a Name?

Helen Keller appeared to be more of an institution than a woman; more an icon than a human being. In her Deaf-Blind information clearinghouse in Wrentham, Helen was the president, but her guardian-promoter Annie Sullivan Macy was chairwoman, vice president, secretary, treasurer, and janitor. Helen was traditional in thinking the woman's sphere is the home, but she believed the home was also the sphere of men. An educated woman should examine the social basis of her life and the impact of her actions upon children, employers, employees, beggars at the door, as well as legislators in Washington. To learn social cause and effect, women needed to self-educate and to educate one another.

Helen rhetorically asked where home is found, why its boundaries were layed, what functions does it contain, and how it could be secured and protected. She argued under coverture, the legal doctrine where a husband covered his wife and controlled household finances and contracts, the female's old "domestic sphere was now an empty shell with its contents removed . . ." (Einhorn, 1998). She envisioned it as a fragile shell where women were no longer safe because of modernity. A woman could be poisoned, starved, and robbed in her shell of a home. The cause of these emerging dangers, Helen argued, lay in how a woman could not "own and direct her own share of the national household" (Einhorn, 1998).

Helen's "shell" was perhaps the best home Annie knew, but the shell was cracking under pressure in the domestic sphere. Annie's husband John

Macy, a beneficiary of the women's work in the household, was the first proponent of this socialist approach, followed by Helen, and then conservative Annie came around. Despite their unconventional approach to housekeeping, the female workers wound up supporting the male intellectual. As her own home faced economic fluctuations, Helen ultimately believed poverty resulted from bad economic practices. She asserted, "The industrial system under which we live is at the root of much of the physical deafness and blindness in the world . . ."

Helen aspired to recreate an operating farm in Wrentham, Massachusetts, like the one her parents had in Tuscumbia, Alabama. She craved functional simplicity in her life. Helen wanted a home among trees, crops, and animals, but the city dwellers did not know how to manage country life. Her Boston bull terrier Phiz, a gift from Radcliffe College classmates, died within a year. Neighbors gave Helen and Annie tame Rhode Island Red chickens, but they became fat from overfeeding. Helen's mother Kate Keller, who managed a chicken farm and manufactured lard, once quipped to Annie, "Of course lard-making doesn't have the charm of sculpture, architecture, or poetry, but I suppose it has its importance in the universal scheme of things."

The power dynamic in this utopian household was not sustainable. The principals involved did not communicate or share vulnerability or intimacy expected in a family. Helen's sentimentality toward her guardian-promoter and John collided with her actual life as an activist. While Annie and John were married, Annie remained Helen's guardian, compelling his to take on a role of dependent. However, it was Helen's good name that brought financial resources into the household.

While Annie was no longer the spirited woman John wooed, he radicalized Helen. John's far more conservative wife Annie, who was visually impaired, doubted a blind individual could achieve a full life. In her mid-forties, Annie had grown stout and moody with her increasingly absentee husband. Increasingly ailing and exhausted from maintaining a household and caretaking duties for Helen, Annie did not have funds to employ help. Helen became less of Annie's student and more of John's puppet.

To articulate on behalf of socialism and give voice on important issues to legislatures, medical associations, and conventions, Helen needed a speaking voice. In 1909, a singing instructor at the Boston Conservatory of Music, Charles W. White, volunteered to coach Helen's in better using her voice. White learned the manual alphabet, and he visited Wrentham every weekend. White coached Helen on breathing methods to strengthen her diaphragm. He discovered Annie's coaching had not strengthened Helen's diaphragm (its contraction increases the volume of the thorax to inflate the lungs that strengthen the volume of the human voice) and may have harmed her speaking voice.

John introduced Helen to a French verismo dramatist named Eugène Brieux, who promoted naturalism in his work about societal ills of the day. Brieux came from humble roots and admired Helen for her 1907 article in *Ladies' Home Journal* discussing venereal disease as a preventable cause of infant blindness. His *Les Avariés*, or *Damaged Lives* (1901) in English, was banned due to its graphic medical portrayal of characters with the venereal disease syphilis. When Helen read Brieux's lips, the connection made him emotional and his tears dropped to her hand. He told Helen, "According to the critics we are not artists, and should be cast out because art has nothing to do with social or political reform. It is an expression of beauty for beauty's sake." Brieux was a reformer. Helen nodded in agreement as he stated, "All things are beautiful to me if they are a real part of human life." He concluded, "Sad, terrible things must also be shown. To realize ugliness, is to suffer and to long for beauty" (Keller, 1929).

Helen was grateful his work had opened her eyes to those challenges in her work for the Blind. After her thirtieth birthday, Helen wrote, "I leave behind thoughts that once looked like reason." She felt her new thinking served her better, like "the rushing, swirling and sometimes inclement atmosphere of the world . . ." Even though her hands could not perceive colors in a sunset, or see depths of the sky, she associated every object in her mind with tactual qualities. Helen combined these bits of information in countless ways that gave her a sense of power, beauty, and incongruity, "For with my hands I can feel the comic as well as the beautiful in the outward appearance of things." She concluded, "It is not physical blindness, but social blindness which cheats our hands of their right to toil" (Keller, 1967).

Many could not imagine how Helen lived without sight and sound. She wrote, "My world is built of touch-sensations, devoid of color and sound" (Keller, 1905, 1929). She paused, "But even without color and sound it breathes and throbs with life." Socialism became a vector lifting Helen into a broader sphere of thought and action. When Brieux returned to France, he wrote to Helen telling her that he was taking an active role in the rehabilitation of blind soldiers.

Helen Keller was real. She stayed on her path to her ideal self like Shaw's Eliza Doolittle in *Pygmalion*, but Annie and John Macy still conspired to make her brand fit their agendas. To improve her appearance, Helen had her natural eyes surgically removed and replaced with glass eyes in 1910. Her new eyes were so realistic nobody could tell they were not natural. While painter Albert H. Munsell could manipulate light in his painted portrait of Helen to de-emphasize her protruding eye, photographs caught everything, so she no longer needed to avert her gaze before cameras.

Helen was an attractive woman. She appreciated beauty through abstraction and through touch. Beauty, Helen argued, is found in

John Macy's Pygmalion

Many speculated whether John Albert Macy or Anne Sullivan Macy was Helen Keller's puppet master. Keller once commented about her detractors, "Let them remember, though, that if I cannot see the fire at the end of their cigarettes, neither can they thread a needle in the dark" (Nielsen, 2004). Keller's speech was a parrot-like squawk similar to the character of Eliza in George Bernard Shaw's play *Pygmalion* (1912). Shaw framed his socialist writing within naturalism or verismo. Helen attended *Pygmalion* in Chicago, Illinois, believing Shaw might "know the password to the silent dark" (Lash, 1980).

Shaw introduced realism to English-language drama to disseminate social and political ideas. Shaw became interested in Alexander Graham Bell's father, who married a deaf woman named Eliza Grace Symonds. Alexander Melville Bell taught physiological phonetics and elocution and developed visible speech to help deaf to learn to speak.

Pygmalion introduced audiences to an important verismo movement theme of recording the endangered local dialects of common people. Shaw mentioned Alexander Melville Bell in his preface to *Pygmalion* and was inspired by Bell and Symonds for his characters of Professor Henry Higgins and Liza. Shaw explored eugenics and class distinction connected to speech communications and language to define what it is to be human.

When Keller and Anne Sullivan Macy traveled in England in 1932, American-born Lady Nancy Astor, who was the first female member of the British Parliament, introduced Keller and Sullivan Macy to Shaw. Keller was thrilled to meet Shaw, who was very cynical during their meeting. Astor, uncomfortable during an awkward silence, stated, "You know, Mr. Shaw, Miss Keller is deaf and blind." The stillness in the room was palatable. Finally, Macy finger-spelled Shaw's response to Astor, "Why, of course, all Americans are deaf and blind" (Lash, 1980)!

experiencing spatial, rhythmic combinations. The Deaf-Blind derive design from the flow of curved and straight lines that are surfaces over all things. Unable to comprehend the authenticity of her experiences, some asked Helen, "What does the straight line mean to you?"

Helen became defensive while explaining how much in life is real or tangible to the Deaf-Blind. She stated, "All palpable things are mobile or rigid, solid or liquid, big or small, warm or cold, and these qualities are variously modified" (Keller, 1955). Helen observed, "The coolness of a water-lily rounding into bloom is different from the coolness of an evening wind in summer, and different again from the coolness of the rain that soaks into the hearts of growing things and gives them life and body." She paused before concluding her definition of a straight line, "It *means* several things. It symbolizes duty. It seems to have the quality of inexorableness that duty has" (Keller, 1955).

Her relationships with philosophers equipped Helen to offer new logic related to the Deaf-Blind community. Helen's metaphorical answer did not relate to the physical; it was represented as a mental characteristic. "When I have something to do that must not be set aside, I feel as if I were going forward in a straight line, bound to arrive somewhere, or go on forever without swerving to the right or to the left." Perhaps the more significant question for her was, "How does the straight-line feel" (Keller, 1905)?

Helen thought for a moment. She came up against straight lines in thinking or resistance to her ideas. She responded, "It feels, as I suppose it looks, straight—a dull thought drawn out endlessly" (Keller, 1905). Moving against the tide of seeing and hearing humanity, Helen understood that lines are seldom straight, and many straight and curved lines come together to become eloquent to the touch. She continued, "They appear and disappear, are now deep, now shallow, now broken off or lengthened or swelling." Helen described how these lines rise and sink beneath a finger's touch. The lines seem to be full of sudden starts and pauses; "their variety is inexhaustible and wonderful" (Keller, 1905).

Helen invited people to participate in her reasoning and to refute her arguments. Like Julia Brace and Laura Bridgman, she used silences to compel people to reflect upon their own actions or to deny experiences common to all human beings. Helen frustrated her family and friends and family with frankness. Smell was a practical sense. "Those I love come and go, and by their odor I know they are near. The odors which cling to their clothes tell me that they have been in the garden and the woods" (Keller, 1929). Her ability to graphically communicate scent added to an arsenal of rhetoric for conveying poverty. Helen argued, "I am surprised that smell or any other sense should be scorned just because sometimes it takes cognizance of disagreeable objects" (Keller, 1929).

Helen wrote to her friend William Wade in 1910, telling him smell prevented her from losing "the sense of human activity and fellowship." In Helen's world, touch, smell, and vibrations gave her information to give names to abstract details of everyday life (Nielsen, 2004). She could not understand why anyone should be discouraged from using and describing their sense of smell. Helen believed denying words about unpleasant scents was as unreasonable as slighting the eye because it receives "visions of trivial, squalid, or ugly things."

John Macy introduced Helen to the British socialist writer H.G. Wells when she started investigating conditions for the Blind. Wells wrote a political tract called *The Misery of Boots* (1907) condemning ownership of private property in land and production. Wells called upon governments to expropriate private property "not for profit, but for service." Published by the British socialist organization called the Fabian Society, *The Misery of Boots* seemed to be more of a realistic novel than political propaganda. George Bernard Shaw appreciated how Wells produced imaginative writing that introduced the Socialist movement to the masses.

Wells's utopian novel *New Worlds for Old* (1908) advocated that service for the community good was productive and just. He rejected the idea of "revolutionary socialism" promoted by German philosopher Karl Marx as flawed. Wells saw socialism as a religion in nature more than a political movement. After reading the novel, Helen agreed, "With confidence I exchanged my old world for his new one." When Helen read Wells's work and summaries of Marx's philosophy, she awakened to new realities. "It seemed as if I had been asleep and waked to a new world—a world different from the world I had lived in" (Keller, 1967). This depressed her. Helen said, "But little by little my confidence came back and I realized that the wonder is not that conditions are so bad, but that society has advanced so far in spite of them."

Helen tried to apply socialist ideas to her life. She wrote, "It is my nature to fight as soon as I see wrongs to be made right" (Keller, 1955). After Helen read Wells and Marx, she joined the Socialist movement, hoping to write for them. "I made up my mind to do something" (Keller, 1967). Helen reveled in the publicity she received as a socialist, but anger toward her controversial views was projected on to Annie and John.

With her yearly stipend, occasional speaking fees, and royalties from writing, Helen, Annie, and John could not live within their means. Seven years into their marriage, John Macy accumulated $2,000 in debts to maintain his public persona in Boston (Lash, 1980). As one of Helen and Annie's longtime supporters, Mary Thaw still offered them the use of her fully staffed woodland cottage in the Allegheny Mountains near Pittsburgh, Pennsylvania. Annie could retreat there without being responsible for Helen's care or household duties. However, this luxury contradicted Helen's claim, "No money belongs to us that is not earned."

John Macy offered few resources to the household as he focused his energy on building his own career as a literary critic. He read and offered feedback on what Helen wrote, but when it came to his career, he did not reciprocate by asking for her opinions. When he worked on his book *The Spirit of American Literature* (1912), he did not share it with Helen. The book made his name as a modern American literary critic, but Helen wrote to her mother, Kate Keller, "He finished his books on American literature; it must be a fine book from what I have heard of it" (Keller, 2005).

John read William James's works to Helen as soon as they were published. Helen gave James a copy of her book, *The World I live In* (1908). James, like Helen's mother, was deeply upset by *The Story of My Life* where Helen described herself, "before her 'consciousness' was awakened by instruction." The psychologist responded with the same concern as Kate

Keller because the passage suggested Helen fit the contemporary definition for an autistic person or someone labeled as "feeble minded." James
asserted that, other than her wildness as a child, she was normal in the
process of living. Helen respected James's thinking; he made her aware of
the weakness of being so fixed in her views. "He was not a mystic—his
mind could not thrive on air as mine does" (Keller, 1929). James compli-
mented Helen's literary abilities, asserting, "The sum of it is that you're a
blessing, and I'll kill anyone who says you are not" (Lash, 1980).

John Macy recruited Helen to his cause, believing inter-Socialist conversations were intended to inform. When John applied for membership to
the International Workers of the World (IWW), he was admitted as a
middle-class bohemian. John described himself as a "parasitic journalist,"
so members in a local union welcomed him as a wage earner and not an
employer of labor . . . and as a good communicator (Macy, 1916). John
believed leading socialists attacked the IWW because only wage earners
were admitted and there was no place for middle-class politicians and lawyers. With his views on politics public, John was denied membership in the
Harvard Club of New York, and the Justice Department watched him.

In Lawrence, Massachusetts, an immigrant community was located,
about seventy miles from Wrentham. During the Lawrence Strike of textile workers from January 11 to March 12, 1912, Helen discovered the
IWW strategy was "not only to better conditions, to get them for all people, but to get them at once" (Keller, 2005). Over 25,000 workers mounted
a landmark strike of the American Woolen Company in Lawrence, Massachusetts, in early 1912 after 146 sweatshop workers, mostly underaged
girls, burned in a fire. Mill workers who lived in squalid tenement conditions did not earn living wages. When strikers, including children, began
to starve, the IWW transported them to food centers and were subsequently attacked and arrested.

Helen Keller applied to become a member of the IWW in 1912, sensing
the Socialist Party was moving too slow on her issues. The IWW was a
more radical labor trade union organizing unskilled immigrant laborers to
overthrow capitalism. A silent film called *The Cry of Children* (1912) was
based upon a scenario inspired by an Elizabeth Barrett Browning poem
illustrating the evils of child labor. Helen with her disabilities kept off the
picket lines, so her actions occurred with a typewriter. Helen sent earnings
from her writing (not her trusts) for the legal defense of jailed strikers.

Another strike involving textile workers from Eastern European countries living in tenement conditions in Little Falls, New York, occurred
between October 1912 and January 1913. Helen who had earned $87.50 in
royalties from composing holiday message greetings for Christmas cards
sent it all to John in Little Falls, with a note, "Will you give it to the brave
girls who are striking so courageously to bring about the emancipation of

the workers of Little Falls . . . If they are denied a living wage, I am also defrauded. While there are industrial slaves, I cannot be free" (Lash, 1980).

John traveled to Schenectady, New York, where a Socialist mayor established a board of public welfare, hoping to draw Helen to create awareness of issues related to local poverty. Helen did not fit any category for IWW membership as she was perceived as middle class, but her rhetoric fit. "The true task is to unite and organize all workers on an economic basis, and it is the workers themselves who must secure freedom for themselves, who must grow strong" (Keller, 2005). Helen was open to the post in Schenectady. Once ideas of social justice found in socialism entered her consciousness, they were not dislodged. Helen stated, "I preach love, brotherhood, and peace, but I am conscious of antagonisms, and lo! I find myself brandishing a sword and making ready for battle" (Keller, 2005).

*   *   *

Industrialist Andrew Carnegie and his family invited Helen and Annie to tea. Helen's difficult financial situation had become known to his wife, Louise Whitfield Carnegie, and daughter, Margaret Carnegie, who remembered Helen raising money for Thomas Stringer's education at the kindergarten at Perkins Institute for the Blind. Carnegie had earlier offered Helen an annuity, and she had turned it down because he was a capitalist. He asked his guests, "Margaret is the philanthropist here, she is the good fairy that whispers in my ear that I must make somebody happy" (Keller, 1929).

Helen smiled toward Margaret. Carnegie not one to beat around the bush asked, "Do you still refuse my annuity?"

Helen responded, "Yes, I haven't been beaten yet." She did not think of her writing as work; writing was a tool to communicate her ideas and name brand. Already a successful writer, Helen could not support her desired lifestyle; she was frustrated about her reliance upon philanthropy to sustain her daily needs.

Carnegie looked at Annie, who shuffled in her seat when he stated, "Fate has added my burden to those that you live with, you must think of your loved ones."

The idea she might die before Annie weighed heavily upon Helen's heart since she was a teenager as she feared Annie would be left destitute because her major trust would go to a charity. Helen was responsible for the loved ones she was dependent upon. Margaret saw a change in the countenance of their guests and made a sound to alert her father he was being too blunt. Carnegie cleared his throat. "The annuity is yours when you want it; everything has been arranged."

Carnegie had already developed a pension for William James for his intellectual contributions to the world. The industrialist provided a counterpoint to John Macy's rhetoric when he argued, "Socialism versus Individualism is the race between the hare and the tortoise . . . with the Individualist being the tortoise found upon a path that he has made and making steady progress." Darwin's theories became part of this view. "While wealth and capitalist competition can be hard for the individual, it is the best for the human race because it insures survival of the fittest" (Carnegie, 1908).

Carnegie drew eugenics into his discourse. "The 'survival of the fittest' means exceptional plants, animals, or man possess needed *variations* from common standards which are fructifying or productive forces to leaven the whole" (Carnegie, 1885). The Carnegie Institution and the Rockefeller Foundation fostered the American eugenics movement. Andrew Carnegie's *Triumphant Democracy* (1885) included statistics related to disability for the United States that was 1:2,720 Blind and 1:2,094 Deaf/Mute, whereas in Ireland it was 1:884 Blind and 1:1,340 as well as 56 institutions for the deaf, 30 institutions for the Blind, and 13 schools for the developmentally disabled (Carnegie, 1885, 136–137).

Helen Keller embodied Carnegie's idea of America's strong free government, where an education was every individual's birthright as a means to accomplish the American dream. That collective national ideal asserted all Americans were equal in aspiring to individual goals. Carnegie shifted in his seat and changed his position. "Say, is it true that you have become a Socialist" (Keller, 1929)?

Helen, as a Georgist socialist, believed American political economist Henry George's notion of people owning the value for what they produce themselves. The economic value, in George's view, which was derived from natural resources including land, should belong equally to all members of society (Keller, 1929). George saw a correlation between advancing poverty and advancing wealth: "With the growth of population, land grows in value, and the men who work it must pay more for the privilege" (George, 1879). The paradox of the poor residing in long-established cities being worse off than the poor in less developed regions struck George, who argued wealth is created by social and technological advances in a free-market economy controlled by landowners and monopolists fostering poverty. That private profit was earned from restricting access to natural resources while productive activity was burdened with heavy taxes seemed socially unjust. George argued such a system was equivalent to slavery, or *wage slavery*. Considering this paradigm, Helen responded with an energetic "yes!"

With Helen's affirmation, Carnegie made a playful growl for effect. "I should take you across my knee and spank you if you do not come to your senses" (Keller, 1929).

Not to let him have the last word, Helen stated, "But a great man like you should be consistent . . . you believe in the brotherhood of man, in peace among nations, education for everybody. Those are all Socialist beliefs." Helen told Carnegie that she would send him a copy of *Out of the Dark* where she had explained why she became a Socialist.

The industrialist rolled his eyes, knowing she would; then he changed the subject, "Say, I heard you and Mrs. Macy were on the lecture circuit. What do you lecture about?"

Helen smiled inwardly. "Happiness . . ."

With a guffaw, Carnegie quipped, "Good subject, there's plenty of happiness in the world if folks would only look for it." Then as a practical businessman, he asked, "How much are tickets to your lectures" (Keller, 1929)?

Helen responded, "A dollar and a half."

This agitated Carnegie. "Too much, way too much, you would make more money if you charged fifty cents and no more than seventy-five cents! Why aren't you writing more" (Keller, 1929)?

"Writing is hard," Helen responded. "Editors only want me to write about my own experience." Carnegie was quiet for a moment remembering how "The Frost King" incident of plagiarism had spiraled out of control. He wondered if the literary critic John Macy was erecting his bohemian socialist "air-castles in the sky," while the women in his life dealt with hard money matters. Helen Keller and Mrs. John Macy should not be out on the lecture circuit . . . on display like actresses on the stage . . . it was not respectable. Why did they need more money to manage when they already received multiple trust funds?

Louise Whitfield Carnegie, like other affluent married women of her time, was known to the world only by her husband's name, Mrs. Andrew Carnegie. Miss Helen Keller, despite her guardian's ignorance, always demonstrated integrity. She was an independent thinker who garnered unprecedented name recognition as a writer, and she was only obscured by her disabilities and the guardianship of Mrs. John Macy, who was no longer employed as a teacher but kept as a gatekeeper. Louise had heard many of the stories of Annie standing in the way of supporters who wanted to help Helen, but she remained silent in this conversation to let her husband speak for them both.

"Writing is hard for everyone except for in rare moments of inspiration," Carnegie observed. "Labor must go into anything that's worthwhile" (Keller, 1929).

Annie's eyes narrowed cautiously. Carnegie remembered, "When I was young, fifteen hundred dollars a year, enough to live on and support my parents in their old age, was my idea of wealth" (Keller, 1929). Mrs. John Macy remembered when she had nothing. Carnegie drew her back to the present, when he said, "But Fate gave me so much more than that . . . I see that fickle goddess laughing in her sleeve sometimes."

Helen observed, "Fate's been good to you, in that your dream came true when you were young and full of the joy of life" (Keller, 1929).

"That's right, only sometimes I cannot believe it . . . it's too much." He paused, trying to compose his thoughts. Helen could unnerve the industrialist with the cool moral gaze of her glass eyes. Carnegie added, "I spend my happiest hours these days in the garden."

Helen, in accord with his sentiment, laughed. "You are an optimist" (Keller, 1929).

The industrialist thought of Helen's friend Mark Twain, who had been a skeptic about the Gilded Age when Carnegie accumulated his wealth. "A pessimist has a poison tongue . . . I would banish everyone, had I the power. Good cheer is worth money."

"Ha!" Helen locked him in a *checkmate*. She exclaimed in her squawking voice, "Not very much! Didn't you just tell me my lecture on happiness is worth only fifty cents" (Keller, 1929)?

The conversation was interrupted with the entrance of an associate. Carnegie announced drolly, "This is one of the twelve men I have turned into millionaires" (Keller, 1929). He told Helen and Annie his life became much more interesting and worthwhile once he left the moneymaking to other people. "I would not have had time to talk to you in the old days, but having time to think, I have changed my views on many things."

*   *   *

Shortly after their conversation with Andrew Carnegie and his family, Helen and Annie initiated their first lecture tour in Montclair, New Jersey, in February 1913. Helen's voice halted when she froze under the pressure. Helen and Annie purchased fashionable dresses beyond their budget. Helen and Annie started off on a lucrative and well-attended lecture tour along the East Coast, and audiences responded to Helen's smile. Alexander Graham Bell introduced Helen in Montclair, New Jersey, and former president William Howard Taft introduced her at New Haven, Connecticut. Celebrities including Henry Ford and Thomas Edison were eager to meet Helen.

Lecturing brought Helen into contact with a new generation of thinkers and their ideas even if she could not benefit from the new technologies. Around this time, Thomas Edison engaged the deaf community with his "vitascope" projection device. He chose a deaf woman as one of the first subjects for his invention so he could employ sign language to demonstrate the potential of silent films. The National Association for the Deaf (NAD) hoped to use the technology to combat the "oral movement" or speech-only movement Alexander Graham Bell supported by creating sign language films with no captions other than titles and credits (Padden and Humphries, 2005). Helen had created a special bond with Thomas Edison, who was deaf when they met. Edison could understand Helen's vowels but

DEAF-BLIND WRITERS

Deaf-Blind writing historically sustained an international community, corrected stereotypes, and preserved cultural memory. William Wade introduced Helen Keller to Madame Berthe Galleon, a French playwright who also found the challenge of deafness more difficult than blindness. Galleon had lost her sight and hearing when she was ten years old, but her early reservoir of memories of music and language allowed her to express herself through words.

Keller was not alone as a Deaf-Blind writer. Laura Bridgman wrote poetry in a journal as an expression of her ideal self. When she attended the World's Columbian Exposition in Chicago, Keller met Clarence J. Selby who was a poet and author of *Flashes of Light from an Imprisoned Soul* (1898). Keller corresponded with another Deaf-Blind woman named Emily Theodocia Pearce, who also suffered from curvature of the spine after an attack of meningitis (Rocheleau and Mack, 1930).

Pearce wrote letters to Keller in the form of poems. Inspired by her pen friend, Pearce started writing short fiction in high school, which was first published in the *Canadian Magazine*. She relocated to New York to pursue a literary career and was beginning to win recognition when she died suddenly. Pearce dedicated *Lights from Little Lanterns* (1926) to Helen: "To one whose life has been my constant inspiration . . . Helen Adams, Keller."

The volume included a poem:

Aspiration . . . To Helen Keller

One cried . . . I would mount to the heights and there
Pour down my treasures to the world below,
That some might upward look from their despair
And high hopes come to know.
But you have cried . . . I seek no place above,
It is my joy to walk the thronged street,
And give the full free measure of my love,
To all I chance to meet.

(Pearce, 1926, 43)

could not make out her consonants. She sat next to him and read his lips with her fingers as he told her of his hopes to develop a machine to use for talking pictures. Ironically, Helen asked him if he thought this technology could be used for helping the Blind to read regular printed books. Edison responded, "Yes I do" (Lash, 1980).

Despite having a talent agent Mr. Glass, the lecture circuits were a financial risk for female performers because Helen and Annie paid travel expenses, but theater managers often did not pay them. Helen looked at happiness from the inside out (Lash, 1980). The realities of Helen and

Annie's situation were increasingly dire even with considerable assistance from Mary Thaw and two trust funds. In her heart, Helen felt it was her poverty and not her will that consented. For some time, lack of money had only been part of her worries. John was thinking of leaving them. He was wearying of the struggle of being a counterfeit head of household led by two strong women... he wanted to live his life without scrutiny.

While on tour, Helen remained in tune with her audience. She adapted the scripts of her talks to fit local interests. Audiences preferred her to describe flowers rather than a realistic stench of poverty. Helen described her audiences as "handicapped in the race of life," so she strove to offer encouragement to the poor, young, deaf, and blind. She addressed themes of happiness or the value of the

Helen Keller and Anne Sullivan Macy examine an eagle display at the New York City International Flower Show in April 1913. Keller and other Deaf-Blind individuals were often granted special access to museums, world fairs, and public events. Keller's sense of smell would have made a flower show a delight; she could identify the difference between blue and white lilacs from the subtlety of their fragrance. (Library of Congress)

senses and the "intimate dependence of human beings one upon another in the emergencies of life."

Helen delivered speeches starting with themes related to the challenges of Deaf-Blind people and then transitioned to difficulties of working people. She explored themes of social blindness and deafness in her lectures, and her rhetoric inspired wry cynicism and sarcasm. Helen's speeches contained metaphors related to war and peace, disease and cures, contextualized by her sense of vertical and horizontal space.

Helen viewed creations and speech as interrelated, crediting speech with transforming her from merely existing to actively living. By involving her audiences while moving from narrow to broad themes, she reached to identify with them. Thoroughly familiar with rhythms and themes from the Bible like other great orators including Abraham Lincoln, Helen utilized clear, simple sensory language to evoke listeners to see, hear, smell, tastes, or feel her boundaries vicariously.

Helen wore a broad smile with fancy dresses that obscured her inability to make her physical body match society's dominant ideal of womanhood. She used pithy and picturesque figures of speech because they were difficult to forget. Her poetic voice differed from John and Annie because it was primitive and inclusive without being folksy or condescending. Helen stated, "Deafness, like poverty, stunts and deadens its victims, until they do not realize the wretchedness of their condition" (Keller, 2005). For Helen, deafness was her biggest disability because it separated her from the voices of people. Helen stated, "Let us here and now resolve that every deaf child shall have a chance to speak, and that every man shall have a fair opportunity to make the best of himself" (Keller, 2005).

Annie collapsed with the flu in Bath, Maine. She and Helen were staying in a hotel, and Helen was unable to use the telephone and unable to move about without a sense of direction. After a few days, Annie summoned a doctor, and the hotel managers helped them to board a train for home. Helen remembered, "My helplessness terrified me" (Keller, 1929).

Annie was misdiagnosed with consumption, the disease that killed her mother. Tuberculosis was a common but serious infectious disease affecting the lungs of the poor in neighborhoods where families lived in tightly packed conditions. After Helen realized how dependent she was upon her guardian, she telegraphed Carnegie and accepted his offer of a semiannual annuity. He replied: "Mrs. Carnegie and I are so glad. One likes to have his words of wisdom appreciated . . . there are few great souls who can rise to the height of allowing others to do for them what they would like to do for others" (Keller, 1929).

*   *   *

Helen's celebrity status was as an innocent, pure female, but she was not an institution; she was very human. John was called back to Wrentham when Annie needed life-saving surgery (possibly a hysterectomy), necessitating a period of recovery. John remained in a position to undermine Helen and his wife, Annie, to forward his own agenda and protect his interests. However, a subtle change in tone emerged as with what Michael Anagnos, John Wright, Arthur Gilman, and others saw in connection with Annie limiting Helen's independence.

Helen was exiled to the home of her college friend Lenore Smith in Washington, D.C. Having a "radical" celebrity in the house challenged Lenore, who took little jabs from Helen for her more conservative political views

(Lash, 1980). Used to Annie's domineering attitude, Helen simplified the difficulties of Lenore's support role like she did with her mother, Kate Keller.

Lenore tolerated Helen's taunts as she took on caretaking while her husband Philip Smith was out of town on business. Lenore was not a socialist, so Helen's political convictions became frustrating. Helen's condescending air toward many government workers reflected upon Lenore's husband who was a government employee. Helen also became anxious she was becoming a burden to her college friend when organizations badgered Lenore for access.

Lenore took Helen to some of Washington's poorest neighborhoods to see if she could help the poor during the winter months. Helen asserted, "Blindness does not shut me out from what is going on around me . . . I have the advantage of having an education that trained my mind to think. That's the difference between me and most people, not my blindness and their sight" (Lash, 1980).

Helen felt women should ask why in a nation of plenty there is such great poverty. She wanted women to study life in their immediate surroundings and in society, to understand all segments of society are dependent upon one another. She wanted women to ask: if one part of the world is suffering, was it because other parts are not governed right? Helen believed if she ever wrote a book for the Socialist movement, it would be called "Industrial Blindness and Social Deafness." When Phil returned, Helen decided it was time to return to Wrentham where she could express her opinions openly.

Helen and Annie traveled by car, and Helen enjoyed the sensations of the open road during their first lecture tour. Helen felt her body was tethered, but the very act of continuing the journey satisfied her. American poet and humanist Walt Whitman wrote about sensations of going beyond empty spaces, times, to reach beyond familiar horizons to understand something beyond a person's current senses communicated the awaiting future. Whitman's "Song of the Open Road" "The Open Road" conveyed, "To gather the minds of men out of their brains as you encounter them, to gather the love out of their hearts . . . to know the world itself as a road, as many roads to hope, as roads for traveling souls."

Helen's thoughts developed independent of her guardian and secretary. She once believed individuals were masters of their own fates and one could sculpt a life in any desired form, but this changed as she encountered different cultures. As she traveled through the United States, Helen realized she spoke with confidence about a topic called "happiness" she knew little about; her success was built upon environmental advantages gleamed from others.

While staying with Lenore, Helen wrote to John asking if Annie was bossing him around, giving him "directions every minute of the day"

(Lash, 1980). John increasingly resented his wife's loyalty to Helen. Helen and Annie found little peace when John Macy returned to Wrentham, but he made himself useful renovating Helen's study, adding a fireplace with a white marble mantle, red tile, and a glass door for her study. He was worn down emotionally. They added a sewing room, and he thinned out some trees, giving others more space to grow. John and Annie started having violent quarrels, after which, Annie would retreat to her room in tears and John retreated to the bottle.

Annie loved dogs, so they acquired a Great Dane they named Thora. Annie hired additional staff, a Swiss maid with a baby and a Russian born immigrant named Ian Bittman. Annie trained him to be a chauffeur, but John enjoyed driving and took on that role as he started work on a new book *Socialism in America*. Helen, Annie, and John took a break and visited Italian-born union leader, who had led the 1912 Lawrence textile workers strike, named Arturo Giovannetti and his wife, Caroline, in New York City, and Helen took her first subway ride. While imprisoned, Giovannetti wrote activist poems including "The Walker" (1914), recounting his experiences while incarcerated that garnered him the name the "Bard of Freedom."

Financially, Helen and Annie received help from her annuities and a refuge if they needed it from Mary Thaw. However, Mrs. Thaw became distracted with ongoing dramas related to her mentally ill son Harry Kendall Thaw who had murdered New York City architect Stanford White over a relationship with his trophy wife model, Evelyn Nisbet Thaw. Mary Thaw fiercely defended her son by hiring the best lawyers and attempting to get him into a private sanatarium instead of mental institutions. Eventually, he was released and returned to violent predatory behavior he had accused Stanford White of, and Mary Thaw could not ignore the evidence or cover it up. As Helen gave up the notion of supporting herself as a writer, she accepted her controversial politics gave her name recognition editors did not want to pay for. Mrs. Thaw never stopped supporting Helen and Annie, who may not have shared her background or politics, but they were not controversial in their behavior.

When John became literary editor for the *Boston Herald*, he hired a secretary, Peter Fagan, who was also a socialist. Despite growing tensions, John negotiated a lucrative deal for Helen's book, *Out of the Dark*, in January 1913. It contained Helen's opinions as a social critic in essays published earlier and led many critics to delineate Helen as John's puppet and not Annie's. John entrenched himself at the St. Botolph Club in Boston again when Annie hired additional help.

John Macy's assistant, Peter Fagan, entered Helen and Annie's lives when John left alone for Europe in May 1913 for four-and-a-half months. John left the two women behind with his trusted secretary, and Fagan gave

John news of Helen and Annie's adventures. Desperate to hold on to John, Annie deposited earnings from the lecture tour to pay for his trip.

When he returned, John rented an apartment along Boston's Fenway while Helen, Annie, and Kate Keller continued to tour. John left a cigarette burning in the apartment, causing a fire that burned some of Annie's mementoes. His worst nightmare was the strength of Annie's loyalty to Helen, but Fagan's reports made him feel he could not be replaced. John purchased a home in Maine, hoping to persuade Annie to relocate there, but this was an unrealistic expectation. While Helen and Annie supported his bohemian lifestyle, Annie could not leave Helen Keller, the institution, who was her creation and reason for name recognition.

Annie and John Macy remained at odds, unable to separate and unable to live together. John's glimpses into Annie's tumultuous early years gave him insights but no definitive answers. Like so many other men that Annie manipulated then cast aside, John tried to give Helen clues of how Annie was not loyal to anyone but herself. John wrote, "To be married to a woman and never get close enough to share the good and bad, to not truly know her" (Lash, 1980).

John knew the extent of the household's financial resources: Annie was now managing a household with income from an Andrew Carnegie pension, a Henry H. Rogers annuity, remnants of William Wade's educational fund, and generous support from Mary Thaw. He assumed that was enough to live in comfort and allow him to pursue his own interests. John wrote to Helen, "I can never explain what my life with Annie has been like" (Lash, 1980).

Miss Spitfire was the same with family members as with adversaries: she could be imperious, changeable, and quick-tempered. Helen reminded John of their shared work and told him she suffered as much from Annie's failings as he did. However, Helen's loyalty to Annie never wavered. Helen wrote to John, "If we were not a trouble to each other, we would not love as we do" (Keller, 2005).

Helen and John traveled to utopian intellectual and literary roads together, which were not shared with Annie. John's alcoholism did not allow him to continue enjoying Helen's utopian life; he could not see beyond his own desires. He rebutted, "She has never been a wife to me or done any of the things a woman might be expected to do" (Keller, 2005).

This was a rare insight into their marriage, what Reverend Edward Everett referred to as an "extraordinary triangle" of three people (Day, 2013). Helen innocently countered, "But we have shared everything we have with you" (Keller, 2005).

Out of frustration, John asserted, "She dominates you." As so many of Annie's previous protectors who also wanted to control Helen Keller, John lost his usefulness and resented falling into a trap he had helped to set for other men. He thought Annie would share access to Helen Keller even with a prenuptial agreement. John added, "She is playing a game and has not been true to me" (Keller, 2005)!

Helen naively told John how Annie hated the travel on the lecture tour, but she continued to do so to give him the chance to write and travel. John just wanted out of the situation, but he did not want to lose face by showing he had caused the problem. Helen replied astutely, "That's no more than you have done, and I love you all the more for it" (Keller, 2005).

Helen had a special bond with John, who in many ways had taken on the role of *teacher* when he came into their lives. She did not want the remnants of their life to shatter. "With such a love I cling to you and I cling to Annie." John Macy connected her to a community of socialists, "You and I are comrades journeying hand in hand to the end" (Keller, 2005).

John stated, "It has become a poor life, Helen" (Keller, 2005).

Helen did not want him to leave. "When the way is dark, and the shadows fall, we draw closer" (Keller, 2005). Her arguments were futile as Annie would not change. Helen asked John, "Do you remember the day that you asked me to trot in the same team with you before you and Annie married?" She added, "Well now I ask you the same question. Whether you choose to or not, I promise that you shall not find me unchanged" (Keller, 2005).

Annie relied upon plans that exploited John's white male position in society, but the life that Annie dreamed of with him was falling about her in ruins. Helen's mother, Kate Keller, who understood how difficult a bad match could be, attempted to help the couple reconcile. In a fit of anger, Annie charged out of John's apartment one night, vowing never to return. John, still hoping to tap into Helen's name recognition and financial resources, used Annie's words to establish her as the initiator of their separation, instead of him. He filed for divorce from Annie in January 1914.

*   *   *

Helen and Annie had a story to tell. In January 1914, Kate Keller joined her daughter Helen and Annie on their first cross-country tour. It started in Ottawa, Canada, traveling a circuit through Toronto and Ontario before crossing the border into Michigan and traveling to Minnesota and Iowa in the Midwest. Wherever they went, Socialists greeted them warmly.

Helen kept in touch with John and his assistant, Peter Fagin, from the road. Over the years, John called Annie "Bill" and Helen "Billy" for nicknames (Keller, 2005). The loss of John led Bill to lean more on Billy as Annie's sight worsened and she gained weight to the point of discomfort. Annie was devastated and haunted by John's accusations when she read them . . . and she read everything coming to Helen.

American industrialist Henry Ford started developing the assembly line model of mass production for the automobile industry in order to produce affordable cars for middle-class Americans. Ford was a pioneer in welfare capitalism that improved the quality of life for his employees, which enabled him to keep the best workers. In 1914, Ford offered employees double the minimal daily pay rate of most of workers. Ford, like Helen, opposed the war, viewing it as a waste of human resources. When Helen toured a Ford Motor plant in Detroit, Michigan, she was impressed by Ford's handshake, feeling his reserve energy through touch.

Ford told Helen he employed seventy-three blind men in his plants because they were efficient workers. He showed Helen the plant, guiding her fingers with alertness and communicating with pleasant simplicity. He observed, "The trouble with most folks who have ideas it that they don't know what to do with them" (Keller, 1929).

Visiting manufacturing and mining towns, Helen realized poor workers in unwholesome industrial environments were creating items of comfort and beauty they could not afford for their own households. Helen paused, "It's all well and good to have ideas, but what are they worth if the idea is never put into actual service" (Keller, 1929).

Ford left Helen pondering upon what the world would be like if it were run like a Ford plant. She liked the idea at first, but then an image of a hard-headed businessman in charge lost its utopian appeal when another image flashed in her mind of thousands of men working in unison with each man a cog or screw in the machine. Helen received a revelation: with progress, humans developed more advanced tools, yet they were losing sight of the satisfaction coming with happiness and personal development, "It was terrible to realize that the very forces which were meant to lift him above drudgery were taking possession of him" (Keller, 1929).

As Helen, Annie, and Kate traveled through Utah, Helen received an angry letter from John accusing them of not wanting to stay in his Boston apartment. Helen grew impatient with his alcohol-induced words; he called her a fool in a letter to Kate. John wrote how he hated their money and accused Annie of stinginess in sharing income. Helen countered, "Do you think it is fair or generous or consistent to say you 'hate our money,' and in the very same letter tell us that you deposited a thousand dollars of that 'hated' money for yourself" (Keller, 2005)?

John changed so much Helen did not know how to deal with him anymore. He wrote to Helen about how Annie wrecked their happy home when she stormed out of their Boston apartment. Helen told him Annie had left to fulfill a tour contract. She accused John of creating arguments to fit with his wishes. "I imagine that is possible for a woman to tell her husband that she thinks they should separate without wishing to leave his domicile" (Keller, 2005).

FAMILIAL REHABILITATION FOR A DEAF-BLIND ADULT ENGINEER

Helen Keller was critical of companies creating conditions where industrial accidents could occur because victims were too old to get special education through schools. Born in Philadelphia, Pennsylvania, on February 12, 1886, Harry Thurlow was an engineer who designed buildings and supervised construction (Rocheleau and Mack, 1930). In Spring 1913, while employed as a foreman at a plant manufacturing explosives, a nitroglycerine explosion left him Deaf-Blind and without four fingers. Thurlow had a wife and two children. His wife penciled a braille nursery tale to teach it to him.

Thurlow used construction skills to remodel his home, laying cement floors and walks to accommodate his needs. His wife worked with him on carpentry and plumbing, who he credited. "She is a personality all by herself, standing out clearly without any aid" (Rocheleau and Mack, 1930). Thurlow remarked, "No aspiring youth wants to include deaf-blindness among his ambitions. But having it saddled on to him, it need not stop any man. Bad as it is, it simplifies life, leaving but two problems: work and play" (Rocheleau and Mack, 1930).

Thurlow's sense of humor helped him to adjust to dramatic shifts in disability and loss of income. He described how he adapted, "For work, I must do what is at hand, not matter how little it earns, or how long it takes, else . . . I am out of a job" (Rocheleau and Mack, 1930). He changed careers by purchasing a typewriter. He memorized the keyboard so he could type letters to start a mail order business selling books and magazine with his wife. For play, Thurlow stated, "I have two lively children, or I read or converse with wife and friends. Conversation is carried on with the manual alphabet, or by folks printing ordinary letters on the back of my hand" (Rocheleau and Mack, 1930).

A bad loser, John accused Annie of dishonesty and harassment and stated the marriage was irredeemable. He was simply no longer the John that Helen knew, but she desperately missed news he had transmitted about her hero Arturo Giovannetti. John was blind to anything to heal the rift. Annie and Kate did not want Helen to continue any correspondence with John.

In early March 1914, Helen asked John to allow his secretary, Peter Fagin, who had learned to finger-spell, to attend to her correspondence. Helen concluded, "If you don't want to, why not let Mr. Fagin write me the home news and straighten out details for my return home" (Keller, 2005)? She added a little dig. "I love to be of use to others, and I do not let anyone spare me in my tasks, and I never shall" (Keller, 2005).

Arriving in California seemed to bring out Kate Keller's poetic soul (Keller, 1929). In San Francisco, Kate revealed she felt happiest traveling with her daughter and Annie. She enjoyed crossing and re-crossing San

Francisco Bay at night when the city's skyline was lit. Kate's words spelled into Helen's hands sparkled when she described how the sun set its shafts through the Golden Gate before the bridge was built as it journeyed westward over the Pacific Ocean.

Visiting Mount Tamalpias north of San Francisco in Marin County, Kate stood reverent in the majestic heights, worshipping nature's monarchs, the Redwoods. The Southern mother and her daughter bonded when they visited Muir Woods. Beneath the ancient trees on the floor of the grove were modest flowers: redwood oxalis with exquisite leaves and lovely blossoms; trillium; violets with tall leafy stems; toothwort, which was common in California; wild ginger with grotesque long horned blooms; and a little wild rose.

Helen returned to the Redwoods over the years. "Every time I touch the redwoods I feel as if the unrest and strife of earth are lulled . . . I cease to long and grieve . . . I am in a holy place, quiet as a heart full of prayer" (Keller, 1929). Kate became aware of the passing of generations from ancestors with the largest redwoods seeming to stand alone. Clusters bolstered the ancients: the largest trees in the middle, and two to four large trees supporting the center giant, circled by the younger trees.

There was a different way of describing these giants: in the city, they used the term "timber" as redwood groves not of Muir Woods had been harvested to rebuild San Francisco after the great 1906 earthquake and fire, but in New England, the term was simply "woods." Helen spoke on behalf of the Blind at the home of William Kent, who bought the grove of mighty redwoods to save them from destruction. Kent gave the grove to the United States as a park. President Theodore Roosevelt wanted to call them Kent's Woods, but Kent asserted, "I suggest that we call them Muir Woods after John Muir the great naturalist" (Keller, 1929). Before they continued on the lecture tour, Kate drew Helen near in an embrace and gently finger-spelled, "This is reparation for all the sorrow I have ever known" (Keller, 1929).

When they returned to the East Coast, Helen and Annie were compelled to rethink about their household arrangements because they could no longer support staff in Wrentham. Kate stayed with them during the transition; she regained a position in Helen's life when John Macy exited it. Annie spoke to Helen in the silence of the night about nightmares pursuing her. Helen later remembered, "For days she would shut herself up almost stunned, trying to think of a plan that would bring John back or weeping as only women who are no longer cherished weep" (Lash, 1980).

Joanne Sullivan had started life with a simple name. Her family called her Annie. When she attended Perkins Institute for the Blind, she gave herself a middle name "Mansfield" to appear more sophisticated. When she married John Macy, she garnered the title Mrs. John Macy but lost the strength of her feme sole identity. While John physically left the household, his named remained, and Annie tried to leverage it to her advantage, but John Macy was not a man of impeccable character. Mrs. Kate Adams Keller bluntly told her daughter, "I do not believe, Helen, that fate deals more kindly with a handsome, brilliant woman who has been drawn into marriage than it does with other women" (Lash, 1980). However, the name Miss Helen Adams Keller never changed . . . it only became more powerful with time.

9

Preparedness and Paradoxes

Power to rise in America was not guaranteed for everyone in the early twentieth century; it was more likely with a good name, education, family connections, and the influence of friends. Helen Keller was lucky in these areas, but she discovered a poignant lesson about being disabled: she could be recognized as an intellectual, disabled women when she stood with the majority, but once she opposed the majority with strong rhetoric, she became an ignorant woman. As her powerful friends and benefactors died, Helen Keller's bond strengthened with her mother Catherine "Kate" Keller, who still offered her insights as to what she could accomplish as a Deaf-Blind woman.

With America's changing economic climate, there was a men's club very different from John Macy's St. Botolph's Club in Boston. It grew across the country and was made up of vagrant men with their own code of ethics (Hunter, 1904). This group was a by-product of capitalism; its mass majority of members were recognized by pot bellies, curvature of the spine, dirty fingernails, and sweaty hands. Helen and Annie knew a second type of vagrant who did not work on principle and operated on different code of ethics. This second vagrant would debate the works of William Shakespeare like John Macy and Mark Twain, and he delighted his companions with his wit, but he was a charming parasite (Hunter, 1904).

This kind of vagrant could find his way into Helen's heart because it had been so sheltered for so long and her heart was not immune to worldly affectations. Helen and Annie did not conduct background checks on employees or new friends. John Macy's assistant, Peter Fagan, accompanied Helen Keller and Mrs. Annie Sullivan Macy on their second Chautauqua tour (Lash, 1980). Fagan was loyal, and he kept John informed on news of Helen and Annie's adventures.

During their travels, Helen experienced regions even within cities by smell. "There are as many smells as there are philosophies." She thought about places in reference to their smells. Fifth Avenue in New York harbored a different smell from other parts of New York; it was a very onerous street with an aristocratic smell. Helen wrote, "As I walk the pavement, I recognize the expensive perfumes, powders, creams, choice flowers, and pleasant exhalations from the houses."

In the residential neighborhoods, she smelled the delicate food smells, silken draperies, and rich tapestries. Sometimes a door opened, and Helen recognized what kind of cosmetics the occupants used. She wrote, "I know if there is an open fire, if they burn wood or soft coal, if they roast their coffee, if they use candles, if the house has been shut up for a long time, if it has been painted or is newly decorated, if the cleaners are at work in it" (Keller, 1929).

In the Midwest, Helen smelled regions with oil wells, the wafting scents of breweries, and the fumes of whisky stills. Small town grocery smelled of rancid butter, potatoes, and onions. Houses often had a musty, damp aura. Southern towns had odors of fried chicken, grits, yams, and cornbread. Northern towns had smells of fresh doughnuts, corn beef hash, fish balls, and baked beans.

Annie Sullivan Macy hired Scottish-born Polly Thomson to be Helen's secretary in October 1914. Annie loved her strong Glasgow accent, but Polly could not type (Lash, 1980). She was solid, practical, and learned to do hairdressing and manicures to save money on the road. Five years younger than Helen, Polly came from a middle-class family. When she was twelve years old when her father, a draftsman, died. Polly never had a college education, so she developed a sense of inferiority despite being very self-possessed. Polly accompanied Helen and Annie on the remaining lecture tour in place of Kate.

Helen's mother Kate Keller, despite being immersed in Southern culture, lived among a generation of women who had organized during the Progressive era when reformers used social science to solve societal issues. Hull House activist Jane Addams contracted tuberculosis of the spine when she was four years causing a curvature in her spine, giving her a limp and a lifelong awareness of public health issues. Addams, like Helen, had big dreams; she wanted to do something useful in the world, and reading the works of Charles Dickens inspired her to work with the poor. Addams was instrumental in working with General Federation of Women's Clubs to lead the Federation's Child Labor Committee to work to improve child labor laws.

American child welfare reformer Julia Clifford Lathrop, another Hull House pioneer, became the first woman to head a federal bureau when she served as director of the United States Children's Bureau in 1912. Lathrop developed her own multidisciplinary studies in statistics, institutional history, sociology, and community organization and graduated the year Helen was born.

The women at Hull House actively campaigned to persuade Congress to pass legislation to protect children. During the 1893 depression, Lathrop served as a volunteer investigator of relief applicants, visiting homes to document the needs of the families. When President William Taft appointed Lathrop to direct the Children's Bureau, she worked with women's groups across the country to direct systematic research into child labor, infant mortality, maternal mortality, juvenile delinquency, and mothers' pensions. For many conservative women, the Children's Bureau's focus gave them a role in politics before women garnered the right to vote nationwide.

Lathrop agreed with Helen's notion that preventative measures should be funded by government rather than charity, "It is a profoundly important public concern which tests the public spirit and the democracy of a community." Over two thousand women's clubs participated by focusing on infant and maternal mortality, birth registration, and public health facilities. The Children's Bureau chose not to address high mortality rates among babies in families of color. In the South, much of the public health campaigns were undertaken by Black clubwomen working within segregated communities.

When Helen's obsession with the war in Europe grew, Kate purchased a braille typewriter so she could write directly to Helen as she continued on the lecture circuit. The sinking of the RMS *Lusitania* on May 7, 1915, became a catalyst for organizing the Preparedness Movement to enter World War I. Former president Theodore Roosevelt supported American military buildup, while President Woodrow Wilson pressed for unarmed neutrality. The Socialist Party, antimilitarists, and pacifists like Helen Keller opposed the Preparedness Movement. The IWW opposed it, believing workers should not be forced to serve in the military for a war they did not support. During the summer of 1915, a series of military training sessions occurred in San Francisco's Presidio and other locations, and objectors were accused of disloyalty.

Helen's revelation within her own isolation determined only a few people were truly interested in her personal aspirations. Unlike Thomas Higgins, who never understood how racism made him a popular performer more than his natural talent (O'Connell, 2009), Helen understood prejudice on an abstract and personal level. The simplest variety of prejudice resulted from ignorance of unfamiliar cultures as well as a plain dislike or a hasty conviction that runs ahead of evidence or disregards it.

Helen would not remain silent in 1916, a year that would transform her life. In January, she first spoke up against Preparedness at Andrew Carnegie's shrine to the arts, Carnegie Hall in New York.

Helen believed Preparedness proponents wanted to distract Americans from the high cost of living, low wages, and uncertain employment. Helen and Annie invaded Andrew Carnegie's fine arts venue, Carnegie Hall, in midtown Manhattan in New York City on January 15, 1916. Helen spoke plainly, "We are not preparing to defend our country . . . Congress is not preparing to defend the people of the United States. It is planning to protect the capital of American speculators . . ." (Einhorn, 1998). She asserted, "Every modern war has had its root in exploitation." Helen asked the crowd, "Will workers walk into this trap?" The Deaf-Blind woman from Alabama demanded, "Be not dumb, obedient slaves in an army of destruction. Be heroes in an army of construction" (Einhorn, 1998).

A Jewish American poet named Anna Strunsky Walling, who was part of a California group of Socialists called "The Crowd" with Jack London, was in attendance at Helen's Carnegie Hall lecture that was free to the public. She wrote down her impressions of Helen as a modern Joan of Arc:

You walked forward as if you wanted to run:
Eagerness was in your feet, in the lift of your head, in your brilliant
*   smile.*
You walked forward and took your place at the edge of the platform,
*   facing the great audience . . .*
Oh, unforgettable experience of my soul when first the effulgence of
*   your courage and your youth laid its spell upon me!* (Lash, 1980)

The following day Helen explained to interviewer Barbara Bindley why she had joined the International Workers of the World. She explained how her motivation for activism came from concern about the connection between industrial greed and blindness and other disabilities. Helen told Bindley, a reporter with the *New York Tribune*, "I am in the fight to change things."

Helen clutched Barbara's knee to emphasize the point, and her voice became shrill in excitement, "I may be a dreamer, but dreamers are necessary to make facts" (Keller, 1967)! Helen exemplified a continuing verismo notion when she said, "Reality, even when it is sad is better than illusions."

Helen lost some of her illusions about the world as she realized Victorian sentimentalism was at the mercy of any winds that blow. "Real happiness must come from within, from a fixed purpose and faith in one's fellow men" (Keller, 1967). IWW learned discipline and tactics in activist trenches. Speaking with passion, Helen exuded radiance and glory as she told her interviewer, "I feel like Joan of Arc at times" (Keller, 1967). Mark Twain had first likened Helen to the French heroine from an obscure village, who had raised French morale during the Hundred Years' War. Helen continued, "My whole becomes uplifted. I, too, hear voices that say 'Come,' and I will follow, no matter what the cost, no matter what the trials I am placed under. Jail, poverty, calumny—they matter not" (Keller, 1967).

Kate Keller's only son, Phillips Brooks Keller, was eligible for the draft; she was afraid of the ramifications of her daughter's revolutionary speech at Carnegie Hall when she revealed to the world her membership in the IWW. Helen wrote to comfort her mother about her motives for getting involved with social justice issues seeming "so wholly outside the 'limits of my personal world'" (Lash, 1980). She described her impressions on visiting slums, sweatshops, and factories during lecture tours.

Kate supported women's suffrage. Helen wrote, "My family all belonged to the master class, and were proud of their birth and social prestige, and they held slaves" (Keller, 2005). Helen explained how disability and dependency upon the uprooted plantation economy tied her to another marginalized community. "Now, even since childhood, my feelings have been with their slaves. I am dispossessed with them. I am disenfranchised with them, I feel all the bitterness of their humiliation when a white man may take a job or home he wants, while they are driven out of houses and churches—nay, and are even terrorized and lynched if they compete in doing profitable work for the master class" (Keller, 2005).

Helen needed to strengthen her relationship with her mother even if they approached conversations from different perspectives. Helen had grown dramatically from her relationship with John Macy. He gave her insights to her guardian even if she did not want to concede to the truth. Helen became a stronger woman for having a weak man in her life. She noted to her mother how Annie did not support votes for women. "She still expects men to look after her affairs and protect her. I do not believe that any sex, class, or race can safely trust its protection to any hands by his own" (Lash, 1980).

Helen Keller condemned Southerners calling themselves Christians, who oppressed Blacks and profited from economic institutions and laws, giving whites unfair advantages. She believed Christ's ministry proclaimed, "The souls of all men are alike before God." Helen wrote she was ashamed in her very soul for the tears of the oppressed in her "beloved south-land" (Lash, 1980). Feeling Blacks were being pushed back into involuntary servitude, Helen sent a check for one hundred dollars with a letter to Oswald Garrison Villard to donate the money to the National Association for the Advancement of Colored People in February 1916. W.E.B. Du Bois published Helen's letter in the NAACP publication called *The Crisis.*

THE AFRICAN AMERICAN DEAF-BLIND EXPERIENCE

When Kate Keller explored educational options for Helen in Alabama, she discovered they were segregated. However, Maryland had a large African American population, and it became a center for Deaf-Blind education. A Black Deaf-Blind man named Albert Jobes resided in Chester, Maryland. Jobes entered the Maryland School for the Blind in 1892 and learned how to weave complex caning for furniture. Jobes was thrifty; he was able to save money working at the Maryland Workshop for the Blind and boarding with an older woman, so he could pursue his own interests and remain self-sufficient.

Frances Leo Brawner, a Deaf Black man who became visually impaired when he was six years old, resided in Maryland. After graduating from the Maryland School for the Blind, he worked for a plumber. Brawner later lost his hearing and became despondent when he thought he could not work again. He attended the Maryland Workshop for the Blind and mastered chair caning and earned a modest wage. He lived with his sister to save money and found companionship at church.

Louis Ewalt was born to a poor Black family in Baltimore. His mother left his father, taking Louis and his six siblings. She found each child positions in manufacturing as soon as they could work. Louis labored in a canning factory before getting a job in the Baltimore Rolling Mills where machines rolled metals into sheets. Ewalt was nine years old working a night shift when a furnace exploded, leaving his face and neck badly burned, causing him to become Deaf-Blind. Louis attended the Maryland School for the Blind to learn how to make brooms. He never mastered spelling to benefit from the manual alphabet. Ewalt attended a Presbyterian church where he enjoyed human contact. After his mother died in 1915, he resided with a sister (Rocheleau and Mack, 1930).

Helen's mother, Kate Keller, pleaded with Helen to modify her position because her family lived in a Democratic stronghold. *The Selma Journal* retaliated, accusing Helen with the utmost animosity of being a traitor to fellow white Southerners, stating she had proclaimed lies, "full of fawning and bootlicking phrases" (Lash, 1980). Helen responded without altering her basic stand. Kate Keller, like Helen, moved beyond their familiar boundaries while accompanying her on the lecture tour.

While John Macy advised her with his agenda and Annie advised her based upon childlike dependency on coverture where women rely on male protectors, Kate Keller advised her based upon her "beloved south-land" of Ivy Green where Helen formed meaningful relationships with Blacks. In deference to her mother, Helen started to self-censor, but in a letter to the news media, she clarified her point, "The equity I advocated in my letter is the equity of all man before the law" (Lash, 1980).

Helen, Annie, and Polly continued to drive to lecture venues in the early morning hours through towns and across prairies with sunflowers as tall as trees; audiences wanted Helen to talk about happiness. They presented lectures in town halls as well as big noisy tents and at lakeside camps for country folk. Their little Ford carried them through thunder and lightning storms mirroring the broader international changes approaching. During the summer of 1916, the tour was not successful; audiences became indifferent to the question of war in Nebraska, Kansas, and Michigan.

The news media typecast Helen as the "arch priestess of the sightless," but resisted printing any of her political views against the mainstream support of Preparedness Movement (Lash, 1980). President Woodrow Wilson started a campaign to promote patriotism and support for the war. The news media created a picture of Helen in the clutches of unscrupulous entities taking advantage of her isolation. Despite John Macy's absence, they suggested Helen was just a mouthpiece for radical socialist agendas. By fall of 1916, John Macy was out of Helen and Annie's lives, except when he contacted them for money, but he remained listed as a member of their household in the 1920 census (Lash, 1980).

Audiences and newspaper readers did not want to have their peace of mind disturbed by a Deaf-Blind woman talking about the dangers for workers in entering war. Helen sensed the vast majority of audiences believed America would never enter the war. She spoke her mind and accepted the consequences. Helen was willing to receive criticism as long as she was treated like an independent-thinking human being.

When Kate experienced a revelation in the diversity within the groves of California Redwoods, it transformed their relationship, somewhat moderating how Helen communicated. She remained a pacifist like her cousin Edward Everett Hale and held her course, but she shifted the methods knowing she could offend some, "My love for America is not blind . . . One of the painful consequences of holding to one's course, if it is unpopular, is the division it causes between friends" (Lash, 1980).

Nobody wanted to hear Helen speak on politics. When Helen, Annie, and Polly returned to Wrentham after their failed lecture tour, Ian Bittman, a Russian immigrant working as their houseman, prepared for their return. Annie trained Ian to cook as Kate had once taught her. However, Helen was lost in the disruption, disoriented. She could not work or think calmly. She did not want to go on; was it a folly to be alive? Helen did not know how to help Annie, who increasingly suffered from inflammation in her legs that affected her mobility. She thought about how bleak her world would be without Annie.

Helen believed limiting free speech led governments to disturb legitimate influences of democratic principles in preparing for wartime conditions. Psychologist Josef Jastrow, who had studied Laura Bridgman and

Helen's dreams, also looked at the paradoxes of pacifists. Jastrow argued that during the overwhelming moments of war reason was decentralized (Jastrow, 1918). War imposed restrictions of speech and influence at every point, meaning there was no business as usual, or pleasure as usual, or occupation as usual, or as Jastrow stated, no "insistence upon privilege as usual" (Jastrow, 1918). Individuals sublimated personal beliefs for a larger national good. "Points of view permeate even in the trenches and prepare the minds of men for the negotiations of the future" (Jastrow, 1918).

Helen reflected this pacifist paradox, but she asserted workers in the trenches learned tactics to use in activism when they returned to civilian life. Jastrow observed women's rights and working-class labor rights activists sometimes approved the cause and disapproved the means. Jastrow observed, "Before 1914 the most militant operations reported in the daily press were those of a group of women claiming equal suffrage. On other occasions advocates of the rights of labor have resorted to militaristic methods" (Jastrow, 1918).

Helen's involvement with women's and labor movements was not physically but ideologically militaristic. Jastow argued that when an avowed pacifist enlisted in the military, he or she appeared inconsistent in adhering to pacifism even if their actions were derived from separate but not unrelated personal values. The distinction involved a simple and pragmatic process moving from action to principle. Jastrow argued that while "actions speak louder than words" is the common conclusion, in the case of a pacifist, it is reversed, which is the paradox.

The effect of war, as with any great sweeping nationalistic emotion, results in the level of critical reasoning being lowered. He used the analogy of vegetarianism to establish pacifism as a practical daily choice. "It is a practice related to an individual's philosophy related to food and it is free from the broader social order; and vegetarianism embodies actions individual actions that speak louder than words. However, militarism and pacifism are tied to collective social bearing" (Jastrow, 1918). The pacifist's actions got ignored, hushed, or misinterpreted, because of the individual's label from the dominant society. According to Jastrow, "Bystanders look at the banner and not at the procession" (Jastrow, 1918).

When the United States joined World War I on April 6, 1917, Kate Keller could not bring herself to communicate about it even with her daughter, Helen. She saw thousands of young men encamped near Montgomery, Alabama, where she now resided. Kate feared the draft would take her son, Phillips Brooks Keller. However, Helen continued to argue she was qualified to speak on issues with meaning to her and the disabled. "My blindness does not shut me out from a knowledge of what is happening about me" (Nielsen, 2004).

Raising the Stakes on Pacifism

Despite her personal views of war, Helen Keller visited blinded soldiers at U.S. General Hospital, No. 7, in Baltimore, Maryland, during World War I. She offered no empty optimism but advised veterans about dealing with the loss of personal liberty and how to find pleasure in reading books. One man told her, "Gee, I read about you in school, but I never thought I would be blind myself" (Harrity and Martin, 1962).

As the United States entered World War I, Edward Everett Hale's Civil War story was produced as a patriotic silent film with the same name *The Man without a Country* (1917). Hale was a pioneering peace advocate, but this silent film depicts pacifists or conscientious objectors as traitors. Helen Keller would not have experienced it without someone to finger-spell it for her.

An orphaned young woman Barbara Norton (Florence La Badie) and brother Tom Norton move in with a pacifist relative. Produced before women garnered the vote, Barbara becomes engaged to pacifist John Alton/Philip Nolan (Holmes Herbert) wearing a pacifist pin, "Peace at any price." Patriotic Barbara dons a "Stars and Stripes" ribbon, breaking their engagement before becoming a Red Cross nurse in France. Alton gets shunned at home for not supporting "The Cause." Barbara, thought to be on board the ill-fated SS *Tauric*, and presumed drowned, motivates her brother to enlist.

An allegorical vision of Barbara as "Columbia," the female personification of America, leads Alton back to his past life as Philip Nolan. John soon experiences a change of consciousness and trades his pacifist pin for a patriotic ribbon before enlisting. Barbara is alive, and the couple reunites before Alton and Tom sail for the warfront (Jewel Productions, 1917).

Annie pushed push men away from Helen if they became too attached. Both Kate and Annie discouraged Helen from marrying and having children. Alexander Graham Bell once told Helen, "You will change your mind when the right man comes a-wooing" (Gray, 2006). When during a June 1916 interview for the *Chicago Tribune*, thirty-six-year-old Helen mentioned she was involved in a romance, people took notice (Nielsen, 2004). She claimed a certain young man was attentive, and she described wanting a relationship with a handsome man, but she wanted a partner who was a straight thinker. Helen did not need a rich man; in her view, she earned her own way through the world, and she was proud of it (Nielsen, 2004).

Twenty-nine-year-old Peter Fagan could make folks laugh with his humor, and he was a radical, passionate socialist (Lash, 1980). Annie hired John Macy's former assistant to be Helen's secretary when Polly needed to return to Scotland on family business. Fagan knew the manual alphabet and braille. Marcia Stevenson, the manager for the "Tour of Helen Keller and Mrs. Macy," had liked him in the secretarial role. Annie was not entirely comfortable with John's former assistant as part of her support system. However, Kate Keller mistrusted Fagan for fostering Helen's radicalism during tumultuous times.

Annie was unaware of the growing bond between Helen and Peter Fagan, but she was seriously ill and preparing to travel with Polly in September 1916 (Lash, 1980). Annie had remained depressed about the breakup of her marriage, and her health deteriorated. Annie's physician advised rest at Lake Placid in the Adirondack Mountains in northern New York state. Polly accompanied Annie to recuperate, so they played off their housekeeper, Ian Bittman, because they could no longer afford to employ him.

Helen, aware of her own isolation, telegraphed her mother to come help lighten the atmosphere. Annie had caught a bad cough initially misdiagnosed as tuberculosis, the disease that killed her mother. However, the diagnosis was changed to pleurisy because she was anxious and exhausted. Peter Fagan picked the perfect moment to secretly propose to Helen.

Fagan took Helen for long walks that autumn in her woodlands and read to her. Helen was happy in his company. He learned about her inclinations, while John described her temperament as only a brother could. Nobody knows *exactly* what motivated John Macy, but with his encouragement, Fagan covertly wooed Helen under her guardian's nose.

Full of plans for Helen's future, he came and sat next to her in her study. For a long time, he held her hand in silence; then he began to finger-spell into her hand tenderly. Helen was surprised to learn he cared so deeply and found sweet comfort in his loving words. She was all atremble when Peter offered plans for her happiness. "If you marry me, I will always be near to help you in all of your difficulties in life" (Lash, 1980).

Helen was stunned. Was it too good to be true how a young man would appear in her moment of need?

Fagan's warmth was a bright light that shone upon Helen's apparent helplessness. The sweet notion of love enchanted Helen, and she trustingly yielded to her deep longing to be part of a man's life. Then he promised, "I will be the one to read to you, do research for you, and do the work that Teacher has done for you" (Lash, 1980).

Helen's mind filled with a web of lifelong imaginings about married life. She was not like her guardian . . . not bossy or domineering with men. Helen immediately wanted to share her joy with her mother. Fagan, not wanting to be discovered, advised, "Better wait a bit, we can tell them together. We must try to realize what their feelings will be" (Lash, 1980).

"Oh no," Helen spelled.

"Certainly," Fagan suggested. "They will disapprove, at first" (Lash, 1980). He read Helen's downcast face, as her expressions transparently revealed her openness to love. "Your mother does not like me, but I shall win her approval by my devotion to you" (Lash, 1980).

Helen exclaimed, "She does like you" (Keller, 1929)!

"Your teacher is too ill to be excited just now," he continued. To let Miss Spitfire know now, would give her an opportunity to create trouble. Fagan suggested, "We must tell her first when she is better" (Keller, 1929).

Peter Fagan offered to do the work Helen's guardian did. If Helen married, under coverture, her husband would become her guardian/protector under the law. Under coverture, the husband covered the wife, and he could use her good name to obtain credit, control her income, and sign contracts and deeds for her. If Miss Helen Keller married, Mrs. Annie Mansfield Sullivan Macy, as Helen's guardian, would no longer be needed. Annie would lose all financial support from Helen's various trusts unless Fagan signed a prenuptial agreement as John Macy had done.

Being a direct woman, Helen suffered to keep this secret from her mother and Annie. The secret started eating away at her joy of being loved, and yet the couple plotted a strategy. This was the first time Helen was offered an opportunity to be independent of her teacher. Fagan and Helen filled out an application for a marriage license; then Fagan disappeared to Boston to file it. As Fagan prepared to leave, Helen told her lover she planned to tell Kate about their relationship in the morning.

Fate interceded as Annie and Polly prepared to leave for Lake Placid. Ian Bittman approached Annie, telling her how unhappy he was (Lash, 1980). Annie misunderstood, thinking the servant was anxious about his imminent layoff. She told him she would hire him back when she was able to. Annie was shocked when Ian informed her how he and the chauffeur, Harry Lamb, had learned Helen and Fagan were preparing to elope. Annie called for Kate.

The *Boston Globe* announced Fagan had applied for a marriage license. Kate read the news and stormed into Helen's room as she dressed. "What have you been doing with *that creature*" (Lash, 1980)?

Helen did not respond; she stood by the window in her study, as cool as a cucumber. Kate uncharacteristically ranted, "The papers are full of a dreadful story about you and him. What does it mean? Tell me" (Lash, 1980)!

Kate Keller and her daughter had started bonding once John Macy left the household. Now Kate's eyes narrowed dangerously. She believed that Peter Fagan was incapable of wooing Helen without significant guidance. Helen sensed Kate's hostility toward her fiancé. Panicking, she pretended not to know what her mother was talking about.

Kate would not back down. She demanded with her voice rising to an unfamiliar pitch, "Are you engaged to him? Did you apply for a marriage license" (Lash, 1980)?

Well prepared, Helen sought to shield Peter. Totally comprehending what was unfolding before her mother, Helen denied everything. She lied to Annie, fearing her guardian would interfere if she confessed her love for John's former assistant.

Kate Keller ordered Fagan to be banned from the house. Kate opposed Helen marrying for eugenic reasons, despite the arguments Alexander Graham Bell gave to Helen in favor of her having a husband and possibly children: Helen Keller did not lose sight or hearing due to heredity; the cause was a childhood illness (Nielsen, 2004). Kate Keller demanded Helen issue a statement to the press through their lawyer denying the relationship. Helen complied. Kate forbade Fagan from speaking to Helen, but he managed to slip Helen a note in braille with his address, begging her to keep in touch.

Upon the advice of Annie's lawyer, Helen continued to deny the relationship until Annie left for Lake Placid with Polly. Fagan also denied the story, saying he was engaged to another woman. However, the Boston City Registrar Edward McGlenen described in detail how the marriage license was signed by Helen and Fagan (Lash, 1980).

An anonymous source, most likely John Macy, told the *New York Times* how Peter confided, "The denials were necessary in order to soothe Mrs. Macy's feelings. Fagan told me he was going to marry Miss Keller" (Lash, 1980).

Kate booked boat passage to take Helen home to Montgomery, Alabama, where Helen's sister Mildred lived with her husband, Warren Tyson. Kate begged Helen not to write to Annie about the extent of the situation until she was stronger.

Fagan did not let up; he consulted with a marriage and family lawyer about laws in the South and booked a boat fare. The lovers set adrift continued to secretly plot to elope under the cover of a kidnapping scheme. While Helen and Kate traveled by boat to Savannah, Georgia, Fagan would kidnap her, and they would escape via train to Florida, where they planned to marry.

In November 1916, Kate discovered the scheme and changed their plans of traveling by train. Fagan was not easily deterred; he showed up several times once Helen and Kate reached Montgomery.

Fagan tenaciously continued weaving a web of falsehood and misinformation, planning to meet up with Helen at her sister's house. On one occasion, he was caught fingerspelling into Helen's hand, but Mildred's husband rushed out with a gun and scared him away.

Sometime later, Helen was discovered alone waiting on the porch in the early morning hours with her bag packed. Nobody will ever know what went through Helen's mind as she shed tears expecting Fagan, who never showed up. Soon he appeared to fall away altogether, and Helen spent the next five months with family in Alabama. Unable to escape, she eventually consoled herself in the thought her problem was not in the loving, but in the circumstances. The affair showed how despite her determination and courage Helen was a captive of protectors and guardians. Moving forward, ideology shaped Helen's view of love as she sublimated her sexual energy into her causes.

* * *

Helen and Annie floundered in their separation as their economic troubles did not dissipate (Nielsen, 2004). Annie's stay at Lake Placid was extended as doctors decided she needed a year to recuperate. Helen was bored in Alabama with her family. She grieved over Peter Fagan and John Macy, as she slowly repaired her fractured relationship with her mother. Annie, oblivious of the extent of the affair and unable to bear her doctor's restrictions, read a magazine travel advertisement, and soon she and Polly set out for Puerto Rico, hoping to enjoy some healthful idleness in the sun.

As Annie and Polly luxuriated, Helen worried where her life was going (Lash, 1980). Helen felt alone and compared her situation to that of the Deaf-Blind poet Madame Berthe Galleon, who had a husband and grown daughter. The financial situation again appeared to be dire when it was not: Helen and Annie had about $15,000 invested in utility stocks, an annual income of $5,600 from trusts (with purchasing power of about $142,000 in 2021), and frequent money infusions from Mary Thaw. Their annual income would have been sufficient for a family with a stable lifestyle, but cash savings were so depleted they were obliged to sell their home in Wrentham.

Helen remained isolated with her family in Montgomery, Alabama. Used to reading extensively in braille about the world and conversing with contemporary thinkers, her family did not recognize she was alone in the knowledge of her potential. Helen once wrote, "I have the advantage of a mind trained to think, and that is the difference between myself and most people, not my blindness and their sight" (Nielsen, 2004). In a rare strategic move following her failed escape from Annie, Helen wrote to her guardian in Puerto Rico, reminding her of their shared financial resources. Helen asked Annie how she should deal with investments so Annie would remain the beneficiary if Helen were to die before her. Annie, uncharacteristically carefree, reassured Helen she was getting better and denied Helen would need anyone to help her because of the presence of her biological family. Annie wrote to Helen, "Besides you believe in a Heavenly Father. (I have not that consolation, but I am deeply glad you have it)" (Lash, 1980).

Something had prompted Helen to test her guardian who remained outside of the country on an extended holiday. She hoped to write a book about the Blind, but she actually needed to be bossed; she missed Annie's prodding, and she could not afford to hire an assistant. Helen informed

Annie about visiting a nineteen-year-old Jewish girl Rebecca Mack from Cincinnati, Ohio, with her family living nearby in Montgomery (Koestler, 1976). Helen coyly wrote she did not understand why Rebecca was so interested in her because of their age difference. She informed Annie the young woman had compiled information on Helen, Annie, and John into scrapbooks. Helen reported Rebecca was interested in special education and hoped to become her self-appointed companion in Annie's absence. Mack visited daily to share the scrapbooks, and Kate poured over them with great care.

When Annie escaped her partnership with Helen, she enjoyed a cheaper lifestyle living with Polly in Puerto Rico. Meanwhile, family bolstered Helen during her time in Montgomery, Alabama, after her Fagan heartbreak. She walked about six miles daily with her sister Mildred Tyson and ate healthy food. The less frenetic pace of life calmed Helen and relaxed her vocal cords so she could speak better. By the end of January 1918, Annie had written to Helen telling her of plans to return to the United States in April. She suggested settling near New York City. Annie could not give up the power she has as Helen's gatekeeper, and she pointed out, "Dear, I do want to get well for your sake. You do need me still" (Lash, 1980).

Annie Sullivan decided to return to her old life because there was no space for a young woman determined to teach the Deaf-Blind from Ohio to be Helen's companion, just as there was no room for Peter Fagan, John Macy, Arthur Gilman, Michael Anagnos, or any person who would undermine Helen's dependence upon Annie. Peter Fagan had changed the power dynamics at Wrentham by convincing Helen she could be an actor for change *in her own life*. Helen saw her need for a plan and for the first time truly challenged, disobeyed, conspired, and deceived to escape her dependence upon Annie.

On April 6, 1917, President Wilson signed a war resolution meaning Americans would enter a war in Europe with new brutal tactics. The power dynamics irrevocably altered with separation, showing Annie to be emotionally dependent upon Helen. Helen and her mother traveled to New York City to greet Annie and Polly. They sold the farmhouse in Wrentham, which they could not afford with wartime inflation. A Boston department store Jordan Marsh purchased the property as a rest home for its employees. Annie, unaware of the changes in Helen, told her, "Each time you fail, just start over again and you will grow stronger" (Lash, 1980).

Annie had confronted Helen's strong will over the years, but it was harder for her to control Helen radicalized by John Macy and Peter Fagin. Annie told Helen, "Dear, you are an impassioned reformer by temperament." She paused, "We both fight for peace like soldiers on a battlefield." Annie's fingers again stilled. "How often have I said that we both make too much of a battlefield of life" (Lash, 1980)! She poured some tea with a sweet smile Helen could feel. She next finger-spelled, "Maybe there would be more peace in the world if we cultivated the gentler virtues."

In 1917, Mary Thaw was publicly humiliated as her son, Harry Thaw, resurfaced in the newspaper headlines (Baatz, 2018). The parents of a young male victim gave evidence that Harry had lured him to New York City on the premise of paying for his college education. Once the young man arrived, he was trapped and whipped before he could escape and return home. At last, Mary stopped contesting the need for Harry to be committed to a mental institution. In Helen and Annie, Mary Thaw found a space where she could be a noble society philanthropist without fearing scandal.

*   *   *

In October 1917, Helen, Annie, and Polly moved with their dog Sieglinde (daughter of Thora) into their new home in Forest Hills, now Queens, which was an affordable suburb of New York City. They called their small brick house on the wrong side of the tracks the "Castle on the Marsh." An American Jewish Georgist author Horace L. Traubel with a wild mane of white hair and a mustache befriended Helen. He visited Helen and Annie to share insights on the great thinkers. Traubel was a leader in the Arts and Crafts movement and edited a literary magazine, *The Artsman*, and a socialist magazine called *The Conservator*. He believed people should own the value of what they produce themselves.

Happy to be out of the public life, Helen and Annie settled in by planting vines and trees in a little philosopher's garden for Helen. She missed John who gave her news of Arturo Giovannetti. Helen had a small study on the top floor, where she began to study Italian to read the great Italian poets Dante Alighieri and Francesco Petrarch in their original language as well as talk to Giovannetti who now lived close. She reflected upon what Dante meant when he wrote, "There is no greater sorrow than to be mindful of the happy time in misery."

Helen's garden was actually a narrow-walled enclave turned into a humble, rustic green nook, a refuge in every kind of weather. Petrarch offered Helen wisdom, "A good death does honor a whole life." Helen understood the meaning of honoring a whole life. Dante wrote, "Consider your origin, you were not born to live like brutes, but to follow virtue and knowledge." Helen knew the ups and downs of the early twentieth century. Meanwhile, bills mounted, and while her goodwill brought resources, Annie and Polly, a maid, a herd of dogs, a chauffeur, and cook all cost money. Helen was truly cash broke, and she knew that her political views were costing her support.

Helen wrote a letter to President Woodrow Wilson on December 12, 1917. She stated her sympathy and affiliation with IWW activists Arturo

Giovannetti, Elizabeth Gurley Flynn, and Carlo Tresca, two months after the 3, along with 166 other activists, were indicted in Chicago for violation of the "Espionage Act" of 1917 penalizing perceived disloyalty. Likewise, the "Sedition Act" of 1918 made it a federal offense to use "disloyal, profane, scurrilous, or abusive language" about the Constitution, the government, the American uniform, or the U.S. flag.

The Supreme Court case *Schenck v. United States* (1919) defined the limits of the First Amendment right to free speech, particularly during wartime. Helen argued prejudiced, self-appointed people sat in judgment of the words and acts of others. She felt the most fatuous utterances in the name of patriotism were hailed with unchallenged reverence. Helen argued, "Rights we had thought ours forever—rights hallowed by the blood and fortunes of our fathers—rights we had been taught were the very bulwarks of our liberties—rights guaranteed to us by the Constitution of the United States, are being violated every day."

Gatherings of protesters were violently broken up; newspapers expressing radical opinions were debarred from postal delivery; individuals were threatened and clubbed for expressing opinions against the war; many were imprisoned with excessive bails. Helen felt intolerance amounted to fanaticism. Having inaccurate articles written about her, Helen stated, "The voice of authority commanding silence has downed the voice of justice." She concluded, "Wars are disastrous to the welfare and happiness of the working-people, their struggles, their aspirations and their liberties."

Millions of poor in America remained socially invisible. Helen argued American society was blind about the impact of poverty. The poor were not part of the consciousness of the nation. She supported industrial democracy as a solution to economic problems. A decade earlier, in her poem *The Song of the Stone Wall*, Helen wrote about walls, and now she updated her iconic rhetoric. "We grope for the wall—the wall that shall support our weakness; we grope as those who have no eyes; we stumble at noonday as in the night; therefore is understanding far from us, and justice doth not overtake us." Helen's affinity for activists following ideals in the way of self-denial and danger led her to state, "I am bound to these thinkers by many holy interests, affections, hopes, visions, and desires."

*   *   *

Helen did not want people to offer her pity related to her disabilities, but Hollywood soon offered Helen a promise to earn fast money and star in a motion picture about her life. American writer and filmmaker Dr. Francis Trevelyan Miller suggested a scenario for producing a silent movie about Helen and Annie that would be a precursor to the documentary, blending two acts with actors and a third with Helen and close associates. Miller suggested Helen could earn $50,000–$100,000 with the film, enough to provide handsomely for the household. Annie, as Helen's guardian, authorized the deal in February 1918.

Director George Foster Platt devised a communications system of taps Helen could follow, allowing Polly to interpret his instructions. Child actress Etna Ross played young Helen and Ann Mason played college-aged Helen. Actors portrayed many of Helen's early mentors: Henry H. Rogers, Mark Twain, Oliver Wendell Holmes, Edward Everett Hale were dead, and other friends had aged so much they would not appear in cameo roles.

Filming started in early June 1918 as thousands of soldiers were deployed to Europe each month to serve in World War I (Lash, 1980). Actresses played Helen, but she portrayed herself later in maturity. Helen wore a wig, thick white makeup, and restricting costumes. Communications were difficult: she was instructed to act natural, but she did not understand how to portray natural. The work was not glamorous, and the film plot soon took bizarre turns. The director gave Helen cues by tapping on the floor.

Helen's life was not visually dramatic, so the director staged a metaphorical scene between "Ignorance" and "Knowledge" outside of a "Cave of Time" over the spirit of baby Helen. Elaborate dream sequences introduced Helen meeting crowds in Jerusalem, Helen with a mythical lover Ulysses, Helen as Joan of Arc riding a white horse while holding a trumpet in her mouth. There was also a scene with Helen flying in the open cockpit of an airplane.

Helen wrote to Alexander Graham Bell, asking him to participate in the film project about her life. Bell expressed an aversion of appearing in a moving picture. Helen hoped to present friends in a symbolic way, but the producers envisioned Helen on an acacia walk among loved ones, past and present. Filming the scene for Helen felt like a great grotesque banquet with Helen's father Arthur Keller, Edward Everett Hale, Bishop Phillips Brooks, Oliver Wendell Holmes, Bell, Mary Thaw, Henry H. Rogers, and Joseph Jefferson played by actors.

Helen felt like she had died, sensing her deceased friends who had helped her, so she again emotionally mourned their loss. When Helen grasped the actors' hands, they seemed too substantial compared to how she remembered her friends. "They did not resemble the hands of the friends they were impersonating" (Keller, 1929).

Although Helen was used to being scripted, going by someone else's script was jarring. Despite having a script, Helen's expectations from real life differed from scripted conversations: she remembered the actors "did not have the flavor of the talk that I remembered" (Keller, 1929). She was shocked by every scripted comment; when the actor portraying Mark Twain made a witty or complimentary speech, Helen recalled, "I did not know whether to laugh or cry" (Keller, 1929).

With her mother, Kate Keller, and brother, Phillips Brooks Keller, watching from the ground, Helen flew as a single passenger in an open airplane in the film's last act at a time when the commercial airline industry was just taking off the ground. Sitting in an airplane Helen, felt many sensations: the throb of the motor like a drum, the engine trembling the plane alive. She felt the plane straining and tugging upward like winds tug at a tree.

As a pandemic known as the Spanish Flu raged, Helen led a Liberty Bond rally in Los Angeles, and Mary Thaw telegraphed her support and a pledge to subscribe to the program (Lash, 1980). She also visited shipyards at San Pedro, where she stood in the midst of shipbuilders preparing to launch a ship they were finishing. Helen felt the reverberations of the rhythmic thunder of the triple hammers in the forge and the quick blows of men driving in rivets. The workmen paused and watched the famous Deaf-Blind woman. Their bosses ordered them back to work, but they wondered what she was doing among them. Helen christened the boat by breaking a bottle of champagne upon its bow. At noon, the ship workers shared their lunch.

Deliverance cost $250,000 to produce, and the rift between creative minds and their consultants Helen and Annie grew (Lash, 1980). Mary Thaw stepped in to broker a solution after Helen wrote to her that she and Annie wanted an honest film about her struggles, triumphs, and aspirations. Thaw forwarded her letter to steel magnate Charles M. Schwab, who had originally invested money to create the Helen Keller Film Corporation (Lash, 1980). After that, Helen and Annie received $10,000 (worth more than $150,000 in 2021) for signing on as consultants. Thaw threatened to file an injunction if fundamental changes were not made to the picture before it was released in August 1919 in New York City.

The film was a hodgepodge of different scenarios reflecting shifting events, gimmicks, and fantasy used to turn Helen into a glamorous disabled woman. They had a vision of a commercial "thriller" while Helen and Annie wanted a "historical record" of their real experiences (Keller, 1929). The producers wanted to depict Helen's two deliverances: her intellectual release from being Deaf-Blind and her later release from social blindness.

Deliverance was released at the end of the pandemic when those who were infected had either died or developed immunity. Audiences were eager to return to theaters and loved Helen, but the film was a box-office failure because it coincided with the conclusion of World War I. Helen refused to cross any picket line, so she did not attend the New York premiere because of an Actors' Equity strike. Helen, Anne and Polly had to borrow funds to return to Forest Hills. Helen later quipped, "We are the kind of people who come out an enterprise poorer than when we enter it."

Annie once told Helen, "No matter what happens, you keep on beginning and failing" (Lash, 1980). Thoroughly frightened now by their lack of money, Helen and Annie decided to try the solution Captain Arthur Henley Keller had identified when Helen was still a minor. Annie taught Helen to perform for benefactors, so it seemed a natural progression to do vaudeville. Their act was simple: Annie, who had a smooth pleasant voice, described the miracle of Helen learning language.

Vaudeville, or continuous-performance theaters, offered American variety shows that reached their heyday as part of an emerging populist consumerism, and it offered Helen a new, real prism into the human condition. The entertainment industry was big business built with capital

---

How the Parrot Spoke to the Masses

Helen Keller and Anne Sullivan Macy developed a twenty-minute vaudeville act (Harrity and Martin, 1962). Macy explained how Keller acquired language, using a seventeen-page script, and answered questions from the audience.

When asked if any government wanted peace, Keller responded, "The policy of government is to seek peace and pursue war."

When asked who the most unhappy people were, Keller replied, "People who have nothing to do."

Keller was asked, "Do you think that America has been true to her ideals?" Her answer included a prison slang term "ducking," meaning she might face coersion, "I'm afraid to answer that, the Ku Klux Klan, might give me a ducking."

Someone asked who Keller's favorite heroine was, and she explained, "Kate O'Hare because she was willing to go to jail for her ideal of world peace and brotherhood." Kate O'Hara was a member of the American Socialist Party who unsuccessfully ran for Congress representing Kansas in 1910 and was later imprisoned during World War I under the Espionage Act of 1917 for giving an anti-war speech in Bowman, North Dakota. Her sentence of five years was pardoned in 1920.

Keller was asked, "Do you think the voice of the people is heard at the polls?" She responded, "No, I think money talks so loud that the voice of the people is drowned."

She was asked, "What is the outstanding deficiency of Americans?" Keller responded, "Lack of originality. Everything is standardized, even our thoughts. The central motive of all our action is 'What will others think about us?'"

When asked if she desired her sight more than anything else in the world? Keller was quick to respond, "No! No! I would rather walk with a friend in the dark than walk alone in the light" (Harrity and Martin, 1962).

investment and epic, energetic brawn. Helen and Annie, who had toured on the Chautauqua lecture circuit, were "old pros" when they started in vaudeville beginning in February 1920 at the New York Palace.

Harry Weber became their personal manager, and he managed other Blind, Deaf, and disabled performers for the National Vaudeville Association (Lash, 1980). Each membership carried insurance and financial aid in case of unemployment that was internationally accepted. The association also operated sanitariums for members with tuberculosis as well as health resorts in California, Arizona, Colorado and other locations.

Helen enjoyed working-class families attending the circuit, where she came in contact with dancers, singers, acrobats, comedians, magicians, and performing children and animals. Vaudeville audiences offered the "warm tide of human life pulsing" (Keller, 1929, 1955). Keller was extremely conscious of audiences. Before uttering anything, she felt the audiences' breath that came in the form of little pulses to her face. She could detect their appreciation or indifference. Their programs were twenty minutes twice a day, and Helen's theme song was called "The Star of Happiness" (Lash, 1980). Keller next demonstrated how she lip-read and learned how to speak her first sentence: "I am not dumb now" (Helen Keller Film Corporation, 1919). Annie repeated everything Helen articulated so the audience could understand it. Helen, Annie, and Polly became nomads traveling by train. The pay was good, and the weeklong gigs allowed them to remain a while in each location. From 1919 to 1922, they performed nearly daily in elegant evening gowns on a set of a drawing room with a fireplace.

Helen and Annie visited a very ill John Macy living in Boston. Helen wrote to her mother, "He looked dreadful, and seemed like a frail old man" (Lash, 1980). Helen was angry that he still demanded money for a life of "selfishness and alcohol." Then when Annie became too ill to go on stage in Toronto and she slowly withdrew from the act, Polly Thomson with her Scottish accent soon stepped into the act.

Kate wrote to Helen, expressing her love in March 1920. Seemingly aware of her mortality, Kate promised her daughter when she died, she would see her in the world to come. While Kate's actions propelled Helen onto a world broader stage, Helen's book *The Story of My Life* and the film *Deliverance* overlooked her functional role in Helen's life. Mrs. Kate Keller and Mrs. Harmony Bridgman had transferred care of their Deaf-Blind daughter to guardian-promoters, and consequently, both were written out of the histories. Indeed, *Deliverance* depicted Annie as Kate's social superior, a Northerner who came to the rescue of Helen and her Southern mother who could not cope.

Helen Keller and Annie Sullivan prepared to go on stage as usual in Los Angeles, California, in November of 1921. Two hours before the performance, Helen received a telegram from her sister Mildred Keller Tyson notifying her of Kate Keller's death. The act went on. Kate Keller had reached beyond Harmony Bridgman's grasp to develop an adult relationship with her Deaf-Blind daughter to lend strength when needed. Kate Keller negotiated a relationship with Helen Keller for her to carry on some core family values of grace when attending difficult duties.

10

Between Persona and Image

With her mother Catherine "Kate" Adams Keller dead, Helen Keller's defining relationship remained with her teacher, guardian, and promoter Annie Sullivan Macy. Kate Keller's simple grave marker attested to a life lived beyond her famous daughter. Mrs. John Albert Macy would not have lived a memorable life if it were not for her famous student who defined her existence, but now Annie Sullivan Macy was tied to Helen's by financial trusts. Despite being her greatest achievement, her single student Helen Keller was the only extant evidence showcasing Annie's abundant creativity and intelligence. However, Helen Keller, Kate's "Little Bronco" possessed and embodied persona without Annie Sullivan Macy. Even though her apparent disabilities were plainly visible to the world, Helen Keller was a complete normal human being regardless of contrived realities of anyone who might profit.

Annie could not let go of her first and greatest achievement. Annie repeatedly attempted to turn Helen into an institution, even recruiting an absentee husband John Albert Macy, to project her image as a great educator, but nobody could deny the Deaf-Blind woman's humanity and soul. Vaudeville played itself out for Helen and Annie after a few seasons. The industry declined with the popularity of silent films. Sadly, in her desperation to keep the past alive, Annie failed to exploit how her partnership with Helen laid groundwork for Deaf-Blind activism. Therefore, in promoting herself, Annie created roadblocks for establishing resources and services to serve the most marginalized group within the disabled community.

While Helen and Annie's twenty-minute scripts varied geographically with audiences, the act offered only one trick: the process Annie used to teach Helen to speak.

Needing to create an image for herself, Annie, who had her own disabilities, developed an image of dependency for Helen in order for the aging teacher to define *herself.* Annie managed to continue to publicly diminish Kate Keller's role in her daughter's life. Kate remained on the geographic sidelines of Helen's public image until she could reenter Helen's life as a mature role model of productivity. With Kate Keller dead, there was no motherly individual to compete with for Helen's devotion, but if Helen was not completely devoted to the teacher-guardian-promoter who undermined her equilibrium, she never conveyed any disloyalty. Sadly, Mrs. Annie "Mansfield" Sullivan Macy was so successful in creating a public image for Helen Keller, unnecessary for an individual with a true persona, she painted her own creative and intelligent self into a corner where there was no space for sweet, loving Annie to grow and flourish.

When Helen and Annie's vaudeville act played in Pittsburgh, Pennsylvania, their longtime friend and financial supporter Mary Thaw reserved all of the boxes in the theater to fill with friends and family. Mrs. Thaw had long held an aversion to women performing on the public stage ever since her daughter-in-law, Edith Nesbit Thaw, proved to be a catalyst in her family's downfall by disclosing sordid court testimony about her son's mental illness. To Mary Thaw's shock, Helen and Annie's vaudeville act was sandwiched between less-than-respectable acts with dancers, acrobats, and trained animals (Lash, 1980).

While on a vaudeville circuit in Syracuse, New York, Helen, Annie, and Polly met up again with their Deaf-Blind friend Thomas Stringer in his home. During one of Helen's earliest public speaking appearance at the Perkins Institute for the Blind, she helped to build a trust fund established by Michael Anagnos for Stringer. Unlike Helen, Tom became an early Deaf-Blind individual to attend a public school to get assimilated with seeing-hearing students. Tom's guardian, a grocer, encouraged Tom to utilize carpentry skills to manufacture lettuce crates and picture frames to build independence. Stringer owned a room full of tools he used to invent things out of his own head as a means of self-expression (Rocheleau and Mack, 1930).

Thinking related to educating the disabled changed as a result of Annie's expensive one-teacher-to-one-student pedagogy to include adult rehabilitation training to build practical skills designed to carry the Deaf-Blind into activities with broader communities. With Thomas Stringer and other Deaf-Blind people, young and old, Deaf and Blind activists explored rehabilitation as a means to build and restore independent lives through education and therapy. While Thomas Stringer developed a quiet persona, as long as Helen was responsible for maintaining Annie and Polly Thomson financially, she remained confined to *the act.*

Helen's character development trajectory naturally led her to her ideal self: her *persona* despite disabilities remained grounded in her remaining senses of touch, smell, and taste. Helen did not wear her fancy gowns at home; she dressed in functional, comfortable, somewhat frumpy clothes and contentedly sat on the floor to read her Bible or news. Still, Helen secretly thrived in her *image* as a Deaf-Blind performer within the vibrant vaudeville community where she connected with working-class families. Reporters sometimes asked Helen why she went into vaudeville, and Helen responded with a favorite one liner, "For the money . . . I don't seem to hold onto it" (Keller, 1955). That was not the truth; Helen Keller was trained to *not* deal with money and was encompassed by her guardian's fiscal dysfunctionality.

Annie, on the other hand, locked into her cultivated image of Teacher, never transcended childhood traumas experienced in impoverished New England backwaters. Annie's life peaked only when she traveled to a greater boondock in Tuscumbia, Alabama. She took a "big city" educational idea of tactile learning and embellished it with a desperate love and tenacious creativity to achieve her great communications breakthrough with Helen. Annie could only break out of the fictions she created by undermining the work of other teachers and alienating her student's well-intentioned friends when they threatened her authority. Annie once confided condescendingly to Helen, "Left to oneself, one's intellect can be ruthless, and one frets at the stupidity of most minds" (Lash, 1980).

Mrs. Macy, fettered in body and spirit, could not express her creativity and passions as she had done before she married John Macy. Despite what Annie and her husband reported to the public, Helen Keller was never *a ball of clay.* Helen in childhood demonstrated a wily, wild intelligence. In her solitary moments, Helen traveled unhindered through the world of ideas, undeterred by Annie's fretting of what others thought of her image.

As the Roaring Twenties commenced, new visions emerged with women taking on new social, economic, and political roles. Having been somewhat predatory with male protectors when she was young and flirty, Annie was no Kate Keller; she retreated into a passive-aggressive vaudeville stage mother role exploiting past victories without building secure foundations for the future. Helen and Annie occasionally performed on radio when it became commercially viable between 1920 and 1923. Radio studios offered no life vibrations, no shuffling of feet, no echoes of applause, and no odor of tobacco or makeup, only a blank void in which her voice floated so Helen felt like she was talking to ghosts.

Helen, Annie, and Polly visited John Macy once again before he relocated to Greenwich Village in New York. John, still legally married to

Annie because she had refused to sign the divorce papers even after *his mother* pleaded with her to do so, lived a bohemian lifestyle. Mrs. John Albert Macy was just another one of Annie's fabrications. John worked as an editor at *The Nation* and lived with a Deaf-Mute sculptor named Myla and their bastard daughter who occasionally accompanied him to the office. Myla died leaving John as an alcoholic single parent, and he aged quickly (Lash, 1980).

Life without John was not the same for Annie, but she tried to remain a pragmatic survivor as she still controlled Helen. Annie ironically told Helen, "You know that I am a chameleon. Let us adjust our lives to the actual. Let us be useful to someone else" (Lash, 1980). Helen prided herself on developing an authentic poetic vision and channeling it into a unique career of rhetoric and activism. Her aborted romance with John's socialist friend Peter Fagan was illuminating; it opened her eyes to her isolation. Mrs. Macy still lived in the past century when women relied upon male protectors for status and image, and she refused to move to the present. Annie seemed to project her own ideals to her charge when she told Helen, "Life is boring for highly cultivated people unless they have poetic vision" (Lash, 1980).

Annie's eyesight continued to decline, so within the household, the Blind led the Deaf-Blind. Annie resented thinkers greater than herself. However, before she died, the retiring Kate Keller fought for Helen like a smart Southern woman by subtly passing on a social lesson from her father, Captain Arthur Henley Keller, who was known for inviting people into his world throughout good times and bad. When Annie closed up, Helen opened up to new relationships and communities.

For every relationship Annie sabotaged, Helen mended or established more strategic alliances as if she were playing a checkers game with an old friend. When World War I made Annie's poetic vision obsolete, Helen asserted, "When one door of happiness closes, another one opens, but often we look so long at the closed door that we do not see the one which has opened for us" (Lash, 1980). After striving for an advanced education, Helen was not blind to her guardian's challenges. She knew they were bound together financially for life, and like with John Macy, she ultimately believed, "If we were not a trouble to each other, we would not love as we do" (Keller, 2005).

Throughout their life together, Helen chose to overlook or cover her guardian's insecurities and indiscretions. Helen was never ignorant in recognizing faults in herself and others; her courage was demonstrated in recognizing what Annie Sullivan brought to her life and navigating the areas of their shared lives. Helen Keller's Southern hospitality welcomed and integrated the orphans and vagrants entering their lives to create a unique living mosaic within her household.

When Helen, Annie, and Polly left vaudeville, the three women remained at a crossroads. Without Kate Keller to serve as backup when crisis arose, Helen's college friend Lenore Smith stepped in when needed. There was a void. Kate and Helen had not agreed on everything; it was not an easy relationship, but Kate's instincts protected her daughter and were selfless. Nevertheless, Annie kept telling Helen, "You will be glad of my merciless prodding one day" (Lash, 1980).

Annie's temper was often aimless, coming from her desperate fear of returning to poverty. From their earliest years together, Annie told Helen, "You will find that you will accomplish something; it may not be what you started, but you will find that you have done something you will be glad to remember" (Lash, 1980). Annie's roundabout methods impacted perceptions of Helen Keller. Despite Helen's activism beginning in 1906, Dr. Harry Best, who compiled a massive treatise *The Blind* (1919), did not mention Helen Keller or her teacher, who he did not taking seriously in an age of social science determining public policy. Helen Keller, after all, was the star of a financially unsuccessful silent film and a mere vaudeville act, whereas Laura Bridgman (who was named) was the product of Dr. Samuel Gridley Howe's professional training.

Soon Helen, Annie, and Polly were drawn into a new adventure after Blind activists established the American Foundation for the Blind (AFB) out of the need to create economic stability for the Blind. The AFB, a national clearinghouse for information, books, and education for the Blind, was established in New York City not far from the suburb of Forest Hills where Helen and Annie lived.

Blind activists identified Charles F. F. Campbell, who had recruited Helen as a Blind activist after she graduated from Radcliffe College, as the most effective advocate for the establishment of the American Foundation for the Blind (Koestler, 1976). Inspired by former Perkins Institute director Michael Anagnos, who had employed Annie and then Helen to cultivate the media to raise money and awareness of Perkins Institute for the Blind, Campbell recognized how Helen could build nationwide support for the AFB. His notion involved Helen and Annie adapting their vaudeville act to recruit donors in *intimate* drawing room meetings of wealthy supporters.

Campbell understood the image of "Helen Keller" held power because it was her real persona. He convinced her to support AFB's mission. Helen, Annie, and Polly started a pilot campaign in the New York area in 1921. The campaign proved to be successful as Campbell predicted, but the AFB did not know how to compensate the three women for their work. They recognized, as William Wade earlier saw, Helen's total dependence upon Annie did not reflect the new model for educating and rehabilitating the Blind and the Deaf-Blind for independent living. Helen appeared fiercely independent, but she visibly remained totally dependent upon someone to serve as her eyes, ears, and voice.

Helen often became the purpose for being to somehow surrounded her (Nielsen, 2004). An editor at Doubleday Publishing, thirty-year-old Nella Braddy, was assigned to write about Helen Keller and her teacher. Georgia-born Braddy was a Southerner, but she possessed a temperament of a New Englander: she was a diligent and calculating woman who recognized the void left by Kate Keller's death. Braddy seemed to have the perfect grounded temperament needed to navigate the institution of Helen Keller; she was a keen observer who was intellectually, emotionally, intuitively, and sensitively perceptive.

Like John Macy, Braddy was self-taught and appreciated irony; like Annie and Helen, she was generous and loved nature and animals. Braddy was not like Polly Thomson when she met and befriended Annie in 1922. Braddy lived in a Garden City boardinghouse in Garden City, New Jersey, where the headquarters of her employer, publishing powerhouse Doubleday, Page and Company, was located. Braddy was dispatched to work with and cultivate Helen and Annie. Braddy learned the manual alphabet to communicate directly with Helen, who was the key to her successful literary career.

Annie, despite various health challenges, tenaciously negotiated a generous salary for Helen, Polly, and herself in 1923. The AFB soon discovered what Mark Twain, Henry H. Rogers, and their capitalist friends had earlier found: Helen rarely handled money, and Annie could not budget resources. After the campaign in 1925, the three women vacationed in California for several months. Upon their return to Forest Hills, New York, they discovered their finances were depleted and their home was in need of major repairs.

The AFB could also see Helen would never exchange her ideals for a paycheck. She continued to speak out on the impact of the capitalist system on the disabled in ways undermining fundraising efforts of the new organization established by Blind activists to serve the Blind. Helen argued, "Superficial charities make smooth the way of the prosperous: but to advocate for all human beings should have leisure and comfort" (Koestler, 1976). As a socialist, she was contradictory within AFB's philanthropic campaigns because they were dependent upon large donations from capitalists. Helen found herself caught between her image and her persona when she asserted, "But it is not fair fighting or good arguing to find that Helen Keller's mistakes' spring out of the limitations of her development" (Lash, 1980).

The challenge of paradoxical Helen's attitude about charities arose after AFB president "Major" Moses Charles Migel tried to provide personal financial help for Helen's household beyond her AFB salary. Migel was a retired silk merchant who was the same age as Annie. Like other institutional managers, Migel discovered how prickly "Miss Spitfire" could be, yet he still chose to help with her mounting medical bills because the trio added significant value to AFB objectives.

When Migel negotiated with Annie, she was terse from the start as her weaknesses made her more formidable. Annie protected the household's interest while Migel hoped to conserve AFB's funds accepted with the understanding they would be used for services for the Blind. The six-month pilot resulted in $100,000 donations, and essentially fifty cents for each dollar raised went to expenses including salaries for Helen, Annie, and Polly. Many major cities railed against national fundraising campaigns that featured Helen when they wanted assurance that funding raised locally would serve local communities.

Migel offered the three $750-plus expenses per month (Koestler, 1976). Annie was outraged and countered that she, Helen, and Polly were worth $2,000 per month for a six-month campaign to raise $2 million for an endowment. While Annie appeared to embrace AFB work for its philosophy of service to the Blind that allowed individuals to discover their best selves, when Migel reported their actual outcome, it gave her cause for pause.

Annie, remembering the subscription campaigns spearheaded by Helen's capitalist benefactors and Mark Twain, suggested the AFB develop a grassroots pledge drive where "common people" could pledge twenty-five cents per month for a year. When AFB failed to respond to her idea, she attacked Migel in the letter saying he was trying to exploit the threesome by getting their "labor as cheaply as possible."

Robert B. Irwin, who was closer to Helen's age, became the Director of Research and Education of the AFB in 1925. Irwin was blinded at five years of age and went on to earn his highest degree at Harvard University in 1907, where he concentrated on education, government, and history studies. Irwin started his career in 1910 as the supervisor of the classes for the Blind and visually impaired in the Cleveland Public Schools.

Migel found it challenging to cope with continuing pushback from Annie and retreated from active negotiations with her and Helen. Irwin stepped up with a smoother touch to lead AFB relations with Annie, Helen, and Polly. He envisioned Helen spearheading a fundraising campaign to endow the AFB. His plan was for Helen to speak in the high society homes of AFB supporters to solicit funds. The Foundation would pay for the expenses for Helen, Annie, and Polly's travel. However, Annie's unrelenting negotiations pitted the three against the Foundation's board, but they eventually agreed to pay the trio $2,000 per month, worth almost $30,000 in purchasing power in 2021). Helen and Annie spoke to ten thousand people during seven gatherings and collected almost $8,000.

*   *   *

The news media pigeonholed Helen to only discuss Deaf-Blind issues. Helen could tolerate having her ideas attacked, opposed, and ridiculed but not her ability to speak out because of disabilities. She wrote, "As political speeches and editorials of our 'best' papers are transmitted to me, I am amazed at the power which stops the ears and clouds the vision of society." Helen explained her paradox, "The decencies and refinements of life, is a Utopian dream, and one who seriously contemplates its realization must indeed be deaf, dumb, and blind" (Lash, 1980).

Almost a century ago, Helen had challenged the validity of the two-party political system. She felt that a constitution could not be final as an effectual guide to the nation's conduct in the shifting circumstances when the United States acted on a dynamic world stage. Helen wrote, "I believe we have heard the swan song of the old parties. The muddling of their leaders has brought the world to the brink of chaos. The progressives insist upon taking matters into their own hands. They see that the government must be revitalized" (Keller, 1955).

Helen wrote a rousing letter in 1924 in support of Robert M. La Follette, Sr. a pacifist running for President of the United States on the Farmer-Labor ticket (Nielsen, 2004). John Hitz had earlier introduced Helen and her mother Kate Keller to "Fighting Bob" when they visited Washington, D.C., and she saw his success as an answer to many social issues. La Follette ran one of the most successful "third-party" campaigns in U.S. history before his death in 1925, leaving his son to take his senate seat. The La Follettes led efforts to establish rehabilitation programs in Wisconsin as this approach to disability grew in stature.

While the AFB offered Helen, Annie, and Polly new financial stability, they were not pleased with Helen's socialist politics since she never remained silent as she crisscrossed the country, making as many as five speeches per day. Helen wrote to her sister Mildred Keller Tyson, "I know of nothing more fatiguing than this business of threshing out plans, objecting, suggesting, negotiating, and explaining matters to strangers. We do not know the personnel of the Foundation well yet, and so we are feeling our way all along most cautiously" (Keller, 2005).

The AFB benefitted from Helen Keller's name recognition and her vast network of friends. Her ongoing supporters Edward and Mary Louise Bok as well as Mary Thaw remained woven through her life whether or not they agreed with her politics. Edward, who had invited Helen to write controversial articles for *Ladies' Home Journal* at the century's start, contributed $5,000 to launch the AFB campaign for the Blind in America in November 1924.

The AFB mobilized lobbying efforts for rehabilitation services to support the newly Blind in adapting to new situations. Helen lobbied legislatures in eighteen states to establish commissions to examine issues related to education, travel on public transportation to allow a Blind individual and a guide to board with one ticket fare, and funding for braille books. The AFB recruited Helen to talk to the members at the annual convention of Lions Clubs International, a male service organization in Cedar Point, Ohio, on June 30, 1925.

Helen demonstrated her Southern charm when she stated plainly, "I am knocking on your door. I want to be adopted" (Einhorn, 1998). She asked the Lions to imagine themselves becoming blind and suddenly losing independence. Helen invited the Lions to foster awareness about the issues of the Blind in local chapters and invited the organization to foster and sponsor AFB work. Helen challenged the Lions to constitute themselves as "Knights of the Blind in this crusade against darkness." The Lions accepted Helen's challenge to include programs to address preventable blindness, and they continue to work on these projects today.

As Helen continued to promote fundraising efforts for the AFB, she toured California in 1926, where she met a Massachusetts-born horticulturalist named Luther Burbank in his garden in Santa Rosa, California. Burbank developed a potato that could be rapidly cultivated. Burbank was a proponent of the Eugenics movement, and he believed the idea that civilized human society was comparable to plants in a hothouse or a carefully cultivated and weeded garden (Burbank, 1915). The horticulturalist argued, "The inherent affinities in the selection of marriage partners might be construed as being eugenic providing that legal restrictions do not interfere with the freedom of choice" (Burbank, 1915).

Burbank, who received support from Thomas Edison and Andrew Carnegie to patent and profit from his innovations, believed "human" weeds should be removed along with "unfit" dependent members of communities. This suggested the disabled and poor should be prevented from having children. Burbank stated societies of classical antiquity, including Italy, employed principles of eugenic selection with "rigor."

Burbank, who connected plant propagation by humans to patterns in the natural world, wrote an essay called "The Training of the Human Plant" (1907), suggesting ways of improving the lives of children. He believed that poverty in the United States could be eradicated by clearing out tenements. He argued city planners should develop conducive environments where city dwellers growing up in congested, dark, unventilated tenements could be transplanted like flowers bred in rich, well-watered, and carefully weeded garden soil.

Burbank viewed education as important to developing the human plant: "As a twig is bent, the tree is inclined" (Burbank, 1915). Burbank raised a deeper question about whether Deaf-Blind women including Laura Bridgman and Helen Keller were worth the effort and cost of their educations and lifelong care. He asserted Laura (who was a hothouse grown in an earlier generation) and Helen (who was more naturally grown in the modern world) were exceptions to his extreme example of children who become Blind and Deaf at a young age due to accident or illness becoming *congenital idiots.*

While Helen's friend who conducted the first census of the Deaf-Blind William Wade argued every Deaf-Blind individual was worthy of assistance, he believed they should be educated or rehabilitated to live independent lives. Burbank observed through great effort the other senses could be developed to compensate for "the all-importance of the environing influences that we commonly speak of as 'educational' in completing the work which heredity carries only to the nascent state of development" (Burbank, 1915). During her visit, Burbank gave Helen a generous donation for the AFB.

During the 1910s, Helen and Annie's lectures inspired several young women to explore service careers. A special education teacher from the Midwest named Rebecca Mack, who compiled scrapbooks of Helen and Annie's adventures, picked up where William Wade left off to develop another census of the Deaf-Blind. Annie carried a grudge against Wade for many years because he had opposed the idea of starting a school for the Deaf-Blind in their Wrentham home, so she stonewalled Mack's efforts. In 1927, Mack collaborated with Corrine Rocheleau to chronicle almost four hundred Deaf-Blind in the United States with the needs of school-aged children to access instruction. However, the Deaf-Blind community was thought to have a number closer to two thousand people.

As Helen Keller dug deeper into her work for the AFB, her disappointments with unsuccessful campaigns of radical friends and her inability to communicate her own thoughts frustrated her. She believed if a Deaf-Blind person learned to speak early, their voice could be preserved even if this was not her experience. Helen wore a mask in her public duties as she and Annie became aggressive in their negotiations with Robert B. Irwin and Migel. Helen quipped, "The grateful smile that I wear on all occasions is becoming 'fixed' on my face and won't come off when I go to bed."

Irwin increasingly became important in her life; he gained notoriety as an effective activist for the Blind when he headed a Uniform Type Committee of the American Association of Workers for the Blind to adopt a single system of embossed print in the United States. He developed an efficient braille-printing machine that reduced the bulk and cost of braille books by about 40 percent. When the AFB announced new technology of

HELEN MAY MARTIN: THE DEAF-BLIND PIANIST

Helen Keller took a few piano lessons to see if she would take to it, but she only retained a mechanical knowledge and decided not to continue lessons. Another Deaf-Blind woman named Helen May Martin born on December 18, 1893, became a pianist (Rocheleau and Mack, 1930). Martin's mother was her teacher and companion through her formative years as she was home-educated.

From the time when she was very young, Martin showed an interest in music and would sit for hours at the piano drumming or listening using her hands while others play. Similar to Keller, music came to Martin through perception of vibrations to her hands and feet. Martin's mother witnessed an inclination toward music and gave her some piano lessons, teaching her a simple melody, and Helen would reproduce it. Martin's progress was steady, and soon she had other teachers until friends urged her to give a public concert in her hometown.

When Martin was eighteen years old, she entered the Kansas School for the Deaf at Olathe, Kansas, which became her home. Martin started performing in public concerts in several Midwest cities in 1922. She read and memorized music scores embossed in New York point. When Martin played, she "listened" with her left foot placed on the soft pedal, and when listening to others play, she placed her hands on the piano's sounding board.

Martin's favorite composers were Ludwig von Beethoven and American composer Edward MacDowell (1860–1908) who was known for his tone poems for the piano including *Woodland Sketches* (1896).

After a performance, a little girl in the audience approached Martin, telling her, "I feel as if love has been poured all over me." A special education teacher Rebecca Mack established a fund so that Martin could develop her musical talent.

talking books for blind adults, Irwin approached Helen and Annie to join efforts to get legislative support.

When Thomas Edison patented his Tin-Foil Phonograph in 1877, one of its listed uses was as a phonograph book to "speak to Blind people without effort on their part." The growing popularity of the radio created a new use for recordings as radio networks prerecorded programing to send out to local broadcasting markets. In the late 1920s, "talking" motion pictures also required sound tracts. Irwin brought Thomas Edison's idea of using 33-rpm long-playing records for talking books to fruition in service to the Deaf-Blind and promoting it nationwide as a library service to supply them to the Blind.

Talking books were not a priority for Helen because she did not benefit from the technology as a Deaf-Blind person, but she continued to speak

---

KATE M. FOLEY: THE BLIND LIBRARIAN

Kate M. Foley (1873–1940) was an American librarian and advocate for Blind literacy working with the California State Library (Koestler, 1976). Like Anne Sullivan Macy, Foley's parents were both Irish immigrants. Blinded in infancy, Foley was six years old before she understood what it meant to be blind because someone always held her hand. Foley attended the California Institute for the Deaf and Dumb and Blind, graduating in 1895. Foley remembered, "My ears and fingers continued to flood my mind with knowledge, and the want of eyesight did not distress me." Foley continued, "When I touched an object, or listened to a lesson, my mind stored it away for future reference."

Helen Keller admired Foley for her optimism in working with the newly Blind and for her ongoing work to prevent blindness (Keller, 1929). Foley worked as a home teacher of the Blind in the Books for the Blind Department of the California State Library beginning in 1917, which provided her with a platform to establish public school classes for blind children, train teachers to assimilate blind students into public schools, train California clubwomen to transpose texts into braille, and work with blind prisoners at San Quentin.

Foley was a major proponent of radio for teaching the Blind and the talking book. When Keller and Robert Irwin led efforts to get senators together to raise money so that the American Federation for the Blind could purchase equipment that would enable them to double the output of talking books after Anne Sullivan Macy's death, Foley had mobility challenges in addition to her blindness. Foley lost her sister shortly after Sullivan died, so the two felt empathy for each other. Keller observed, "Kate is quite as much alone as I am on the dark trail" (Keller, 1929).

---

about funding issues. In addressing the Iowa State Legislature in 1927, Helen supported developing a committee to allocate separate funds for the Blind from agencies supporting people with other disabilities in general welfare budgets. Helen asserted that with education and special aid, the Blind could become self-supporting citizens.

Migel led talking book lobbying when he met with Thomas Edison's son, Charles Edison, at the Edison Laboratories in West Orange, New Jersey, to promote the idea of talking books. Irwin soon envisioned libraries for the Blind stocked with recordings instead of braille books, but it was the Great Depression, and Edison Laboratories did not consider the project to be a profitable enterprise to develop. Migel next approached the Carnegie Corporation, established in 1911 to advance the diffusion of knowledge and information that supported public library work.

Helen paused in her lobbying efforts to write *My Religion* (1927), describing how Swedenborg's writings shaped her faith. She asserted, "To one who is Deaf and Blind, the spiritual world offers no difficulty." Annie retired from public appearances in 1927. Annie did not confide her traumatic past to Helen like John Macy had not shared his professional writing with her. Annie, like her father Thomas Sullivan, was a wonderful storyteller. She wove Irish stories about the little people in Ireland filled with terrific imagery. Other than the stories from her parents' homeland Ireland, Annie never spoke of her father.

After marrying Keith Henney in 1926, Nella Braddy Henney joined Helen's entourage and started deeper conversations with combined aggression and sensitivity between Helen and Annie concerning their lives (Nielsen, 2004). Henney was fascinated with Helen's thought processes. Annie, who wanted to dig up information for her own biography, offered Henney a roadmap into interrogating Helen. In conversations, Annie started Helen with object lessons of her past: "horse," "city," and then "house." The abstract notion of "house" solicited the domestic geographic memories Helen used to remain in balance. Helen described the houses where she was happy because there were many objects her fingers could touch and remember. Although she spent a lot of time in Mary Thaw's Pittsburg home, the housekeeping staff probably kept it spotless, so Helen could not recall details as she would from Wrentham or Edward Everett Hale's cluttered office.

Henney and Annie asked Helen what her friends meant to her. Helen responded, "A touch of the hand . . . the footsteps . . . the feel of a face . . . of the skin" (Lash, 1980).

Henney needed to be able to translate Helen Keller to write Annie's story. Henney used what she had learned not to be close to Helen as a friend, but to advance her writing career. Worn down by life, Annie's disillusionment in life stemmed from disappointments with men. With important matters of the heart, Annie was secretive; she was in her sixties before Helen learned about the hardships of her guardian's early life. Prior to those revelations, Annie simply had told Helen she was born in the village of Feeding Hills, Massachusetts, and she lost her mother, Alice Sullivan, and younger brother James "Jimmy" Sullivan at an early age.

While Helen adopted a philosophical approach to her disabilities, Annie viewed her own vision loss as karmic (Lash, 1980). For all their closeness, Helen and Annie did not confide their deepest emotions to each other. As Henney collaborated with Helen on a second autobiography called *Midstream: My Later Life* (1929), Annie resisted having her early story told. Annie asked Henney to keep an eye on Helen's writing in 1928, while she asked Migel to finance a trip to Feeding Hills and Tewksbury to jog her memories, but she did not want the purpose of the visit made known to AFB.

Once Henney edited a chapter, she read it to Annie, who translated it to Helen with fingerspelling, a triangular process just as she had done with

John during the work on *The Story of My Life*. Helen remembered, "I am not an easy, prolific writer . . . it is with pain, not joy; for I cannot forget the stern labor that went into them" (Keller, 1929). Hammering out ideas was exasperating. Helen developed her own system for staying on pace with writing projects: she used hairpins to prick appropriate phrases on type-written pages.

Midstream (1929) illustrated how Helen's sensory skills were not remarkable. Touch was Helen's chief vector to the outer world with sensations including heat, cold, friction, smoothness, roughness, pain, and vibrations playing upon her skin. Henney's boss Frank Nelson "Effendi" Doubleday, founder of Doubleday & McClure Publishers, persuaded Helen to submit to sensory testing. A professor of neurology at Columbia University Dr. Frederick Tinley tested Helen's remaining senses. He wanted to understand how she received impressions of her environment. Tactile sense travels throughout the body via the nerve system and under the urge of necessity tactile sense becomes discriminating, so the feeler's mind can draw conclusions from the revealed sensations.

Helen remembered how one technician counted her breaths, one took her pulse, and another gauged her body temperature. Tests determined if Helen blushed, laughed, or cried and if she demonstrated fear and anger or experienced taste under certain circumstances. Helen whirled about like a large wooden top in an apparatus to see how she would react when zapped with electric currents, while bound at the wrists with rubber cuffs. With her head in a vicelike apparatus, Helen's fingers and joints were rapidly moved up and down. Technicians asked Helen which finger moved, and what joint moved, and in what direction. She responded for hours with whatever came into her thought and hoped her responses matched what the machine recorded.

Scientists determined Helen's reactions were untrustworthy, and the machines reported she fell short in the scientists' expectations. This undermined Helen's equilibrium because much of her self-identity was established with her remaining senses of touch, taste, and smell. In trying to understand if Helen's remaining senses were better than her seeing and hearing counterparts, she received the same feedback she received from childhood playfellows: Helen was the same as everyone else, only she was Deaf and Blind. Helen's impressions were not derived from senses alone; they also came from the association of abstract ideas and imagination. Helen learned from experience that ideas entered her mind as detached, these chaotic physical experiences she synchronized into harmonious concepts of the world.

Testing revealed Helen's sense of smell was well preserved, her sense of taste was moderately preserved, but her senses of smell and touch combined, offering her information about her environment (Keller, 1929).

Odors and vibrations communicated aesthetic information. Helen told Tilney, "The sense of smell is the aesthetic sense, I think, even more than sight. I know that odors give me a vivid conception of my surroundings."

Helen associated certain smells with poignant memories, deep emotions, and poetry. She reported to Tilney about her sensitivity to unpleasant odors, "Bad smells have a depressing influence upon me; for they suggest all manner of dreaded things—disease, accidents, coming evil, and unhappy lives. Sometimes, when such an odor comes between me and a beloved object, a nervous tremor seizes me, and I find it difficult to control myself" (Keller, 1929). Tests revealed Helen possessed no sense of sight and no perception of light or dark. Helen's glass eyes were implanted in 1910, so no retinas remained, and she was completely Deaf; she had no bone or air conduction in either ear.

Helen and Annie were not money people. As Annie's health deteriorated, the AFB grew concerned about who would manage Helen's affairs when Annie died. Annie reported how Helen painstakingly worked for the AFB's letter writing campaign, sometimes retyping letters five or six times to get each right. Helen inscribed over seven hundred books over a three-month period with either Annie or Polly standing over her to make sure they were straight. While Polly was called a secretary, Helen was the only typist, and they needed a stenographer.

Meanwhile, doctors removed Annie's left eye to relieve pain, but surgery on the other eye was postponed because it would result in total blindness. Henney soon realized Annie's story was far more compelling than Helen's (Lash, 1980). Once the revelations surfaced about Annie's formative years at Tewksbury almshouse, Helen realized the woman she was frighteningly dependent upon, like her husband John Macy, had never truly confided in her. Helen Keller was humiliated by the revelation.

*   *   *

For two decades, Helen believed capitalistic financial speculation acted like economic parasites feeding upon values and creating none. October 24, 1929, the day known as "Black Thursday," altered the course of many lives. The New York Stock Exchange hailed the Great Depression as a period of global depression of unprecedented scale as even once affluent people lost wealth. Helen, Annie, and Polly returned to New York in the early stages of the Great Depression when millions of people became unemployed, with nearly a quarter of the adult American population looking for work for an average duration of forty-three months in 1933.

Annie was almost completely blind, and it filled her with a sense of desperation and hopelessness. Having little religious faith, Annie felt old age was a pointless struggle. Conversely, Helen developed a deeper faith and approached her disabilities with more courage. Their roles reversed with Polly in the household, so Helen became the guide and breadwinner, and her efforts were always to keep Annie positive. When Mary Thaw died in 1929, she left a generous bequest to her longtime friends Helen and Annie. This money paid for Annie's mounting medical bills and other debts.

Helen and Annie later met theoretical physicist Albert Einstein at the St. Moritz Hotel in New York City. Helen was impressed by Einstein's sympathetic handclasp and shy manner, and he allowed Helen to touch his head, so she could feel the "fraternal aura" of his personality. Helen was outraged that any entity could try to brand Einstein as a "traitor for his humane pacifism" (Lash, 1980). Einstein was intrigued by Annie and told her, "Your work has interested me more than any other achievement in modern education" (Lash, 1980). He gushed, "Not only did you impart language to Helen, you unfolded her personality, and such an achievement borders on the superhuman" (Lash, 1980).

Polly accompanied Helen to Washington, D.C., where she successfully lobbied the Congress to support a bill allocating $75,000 to fund production of braille books for the Blind; this became the first federal program for the Blind. Helen spoke before the House of Representatives Committee on the Library about H. R. 9042 on March 27, 1930, asking to appropriate funds to supply braille books to the Blind. Ruth Baker Pratt, the first female-elected representative to Congress from New York, was on the House Committee on the Library and introduced the Pratt-Smoot Act (1931). Helen argued, "Books are the eyes of the blind." Helen appealed to legislators to consider what it would be like to be blind. "We who face the reality know we cannot escape the shadow while life lasts" (Koestler, 1976).

Helen's preference during her youth was for sudden reform, but with Migel's moderate influence, she developed a desire to transcend political factions through gendered cooperation working with First Ladies. Helen organized and raised money for the conference budget because the Blind were organizing work in their own interests. In early 1931, Helen became a key participant in an international AFB conference in New York for workers for the Blind. Information from twenty-three countries was disseminated, and Helen presented delegates to the First Lady Lou Henry Hoover and met Eleanor Roosevelt.

Migel recognized Helen's work contributed to the early success of the AFB, so he lobbied the Foundation to fund a $6,000 yearly salary and a $1,200 allowance for clerical help for Helen and Annie. Migel convinced Annie to allow him to establish a committee of three men selected by Helen, including himself, to consolidate and manage her trust and financial affairs. The AFB developed the Helen Keller Trust Custody Account consisting of a stock portfolio with shares from Nella Braddy Henney's employer Doubleday, Doran & Co., a New Jersey department store L.

Bumburger purchased by Macy's in 1929, as well as Standard Oil of California and Indiana (Lash, 1980).

President Franklin Delano Roosevelt's policies preserved the power of the trusts established by Helen's capitalist friends. Roosevelt revisited the gold standard for currency as a means to stabilize the economy. Considering how so many struggled during the Great Depression, Helen, Annie, and Polly were in relatively good financial shape. The household already received $5,000 annually from the Carnegie pension, $800 from the Eleanor Hutton Trust for Helen's education, and $600 from the Henry H. Rogers Trust organized by Mark Twain. The Boston lawyer Robert L. Raymond who managed the Eleanor Hutton Trust Fund reported it "came out pretty well through this horrible mess" (Lash, 1980). At this juncture, Helen and Annie agreed that Annie's will should leave the Eleanor Hutton Trust Fund to Polly, as Annie controlled the finances as Helen's guardian.

Surprisingly, Polly was not yet an American citizen, so Helen (not Annie) was obliged to write to officials on her behalf regarding visas when the trio traveled in Great Britain. The global depression gave new relevance to Helen's rhetoric when she told the seeing, "Use your eyes as if tomorrow you would be stricken blind." The effect of this rhetoric was to get people to put aside smaller worries of the day in order to lay foundations for a better future.

A middle-aged Helen Keller offered the young new inspiration to strive for their ideal self in difficult times. Helen delivered the commencement address to students at Queen Mary College in Glasgow, Scotland, in June 1932. She cited Saint Margaret of Scotland to send a message to go "in search not of things that you may own, but in search of your true self, for your own way of thinking and serving, for the lives of other beings" (Keller, 2005). When Helen spoke on Independence Day to the National Institute for the Blind in London, her topic was independence for the Blind. She reminded the audience of times when the Blind were made dependent and had to live life on the "by-ways of beggary and charity" (Einhorn, 1998). Helen asked the crowd, "Am I my brother's keeper" (Einhorn, 1998)? "Yes" was the response.

Helen Keller's power grew as her message related to the disabled meshed with the lives of ordinary people struggling with economic hardship. She asserted society was responsible for those "who by reason of physical disability, are less fitted than their fellows, to participate in the struggle for their maintenance" (Einhorn, 1998). Helen also promoted education and training as the best way to help the disabled and every individual grappling in difficult times: "Men are not honored for the difficulties that beset their lives, but for the overcoming of them." Helen argued community is found in striving for "unity out of the discords created by fear and strife" (Einhorn, 1998).

A few days later, Helen spoke to National Council of Women in London. She stated women have it in their power to bring comfort and happiness to all through making the world safe from war. Women needed to understand the world as it is in the physical environment as well as on a spiritual level. By spiritual, Helen meant women should study economics, industry, and politics to understand how to use wealth for progressive education to benefit humanity.

During the summer of 1932, after traveling in England and Scotland, Helen, Annie, and Polly returned to their rented farmhouse in South Arcan, Scotland. They received a telegram announcing John Macy had died. Annie had never stopped loving John even though they had not lived together since 1914 and he had formed another natural family. Meanwhile, in Forest Hills, neighbor Herbert Haas had started caretaking for the household when Helen, Annie, and Polly were away. Herbert had spent time in his youth in an orphan asylum; he was married with a daughter, but they were separated. Within Helen's household, Herbert was quiet and considerate in his work as driver and butler, and the women appreciated his sense of humor. Annie felt safe leaving Helen with Herbert because he had learned sign language and was happy spending evenings with Helen playing checkers and dominos.

As Helen, Annie, and Polly continued traveling, work on the talking book continued in the United States. The industrial layoff of the Great Depression actually created an opportunity to develop less marketable technologies. In May 1932, the AFB approached RCA Victor and Bell Telephone Laboratories, which emerged out of Alexander Graham Bell's Volta Laboratory in 1925. AFB activists became frustrated when Helen initially opposed participating in fundraising efforts for the talking book because Annie and Polly both were dealing with health issues. On a fundamental level, as a socialist, Helen considered talking books to be a luxury when people were going hungry, and as a Deaf person, the technology did not help her. However, she agreed to publicize the effort when she could.

Helen was awarded a prestigious $5,000 award, worth over $89,000 in 2021, from Pictorial Review for her contributions as a woman to American life over the previous decade ("Helen Keller . . . ," October 19, 1932). Helen's friends, including Henney, advised her to keep the money for her personal use. However, Helen was frustrated by her continual lobbying solely for the Blind and turned the award money over to the AFB, stipulating it be used for the Deaf-Blind as she would direct.

AFT leadership recognized the significance of Helen's action and elected her to their board of trustees. At the award luncheon, Migel's speech, read by his wife because he was sick, recounted when he had sat next to Representative Ruth Baker Pratt (New York) while Helen was giving testimony to support her bill. Migel asked Pratt, "Why are you weeping" (Lash, 1980)?

Pratt responded, "I don't know, why are YOU weeping" (Lash, 1980)?

Migel stated in his speech, "I have often tried to analyze what it is in Helen Keller that so awakens the better part of our natures—the desires to be up and doing for any cause that she espouses. It is not pity—not emotion—it must be the great soul within her . . ." (Lash, 1980).

Helen partnered with Robert B. Irwin on lobbying sessions related to AFB issues. They visited Senate offices to lobby for H. R. Bill 168 regarding talking books. They met David I. Walsh, a Democrat from Massachusetts; Senator Hugo Black, a Democrat and devoted New Dealer who showed Southern courtesy; Senator Royal S. Copeland, a Democrat from New York who was a former homeopathic physician who offered a public health campaign; and Senator Robert La Follette, Jr., who was the son of one of Helen's favorite politicians.

Helen and Irwin talked to Mr. Kent Keller of Illinois and introduced Helen and Irwin to several members of the Committee on the Library who supported the legislation. Some congressmen were equally supportive of the talking book and braille. They also discussed talking books with the head of the WPA and Frances Perkins, Helen's contemporary in age, who became the secretary of labor (Lash, 1980). Helen felt that the talking book would never replace braille but decided it was good for entertainment for older blind individuals. Library of Congress produced the talking books, and the AFB successfully lobbied for free postage to mail braille and talking books in May 1934.

When Franklin Delano Roosevelt was inaugurated as President in 1933, Helen sent the First Lady Eleanor Roosevelt a corsage arranged in her favorite colors. Helen admired how the First Lady visited the poor to discover their challenges firsthand and to offer practical solace. Eleanor Roosevelt offered Helen important lessons: visit constituencies you care about, remember what these people communicate, and keep any promises made. President Roosevelt, in April 1933 ordered gold coin and certificates in denominations over one hundred dollars to be exchanged for currency, finally removing the United States from the gold standard to expand the money supply at the height of the Great Depression.

Migel asked Helen to write a letter in May 1933 to President Roosevelt to develop support for hiring of Blind people to run newsstands in federal buildings so that they had an opportunity for independence and self-respect. She asked Eleanor Roosevelt to host a garden tea party at the White House in 1935 in order to help her to promote talking books that were an adaptation of the phonograph technology. Talking books technology did not help Helen, but it enabled the Blind to listen to books for education and entertainment.

Helen and the First Lady developed a respectful working friendship. Helen explained how the Library of Congress supplied recordings for free once the Blind acquired record players, but unfortunately, many blind could not afford the technology. After the garden party, Eleanor, who had experienced a particularly stressful week, wrote to a friend, "My calm has returned, and my goat has ceased bleating . . . why do I let myself go in that way" (Cook, 1999)?

Henney worked as an editor at Doubleday from 1919 to 1938. She became Helen and Annie's close confident while gathering material for *Teacher: Anne Sullivan Macy: The Story Behind Helen Keller*, which was published on September 13, 1933. Henney's biography revealed Annie's challenging early years in poverty, but Annie barely acknowledged it. She told Henney, "Unexpected good has filled the chinks of frustration in my life. But at times melancholy without reason grips me like I am in a vice" (Lash, 1980).

In 1935, President Roosevelt signed the Social Security Act offering unemployment insurance, retirement pensions, and assistance to children and the disabled. Keller supported the Social Security Act when it was passed in 1935 and allowed her name to appear on an amendment to the Wagner Economic Security Bill, Title X, authored by Robert Wagner (Democrat, New York) to expand funding for vocational training for the Blind in June 1935. "Any blind person who is mentally and physically sound, and with proper training can become at least partially self-supporting."

While the act was passed in August 1935, it was controversial, requiring a lot of negotiation, and did not receive funding until the following year. Helen's work resulted in the Blind being included under the category of "disabled"; they could apply for financial assistance. The act required all earnings and the value of gifts be deducted from relief allowances. This created a dilemma for the Blind who were guided by agencies to seek employment even if it was not a living wage.

The Deaf-Blind was Helen's primary cause, but the Blind was the largest group that she could serve. Helen began to come in contact with an activist for the Blind, Peter J. Salmon, who was working at the Industrial Home for the Blind (IHB) in Brooklyn, New York. He had started as their business manager in 1917 and later became the executive secretary (Keostler, 1976). Salmon argued whether support for the Blind came from private philanthropy or government funding, it should be administered by people who understood the challenges of the Blind.

While Helen and Polly traveled, Herbert took care of Annie as her condition deteriorated. Helen and Annie visited the Catskill Mountains north of New York City during the summer of 1936, on Migel's advice. Helen later rented an ocean side cottage in Greenport, Long Island, as Annie's health further deteriorated. Annie walked into the waves, became dizzy, and collapsed. Helen and Polly helped her back to the cottage, took her to the hospital, and then returned to Forest Hills.

Herbert transported Annie to the hospital. Helen's last memory of Annie was when Herbert was recounting a story of the rodeo he had attended. Annie laughed as she spelled the story into Helen's hands, tenderly fondling them. Before Annie died, she told Herbert, "I leave Helen and Polly in your hands" (Lash, 1980). Annie allegedly told Helen, "Hold out your arms to the Deaf-Blind, forget yourself in them, and be faithful to their cause. That will be your memorial to me." Annie continued, "There may be a wall between you but hammer it down stone by stone, even if you are broken down in the effort" (Lash, 1980). Soon after, Annie drifted into a coma. On October 20, 1936, Annie died with Helen by her side, holding her hand.

Annie's role as Helen's primary link to the outside world ended, and others soon vied for that role. Helen remained strong throughout Annie's funeral, but nobody knew exactly how she would deal with the loss. Annie's ashes were placed in a special memorial at the National Cathedral in Washington, D.C. Annie Sullivan Macy was the first woman to be honored in this way, to later be joined by Polly Thomson and Helen Keller.

Helen told Polly, "I can never, never get used to the house without Teacher . . . from the moment I awoke in the morning until I lie down at night, there is an ache in my heart which never stops" (Lash, 1980).

Polly responded, "Nor can I, not once in all the twenty-four hours does it seem like our home without her" (Lash, 1980). Helen became disoriented by Annie's absence, and she ate and slept minimally. Their new home located in Forest Hills was never part of Annie's life; her personality was imbedded at Wrentham. Helen remembered, "Only her poor tortured body sojourned in this place" (Lash, 1980).

Helen needed to reset her life. Polly piloted their journeys with intrepid sturdy determination. A few days later, Helen and Polly set sail for Scotland. Thanks to many friends, Helen and Polly did not need to worry about money; they were at least financially secure. As close as mother and daughter, more supportive than sisters, Helen Keller and Annie Sullivan Macy had built a more enduring partnership than most husbands and wives. As a team, Annie played offense while negotiating deals while Helen played defense for her guardian. Polly Thomson tried to keep Helen fashionable; then she became increasingly possessive of Helen. However, Kate Keller had given Helen a characteristic of grace with those less fortunate throughout dramatically changing circumstances.

11

Together We Can Do So Much

Helen Keller's faith helped her to maintain an equilibrium throughout her life, and with Annie Sullivan Macy gone, Polly Thomson became her primary caretaker. Annie's original plan for Helen's care in her absence had relied upon John Albert Macy, but he was also dead. A few individuals hoped to insinuate themselves into Helen's life to control her. Helen's siblings Mildred Keller Tyson and Phillips Brooks Keller maintained congenial relationships with her while enjoying their private lives. Herbert Haas modestly became the go-to neighbor doing workman tasks like maintaining the lawn, snow shoveling, shopping, and performing basic maintenance duties; he grew into a trusted friend (Lash, 1980). Helen Keller needed to redefine herself as an individual . . . and she did.

With such a domineering presence as Annie Sullivan Macy gone, Helen needed to discover her new equilibrium. A friend Edward Fitzgerald once recounted a story about his grandfather who kept several parrots. Each parrot had a talent, but one parrot stood out because he could only puff up his feathers like an owl. The little parrot became "the little owl" by fluffing up his feathers. Helen likened her life to that little parrot owl, when she used her talent to draw attention to important causes (Lash, 1980). As Nella Braddy Henney dug deeper into the affairs of Helen Keller, the Deaf-Blind lobbyist railed at how people still tried to control her life and actions.

Helen now took credit for negotiating salaries, stating, "The fact is, I have fought for every increase in pay we have, and I am very proud to earn a salary to which I am entitled" (Lash, 1980). She believed she maintained control over her affairs from the time of her father's death when she was seventeen. However her guardian Annie legally controlled Helen's financial affairs throughout her adult life.

Helen started earning money as a teenager, surrendering thirty-five dollars from her first article for *Youth's Companion* to her insolvent father when she was thirteen years old. Helen asserted, "Of my own accord I have undertaken public responsibilities . . . After Teacher's health broke down, I worked very much alone with Polly's hand to furnish information and her voice to reinforce my halting speech" (Keller, 1955).

Polly Thomson had come to the United States in 1913 searching for work as a paid companion or governess. Helen and Annie resided in Wrentham, Massachusetts, so Polly joined the household as a secretary-housekeeper in October 1914 after John Macy left. Polly was a hard worker who quickly learned to wear a mask to hide her true opinions within the unique household dynamics. With Helen's approval, Polly inherited the Eleanor Hutton Trust Fund worth almost $23,000, worth over $434,000 in 2021, when Annie died. Helen approved this as a message of faith in Polly's abilities to be her primary caregiver.

When she started reading books about geography, Helen seemed to develop a compulsive need to travel. After Annie Sullivan Macy's funeral, Polly escorted Helen to Scotland where her brother Robert Thomson, an ordained minister with the Church of Scotland, offered them much-needed refuge. However, after Annie's death, biographer Henney saw herself as Annie's heir apparent and planned to closely monitor Helen's behavior to suit her purposes. Polly resisted Henney's interference as she grew increasingly possessive of her employer and companion. While Helen needed Henney as a literary agent to advise on contracts, Henney tried to influence her egalitarian life and household according to her more capitalistic values. Helen remembered, "Mother and Teacher knew me better than anyone else ever did, and they never dictated the course of action that I should follow" (Lash, 1980).

Some suggested Helen should return to Alabama to live with her sister Mildred Keller Tyson in comfortable seclusion, but Helen continued on a public journey with its extensive traveling. "Life is a daring adventure or nothing." Helen was determined to stay out the squabbles of those around her. "The mortally wounded must strive to live out their days cheerfully for the sake of others" (Keller, 1955). How Helen used her education led the world to cherish her for other accomplishments. Writing helped her and other Deaf-Blind individuals to express the self. Henney soon encouraged her to keep a journal of life after Annie, to be published by Doubleday, Doran & Company. Helen hoped to demonstrate to the world she could go on as an independent person.

Helen and First Lady Eleanor Roosevelt were about the same age, so she read Roosevelt's book *This Is My Story* (1937) about how she freed herself from social inhibitions and family paternalism. Helen wrote to the First Lady, "I sympathize with your childhood aspirations to independence and the tremendous self-consciousness you overcame . . . the two lessons you took to heart we cannot learn too early—that power cannot last or preserve its beneficence without love for the people . . ." (Lash, 1980). The First Lady responded, "Words of praise from one who stands for the embodiment of courage to all of us means more than I can say" (Lash, 1980).

When Helen and Polly returned from Scotland in 1938, they sold the house in Forest Hills for $9,000 cash and moved into a home built with AFB support in Westport, Connecticut. Their Forest Hills neighbor Herbert Haas relocated with them, taking on an increasingly important role of managing the household, tending the garden with Helen's beloved roses, and repairing the car and Helen's typewriter and braille machine when necessary.

Helen and Polly named their new home Arcan Ridge after a favorite Scottish location Helen, Annie, and Polly had visited. This home offered Helen more autonomy because she required less guidance. Helen selected clothing, dressed, and styled her hair independently. She weeded and tended her garden as her mother had encouraged her to do as a child. During the summer months, she picked the fruit by touch when it was at its juiciest as her father had selected for her before Annie entered her life. The household grew to have eight dogs, and dogfights were common.

Henney introduced Helen and Polly into new social circles that included Katherine Cornell, who sponsored Helen to join the posh conservative women's club called the Cosmopolitan Club, or "Cos Club" in New York City's Upper East Side. Egalitarian Helen Keller, a woman who was comfortable sitting on the floor, enjoyed the new friendships. However, the posh women and their husbands outside of the household did not approve of how Helen and Polly brought Herbert Haas into their household. They tried to burden Helen with their prejudiced think because they still believed a "servant" should not be treated like a member of the family. Helen and Polly loved their orphaned friend Herbert like a member of the family . . . indeed, he was a member of their new family.

*   *   *

Without Annie's constant haggling, the American Federation for the Blind's leadership envisioned Helen working in an international arena. She was energized by meeting people on her travels even though the journeys were exhausting. Throughout her public life, Helen suggested ways to educate school-aged Deaf-Blind children who were widely scattered across the country. During the Great Depression, Helen began to frame special education within the twentieth-century understanding of rehabilitation and lifelong learning. Helen stated, "Each Deaf-Blind child is different from every other, and should, therefore, receive individual attention."

A Blind Japanese writer, Takeo Iwahashi, translated Helen's first autobiography *The Story of My Life* (1903) into Japanese, and he invited Helen to visit Japan in 1935 (Lash, 1980). Iwahashi had become blind while studying at university; he started printing books in braille at home, and then he opened his home to lend books to the Blind, establishing the Nippon Lighthouse for the Blind in 1922. Iwahashi formally invited Helen and Polly to tour Japan in 1937 to conduct a nationwide campaign in Japan, Korea, and Manchuria.

Before leaving the United States for Japan, Helen received President Roosevelt's message while staying at the St. Francis Hotel in San Francisco, California. The president telegraphed Helen, telling her about his complete confidence in her. Roosevelt recognized Helen as a communicator of inspiration to the disabled that traveled beyond American borders, and he asked her to "convey to the Japanese people the cordial greetings of the American people" (Lash, 1980).

Once in Japan, Helen was welcomed in diplomatic and humanitarian ways; everywhere Helen, Polly, and Iwahashi visited, they received enthusiastic welcomes. The Japanese revered Helen because they respected her as a woman of courage who overcame great barriers with apparent humility. She became one of the first women to be allowed to touch a sacred bronze statue of Buddha. Although Helen met the emperor, princes, and politicians, she touched the hearts of the Japanese people.

Thousands of Japanese children waving American and Japanese flags greeted Helen at the port of Yokohama. Politicians devoted events to create awareness for the Deaf-Blind, and Iwahashi acted as Helen and Polly's interpreter. Their tour led to the enactment of the Law for the Disabled Persons and the Compulsory Education System of the Blind Children. The Japanese lecture tour raised an unprecedented 35 million yen for the Blind and Deaf Japanese.

When Helen and Polly returned to the United States, President Roosevelt invited Keller to serve on the Committee on Purchasing of Products made by the Blind, a federal committee created as part of the New Deal effort. The director of the Industrial Home for the Blind in Brooklyn, New York, Peter J. Salmon, established the first vocational placement service for the Blind and designed service models internationally for the Blind (Koestler, 1976). Salmon wrote to M. C. "Major" Migel with the AFB, asking if anything more could be done to create jobs for the blind. Salmon proposed creating more opportunities than getting the federal government to purchase products produced by the blind.

The AFB made the most of Helen's charisma to work with the White House, and she was ready for the work. In Helen's view, President Roosevelt was limited by being paralyzed by Guillain-Barre Syndrome; he was "terribly handicapped by the predominance of politics over administration in the United States" (Lash, 1980). Helen felt Roosevelt was a truly creative statesman. Helen stated in 1938, "Ideas—constructive ideas such as Roosevelt seeks to embody—are lighthouses erected on the misty coast of futurity" (Lash, 1980).

During their travels through Europe, Helen and Polly began to fear the buildup of another war machine. Helen, who grappled with conflicting ideologies during World War I, felt many Americans avoided deep examination of ideas in discussing politics. Helen believed Roosevelt's greatest challenge was working with politicians who sought office to further their own interests. Helen argued the strongest traditions of democracy were once "threatening" new ideas related to religion and the Constitution (Keller, 2005).

Meanwhile, Helen's growing persona as someone with empathy led her to receive a rare honor. The Nakoda Tribe in western Canada (and indigenous to the United States) made Helen a "blood sister" (Harrity and Martin, 1962). Chief Walking Buffalo invested Helen as the second white woman to become a tribal sister in a traditional ceremony. He gave her the name White Plume, delineating a white feather falling from heaven as a message of protection. In many cultures, a white feather symbolizes peace, purification, and faith. Another American woman to receive such an honor was sharpshooting performer Annie Oakley, who was befriended and unofficially adopted by Lakota Sioux Chief Sitting Bull in 1894.

*   *   *

On September 1, 1939, World War II started. The United States entered World War II after the Japanese bombed Pearl Harbor. Helen and Polly traveled extensively overseas during World War II, visiting the sick and wounded in hospitals to support the American Foundation for the Overseas Blind. AFB Executive Director Robert B. Irwin remained in the United States, fostering international cooperation on behalf of all the Blind internationally. He was instrumental in the passage of three laws, which became a great stimulus to the employment of the Blind: the Barden-La Follette Act, the Randolph-Sheppard Act, and the Wagner-O'Day Act. When World War II required special provisions for the war-blinded, Irwin wrote and secured the passage of the bill recognized as "a bill of rights for blinded veterans" (Koestler, 1976).

Between tours, Helen met and befriended Jewish American sculptor Jo Davidson in spring 1942. Davidson, like Eleanor Roosevelt, was about the same age as Helen. He was a sculptor and artist active in socialist circles. While he was an art student, he had learned the manual alphabet from a Deaf sculptor, possibly John Macy's partner after he separated from Annie Sullivan Macy, and retained the skill so he could finger-spell into Helen's hand. Davidson was famous for producing portrait busts and did not require his subjects to formally pose for him; he observed and spoke with subjects to get to know them deeply.

Davidson invited Helen and Polly to his farm only to discover the memory in Helen's fingers, which had so impressed Mark Twain and others (Davidson, 1951). Davidson allowed Helen to wander her fingers over the sculptures in his studio as old friends, and he realized Helen's fingers *saw* his sculptures profoundly. When Helen reached a bronze bust of Albert Einstein who she had met with Annie Sullivan Macy in New York, she observed, "He is like a sunflower." Helen also passed her hand over the sculpted face of President Roosevelt and immediately recognized him. "Not only is he a great American, he is also our most valiant victor over physical handicaps" (Davidson, 1951).

Davidson nodded and finger-spelled his agreement. Davidson also produced portrait busts of leaders including Presidents Woodrow Wilson, Herbert Hoover, and Dwight D. Eisenhower who had met Helen. Davidson discovered Helen's words and thoughts were superimposed on each other with astonishing precision. She continued talking about Roosevelt, "His unfailing sympathy for the Blind, has been such a beautiful experience in my work" (Davidson, 1951). His work synthesized the sitter's personality, and he produced busts of Helen in 1942 and 1945.

Having financially supported the NAACP since the 1910s, Helen continued to respond to the needs of Black Blind and Deaf-Blind individuals. Helen testified on how the African American poor were not adequately served with the Social Security Act before the House Subcommittee on Labor Investigating Aid to Physically Handicapped on October 3, 1944. Helen argued the Social Security Act "has not provided sufficiently for the particular needs of the poorer Blind, or taken into account their severe curtailments in bread-winning opportunities and personal liberty" (Einhorn, 1998).

The meager education and health care options for disabled Blacks upset Helen, who pleaded for assistance for Blind African Americans, "In my travels up and down the continent I have visited their shabby school buildings and witnessed their pathetic struggle against want" (Keller, 2005). Helen exclaimed, "I feel it a disgrace that in this great wealthy land such injustice should exist to men and women of a different race—and Blind at that!" Helen also testified how the most challenged group, the Deaf-Blind, were tragically isolated. "It is difficult to arouse enough interest to soften their fate" (Keller, 2005). Her research revealed while there were agencies for the Blind in every state, not one of these agencies had been organized to rehabilitate and assist the Deaf-Blind.

Helen, who remained a pacifist, was fearful her friendship with the Japanese people was broken, but this did not lessen her efforts (Harrity and Martin, 1962). World War II resulted in heavy casualties. Thousands of war veterans returned home different from when they had left. From 1943 to 1955, Helen at the age of sixty-three years first visited hospitals with her slightly older college friend Lenore Smith, who had accompanied her to her visit to the Massachusetts Association for Promoting the Interest of the Adult Blind when they were students at Radcliffe College. Helen and Lenore first visited Walter Reed National Military Medical Center in Bethesda, Maryland, and doctors reported on the impact of Helen's visits to military hospitals to the White House.

First Lady Eleanor Roosevelt announced Helen's visits with patients in military hospitals, as well as doctors and nurses, were "probably the most healing that can come to them." Soon, other friends including Polly and Jo Davidson took turns in accompanying her on visits to the newly disabled veterans in American military hospitals. Helen offered a special kind of healing for the men wounded in service to the nation. They appreciated her visits much more than those of Hollywood blondes, brunettes, and celebrities. Helen's message was basic: life is not over with disability . . . it is different but not done. One wounded soldier asked her, "What gives your courage to go on?"

Helen responded, "The Bible and poetry and philosophy" (Harrity and Martin, 1962).

The soldier then asked, "How do you feel when God seems to desert you" (Harrity and Martin, 1962)?

Helen answered, "I never had that feeling" (Harrity and Martin, 1962).

Wounded service men and veterans were sometimes bitter. Helen's experiences gave her credibility, and she represented someone to have triumphed over adversity. Helen told another wounded veteran, "I once raged with anger. I was rebelling against my handicap" (Harrity and Martin, 1962).

The veteran found meaning in Helen's gentle touch and responded, "But the braille dots only feel like sandpaper to me" (Harrity and Martin, 1962).

Helen took the soldier's hands in hers, "Your hands will grow softer and more sensitive with time" (Harrity and Martin, 1962).

He asked, "Does it not make you sad, taking all these hands scarred with pain and fatigue" (Harrity and Martin, 1962)?

Helen responded, "No, I love the courage throbbing through them" (Harrity and Martin, 1962).

Though much of her life was devoted to fundraising for the Blind, during World War II, Helen wrote to a friend, saying, "I regard philanthropy as a tragic apology for wrong conditions" (Lash, 1980).

Toward the end of World War II, Helen hoped to develop protective measures for the Deaf-Blind during air raids, but nothing viable could be organized. She visited the newly disabled veterans for media-staged events. The media loved to report on her veteran's hospital visits, but they were mediated so that she only offered messages that veterans should take advantage of work-oriented rehabilitation and retain a positive attitude. An anonymous poet penned a verse about Helen:

Foot, they! They call her blind!
They call her blind, yet she can lead
A thousand soul-sick men
From cold gray stones and make
*   them heed*
The song of wind and rain.

(Harrity and Martin, 1962)

Presidents of the United States served as honorary chairs of the American Federation of the Blind. When President Roosevelt died on April 12, 1945, Helen was touring a naval hospital in Charleston, North Carolina. She remembered, "The company went mute and limp . . . It was an irreplaceable void we workers for the handicapped feel now that the tangible tokens of his sympathy and counsel are withdrawn" (Lash, 1980). Eleanor Roosevelt responded, "As I stood and listened to Miss Keller speak, I thought how wonderfully both Miss Keller and my husband typified the triumph over physical handicaps."

Helen did not see herself as others did; she remained true to her faith. "It is not for us to pray for tasks equal to our powers, but for powers equal to our task" (Harrity and Martin, 1962). Peter J. Salmon organized a luncheon at the Brooklyn Industrial Home for the Blind to celebrate Helen's sixty-fifth birthday in 1945. As a Perkins Institute graduate, Salmon had been Blind from the age of nine years. Keller's story of learning to communicate inspired him to advocate for the Deaf-Blind. IHB pioneered vocational rehabilitation for adults who became blind because they had difficulty finding training for dealing with new disability (Koestler, 1976). IHB first accepted a Deaf-Blind person in 1917 for rehabilitation and was opening a Deaf-Blind department to offer employment training, work, and opportunities for social networking. Helen and thirteen Deaf-Blind participants of the program came together for lunch.

Thinking changed from focusing only on childhood education when Helen was young to also developing modern adult vocational rehabilitation for the Deaf-Blind. Helen believed the Deaf-Blind now could get training to live more independent lives and support themselves. However, the Deaf-Blind remained too scattered to make use of many agency services.

WAR: A CATALYST FOR A NEW GENERATION OF DISABILITY ACTIVISTS

Unknown to Helen Keller and Anne Sullivan Macy, a teenager named Mary Elizabeth Switzer became inspired during one of their lectures held in Boston in 1914 (Walker, 1985). Switzer graduated from Radcliffe College and took jobs working for the Carnegie Endowment for International Peace and the Women's International League for Peace and Freedom, seeking a career in public service. Switzer learned about the work of social reformers Eleanor Roosevelt and Jane Addams on health, safety, and educational needs of Americans.

Switzer observed how First Lady Eleanor Roosevelt interacted with young crowds to learn about their hopes and dreams. She learned how by addressing the struggle of a few, the government could find solutions for thousands. She saw the needs of the poor and the displaced as well as new reform strategies.

Switzer was a pacifist knowing it was an unpopular stand. World War II brought about opportunities when President Franklin Delano Roosevelt proclaimed the Four Freedoms in 1941: freedom of expression, freedom of worship, freedom from want, and freedom from fear. Switzer rose in the federal government employed as an assistant to the administrator of the Federal Security Agency, where she worked with the National Youth Administration.

Helen Keller and Switzer did not cross paths again in person, but they influenced each other in developing rehabilitation services for the Deaf-Blind. Switzer remembered, "As you look over your life and the threads that come together in one period . . . you can see one thing leads to another in a fairly logical sequence" (Walker, 1985). In late 1950, Mary Switzer became the director of the Office of Vocational Rehabilitation, which developed a variety of programs to serve the Deaf-Blind.

Mary E. Switzer, the little girl with long straight hair who was packed in with her socialist uncle Michael Moore in Boston's Ford Hall to hear Helen and Annie lecture on the topic of "happiness" in 1914, was poised in a key federal position to effectively combine rehabilitation services to better serve the Deaf-Blind (Walker, 1985).

The Deaf-Blind community, like Helen Keller, strove for opportunities for self-determination and to have options to live in communities of their choosing. No longer having to adjust her opinions about Perkins Institute for the Blind to suit Annie Sullivan Macy's agenda, Helen suggested a collaboration between the AFB, IHB, and Perkins Institute to be a semiautonomous entity, called the National Council for the Deaf-Blind. She recognized Peter Salmon's work with the IHB for helping the Deaf-Blind to be "independent, earning their own way, and sharing in the support of their families and service to the community" (Koestler, 1976).

Eleanor Roosevelt, like Helen, felt disability offered an opportunity for an individual to develop latent senses. Following Franklin Delano Roosevelt's death, Helen was emboldened in her socialist activities when she became involved with the Independent Citizen's Committee for the Arts and Sciences headed by Jo Davidson. Her involvement in this leftist-liberal group supporting the policies of President Roosevelt led the FBI to compile a file on Helen's socialist leanings.

In 1946, Robert B. Irwin's interest in international work for the Blind resulted in organizing the American Foundation for Overseas Blind, later renamed Helen Keller International known for removing barriers and creating health equity for the Blind. Helen started a world tour representing the AFB. Over the next eleven years, at a time when most people retired, Helen and Polly traveled to thirty-five countries. Irwin's legislative efforts also led to the program of Aid to the Needy Blind under Title X of the Social Security Act and a bill that allowed the Blind an additional exemption on their Federal Income Tax.

During two world wars, Helen witnessed enormous human suffering through her public speaking and interactions. In November 1946, while traveling in Italy, Helen and Polly received news that their Arcan Ridge home had been destroyed by fire. Everything was lost, including correspondence along with notes that Helen had compiled for a biography of her teacher Annie Sullivan Macy. Herbert, who lived over the garage separated from the house by a steel door, did not lose everything. Polly was devastated. Helen took the loss in stride; she felt that so many in Europe had lost everything, and the aftermath of war was worse than anything that she had suffered.

Davidson's Independent Citizens Committee merged with the National Citizens Political Action Committee to become the Progressive Citizens of America (PCA). This group struggled during tensions of the Cold War and fought for racial equality, economic justice, and civil liberties. Important segments of the PCA became the base for Henry Wallace's third party Progressive candidacy for U.S. President in 1948. His Progressive platform called desegregation of public schools, a national health insurance program along with racial and gender equality in the United States.

In 1948, Polly suffered the first of several strokes. As a result, Helen granted Henney her power of attorney. Henney, no longer employed by the publisher Doubleday, tried to insert herself more deeply into the household to gain an income from the AFB. The household was allotted $20,000 annually: Polly earned $5,000, Herbert earned $3,500, general expenses got $5,000, braille books got $1,000, and Henney asked to be added to the household budget for $2,000. Polly was reluctant to train any replacement who might subvert her control over Helen. Those closest to Helen were no longer allowed to spell for Helen, who increasingly was at the mercy of her senile companion. Helen's liberal friends worried circumstances might force her to be in her conservative family's care for the remaining years of her life.

Helen started a new process of introspection as her new role of "elder" in international work grew. "It is no use trying to reconcile the multitude of egos that compose me" (Lash, 1980). A high school student asked Helen what it was like to grow old. Helen responded simply, "There is no age to the spirit. Age seems to me only another physical handicap, and it excites no dread in my mind" (Lash, 1980). Helen Keller loved children, and she retained a natural curiosity from her own childhood. "All my life I have tried to avoid ruts, such as doing things my ancestors did before me, or leaning on the crutches of other people's opinions or losing my childhood sense of wonderment" (Lash, 1980). For Keller maintaining agency and connection to others was her key to longevity, "I am glad to say I still have a vivid curiosity about the world I live in" (Lash, 1980).

Some young people thought Helen Keller was already dead, but at the age of sixty-eight years, she concluded, "It is as natural for me to believe that the richest harvest of happiness comes with age as to believe that the true sight and hearing are within, not without . . ." (Lash, 1980).

*   *   *

In 1952, Helen traveled to France to celebrate the centennial of Louis Braille's death. Blinded as the result of a childhood accident, Braille had developed a tactile code of raised dots that revolutionized communication and education for the Blind, which has been internationally adapted. Braille, like Helen, did not want the Blind to be pitied; he stated, "Access to communication in the widest sense is access to knowledge, and that is vitally important to us if we are not to go on being despised or patronized by condescending sighted people." Helen, who had once locked her mother in a pantry to communicate her own need to connect with the broader world, utilized braille like a *golden key*, in the same way a "spider uses the web" (Harrity and Martin, 1962).

Jo Davidson looked forward to celebrating Helen's seventieth birthday with her in Italy, where she discovered she had a cousin. An Italian culture lecturer at Harvard and the University of Florence, Caetano Salvemini, arranged with the Beaux Arts authorities for Helen and her entourage to visit the Borgello and the Medici tombs in Florence, Italy. Davidson checked out the movable scaffolding the authorities had set up so Helen could pass her hands over the sculptures of Donatello and Michelangelo.

Witnesses watching from below were transfixed as Helen contemplated the sculptures as if they were living personal friends. Davidson had seen the sculptures before but never with the same intimacy of observing

Helen's fingers exploring the forms and peering into the tiniest crevices and over the most subtle undulations as she had done since exploring Oliver Wendell Holmes's library as a child. All of the dignitaries were silent as Helen exclaimed in excitement when she discovered the slightly opened mouth of the young "St. John the Baptist." The group returned to Becheron, where Davidson sketched Helen sitting on the floor, as she loved to do, with Polly fingerspelling into her hand.

Nella Braddy Henney, who beyond writing Annie's biography otherwise worked on encyclopedias as a low-level editor, was determined to remain Helen's editor to make her name in the publishing business (Nielsen, 2004; Lash, 1980). Henney once again started frequenting Arcan Ridge after reading a biography that revealed family scandals about Dr. Samuel Gridley Howe's family written by an unauthorized biographer. Up to that point, the Howes had maintained their story and brand, but Henney told Polly, "Up to now the Howes have done most of the writing about the family, but apparently from here on out, other people are to rake over the coals." Henney surmised, "It is gruesome to think that this time will come for Helen also, but fortunately she has told everything and there will be no licking of lips over revelations" (Lash, 1980).

The American Foundation for the Blind rebuilt the house at Arcan Ridge as Helen went to work on a new book about Annie called *Teacher: Anne Sullivan Macy, a Tribute by the Foster Child of her Mind* (1955). The same year, filmmaker Nancy Hamilton and actress Katharine Cornell produced a documentary about Helen's life called *The Unconquered* (1955). Henney worked as a consultant on the film spotlighting Helen in her home, and it received an Academy Award in the category of documentary.

Henney also introduced Helen and Polly to William Gibson, who was in the process of developing a teleplay *The Miracle Worker* based on Henney's biography of Annie. Henney served as a paid consultant on this project. Helen's trustees became uncomfortable when after Polly's stroke, Henney failed to inform them on details about the negotiations. In a clear conflict of interest, Henney made an agreement where Helen received only 20 percent of Gibson's 20 percent.

The extensive notes Henney took while Annie was alive were likely useful to the project. Gibson, married to a psychotherapist named Margaret Brenman-Gibson, wove a psychological profile framing Annie within her childhood traumas at Tewksbury almshouse into the story. In a reprisal of *The Story of My Life* (1903), the trauma of Catherine "Kate" Keller dealing with her first daughter losing sight and hearing from an illness soon after losing her father as a result of a catastrophic outbreak of yellow fever in Memphis, Tennessee, is eclipsed by the childhood trauma of Annie Sullivan.

Gibson depicted Helen's educational breakthrough and subsequent connection to the broader world as an intervention. Annie Sullivan could

William Gibson's play, *The Miracle Worker*, performed around the time of Helen Keller's birthday on location at Ivy Green in 2010. This annual performance is held in the backyard of Ivy Green, where the iconic nineteenth-century water pump became identified with Helen Keller's communications breakthrough. The play, based upon *The Story of My Life*, reinforced Anne Sullivan Macy as the dominant female figure in Keller's life, but also remains relevant for its message of courage and determination. (Library of Congress)

not reach Helen to teach her the manual alphabet without breaking down her student's former self in a brutal rite of passage that changed Helen profoundly. In *The Miracle Worker*, Annie who demanded total obedience from Helen to the point of separating her from her family to create total dependence upon her. Despite family resistance, Annie immediately instilled discipline to teach Helen to communicate. Annie's tactile approach used fingerspelling (spelling words into her hand), beginning with "d-o-l-l" for the doll she gave Helen as a present.

The story retelling unfolds during the 1880s when the New South was emerging, and women were creating new narratives of a shattered way of life. The teleplay further reinforced Annie and John Macy's mythmaking about the Keller family by glossing over their declining fortunes and emphasizing Annie's drama without considering any possible trauma to Helen. With Polly being vulnerable, Henney took the opportunity to shape Gibson's narrative to once again place focus on Annie. Helen finally worked through continuing challenges to extract herself from people who sought to isolate her to support their own agendas. *The Miracle Worker* effectively marked the end of Helen and Henney's relationship (Nielsen, 2004).

* * *

In March 1960, Helen was with Polly when she collapsed on the kitchen floor and remained there until help arrived. Polly died on March 21, 1960, with Helen by her side. Helen's new assistants Winifred "Winnie" Corbally and Evelyn Siede did not try to control her (Lash, 1980). They were not possessive, and while both were more politically conservative, they did not restrict Helen in self-expression. Siede was frugal and managed to run the household on less money than Polly.

Helen experienced unprecedented freedom and happiness for about a year. In October 1961, she experienced a stroke, which returned her mentally back to happier days at the Wrentham farm with Annie and John Macy. Subsequent strokes diminished Helen's remaining senses. She developed diabetes, impairing her mobility. For the last seven years of her life, Helen was confined to a wheelchair. She retired from her work with the AFB and spent her time in book study.

In 1962, the IHB launched a demonstration project called the Anne Sullivan Macy Service for Deaf-Blind Persons lasting seven years, while working with 171 Deaf-Blind participants (Salmon, 1970). Perhaps partially inspired by the Pictorial Review money Helen had received thirty years before, the project's objective was to test regional resources to demonstrate how with rehabilitation training Deaf-Blind adults could go into communities and establish self-directed homes and somewhat independent lives. Helen Keller's biggest struggle was to gain some autonomy as a Deaf-Blind woman.

The Deaf-Blind, perhaps the most marginalized in the disability community, connected to the Civil Rights Movement on a fundamental level to garner self-determination and access to aspects of public life. The following year, Martin Luther King wrote a letter from an Alabama prison, "In a real sense all life is inter-related. All men are caught in an inescapable network of mutuality, tied in a single garment of destiny. Whatever affects one directly, affects all indirectly. I can never be what I ought to be until you are what you ought to be, and you can never be what you ought to be until I am what I ought to be . . . This is the inter-related structure of reality" (King, 1963).

Money became the basis of the eventual Henney-Keller total breakup. Helen felt that Henney had financially exploited her and her loved ones as a literary agent dating back to when Annie had negotiated the contract for her biography (Lash, 1980). Henney took great pride in the success of *The Miracle Worker*, but she failed to comprehend Helen's anger at being

PASSING THE TORCH, DR. ROBERT SMITHDAS

An American Deaf-Blind educator Robert Smithdas led a more independent life than Helen Keller because the changing technology opened doors to living autonomously. Smithdas was an advocate and author who married a Deaf-Blind woman. He was the first Deaf-Blind person to earn a master's degree in vocational guidance and rehabilitation for the handicapped. His education was similar to Keller's, but he benefited from advances in technology including teletype phones, computers, and pagers. Smithdas agreed with Keller, "Deafness takes you away from people" (Smithdas, 1958).

As a man, Smithdas fought his battles within a white male-dominated world without being silenced for unpopular political views. Journalist Barbara Walters considered Smithdas and his Deaf-Blind wife to be her most memorable interview, and she suggested Keller merely put a dent in barriers (Walters, n.d.), so Smithdas could make the real breakthrough. Smithdas, who attended Perkins Institute for the Blind, worked for the Industrial Home for the Blind from 1950 to 1960 where he met Peter J. Salmon.

Smithdas became pivotal in lobbying Congress to authorize an act in 1967, establishing the Helen Keller National Center for Deaf-Blind Youths and Adults (HKNC) to provide nationwide services for Deaf-Blind people. Federal law mandated individual states take responsibility for Deaf-Blind education until the age of sixteen after which the NKNC took over.

Smithdas directed community education for the Sands Point, New York HKNC, which continues to operate as a residential rehabilitation and training facility. The organization provides independent living skills training, referral, employment training, counseling, and transition assistance for individuals as well as technical assistance and training for service providers. Congressional findings showed the HKNC "is a vital national resource for meeting the needs of individuals who are Deaf-Blind, and no State currently has the facilities or personnel to meet such needs."

exploited when Polly was most vulnerable. Helen regained the power of attorney in literary matters Henney had obtained in 1948, and Henney's role as Helen's literary executrix was revoked in 1963. Henney's papers related to Helen Keller and Annie Sullivan eventually went to Perkins Institute for the Blind in Boston, Massachusetts.

Helen Keller no longer needed to prove anything to the world. Children could spell words into her hands like the "wildflowers of conversation" (Harrity and Martin, 1962). The dramas related to Annie Sullivan Macy were buried, and Helen could sustain her equilibrium. Faith told Helen she would have use of all of her senses in the next stage of her soul's journey. Helen once remarked, "I believe in the immortality of the soul because I have within me immortal longings" (Lash, 1980). In late May 1968, Helen suffered from a heart attack. She drifted off in her sleep on June 1, 1968, with Winnie Corbally by her side but did not reawaken.

Helen Keller was cremated. She would not suffer a postmortem as Laura Bridgman did or be buried in an unmarked pauper's grave like Julia Brace. At last, Helen was no longer a subject for tests measuring her senses or intelligence. Phillips Brooks Keller and Mildred Keller Tyson organized an elaborate ceremony held in the National Cathedral in Washington, D.C., on June 6, 1968. Her siblings invited a conservative senator from Alabama to deliver Helen's eulogy. The Blind and seeing eye dogs were seated in a special section. Sign language, a form of communication that Helen's generation was discouraged from using, was used. The fifty-member choir from Perkins School for the Blind performed there.

In life, Helen Keller's name became a worldwide symbol of what the human spirit can accomplish despite severe physical limitations. Her ashes were interred with the family that life had provided: Annie Sullivan Macy and Polly Thomson. Their spot was marked with a bronze braille plaque, rubbed so many times by admirers it was replaced multiple times.

Helen Keller is remembered for stating, "Alone we can do so little; together we can do so much" (Lash, 1980). When Helen Keller started life in a small Alabama hamlet, she demonstrated a fierce independent spirit even before she had lost her sight and hearing at eighteen months. As a Deaf-Blind woman, like Julia Brace and Laura Bridgman, Helen Keller could not become the great individual alone; she needed sustained help from family, friends, and strangers.

Helen Keller left a quarter of her residual estate to support the IHB Deaf-Blind program. Peter Salmon led a five-year program to add a 1967 provision to federally finance the National Center for Deaf-Blind Youths and Adults through the Vocational Rehabilitation Act. The National Center received twenty-five acres of surplus federal land at Sands Point, Long Island. The Rehabilitation Building was named after Mary E. Switzer, who Helen and Annie inspired as a teenager. Helen Keller together with many like-minded activists finally created an enduring institution to support the Deaf-Blind to live, work, and thrive in communities of their own choosing.

Timeline

April 9, 1865	General Robert E. Lee surrenders Confederate troops to the Union General Ulysses S. Grant at Appomattox, Virginia, ending in Civil War.
April 14, 1866	Joanne Sullivan is born in Feeding Hills section of Agawam, Massachusetts.
1869	The Boston School for Deaf-Mutes (now known as Horace Mann School for the Deaf) is established as the first free public day school for the Deaf under the direction of the Boston School Board.
1871	Charles Darwin's *The Descent of Man, and Selection in Relation to Sex* is published and becomes the basis of the Eugenics movement.
1876	Anne Sullivan and brother are admitted to Tewksbury Almshouse after the death of their mother. Benjamin Franklin Sanborn reports on Tewksbury, "Insane women were placed in unhealthy dungeons, drugged to death, or permitted to die for want of proper care."
1877	The Compromise of 1877, an unwritten deal among United States Congressmen, brings about the end of the Reconstruction, resulting in declining economic changes for the Keller household in the South.

September 9, 1878	In the midst of a yellow fever epidemic in Memphis, Tennessee, General Charles William Adams dies, and within months, his daughter Catherine Adams Keller marries Captain Arthur Henley Keller, who is twenty years older.
June 27, 1880	Helen Adams Keller is born in Tuscumbia, Alabama. The National Association of the Deaf is established the same year to fight discrimination, and the Howe Memorial Press is established at Perkins Institute for the Blind to print books with braille.
October 7, 1880	Anne Sullivan is admitted to Perkins Institute for the Blind after Frank B. Sanborn visits the state poorhouse at Tewksbury, Massachusetts, and she confronts him and asks for help to get an education.
February 1882	Helen Keller becomes ill with an undiagnosed illness resulting in her becoming Deaf, Mute, and Blind.
March 3, 1887	Anne Sullivan arrives in Tuscumbia, Alabama, to instruct Helen Keller. Throughout Keller's life, she perceives the day to be her "soul birthday."
June 20, 1887	Queen Victoria's Golden Jubilee is celebrated, causing a halt in production of English language books produced in braille.
May 1888	Helen Keller and Anne Sullivan arrive in Boston to stay with Michael Anagnos. Keller meets Oliver Wendell Holmes, John Greenleaf Wittier, Edward Everett Hale, and Phillips Brooks.
1889	Florence Howe Hall describes Helen Keller's early education in *St. Nicholas* magazine following another article about Laura Bridgman that is published posthumously.
Spring 1890	Helen Keller begins instruction at Horace Mann School for the Deaf the same year the New England Kitchen opens as a public

community kitchen designed to serve the working-class poor in Boston.

1890   Alexander Graham Bell successfully lobbies the U.S. Census Bureau to use the term "Deaf" instead of "Deaf-Mute" for the census so that the incidence of deafness can be more accurately recorded.

November 1891   Anne Sullivan sends Michael Anagnos a story attributed to Helen Keller, called "The Frost King," which she describes as an original creation.

January 30, 1892   Anne Sullivan informs Helen Keller "The Frost King" has been accused of being plagiarized, and she is devastated.

June 1893   Helen Keller turns the first spade of soil over at the groundbreaking for the new Volta Bureau and library in Georgetown, Washington, D.C.

1893–1897   An economic depression forces Captain Arthur Keller to mortgage all of his property, so the family relocates to a summer cabin in a nearby quarry.

October 1893   Helen Keller visits the Chicago World's Fair as Alexander Graham Bell's guest and describes it in an article for *St. Nicholas Magazine.*

October 1894   Helen Keller and Anne Sullivan begin to attend Wright-Humason School in New York, where they meet Laurence Hutton, Mark Twain, William Dean Howells, Charles Dudley Warner, and Richard Gilder.

August 19, 1896   Helen Keller's father, Captain Arthur Henley Keller, dies. John Hitz, Jr. provides Swedenborgian literature to Helen Keller and converts her to Swedenborgianism. Keller enrolls in Arthur Gilman's Cambridge School for Young Ladies to prepare to enter Radcliffe College. In the landmark decision for *Plessy v. Ferguson*, the U.S. Supreme Court upholds the constitutionality of

	racial segregation laws for public facilities in a doctrine known as "separate but equal."
June 1897	Helen Keller passes Radcliffe entrance examinations.
1899	Helen Keller trains to articulate speech. Only 40 percent of Deaf students in the United States are receiving speech training at this time.
September 1900	Keller enters Radcliffe College and struggles to keep up with the curriculum without special accommodations.
February 1, 1901	Helen Keller writes to the editors of *The Great Round World*, a weekly children's magazine published between 1896 and 1903, thanking them for publishing embossed editions because "the Blind as a class are poor."
1901–1902	Helen Keller writes a series of articles about her life with help from Harvard English lecturer John Macy. The articles later get published in book form as *The Story of My Life*, dedicated to Alexander Graham Bell in 1903.
June 1904	Helen Keller graduates from Radcliffe College cum laude. Helen Keller and Anne Sullivan purchase a home in Wrentham, Massachusetts, and relocate there.
October 18, 1904	"Helen Keller Day" is held at the St. Louis Exposition with the goal of awakening worldwide interest in the education of the Deaf-Blind.
May 2, 1905	Anne Sullivan and John Macy marry at their shared home in Wrentham, Massachusetts. Helen Keller's annuity is cut by half due to the assumption that Macy will support his wife.
October 1906	Michael Anagnos dies, and Helen Keller gets subsequently appointed to his seat on the Massachusetts Commission for the Blind.

February 28, 1907	Mark Twain writes about the controversial Stanford White murder case involving Mary Copley Thaw's son Henry Kendall Thaw for *Harper's Weekly*.
1908	As editors continue to press Helen Keller to write about her own life, her book *The World I live In* gets published.
June 10, 1909	Helen Keller's distant cousin Edward Everett Hale dies.
1909	Helen Keller joins the Socialist Party and becomes a suffragist like her mother, Kate Keller, as women in some states lobby for the right to vote in local elections. Helen Keller's book, *The Song of the Stone Wall*, dedicated to Dr. Edward Everett Hale, gets published.
1910	Andrew Carnegie learns about Helen Keller's financial problems when his daughter asks him to arrange an annuity for her.
1912	Maria Montessori's European pedagogy spreads to the United States, and former President Theodore Roosevelt forms the Progressive Party.
1912	Helen Keller, Anne Sullivan Macy, and John Macy become active in the Lawrence Strike from the sidelines.
February 1913	Helen Keller and Anne Sullivan Macy began a fifteen-month lecture tour in the Northeast to supplement their income, and later that year, Keller's book *Out of the Dark* is published.
February 3, 1913	Ratification of the Sixteenth Amendment enables Congress to impose the Federal Income Tax, meaning Washington legislators have additional fund that start federal lobbying for resources.
May 1913	As the Macy marriage falls apart, John Macy leaves for Europe.
1914	After doing a series of lecture tours that result in financial losses, John Macy leaves

the household, and Scottish-born Polly Thomson joins the household. John Macy writes to Helen Keller, requesting financial assistance. Helen Keller's book *Out of the Dark* discussing her disabilities gets published.

May 7, 1915

The sinking of the Cunard ocean liner RMS *Lusitania* leads a survivor to work with Helen Keller to establish an organization for Blind war veterans.

January 15, 1916

Helen Keller speaks out against the Preparedness Movement in advance of World War I, during a program at Carnegie Hall in New York City.

January 16, 1916

Helen Keller explains to reporter Barbara Bindley why she is a member of the International Workers of the World.

February 1916

Helen Keller creates anxiety in her family by sending a one-hundred-dollar donation and a letter of support to the NAACP.

June 9, 1916

Helen Keller divulges a romance to an interviewer for the *Chicago Tribune*.

November 1916

Helen Keller takes out a marriage license in an ill-fated affair with John Macy's former secretary, Peter Fagan. United States experiences first large epidemic of the polio virus that attacks the central nervous system; children aged five to nine years are hardest hit with an estimated twenty-seven thousand cases and six thousand deaths.

1916

Due to health problems, Anne Sullivan Macy and Polly Thomson travel to Puerto Rico and separate from Helen Keller, who returns to her family in Alabama. Helen Keller meets a teenager Rebecca Mack, who later takes up William Wade's work documenting the Deaf-Blind. Helen Keller and Anne Sullivan Macy sell the Wrentham house and purchase a home in Forest Hills, Long Island, New York.

April 6, 1917	As the United States enters World War I, 80 percent of Deaf students are taught to speak. President Woodrow Wilson, concerned by the high draftee rejection rate, initiates the Children's Year as an initiative to study preventable child health issues.
February 1918–April 1920	The Spanish Flu pandemic, thought to have an origin in the state of Kansas, begins.
November 11, 1918	After Armistice in Europe, veterans return to the United States with disabilities, which leads Congress to pass major rehabilitation program for soldiers through the Vocational Education Bureau.
August 18, 1919	*Deliverance*, a financially unsuccessful silent film produced by the Helen Keller Film Corporation, is produced based upon Helen Keller's life. Women win the right to vote with the Nineteenth Amendment the same day; Helen Keller helps to establish the American Civil Liberties Union (ACLU).
1920–Spring 1924	Helen Keller, Anne Sullivan Macy, and later Polly Thomson perform on the vaudeville stage.
November 15, 1921	Helen Keller's mother Catherine "Kate" Adams Keller dies.
1921	The American Foundation for the Blind is established by Blind activists. A Blind man named H. Randolph Latimer establishes a central clearinghouse for the Blind.
1924	Major M. C. Migel of New York becomes the first president of the American Foundation for the Blind and taps Helen Keller and Annie Sullivan Macy for fundraising efforts. Helen Keller supports Progressive Robert La Follette, Sr.'s "third-party" campaign for the president of the United States.
June 30, 1925	Helen Keller delivers speech to International Convention of Lions Club International, asking them to champion fundraising efforts for the Blind.

1927	Helen Keller collaborates with writer Nella Braddy Henney on *My Religion*, which is her interpretation of Emanuel Swedenborg's writings and not the religion.
1929	Helen Keller's book *Midstream: My Later Life* is published the same year as the Wall Street crash; it contains reflections of her life without knowledge of Anne Sullivan Macy's early life.
June 9, 1929	Mary Copley Thaw, a financial supporter of Helen Keller and Anne Sullivan Macy, dies, leaving them money to pay off debts.
1930	Anne Sullivan has increasing health issues; she is virtually blind after having one eye removed, and Helen Keller travels to Scotland, England, and Ireland.
March 3, 1931	Pratt-Smoot Act is signed into law funding Books for the Blind program with Library of Congress after Helen Keller testifies.
1931–1932	Helen Keller and Anne Sullivan receive honorary degrees from Temple University. Keller travels to France, Yugoslavia, England, and Scotland.
August 26, 1932	John Macy dies, leaving an illegitimate daughter from a relationship with a Deaf sculptor.
October 1932	Helen Keller receives a $5,000 award from Pictorial Review in recognition of her contributions to American life over the previous decade. She gives monetary award to the American Federation for the Blind to use for developing Deaf-Blind services.
November 8, 1932	Franklin Delano Roosevelt, who is paralyzed from the waist down, is elected president.
1933	Keller returns to England and Scotland; Nella Braddy Henney's biography of Anne Sullivan Macy is published revealing her tumultuous childhood.
May 10, 1933	Nazis burn Helen Keller's books in front of the University of Berlin.

1934	Forest Hill, New York, neighbor Herbert Haas joins Helen Keller household as handyman.
1935	The Great Depression strikes the Deaf particularly hard when 44 percent of employed Deaf workers lose jobs. Three hundred disabled people with disabilities establish the League of the Physically Handicapped in New York as the first association of disabled people to protest discrimination by the Works Progress Administration (WPA).
August 14, 1935	President Franklin Delano Roosevelt signs the Social Security Act, establishing a program of permanent assistants for adults with disabilities.
October 29, 1936	Anne Sullivan Macy dies at Forest Hills after experiencing a coronary thrombosis and falling into a coma. Macy is interred in a memorial at the National Cathedral in Washington, D.C.
November 4, 1936	Helen Keller and Polly Thomson leave for Scotland to be with Thomson's family while they grieve.
April 7, 1937	Helen Keller travels to Japan for a two-month tour. The American League for the Deaf-Blind is established in New Jersey as a service organization to help set up homes for Deaf-Blind people and, later, provides braille to print and print to Braille transcription services, shopping services, and a braille lending library.
Fall 1938	Helen Keller sells the Forest Hills house and relocates to a home in Westport, Connecticut, called Arcan Ridge. Keller and Polly Thomson join the social circle of actress Katharine Cornell.
1939	Keller's *Journal* is published. Under the WPA regulations, Deaf workers are considered to be unemployable. With the onset of World War II, Adolf Hitler orders the euthanasia program of individuals with

physical and intellectual disabilities that continue for two years, and Hitler bans Keller's *Journal* because she is critical of his policies.

1940	France falls to Nazi Germany.
1941	Adolf Hitler attacks Soviet Union, and Japanese bombing of Pearl Harbor brings United States into World War II.
1943	Helen Keller tours military hospitals with friends.
1944	Holocaust of European Jews continues, and the G.I. Bill is enacted in the United States.
September 1944	Helen Keller speaks at a rally supporting Franklin Delano Roosevelt in Madison Square Garden, along with Henry Wallace.
August 6–9, 1945	The United States drops atomic bombs on Hiroshima and Nagasaki, Japan, in 1945, and World War II ends.
1946	Helen Keller tours Greece, Italy and the Vatican, France, and Great Britain on behalf of the American Foundation for the Overseas Blind.
November 23, 1946	Helen Keller and Polly Thomson's Arcan Ridge home burns down while they are traveling in Italy, and their possessions are destroyed.
1947	The Truman Doctrine establishes that the United States will provide political, military, and economic assistance to all democratic nations under threat from external or internal authoritarian forces. Helen Keller and Polly Thomson travel to Egypt, England, Syria, Lebanon, and Jordan.
October 14, 1948	While touring Hiroshima and Nagasaki, Japan, Keller describes the horrific conditions of the atomic bombs in the Japanese people. Helen Keller and Polly Thomson also travel to Australia and New Zealand.

1948	Dr. Howard A. Rusk establishes the Rusk Institute of Rehabilitation Medicine in New York City, where he develops techniques to improve the health of injured veterans from World War II. His theories focus on treating the emotional, psychological, and social aspects of individuals with disabilities, later becoming the basis for modern rehabilitation medicine.
1950	Korean War begins. McCarthy claims Communists have too much influence on the U.S. government. Helen Keller and friends are recorded in FBI files.
1950	Television becomes widely available, and disabled veteran and people with disabilities begin the barrier-free movement to create access.
September 1950	Herbert Haas, the caretaker for Keller's household, dies.
1951	Helen Keller and Polly Thomson tour South Africa.
January 2, 1952	Helen Keller's socialist friend and sculptor Jo Davidson dies.
1952	Helen Keller and Polly Thomson tour Egypt, Lebanon, Syria, Jordan, and Israel.
1953	Helen Keller and Polly Thomson tour Brazil, Chile, Peru, Panama, and Mexico.
June 15, 1954	Nancy Hamilton and Katherine Connell produce a documentary called *Unconquered*, about Keller's life with Polly Thomson in their rebuilt home at Arcan Ridge.
1954	*Brown v. Board of Education of Topeka* rules unanimously that racial segregation of children in public schools is unconstitutional. Helen Keller's birthplace "Ivy Green" in Tuscumbia, Alabama, is listed on the National Register of historic places.
1955	Helen Keller's book honoring Anne Sullivan Macy called *Teacher* gets published. Helen Keller receives honorary degree

	from Harvard. Helen Keller visits India, Hong Kong, the Philippines, and Japan.
1956	Helen Keller and Polly Thomson tour Scotland, Portugal, Spain, France, and Switzerland.
1957	Helen Keller and Polly Thomson tour Canada and Scandinavia. The first production of William Gibson's teleplay set in Tescumbia, Alabama, called *The Miracle Worker*, for the television anthology drama series *Playhouse 90*, garners a Pulitzer Prize.
September 1959	Polly Thomson experiences a stroke.
October 19, 1959	William Gibson's three-act play *The Miracle Worker* adapted from a teleplay premieres at the Playhouse Theater in New York, with Anne Bancroft as Anne Sullivan and Patty Duke as Helen Keller.
January 1960	Helen Keller revokes Nella Braddy Henney's power of attorney and fires her as a literary agent.
March 21, 1960	Polly Thomson dies. Thomson is interred in a memorial at the National Cathedral in Washington, D.C., with Anne Sullivan Macy.
1961	Helen Keller experiences her first stroke and retires from public life.
1964	Civil Rights Act passes helping to end discrimination against women and minorities but not making provisions for people with disabilities. President Lyndon Johnson awards Helen Keller the Medal of Freedom.
1965	Medicaid is established to cover medical costs for some individuals with disabilities and low-income families.
1966	National Organization for Women is established.
1967	An Act of Congress establishes the Helen Keller National Center for Deaf-Blind Youths and Adults in Sands Point, New York.

| April 4, 1968 | Martin Luther King, Jr. is assassinated. |
| June 1, 1968 | Helen Keller dies. Keller is interred in a memorial at the National Cathedral in Washington, D.C., with companions Anne Sullivan Macy and Polly Thomson. |

PRIMARY SOURCE DOCUMENTS

Helen Keller, "Sister Mabel," 1890

Helen Keller gained undesired notoriety and an inauspicious introduction to literary society after she sent a story, thought to be original, to Michael Anagnos (1837–1906), the director of Perkins Institute for the Blind on his birthday in 1891. Anne Sullivan had a good relationship with Anagnos until her teaching confronted his institutional authority and the reputation of Samuel Gridley Howe (1801–1876). The Perkins Institute published Keller's story "The Frost King" in 1892, and a scandal ensued when a newspaper reported the similarities to a published story as well as literary flourishes that were most like Sullivan's work. A brutal internal investigation was inconclusive about who was at fault, but it compelled Keller and Anne Sullivan to separate from the institute. As a result of this incident, editors demanded that Helen write about herself: "Do not meddle in matters not related to your own personal experience."

"Sister Mabel" published in St. Nicholas *magazine in August 1890 described an important aspect of Helen's "phantom" life in the South when Caption Arthur Keller would pick the first juicy fruit of the season as a special treat. The story also conveys a Victorian sensibility found in Sarah Chauncy Woolsey's* What Katy Did *(1872) where the protagonist's invalid cousin, also named Helen, teaches the importance of remaining cheerful in adversity.*

Keller later contributed a story called "Edith and the Bees" to an anthology called The Emerald Story Book: Stories and Legends of Spring, Nature, and Easter *(1915). In this story, a girl stung by a bee learns how worker bees contribute to the sustainability of the whole colony. "The Frost King" did not stylistically compare to "Sister Mabel" and "Edith and the Bees." It reflected the first time that Sullivan directly undermined Helen's independence to retain control over her.*

Sister Mabel
By Helen A. Keller.

Harry was twelve years old. He has two little sisters, both younger than himself. Mabel is ten and Kitty is five years of age. They live in a beautiful and quiet village, in a far-away southern country, where the sun shines brightly nearly all the year, and where the little birds fill the air with their glad songs from morning until night, and where each gentle breeze is sweet with the perfume of roses, jasmines, and magnolias. Harry and Kitty have a little garden on the sunny side of the house, which they plant, and carefully tend. Harry digs and plows the ground because he is taller and stronger than Kitty. When the ground is all ready, Kitty helps sow the seeds and cover the lightly with the soil. Then they bring water from the well to sprinkle over them. The little boy and his wee sister are very happy together.

Mabel loves to watch them at play from her window. Mabel is an invalid. She has never been able to run and frolic with her brother and sister; but Mabel is not often sad. She sits by the window with the warn sunshine upon her pretty brown hair and paleface, and chats happily to the other children whiles they work or play. Sometimes a sad feeling comes into Mabel's heart because she cannot run and skip like the other little girls, but she wipes away the tears quickly when she sees her brother or sister coming toward her, and tries to greet them with a pleasant smile; for Mable does not wish to make them unhappy. She often tells Kitty pretty stories she has read, and is always delighted to help Harry with his lessons. I am very sure Mabel helps everybody with her sunny smiles and gentle words. Harry is sure to bring Mabel the first juicy peach which ripens, and dear little Kitty never forgets to give her the first sweet hyacinth which blooms in the little garden. When Harry was ten years old, his father gave him a pretty pony named "Don"; a beautiful pet, and very gentle. Nearly every pleasant morning, after breakfast, Harry and Kitty would go to the stable, and saddle and bridle Don. Then they would lead him around to the side of the house, under Mabel's window, and there he would stand quietly until the other children were ready for their ride, and let Mabel pat his soft nose while he ate the delicious lumps of sugar which she kept for him.

Don has a good friend named "Jumbo." Jumbo is a splendid mastiff with large, kind eyes. Jon is never happy if Jumbo is not at his side. Jumbo will sit on his kind legs and look up at Don, and Don will bend his beautiful head and look at Jumbo. Mabel thinks they have some way of talking to each other— for why should not animals have thoughts and a language as well as we?

Harry would mount Don first, then Kitty's mother would put a blanket before the saddle and place Kitty upon it, and Harry would put his arms around her, and give her the reins, and away they would go! First they would ride through the village and they would take the broad country road. They would sometimes stop Don to admire the green fields and lovely wild flowers that grew by the way. On their way home they would dismount, and gather the most beautiful flowers they could find for Mabel. Then Harry would drive and Kitty would hold the flowers in her lap. The boy and girl made a pretty picture sitting so gracefully on the pony's back and many people looked at them. Mabel always kissed her hand to them when she saw them coming up the path.

Source: Keller, Helen Adams. "Sister Mabel." *St. Nicholas* (August 1890): 892.

Helen Keller, Letter to *St. Nicholas Magazine*, 1892

Helen Keller was a precocious correspondent once she could communicate in written form. This writing sample comes from an article by Abbot Academy student Adeline G. Perry called "A Visit from Helen Keller," in the June 1892 issue of St. Nicholas Magazine, *which describes Keller and Sullivan's visit to the Abbot Academy in Andover, Massachusetts, on May 15, 1891. Perry downplays Sullivan's work with Keller, asserting, "She could advance more rapidly there" (Perry, 1892, 574).*

Helen's letter serves an educational purpose to tell other children about how she communicated and that she wanted to communicate to them. St. Nicholas *was a monthly American magazine for children that ran from 1872 until 1940. It was the brainchild of publisher Roswell Smith (1829–1892) one of the founders of* Scribner's Monthly, *and Smith hired author Mary Mapes Dodge (1831–1905) to edit it.* St. Nicholas *had about seventy thousand subscribers. One of Keller's favorite stories,* Little Lord Fauntleroy *by Frances Hodgson Burnett (1849–1924), was first published as a series in* St. Nicholas *beginning in 1885.*

During the summer of 1890, Helen heard the story of Thomas "Tommy" Stringer (1886–1945), who became Deaf-Blind after contracting cerebra-spinal meningitis. Helen was deeply moved and decided that she, if nobody else was willing, would save the poor boy. After Helen's dog named Lioness was shot in late 1891, friends far and wide raised $300 to purchase her a new dog. Helen accepted the gift on behalf of Tommy to start a fund for his education.

Following the example of her father who was a small-town newspaper editor, Helen wrote newspaper articles addressed to children as well as about eight personalized appeals to newspaper editors a day describing Tommy's needs. Helen abstained from soda water and other luxuries to save money. She created awareness about the needs of several other Blind and Deaf children and helped raise enough money for Tommy to attend Perkins' Kindergarten for the Blind for two years.

Dear St. Nicholas:

It gives me very great pleasure to send you my autograph because I want the boys and girls who read St. Nicholas to know how blind children write. I suppose some of them wonder how we keep the lines straight so I will try to tell them how it is done. We have a grooved board which we put between pages when we wish to write. The parallel grooves correspond to lines and when we have pressed the paper into them by means of the blunt end of the pencil it is very easy to keep the words even. The small letters are all made in the grooves, while the long ones extend above and below them. We guide the pencil with the right hand, and feel carefully with the fore finger of the left hand to see that we shape and space the letters correctly. It is very difficult at first to form them plainly but if we keep on trying it gradually becomes easier and after a great deal of practice we can right legible letters to our friends. Then we are very, very happy. Sometime they may visit a school for the blind. If they do, I am sure, they will wish to see the pupils write.

Very sincerely, your little friend

Helen Keller

> **Source:** Perry, Adeline G. "A Visit from Helen Keller." *St. Nicholas Magazine* 19, no. 8 (June 8, 1892): 573–577.

Helen Keller, "Why Men Need Woman Suffrage," 1915

American citizens vote on measures that state legislatures place on the ballot. Although opponents believe that citizens are not informed enough to decide sound public policy judgments, direct democracy is most actively utilized at the state level when federal direction is lacking on issues.

Direct legislation sets the political agenda in respect to politically charged issues affecting marginalized population groups including abortion, affirmative action, animal rights, bilingual education, disability rights, environmental reform, health care reform, medical marijuana, physician-assisted suicide, school choice, and taxes.

State and local initiatives seldom receive the same attention as candidate elections despite being offered side by side on the same ballot, and candidate races sometimes do not offer views on initiatives unless the ballot measures contain controversial issues, strong ideological undercurrents, or expensive campaigns.

When the California Legislature established the initiative process in 1911, Frederick O'Brien (1869–1932), a self-described hobo and journalist, exclaimed, "It freed the state from the corporate bonds which enslaved it for decades. It gave the people the privilege of making and unmaking their laws, and naming and removing their officials. It made hope spring again in the hearts of men and women who had long been held in the chains of political lawlessness." Keller asks men to include women in this process.

Why Men Need Woman Suffrage
HELEN KELLER

Many declare that the woman peril is at our door. I have no doubt that it is. Indeed, I suspect that it has already entered most households. Certainly a great number of men are facing it across the breakfast table. And no matter how Deaf they pretend to be, they cannot help hearing it talk.

Women insist on their "divine rights," "immutable rights," "inalienable rights." These phrases are not so sensible as one might wish. When one comes to think of it, there are no such things as divine, immutable, or inalienable rights. Rights are things we get when we are strong enough to make good our claim to them. Men spent hundreds of years and did much hard fighting to get the rights they now call divine, immutable, and inalienable. Today women are demanding rights that tomorrow nobody will be foolhardy enough to question.

Anyone that reads intelligently knows that some of our old ideas are up a tree, and that traditions are scurrying away before the advance of their everlasting enemy, the questioning mind of a new age. It is time to take a good look at human affairs in the light of new conditions and new ideas, and the tradition that man is the natural master of the destiny of the race is one of the first to suffer investigation.

The dullest can see that a good many things are wrong with the world. It is old-fashioned, running into ruts. We lack intelligent direction and control. We are not getting the most out of our opportunities and advantages. We must make over the scheme of life, and new tools are needed for the work.

Perhaps one of the chief reasons for the present chaotic condition of things is that the world has been trying to get along with only half of itself. Everywhere we see running to waste woman-force that should be utilized in making the world a more decent home for humanity. Let us see how the votes of women will help solve the problem of living wisely and well.

When women vote men will no longer be compelled to guess at their desires—and guess wrong. Women will be able to protect themselves from man-made laws that are antagonistic to their interests. Some persons like to imagine that man's chivalrous nature will constrain him to act humanely toward woman and protect her rights. Some men do protect some women. We demand that all women have the right to protect themselves and relieve man of his feudal responsibility.

Political power shapes the affairs of state and determines many of the everyday relations of human beings with one another. The citizen with a vote is master of his own destiny. Women without this power, and who do not happen to have "natural protectors," are at the mercy of man-made laws. And experience shows that these laws are often unjust to them. Legislation made to protect women who have fathers and husbands to care for them does not protect working women whose only defenders are the state's policemen.

The wages of women in some states belong to their fathers or their husbands. They cannot hold property. In parts of this enlightened democracy of men the father is the sole owner of the child. I believe he can even will away the unborn babies. Legislation concerning the age of consent is another proof that the voice of woman is mute in the halls of the lawmakers. The regulations affecting laboring women are a proof that men are too busy to protect their "natural wards."

Economic urgencies have driven women to demand the vote. To a large number of women is entrusted the vitally important public function of training all childhood. Yet it is frequently impossible for teachers to support themselves decently on their wages. What redress have these overworked, underpaid women without the vote? They count for nothing politically.

An organization of women recently wanted to obtain a welfare measure from a Legislature in New York. A petition signed by 5,000 women was placed before the chairman of a committee that was to report on the bill. He said it was a good bill and ought to pass. After the women had waited a reasonable time, they sent up a request to know what had become of the bill. The chairman said that had been brought to him signed by 5,000 women. "Oh," replied the chairman, "a petition signed by 5,000 women is not worth the paper it is written on. Get five men to sign and we'll do something about it." That is one reason we demand the vote—we want 5,000 women to count for more than five men.

A majority of women that need the vote are wage-earners. A tremendous change has taken place in the industrial world since power machines took the place of hand tools. Men and women have been compelled to adjust themselves to a new system of production and distribution. The machine has been used to exploit the labor of both men and women as it was never exploited before. In the terrific struggle for existence that has resulted from this change women and children suffer even more than men. Indeed, economic pressure drives many women to market their sex.

Yet women have nothing to say about conditions under which they live and toil. Helpless, unheeded, they must endure hardships that lead to misery and degradation. They may not-lift a hand to defend themselves against cruel, crippling processes that stunt the body and brain and bring on early death or premature old age.

Working men suffer from the helplessness of working women. They must compete in the same offices and factories with women who are unable to protect themselves with proper laws. They must compete with women who work in unsanitary rooms called homes, work by dim lamps in the night, rocking a cradle with one foot. It is to the interest of all workers to end this stupid, one-sided, one-power arrangement and have suffrage for all.

The laws made by men rule the minds as well as the bodies of women. The man-managed state so conducts its schools that the ideals of women are warped to hideous shapes. Governments and schools engender and nourish a militant public opinion that makes war always possible. Man-written history, fiction, and poetry glorify war. Love of country is turned into patriotism which suggest, drums, flags, and young men eager to give their lives to the rulers of the nation. There will continue to be wars so long as our schools make such ideas prevail.

Women know the cost of human life in terms of suffering and sacrifice as men can never know it. I believe women would use the ballot to prevent war and to destroy the ideas that make war possible. In spite of an education that has taught them to glorify the military element in their ideals of manhood, they will wake to the realization that he loves his Country best who lives for it and serves it faithfully. They will teach children to honor the heroes of peace above the heroes of war.

Women are even now more active in working for social legislation and laws affecting the schools, the milk supply, and the quality of food than are the men who have the votes. Fundamentally, woman is a more social being than man. She is concerned with the whole family, while man is more individualistic. Social consciousness is not so strong in him. Many questions can be solved only with the help of woman's social experience—questions of the safety of women in their work, the rights of little children. Yet her peculiar knowledge and abilities are made the basis of arguments against giving women the vote. It is indisputably true that woman is constituted for the purposes of maternity. So is man constituted for the purposes of maternity. But no one seems to think that incapacitates him for citizenship. If there is a fundamental difference between man and woman, far be it from me to deny that it exists. It is all the more reason why her side should be heard.

For my part, I should think that man's chivalrous nature would cause him to emancipate the weaker half of the race. Indeed, it seems strange that when he was getting the suffrage for himself it did not occur to him to divide up with his beloved partner. Looking closer, I almost detect a suspicion of tyranny in his attitude toward her on the suffrage question. And can it be that this tyranny wears the mask of chivalry? Please do not misunderstand me. I am not disparaging chivalry. It is a very fine thing—what there is of it. The trouble is, there is not enough to go around. Nearly all the opportunities, educational and political, that woman has acquired have been gained by a march of conquest with a skirmish at every-post.

So since masculine chivalry has failed us we must hustle a bit and see what we can do for ourselves—and the men who need our suffrage. First of all, we must organize. We must make ourselves so aggressive a political factor that our natural protectors can no longer deny us a voice in directing and shaping the laws under which we must live.

We shall not see the end of capitalism and the triumph of democracy until men and women work together in the solving of their political, social and economic problems. I realize that the vote is only one of many weapons in our fight for the freedom of all. But every means is precious and, equipped with the vote, men and women together will hasten the day when the age-long dream of liberty, equality and brotherhood shall be realized upon earth.

Source: Keller, Helen. "Why Men Need Woman Suffrage." *New York Call,* October 17, 1915.

Helen Keller, "What Is the IWW?" Speech, 1918

The International Workers of the World was established by radical militant unionists, socialists, and anarchists who believed that the great mass of workers were in an economic struggle with an employing class. The IWW promoted worker solidarity, and its motto was "an injury to one is an injury to all." As early as 1840, New England Transcendentalist Orestes Brownson (1803–1876) in his "The Laboring Class," published in the Boston Quarterly Review, *observed during America's first sustained industrial depression that there was a correlation between the different motives of the wealthy capitalists and labor that reached a crisis point.*

John Albert Macy (1877–1932) was an ardent socialist and author of Socialism in America *(1916), in which he updated William English Walling's* Socialism as It Is *(1912) and Helen Marot's* American Unions *(1914). Macy believed the test of the working-class ideal was not found in the damage it causes for the owning classes, but in the "amount of perturbation it excites in the minds of the owning classes" (Macy, 1916, 161). Macy noted that many of the leading socialists attacked the IWW because only wage earners were admitted, and there was no place for middle-class agendas. When joining, Macy who considered himself to be middle-class divulged that he was a "parasitic journalist." A local union took him in because he was a wage earner and not an employer of labor.*

In their most relaxed conversations, Macy read works by Henry David Thoreau (1817–1896) to Helen integrating it into a broader conversation of poverty, socialism, and social justice in America. Macy asserted that Thoreau's principles related to the injustices of contemporary political and industrial life would be condemned as "un-American." Macy also thought that the great changes in relations between workman and their tools, some of Thoreau's individualism, had become obsolete. Keller absorbed these principles and utilized them when describing the IWW in a speech to the New York City Civic Club in January 1918.

What Is the IWW?
Speech at the New York City Civic Club, January 1918

I am going to talk about the Industrial Workers of the World because they are so much in the public eye just now. They are probably the most hated and most loved organization in existence. Certainly they are the least understood and the most persistently misrepresented.

The Industrial Workers of the World is a labor union based on the class struggle. It admits only wage-earners, and acts on the principle of industrial unionism. Its battleground is the field of industry. The visible expression of the battle is the strike, the lock-out, the clash between employer and employed. It is a movement of revolt against the ignorance, the poverty, the cruelty that too many of us accept in blind content.

It was founded in 1905 by men of bitter experience in the labor struggle, and in 1909 it began to attract nation-wide attention. The McKees Rocks strike first brought it to notice. The textile strike of Lawrence, Massachusetts, the silk workers' strike of Paterson, New Jersey, and the miners' strike of Calumet, Michigan, made it notorious. Since 1909 it has been a militant force in America that employers have had to reckon with.

It differs from the trade unions in that it emphasizes the idea of one big union of all industries in the economic field. It points out that the trade unions as presently organized are an obstacle to unity among the masses, and that this lack of solidarity plays into the hands of their economic masters.

The IWW's affirm as a fundamental principle that the creators of wealth are entitled to all they create. Thus they find themselves pitted against the whole profit-making system. They declare that there can be no compromise so long as the majority of the working class lives in want while the master class lives in luxury. They insist that there can be no peace until the workers organize as a class, take possession of the resources of the earth and the machinery of production and distribution and abolish the wage system. In other words, the workers in their collectivity must own and operate all the essential industrial institutions and secure to each laborer the full value of his product.

It is for these principles, this declaration of class solidarity, that the IWWs are being persecuted, beaten, imprisoned, murdered. If the capitalist class had the sense it is reputed to have, it would know that violence is the worst weapon that can be used against men who have nothing to lose and the world to gain.

Let me tell you something about the IWWs as I see them. They are the unskilled, the ill-paid, the unnaturalized, the submerged part of the working class. They are mostly composed of textile mill workers, lumber men, harvesters, miners, transport workers. We are told that they are "foreigners," "the scum of the earth," "dangerous."

Many of them are foreigners simply because the greater part of the unskilled labor in this country is foreign. "Scum of the earth?" Perhaps. I know they have never had a fair chance. They have been starved in body and mind, denied, exploited, driven like slaves from job to job. "Dangerous?" Maybe. They have endured countless wrongs and injuries until they are driven to rebellion. They know that the laws are for the strong, that they protect the class that owns everything. They know that in a contest with the workers, employers do not respect the laws, but quite shamelessly break them.

Witness the lynching of Frank Little in Butte; the flogging of 17 men in Tulsa; the forcible deportation of 1200 miners from Bisbee; the burning to death of women and little children in the tents of Ludlow, Colorado, and the massacre of workers in Trinidad. So the IWWs respect the law only as a soldier respects an enemy! Can you find it in your hearts to blame them? I love them for their needs, their miseries, their endurance and their daring spirit. It is because of this spirit that the master class fears and hates them. It is because of this spirit that the poor and oppressed love them with a great love.

The oft-repeated charge that the Industrial Workers of the World is organized to hinder industry is false. It is organized in order to keep industries going. By organizing industrially they are forming the structure of the new society in the shell of the old.

Industry rests on the iron law of economic determination. All history reveals that economic interests are the strongest ties that bind men together. That is not because men's hearts are evil and selfish. It is only a result of the inexorable law of life. The desire to live is the basic principle that compels men and women to seek a more suitable environment, so that they may live better and more happily.

Now, don't you see, it is impossible to maintain an economic order that keeps wages practically at a standstill, while the cost of living mounts higher and even higher? Remember, the day will come when the tremendous activities of the war will subside. Capitalism will inevitably find itself face to face with a starving multitude of unemployed workers demanding food or destruction of the social order that has starved them and robbed them of their jobs.

In such a crisis the capitalist class cannot save itself or its institutions. Its police and armies will be powerless to put down the last revolt. For man at last will take his own, not considering the cost. When that day dawns, if the workers are not thoroughly organized, they may easily become a blind force of destruction, unable to check their own momentum, their cry for justice drowned in a howl of rage. Whatever is good and beneficent in our civilization can be saved only by the workers. And the Industrial Workers of the World is formed with the object of carrying on the business of the world when capitalism is overthrown. Whether the IWW increases in power or is crushed out of existence, the spirit that animates it is the spirit that must animate the labor movement if it is to have a revolutionary function.

Source: Keller, Helen. *New York Call*, February 3, 1918.

Bibliography

Adichie, Chimamanda Ngozi. 2009. "The Danger of a Single Story." TED-Talks on YouTube. Online: https://www.youtube.com/watch?v=D9Ihs241zeg&feature=youtu.be

Alcott, Louisa M. 1886. "The Blind Lark." *St. Nicholas: An Illustrated Magazine for Young Folks* 12, no. 1 (November): 12–19.

Baatz, Simon. 2018. *The Girl on the Velvet Swing: Sex, Murder, and Madness at the Dawn of the Twentieth Century.* New York: Little, Brown and Company.

Bell, Alexander Graham. 1883. *Fallacies Concerning the Deaf and the Influence of Such Fallacies in Preventing the Amelioration of Their Condition.* Washington, DC: Judd & Detweiler.

Bell, Alexander Graham. 1916. *The Mechanism of Speech: Lectures Delivered before the American Association to Promote the Teaching of Speech to the Deaf, to Which Is Appended a Paper Vowel Theories.* New York: Funk & Wagnalls.

Best, Harry. 1919. *The Blind: Their Condition and the Work Being Done for Them in the United States.* New York: The MacMillan Company.

Bindley, Barbara. 1916. "Helen Keller: Why I Became an IWW." *New York Tribune,* January 15, 1916. Online: Industrial Workers of the World. https://www.iww.org/history/library/HKeller/why_I_became_an_IWW

Brown, Emma E. 1880. "Perkins Institution and Massachusetts School for the Blind." *Some Curious Schools.* Boston: D. Lothrop and Company.

Burbank, Luther. 1915. *Luther Burbank: His Methods and Discoveries and Their Practical Application,* Vol. 12. New York and London: Luther Burbank Press.

Burnett, Frances Hodgson. 1886. *Little Lord Fauntleroy.* New York: Scribner's Sons.

Burroughs, John. 1905. *Ways of Nature*. Boston: Houghton Mifflin.

Campbell, Charles F. F. 1931. *Two Outstanding American Blind Educators: Sir Francis Campbell, Robert B. Irwin*. Address given before the delegates to the World Conference on the Work for the Blind, Cleveland, April 25, 1931. Online: https://archive.org/details/twoout standingam00char/page/n5/mode/2up

Canby, Margaret T. 1873. *Birdie and His Fairy Friends: A Book for Little Children*. Philadelphia: Press of Wm. F. Fell & Co.

Carnegie, Andrew. 1885. *Triumphant Democracy, or Fifty Years' March of the Republic*. Garden City, NY: Doubleday, Doran & Company.

Carnegie, Andrew. 1908. *Problems of Today: Wealth, Labor, Socialism*. Garden City, NY: Doubleday, Doran & Company.

Chamberlin, Joseph Edgar. 1937. *Nomads and Listeners of Joseph Edgar Chamberlin*. Edited by Samuel M. Waxman. Freeport, NY: Books for Libraries.

Cook, Blanche, Weisen. 1999. *Eleanor Roosevelt: The Defining Years, 1933–1938*. New York: Penguin Books.

Davidson, Jo. 1951. *Between Sittings: An Informal Autobiography*. New York: The Dial Press.

Day, Sara. 2013. *Coded Letters, Concealed Love: The Larger Lives of Harriet Freeman and Edward Everett Hale*. Washington, DC: New Academia Publishing.

de Kroyft, Helen Aldrich. 1875. *The Story of Little Jakey*. Cambridge, MA: Riverside Press.

Delano, Marfe Ferguson. 2008. *Helen's Eyes: A Photobiography of Annie Sullivan, Helen Keller's Teacher*. Washington, DC: National Geographic.

Dickens, Charles. 1842. *American Notes*. Gloucester, MA: Peter Smith, 1968.

Einhorn, Lois J. 1998. *Helen Keller, Public Speaker: Sightless but Seen, Deaf but Heard*. Westport, CT: Greenwood Press.

Ellis, William T. 1897. "Helen Keller and Tommy Stringer." *St. Nicholas: A Magazine for Young Folks* 17, no. 12 (October): 996–1000. Online: https://www.disabilitymuseum.org/dhm/lib/detail.html?id=2288 &page=all

Foley, Kate M. 1919. *Five Lectures on Blindness*. Sacramento: California State Library. Online: https://www.gutenberg.org/files/22170 /22170-h/22170-h.htm

Froner, Philip. 1967. *Helen Keller, Her Socialist Years: Writings and Speeches*. New York: International Publishers. [Reprint Leopard Books India.]

General Federation of Women's Clubs. 1922. *Know Your Own Country, Know Your Own Community*. Washington, DC: General Federation of Women's Clubs Headquarters.

General Federation of Women's Clubs, Division of Americanization. 1922. *Americans All.* Washington, DC: General Federation of Women's Clubs Headquarters.

George, Henry. 1879. *Progress and Poverty: An Inquiry into the Cause of Industrial Depressions and Increase of Want with Increase of Wealth, and Remedy.* New York: Modern Library.

Gibson, William. 2008. *The Miracle Worker: A Play.* New York: Scribner.

Gilman, Stella. 1884. *Mothers in Council.* New York: Harper and Brothers.

Gitter, Elisabeth. 2001. *The Imprisoned Guest: Samuel Howe and Laura Bridgman, the Original Deaf-Blind Girl.* New York: Farrar, Straus and Giroux.

Gray, Charlotte. 2006. *Reluctant Genius: Alexander Graham Bell and the Passion for Invention.* New York: Arcade Publishing.

Hale, Edward Everett. 1863. *The Man without a Country and Other Tales.* San Bernardino, CA: Timeless Classic Books.

Hale, Edward Everett, Jr. 1917. *The Life and Letters of Edward Everett Hale.* Boston: Little Brown & Company.

Hall, Florence Howe. 1889. Helen Keller. *St. Nicholas: An Illustrated Magazine for Young Folks* 16, no. 11 (September): 834–843.

Happy Poverty, or, The Story of Poor Ellen. 1817. Hartford, CT: Hartford Evangelical Tract Society. Online: https://www.disabilitymuseum .org/dhm/lib/catcard.html?id=791

Harrity, Richard, and Ralph G. Martin. 1962. *The Three Lives of Helen Keller.* Garden City, NY: Doubleday & Company, Inc.

Hayes, Lydia Y. 1926. "The Education of a Girl Who Cannot See or Hear." *Outlook for the Blind* 20: 12–16. Online at the Internet Archive: https://archive.org/details/outlookforblind1926unse/page/n19

Helen Keller Film Corporation. 1919. *Deliverance.* Written by Francis Trevelyan Miller, cinematographers: Lawrence Fowler and Arthur L. Todd. Distributed by George Kleine System. Online with Library of Congress: https://www.youtube.com/watch?v=zGNeJiYhqrw

"Helen Keller Meeting First Lady Grace Coolidge in 1926" [Newsreel]. Described with captions on YouTube: https://www.youtube.com /watch?v=9Of-9Vo15Xg

"Helen Keller's Visit to the World's Fair." *St. Nicholas: An Illustrated Magazine for Young Folks* 21, no. 2 (December 1893): 174–177. Online: https://www.disabilitymuseum.org/dhm/lib/catcard.html ?id=2292

"Helen Keller Wins Achievement Prize; Gets $5,000 Pictorial Review for Her Work among the Blind, Is 'Surprised and Proud' Says 'A Lot of Good' Can Be Done with the Money to Press Drive for New $1,000,000 Fund." *New York Times,* October 19, 1932.

Henney, Nella Braddy. 1933. *Anne Sullivan Macy: The Story behind Helen Keller.* Garden City, NY: Doubleday, Doran & Company.

Henney, Nella Braddy. 1974. *With Helen Keller.* Eaton, NH: Keith Henney.
     Online: https://www.afb.org/HelenKellerArchive?a=d&d=A-HK01
     -03-B059-F04-044.1.1&e=-------en-20--1--txt--Takeo
     +Iwahashi+book------3-7-6-5-3--------------0-1

Hoyt, Edwin P. 1979. *The Improper Bostonian: Dr. Oliver Wendell Holmes.*
     New York: William Morrow and Company.

Hunter, Robert. 1904. *Poverty.* New York: Grosset & Dunlap.

Hunter, Robert. 1908. *Socialists at Work.* New York: The Macmillan
     Company.

Hutton, Laurence. 1891. *Curiosities of the American Stage.* London: James
     R. Osgood, McIvaine & Co.

Hyde, Clyde Kenneth. 1962. *George Lyman Kittredge: Teacher and Scholar.*
     Lawrence: University of Kansas Press.

Jastrow, Joseph. 1889. "The Story of Laura Bridgman." *St. Nicholas: An
     Illustrated Magazine for Young Folks* 16, no. 10 (August): 12–19.

Jastrow, Joseph. 1900. *Fact and Fable in Psychology.* Boston: Houghton
     Mifflin Company.

Jastrow, Joseph. 1918. *The Psychology of Conviction.* Boston: Houghton
     Mifflin.

Jefferson, Joseph. 1889. *The Autobiography of Joseph Jefferson.* New York:
     The Century Company.

Jewel Productions. 1917. *Man without a Country.* Director Earnest C.
     Warde, Writer "Scenario writer Lloyd Lonergran." Cinematography
     George Webber. Silent Hall of Fame Enterprises.

Keller, Helen Adams. 1890. "The Letter-Box: South Boston, March 1890."
     St. Nicholas: An Illustrated Magazine for Young Folks 16, no. 11
     (May): 608.

Keller, Helen Adams. 1894. "Letter from Helen." *St. Nicholas Magazine* 27,
     no. 2 (January): 950.

Keller, Helen Adams. 1903. *The Story of My Life: with Her Letters (1887–
     1901) and a Supplementary Account.* New York: Doubleday, Page &
     Company. [Reprinted by Middletown, DE: Digireads, 2019.]

Keller, Helen Adams. 1905. "Chat about the Hand." *Century Magazine* 69:
     454–465. Online: https://www.disabilitymuseum.org/dhm/lib
     /detail.html?id=2297

Keller, Helen Adams. 1906. "Christmas in the Dark: As the Blind See the
     Yuletide." *Ladies' Home Journal* 25 (December): 13.

Keller, Helen Adams. 1910a. *Song of the Stone Wall.* New York: The Cen-
     tury Company.

Keller, Helen Adams. 1910b. "The Valued of the Sense of Smell to the Blind-
     Deaf." *Outlook for the Blind* 4: 66–67.

Keller, Helen Adams. 1913. "Tribute to Mr. Wade." *Outlook for the Blind* 47.
     Online: https://www.afb.org/HelenKellerArchive?a=d&d=A-HK01

-03-B088-F08-006.1.1&e=-------en-20--1--txt--william+wade-----
-3-7-6-5-3-------------0-1

Keller, Helen Adams. 1915. "Edith and the Bees." In *The Emerald Story Book: Stories and Legends of Spring, Nature, and Easter,* compiled by Ada M. Skinner and Eleanor L. Skinner, 226–229. New York Duffield & Co.

Keller, Helen Adams. 1920. *Out of the Dark: Essays, Lectures, and Addresses on Physical and Social Vision.* New York: Doubleday, Doran & Company.

Keller, Helen Adams. 1925. "A Visit to Luther Burbank." *Outlook for the Blind* 19, no. 3: 21–24.

Keller, Helen Adams. 1929. *Midstream: My Later Life.* Garden City, NY: Doubleday, Doran & Company.

Keller, Helen Adams. 1938. *Helen Keller's Journal, 1936–1937.* New York: Doubleday, Doran & Company.

Keller, Helen Adams. 1955. *Teacher Anne Sullivan Macy: A Tribute by the Foster-child of Her Mind.* Garden City, NY: Doubleday and Company, Inc.

Keller, Helen Adams. 1967. *Helen Keller, Her Socialist Years: Writings and Speeches.* Edited by Philip S. Foner. New York: International Publishers.

Keller, Helen Adams. 2000. *Light in My Darkness.* Revised and expanded by Ray Silverman; foreword by Dorothy Herrmann. West Chester, PA. Swedenborg Foundation.

Keller, Helen Adams. 2005. *Selected Writings.* Edited by Kim E. Nielsen. New York: New York University Press/American Federation for the Blind.

Keller, Helen Adams. 2009. *The World I Live In & Optimism.* Mineola, NY: Dover Publications.

Kete, Mary Louise, and Elizabeth Petrino. 2018. *Lydia Sigourney: Critical Essays and Cultural Views.* Amherst: University of Massachusetts Press.

King, Martin Luther, Jr. 1963. "Letter from a Birmingham Jail." April 16, 1963. Online: https://www.africa.upenn.edu/Articles_Gen/Letter_Birmingham.html

Koestler, Frances A. 1976. *The Unseen Minority: A Social History of Blindness in America.* New York: David McKay Company, Inc.

Lash, Joseph P. 1980. *Helen and Teacher: The Story of Helen Keller and Anne Sullivan Macy.* New York: Delecorte Press/Seymour Lawrence.

Longmore, Paul K., and Lauri Umanscky, eds. 2001. *The New Disability History: American Perspectives.* New York: New York University Press.

Lyde, Elsie Leslie. 1977. *Trustable and Prehus Friends*. Foreword by Julie Harris and edited by Jane Douglass New York: Harcourt, Brace, Jovanovich.

Macy, John Albert. 1902. "Helen Keller as She Really Is: An Intimate Portrait of Her in Her Daily Life and Work." *Ladies' Home Journal* 19 (November): 1–12, and 55.

Macy, John Albert. 1913a. *A Guide to Reading for Young and Old*. Garden City, NY: Doubleday, Page & Company.

Macy, John Albert. 1913b. *The Spirit of American Literature*. Garden City, NY: Doubleday, Page & Company.

Macy, John Albert. 1916. *Socialism in America*. Garden City, NY: Doubleday, Page & Company.

Marden, Orison Swett. 1905. "Helen Keller: Blind, Deaf, and Dumb, Patient Effort Wins Her Culture and Rare Womanhood." *Little Visits with Great Americans, or, Success Ideals and How to Attain Them*, Vol. 2: 391–401. New York: Success Company.

McGinnity, B. L., Seymour-Ford, J., and Andries, K. J. 2004. *Founders*. Watertown, MA: Perkins History Museum, Perkins School for the Blind. Online: https://www.perkins.org/history/people/founders#perkins

Morris, Amy J. M. 2016. "Illuminating the Darkness: Helen Keller Makes Big Impression on Abbot Academy Students in 1891." *Andover Townsman*, February 12, 2016. Online: https://www.andovertownsman.com/news/local_news/illuminating-the-darkness/article_605a2d93-5575-5b7d-9262-806e7328b866.html

Nielsen, Kim E. 2004. *The Radical Lives of Helen Keller*. New York: New York University Press.

Nielsen, Kim E. 2007. "The Southern Ties of Helen Keller." *The Journal of Southern History*, 73, no. 14 (November): 783–806.

Nielsen, Kim E. 2009. *Beyond the Miracle Worker: The Remarkable Life of Annie Sullivan Macy and her Extraordinary Friendship with Helen Keller*. Boston: Beacon Press.

O'Brien, Frederick. 1911. "What the 1911 Legislature Did." *Los Angeles Record*, March 28, 1911.

O'Connell, Deirdre. 2009. *The Ballad of Blind Tom*. New York: Overlook Duckworth.

Padden, Carol, and Tom Humphries. 2005. *Inside Deaf Culture*. Cambridge, MA: Harvard University Press.

Parsons, Mary A. 1880. "The Boston School for Deaf Mutes." *Some Curious Schools*. Online: https://archive.org/stream/SomeCuriousSchools/Some%20Curious%20Schools_djvu.txt

Pearce, Theodocia. 1926. *Lights from Little Lanterns*. New York: Joseph Lawren. Online: https://www.afb.org/HelenKellerArchive?a=d&d=

A-HK01-03-B078-F12-001.1.23&e=-------en-20--1--txt--theodocia +pearce------3-7-6-5-3--------------0-1

Perkins School for the Blind. n.d. "School Development." Online: https:// www.perkins.org/history/legacy/school-development

Perry, Adeline G. 1892. "A Visit from Helen Keller." *St. Nicholas: An Illustrated Magazine for Young Folks* 19, no. 8 (June): 573–577. Online: https://www.disabilitymuseum.org/dhm/lib/detail.html?id=2289 &page=all

Rocheleau, Corrinne, and Rebecca Mack. 1930. *Those in Silence: The Deaf-Blind in North America A Record of Today.* Washington, DC: The Volta Bureau.

Roosevelt, Eleanor. 1958. *On My Own.* New York: Harper & Brothers Publishers.

Royce, Josiah. 1904. *The World and the Individual.* New York: Macmillan Company.

Salmon, Peter J. 1970. *Out of the Shadows: Final Report of the Anne Sullivan Macy Services for the Deaf-Blind Persons: A Regional Demonstration Project, 1962–1969, conducted by the Industrial Home for the Blind.* New Hyde Park, NY: National Center for Deaf-Blind Youths and Adults.

Selby, Clarence J. 1898. *Flashes of Light from an Imprisoned Soul.* Chicago: A. L. Fyfe.

Showalter, Elaine. 2016. *The Civil Wars of Julia Ward Howe: A Biography.* New York: Simon & Schuster.

Smith, Nora Archibald. 1925. *Kate Douglas Wiggin as Her Sister Knew Her.* Boston: Houghton Mifflin.

Smithdas, Robert J. 1958. *Life at My Fingertips.* Garden City, NY: Doubleday & Company.

"Stranger Than Fiction: How Helen Keller, a Little Girl Deaf, Dumb, and Blind, Raised Subscriptions to Help a Child Similarly Afflicted; Marvelous Results of Patience and Teaching." *The Illustrated American* 9 (July 9, 1892): 369–371.

Tilney, Frederick. 1928. "The Mind of Helen Keller: Brain Specialist Analyzes Her Marvelous Senses of Touch and Smell." *Personality* 2, no. 6 (October). Online: https://archive.org/details/mindofhelenkelle00 fred/page/n1

Torrey, Bradford. 1893. *The Foot-path Way.* Boston: Houghton Mifflin.

Torrey, Bradford. 1900. *Birds in the Bush.* Boston: Houghton Mifflin.

Torrey, Bradford. 1906. *Friends on the Shelf.* Port Washington, NY: Kennicat Press.

Trobridge, George. 1907. *Swedenborg: Life and Teaching.* New York: Swedenborg Foundation, Inc.

Tuttle, Dean, and Naomi Tuttle. *Charles F. F. Campbell.* Online: https://sites.aph.org/hall/inductees/campbell/

Twain, Mark. 2001–2015. *Autobiography of Mark Twain,* 3 vols. Berkeley: University of California—The Mark Twain Project.

Wade, William. 1901. *The Deaf-Blind: A Monograph.* Indianapolis: Hecker Brothers. Online: https://archive.org/details/deafblindmonogra00will/page/n5

Wade, William. 1904. *The Deaf-Blind: A Monograph,* 2nd ed. Indianapolis: Hecker Brothers.

Wade, William. 1908. *The Deaf-Blind: A Monograph: Supplement.* Indianapolis: Hecker Brothers.

Wagner, David. 2012. *The "Miracle Worker" and the Transcendentalist: Annie Sullivan, Franklin Sanborn, and the Education of Helen Keller.* Boulder, CO: Paradigm Publishers.

Walker, Martha Lentz. 1985. *Beyond Bureaucracy: Mary Elizabeth Switzer and Rehabilitation.* Lantham, MD: University Press of America.

Walters, Barbara. n.d. "Bob Smithdas Interview with Barbara Walters [partial interview]." Online: https://youtu.be/P8h8aPs4mPY

Wiggin, Kate Douglas. 1889. *The Story of Patsy.* Boston: Houghton, Mifflin.

Williams, Job. 1892. "Is Helen Keller a Fraud?" *American Annals of the Deaf* 37, no. 2: 156–159. Online: https://www.disabilitymuseum.org/dhm/lib/detail.html?id=2430&page=all

Index

About the Author

Meredith Eliassen, MSLIS, is special collections librarian and university archivist at San Francisco State University, San Francisco, California. She has an interest in local history and folklore and is also a designer for MME Designs (https://mmedesigns.net/). She is the author of *San Francisco State University* (2006).